STACKPOLE BOOKS

An imprint of
The Globe Pequot Publishing Group, Inc.
64 South Main St.
Essex, CT 06426
www.GlobePequot.com

British Library Cataloguing in Publication Information available

Library of Congress Cataloging-in-Publication Data

Names: Gunnarson, Jacob author | Polmar, Norman author
Title: Submarine aircraft carriers : from World War I to the age of drones
    / Jacob Gunnarson and Norman Polmar.
Description: Essex, Connecticut : Stackpole Books, [2025] | Includes
    bibliographical references and indexes
Identifiers: LCCN 2025019796 (print) | LCCN 2025019797 (ebook) | ISBN
    9780811777292 cloth | ISBN 9780811777308 ebook
Subjects: LCSH: Submarines (Ships)—History | Aircraft carriers—History |
    Naval history—20th century | BISAC: HISTORY / Military / Weapons
Classification: LCC V857 .G86 2025 (print) | LCC V857 (ebook) | DDC
    623.825/7—dc23/eng/20250616
LC record available at https://lccn.loc.gov/2025019796
LC ebook record available at https://lccn.loc.gov/2025019797

CONTENTS

PERSPECTIVE

Two remarkable inventions that appeared at the beginning of the 20th Century became weapons that revolutionized warfare: the submarine and the aircraft. By the outbreak of the Great War—World War I—in August 1914, several nations had developed those two platforms into deadly weapons. Both weapons had major roles in that conflict.

During that war the German and British navies took primitive steps to combine the two weapons, primarily to extend the range of aircraft by carrying them to sea on the decks of submarines. Germany also devoted considerable effort toward developing aircraft that could be disassembled and stored within the submarine, and assembled and launched to seek out targets beyond the submarine's limited range of vision. Although those weapon "systems" never reached operational service, the threat of their use against the United States led to large-scale panic in New York City in 1918. The armistice of November 1918 prevented the German submarine-carried aircraft from seeing combat.

In the period between the world wars several countries undertook aircraft-carrying submarine projects. Extensive experiments were carried out by Great Britain, France, Japan, and the United States. All of those nations modified submarines to carry aircraft to sea. The Soviet Union, Italy, and Poland considered designs for such aircraft and submarines, but those three nations abandoned their efforts without at-sea experiments.

When global conflict erupted again in 1939, France and Japan had submarines at sea that could carry and launch aircraft. The French effort—the large submarine *Surcouf*—ended precipitously with the loss of that submarine, possibly through collision with a merchant ship. She had never flown her aircraft operationally.

During World War II only the Imperial Japanese Navy employed submarine-launched, fixed-wing aircraft to undertake reconnaissance missions and to attack land targets. A Japanese submarine-launched floatplane made the only air attacks on the contiguous United States during the war with two strikes against targets in Oregon. And submarine-refueled flying boats carried out the second Japanese air attack that targeted the U.S. bases at Pearl Harbor.

The Japanese planned highly ambitious submarine/aircraft attacks on American "strategic" targets including New York City and the Panama Canal. Those operations were not carried out as the tide of war shifted against Japan before they could be undertaken. The submarines built specifically to carry out those attacks—the *Sentoku* Type or *I-400* class—were the largest non-nuclear submarines to be constructed by any nation. Indeed, they dwarfed the world's early nuclear-propelled submarines. Those Japanese giants never launched aircraft in combat.

During World War II the German Navy developed towed rotary-wing/ autogyro aircraft for operation from submarines to extend the "eyes" of their lookouts when the U-boats were on the surface. They were intended to seek out shipping targets. But their flights made the submarine more vulnerable to Allied detection and the autogyros were rarely flown from U-boats beyond their initial trials.

The concept of submarine-launched aircraft persisted into the Cold War era, with both the Soviet Union and United States developing proposals for aircraft-carrying undersea craft. However, the advent of cruise (guided) and ballistic missiles quickly terminated interest in those submarine/aircraft concepts, except for the occasional helicopter operating with a submarine and, significantly, submarine-launched unmanned (drone) aircraft.

The authors are in debt to several individuals for their assistance in the research, writing, and publishing of this book.

Steve Coates, an expert on World War II–era German helicopters, supplied us original documentation on the Fl 282 and Fa 330 and gave valuable feedback. Richard Douglass shared his research on covert Central Intelligence Agency balloon operations. Eugene Handler provided a firsthand account of his role in the development of Convair's Sub-Plane. Emily Knott traveled to the British National Archives to access and photograph original documentation on the submarine M-2. Capt. Jerry Mason, USN (Ret.), administrator of the online U-boat Archive, contributed copious amounts of material on German submarine operations during World War II.

Yuta Norden aided in translating Russian sources, and David Gunnarson assisted in archival research. We are grateful to Chris Gibson; Scott Lowther; *Kommandørkaptein* Hans Petter Oset, Royal Norwegian Navy; Capt. Don Walsh, USN (Ret.); and Ziyuan Zhao for providing us with additional material.

Ryo Dobashi, Alan Reddig, Tetsukuni Watanabe, and the staffs of the Glen L. Martin Maryland Aviation Museum, Kure Maritime Museum, and Royal Navy Submarine Museum provided photographs to use in this book.

We would also like to extend our thanks to the staffs of the U.S. National Archives and Records Administration, National Naval Aviation Museum,

Naval History and Heritage Command, Smithsonian Air and Space Museum, and the Hamilton Library at the University of Hawai'i at Mānoa for facilitating our research.

The staff of Globe Pequot and Stackpole Books made this book a reality, especially Dave Reisch, Felicity Tucker, Jason Rossi, and Jo-Ann Parks.

In addition, Jacob Gunnarson is in debt to his family and friends for their encouragement and advice throughout the course of this project, particularly for the dedicated support of his parents, David and Sarah.

—Jacob Gunnarson
—Norman Polmar

SHIP DESIGNATIONS

The following U.S. Navy ship designations are used in the text.

AG   miscellaneous auxiliary
AGSS   auxiliary submarine
AMS   motor minesweeper
AO   oiler
AOSS   submarine oiler
APS   transport submarine
APSS   transport submarine
AS   submarine tender
ASSP   transport submarine
AV   seaplane tender
AVD   seaplane tender—destroyer
AVP   seaplane tender—small
BB   battleship
CA   heavy cruiser
CL   light cruiser
CV   aircraft carrier
CVA   heavy aircraft carrier
CVE   escort aircraft carrier
DD   destroyer
DE   destroyer escort
DMS   destroyer minesweeper
LCS   littoral combat ship
LPSS   transport submarine
SC   cruiser submarine
SF   fleet submarine
SM   submarine minelayer
SS   submarine

SSBN   ballistic missile submarine (nuclear-propelled)
SSG   guided missile submarine
SSGN   guided missile submarine (nuclear-propelled)
SSN   attack submarine (nuclear-propelled)
SSP   transport submarine
SSRN   radar picket submarine (nuclear-propelled)

ABBREVIATIONS

Armstr. Sidd.	Armstrong Siddeley
ASW	Anti-Submarine Warfare
BOSS	Border and Offshore Submersible Sentry
BuAer	Bureau of Aeronautics (U.S.)
BuShips	Bureau of Ships (U.S.)
BuWeps	Bureau of Naval Weapons (U.S.)
CIA	Central Intelligence Agency (U.S.)
DARPA	Defense Advanced Research Projects Agency (U.S.)
H.-B.	Hansa-Brandenburg Flugzeugwerke
hp	horsepower
JATO	Jet-Assisted Takeoff*
kn	knot
LFG	Luft Fahrzeug Gesellschaft
MG	machine gun
mph	miles per hour
NARA	National Archives and Record Administration (U.S.)
NASM	National Air and Space Museum (U.S.)
NATO	North Atlantic Treaty Organization
NavAir	Naval Air Systems Command (U.S.)
NKVD	*Narodnyy komissariat vnutrennih del* (People's Commissariat for Internal Affairs; Soviet Union)
nm	nautical mile
Recon	reconnaissance
SAC	Strategic Air Command (U.S.)
shp	shaft horsepower
SLAM	Supersonic Low-Altitude Missile
SLUAS	Submarine-Launched Unmanned Aerial System
STARE	Submarine-launched Tactical Airborne Reconnaissance Expendable

---

* These were rocket boosters, not turbojet devices.

STOL	Short Takeoff and Landing
TNA	The National Archives (Britain)
TsKB	*Tsentral'noye dizaynerskoye byuro* (Central Design Bureau; Soviet Union)
UAV	Unmanned Aerial Vehicle
UDT	Underwater Demolition Team
VTOL	Vertical Takeoff and Landing

CHAPTER 1

The Early Efforts

Two brothers in the small German town of Lüdinghausen probably were the first persons to conceive of a combination of two new and revolutionary military technologies: the submarine and the aircraft. The age of practical submarines had begun at the start of the 20th Century and the Wright Brothers' pioneering flight had occurred at almost the same time. Ernst Bielefeld, an engineer, and his brother H. Bielefeld, an accountant, submitted their concept for a submarine carrying two disassembled floatplanes to the Imperial Patent Office in November 1912. They christened their proposed undersea craft the *U-Boot-Flugzeug-Mutterschiff*—the Submarine Aircraft Mothership.

The floatplanes were to be pulled out of hangars fore and aft of the conning tower and assembled on rotating platforms on the submarine's deck, then hoisted into the water by a deck-mounted crane. The brothers intended their submarine aircraft carrier to extend the range of floatplanes beyond their coastal seaplane bases.[1]

The Bielefelds' patent was prophetic. Within three years a floatplane would be carried to sea on the deck of a submarine. And within five years the German Navy would use the brothers' patent as inspiration for its submarine designs. Little could the Bielefelds have known that their idea would become a concept studied by all of the major navies of the world.

Three months after the outbreak of World War I in August 1914, the German Army captured the Belgian port of Zeebrugge on the North Sea. The port was located close to shipping lanes in the English Channel and the North Sea, making it an ideal base for German submarines to prey on Allied merchant ships. In November 1914, five U-boats sailed from German ports to Zeebrugge's mole, a curving breakwater stretching one and a half miles out into the North Sea. First to arrive was the *U-12* under the command of

Section at A

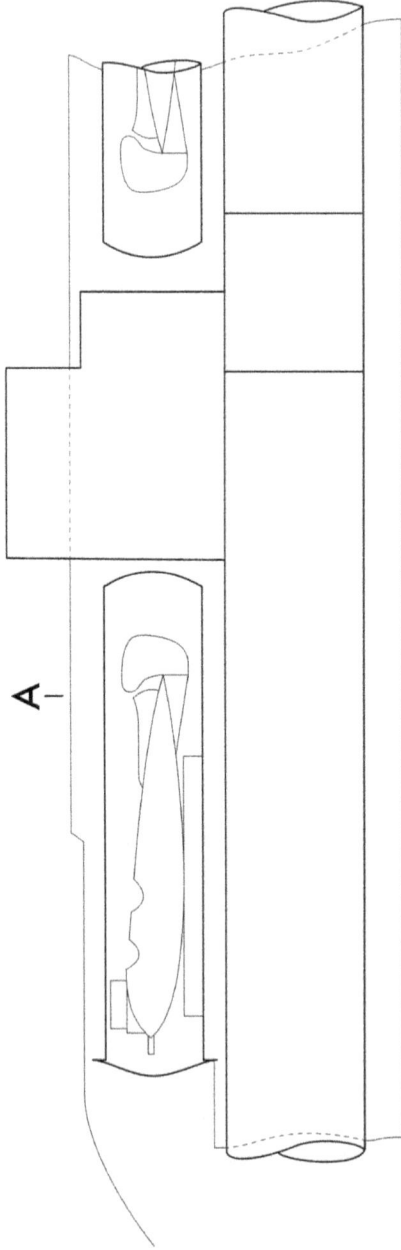

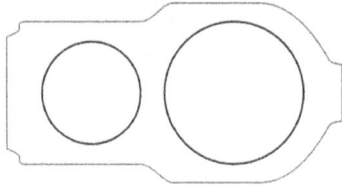

The Bielefeld brothers' 1912 concept for a "submarine aircraft mothership." The craft was intended to transport seaplanes out to sea so that they could operate beyond their coastal bases. (©JACOB GUNNARSON)

Kapitänleunant Walter Forstmann. Although the thick smoke that bellowed from her four kerosene engines made the *U-12* a conspicuous target on the surface, she was a potent threat to Allied ships when submerged and driven by battery-powered electric motors.

German aircraft arrived at Zeebrugge shortly after the U-boats. On 6 December, Naval Aviation Division 1 became the first contingent of German naval aircraft stationed at the port. Its new base on the mole was decidedly makeshift: a railroad shed converted into a hangar near the submarine base. *Oberleunant zur See* Friedrich von Arnauld de la Perière commanded the division of three other officers and 55 enlisted men. They flew two Friedrichshafen FF 29a floatplanes—unarmed, two-seat biplanes with a maximum speed of 60 mph.[2]

Von Arnauld's mission at Zeebrugge was unclear. "Nothing was known at that time about the use of a sea-flight station near a land front line," he recalled.[3] With no specific instructions forthcoming from naval headquarters, the unit formulated its own missions and tactics. By December, two additional FF 29s had arrived, and the planes each were fitted to carry two 26-pound bombs. They began long-range reconnaissance missions over the coasts of France and England, flying 26 missions that month. On Christmas Eve 1914, an FF 29 attempted to bomb England's Dover harbor: the bombs struck a few hundred yards offshore.[4] On Christmas Day an FF 29 with von Arnauld at the controls and *Oberleunant zur See* Hermann Moll as his observer set out to bomb the British capital—London. They were forced to drop their bombs ten miles west of the city to escape British fighters.[5] *That was the first confirmed aerial bombing of British soil.*[6] No deaths and little damage resulted from those attacks, but they heralded the beginning of the German air attacks on Britain.

Von Arnauld's raids were limited by the low reliability and short range of the aircraft. The temperamental Mercedes engines of the FF 29 forced many of the aircraft to come down at sea.

The submariners and airmen shared the Zeebrugge base and, despite the difference between their "machines," they bonded over the still experimental nature of both aircraft and submarines. In that spirit of camaraderie, Forstmann of the submarine *U-12* and von Arnauld conceived of a way of increasing the range of the seaplanes by using the submarine: The idea of strapping von Arnauld's Friedrichshafen to the U-boat seemed sensible. The aircraft easily could be launched by submerging the submarine and floating off the aircraft; it could be recovered by the U-boat surfacing beneath it. As an improvised aircraft carrier, the submarine needed no modifications. It is not known if those involved were aware of the Bielefeld Brothers' earlier patent.

At 0940 on 6 January 1915, an FF 29 was lowered by crane onto the deck of the *U-12*. The aircraft was No. 204, which von Arnauld had previously used

The German submarine *U-12* carrying an FF 29a floatplane out to sea on 6 January 1915. This photo was taken inside the port of Zeebrugge's breakwater or mole. One hour later, after the *U-12* had sailed out to sea, the submarine submerged, and the floatplane took off. After flying to the coast of England, the FF 29a returned to Zeebrugge. (AUTHORS' COLLECTION)

to bomb England. Von Arnauld was in the pilot's seat with Moll again as his observer. Because the space between the aircraft's floats was wider than the submarine's deck, it was placed on deck sideways, near the bow. Moving out into the harbor, the *U-12* trimmed down and let the aircraft float free to taxi on the water. With that trial successfully completed, the FF 29 was picked up by the submarine and the *U-12* sailed out past the mole and out to sea. Although it was a clear day with excellent visibility and light winds, there were large swells outside of the breakwater. The sea state was no issue for the submarine, but the waves proved too violent for the fragile seaplane.

Forstmann became increasingly concerned for the safety of the aircraft and at 1040, when the submarine was 19 miles from Zeebrugge, he decided to submerge the submarine to launch the aircraft. Von Arnauld took off without incident and flew 70 miles to Kent on the English coast. Unseen by the British, he then headed back toward Zeebrugge. While he and Forstmann had planned to rendezvous at sea, von Arnauld decided that the conditions were too rough to alight on the open water and flew directly to Zeebrugge. The *U-12* remained in the rendezvous area for two hours, returning to port at 1430.[7]

Both Forstmann and von Arnauld considered the operation a successful proof of concept. Still, future missions would need calmer seas and a more robust method of attaching the aircraft to the U-boat. Both officers were eager to try again—and with bombs carried on the Friedrichshafen. However, the

Navy's leadership did not approve of the informal experiment, impressing upon von Arnauld that "U-boats operate in the water, airplanes in the air; there is no connection between the two."[8] Hence there was no further development of aircraft-carrying submarines at Zeebrugge.[9]

The *U-12* was not the last U-boat to carry a floatplane on her deck. On 22 May 1915, a Rumpler 4B floatplane was strapped down to the bow of the *U-22* at the shipyard in Wilhelmshaven for a pierside experiment.[10] The submarine did not go to sea with the aircraft.[11]

Sometime after the historic flight at Zeebrugge, the *U-25* rescued an FF 29 that had alighted on the water off the North Sea coast of Germany because of engine trouble. Carefully surfacing beneath the floatplane, the *U-25* returned the Friedrichshafen to its base at Borkum.

The Royal Norwegian Navy performed an aircraft-submarine rescue in 1917. Norway, a neutral country during World War I, had produced a handful of military aircraft. Hans Fleischer Dons, believed to be the first Norwegian to fly an aircraft, was an officer from the submarine *Kobben* (later renamed the *A-1*).

Among the Norwegian military aircraft were two MF2 floatplanes. On 21 July 1917, one of the MF2s damaged a float when it alighted in Trondheim harbor. The submarine *A-4* was sent into the harbor carrying a new float on her deck. After raising the *A-4*'s submerged stern beneath the aircraft, the airmen were able to replace the broken float, and the MF2 was set back on the water as the submarine submerged.[12]

BRITISH EXPERIMENTS

On Christmas Day 1914, the Royal Navy carried out a ship-based air attack on the German Zeppelin hangars at Cuxhaven on the North Sea coast. Although launched from surface ships, not submarines, the raid demonstrated that ship-based aircraft could strike targets beyond the range of aircraft flying from bases in Britain. (The Japanese had conducted a similar ship-launched attack against the German-occupied port of Tsingtao, China, in September 1914.)

In January 1915, the Zeppelins began bombing raids on England. The airships bombed from high altitudes, above the ceiling of the defending fighter aircraft. Antiaircraft guns would only score an occasional hit on the airships. British warships in the English Channel and North Sea observed that the Zeppelins only rose to high altitudes over land, flying close to the water during their transit over the sea. The British realized that defending fighters could intercept the airships while they were low over the North Sea and thus vulnerable.

In early 1916, the Royal Navy modified the submarine *E-22* to carry seaplanes to intercept Zeppelins. Two Sopwith Schneider floatplanes would rest on sloping rails installed behind the conning tower; to launch the aircraft the

The British submarine *E-22* carrying two Sopwith Schneider floatplanes on 24 April 1916. Two parallel rails were installed on the submarine's deck to enable the aircraft to slide into the water. The *E-22* was sunk by a German U-boat on the following day, putting an end to the trials. (AUTHORS' COLLECTION)

E-22 would trim down by the stern and the Schneiders would slide down the rails into the water.

The Schneiders, from the naval air station at Felixstowe, were smaller than the German Friedrichshafens and more delicate, requiring calm weather for their water takeoff. The aircraft would be carried into the North Sea by the *E-22*, takeoff, patrol over the Helgoland Bight searching for Zeppelins, and then fly back to Felixstowe. On 24 April, two Schneiders were loaded onto the *E-22* after alighting on the calm waters of Felixstowe harbor. Still close to shore, the submarine submerged her stern, and the aircraft slipped off to fly back to Felixstowe.

The next day, at sea off the eastern coast of England, the *E-22* was torpedoed and sunk by the German submarine *UB-18*, putting an end to that line of experimentation. By the end of the war in November 1918, Zeppelins were being intercepted by seaplanes launched from surface ships and by land-based fighter aircraft.

The British briefly experimented with submarine-towed, lighter-than-air craft. In 1918 the *K-5*, one of the large, steam turbine-powered K-class submarines, towed a Sea Scout Zero airship in an effort to increase the blimp's range.[13] The blimp was intended to be a convoy escort, planned to sight surfaced U-boats at a distance. Several British C-class submarines also towed manned balloons to sea in another effort to spot surfaced U-boats.[14]

STORABLE SEAPLANES

The German and British experiments proved that carrying seaplanes on the decks of submarines was a dangerous endeavor for both machines: The submarines risked being caught on the surface by the enemy, while the seaplanes were in danger of being swamped by the sea or unable to take off in rough seas. If the submarine had to quickly submerge, the attached seaplane could be lost or damaged beyond repair.

Those problems could be alleviated if the seaplane could be disassembled or "folded up" and stowed in a pressure-tight container mounted on the submarine. In 1915 British aircraft designer Pemberton Billing—whose company would later become Supermarine—submitted a design to the Admiralty for a flying boat that could be stored on board submarines.[15] Billing's design probably was designated PB27; only a scale model was made.

That same year, Rear Admiral Sir Robert Arbuthnot proposed that submarines carry aircraft stowed in watertight hangars. The idea was considered by an Admiralty subcommittee, but nothing came of his proposal at that time.[16] Britain would only experiment with aircraft-carrying submarines again after the war.

As World War I continued, Germany began to construct larger U-boats for long-range operations. In early 1916 the North German Lloyd company and Deutsche Bank built the cargo-carrying submarine *Deutschland*, intended to bypass the British blockade of German ports to transport critical materials such as rubber and nickel from the United States, which was neutral at that time. She was the world's largest submarine, displacing 1,820 tons submerged and able to carry 790 tons of cargo. As a "civilian" submarine, the *Deutschland* undertook two highly successful voyages from Germany to Baltimore, Maryland, and to New London, Connecticut, in the summer and fall of 1916, respectively. Her sister ship *Bremen*, completed in July 1916, attempted a similar journey to Norfolk, Virginia. She sank en route due to unknown causes. Six additional *Deutschland*-class submarines were ordered as cargo carriers.[17]

Following the Battle of Jutland in May 1916, Germany's main surface fleet was penned up in port by the British blockade. A large submarine with a heavy gun and torpedo armament could fulfill the raiding cruiser role, bypassing the British blockade and attacking the important merchant shipping in distant waters. Several such "cruiser" submarines were laid down by the end of

The German cruiser submarine *U-155*, formerly the cargo submarine *Deutschland*. She undertook two voyages to the United States as a cargo submarine, circumventing the blockade of German ports imposed by the British. The *U-155* was converted to a military submarine with the addition of six torpedo tubes and two 5.9-inch (150-mm) guns. (U.S. NAVY)

1916. However, those U-boats would take considerable time to build, thus the *Deutschland*—renamed the *U-155*—and her five sister ships were taken over by the German Navy and converted into makeshift cruiser submarines with the addition of deck guns and torpedo tubes.

The potential role of those large submarines as commerce raiders prompted a reevaluation of the concept of operating seaplanes from submarines. Some officers in the German Navy were aware of the Bielefeld Brothers' patent for a submarine with floatplane hangars. The idea met with resistance from the officials of the U-boat Inspectorate. In December 1916, the assistant chief of the U-boat Inspectorate wrote to the Imperial Naval Office expressing a dim view of the concept of an underwater aircraft carrier:

> The construction of a submarine mothership [for aircraft] presents numerous difficulties, and its practical implementation offers even more. Ultimately the value of the few aircraft that can be carried by such a craft is small in comparison to the expense.[18]

Naval aviators were more excited about the prospect: In January 1917, after being shown the Bielefeld Brothers' patent, the commander of the Naval Aviation Division asked the U-boat Inspectorate if a small seaplane could be stored inside of a pressure hull. Instead of using the submarine to extend the seaplane's combat range, he considered the seaplane an essential reconnaissance tool for the submarine to find targets. The U-boat Inspectorate remained pessimistic, replying that submarines already were cramped and that their hatches were too small to fit an aircraft fuselage or engine.

However, the concept of an aircraft-carrying submarine spread within the German Navy and began to find advocates in submarine officers. *Kapitänleunant* Lothar von Arnauld de la Perière, then the commander of the *U-35*, was undoubtedly aware of his brother Friedrich's experiment with the *U-12* and became an outspoken supporter of the concept:

> A significant disadvantage of the submarine is its low vantage point and consequently short range of vision. . . . On the new U-boats of large displacement which are now under construction, features must be created that expand the effective radius of action and increase their success. This is all the more necessary if the U-boats are to work in the Atlantic, where the merchant ship routes are far apart and are therefore more difficult to find than near the coasts. The U-boat will only be fully exploited in the trade war if it can be given an aircraft. I think this is constructively feasible.[19]

In March 1917, shortly after Lothar von Arnauld's letter advocating the aircraft-carrying submarine, the U-boat Inspectorate began investigating an aircraft that could be stored on board a converted *Deutschland*-class submarine. The Hansa-Brandenburg Flugzeugwerke offered a twin-float monoplane that easily could be disassembled into component parts: the engine, fuel tank, wings, floats, propeller, and fuselage. All would be stored either inside of the pressure hull or in small containers underneath the U-boat's outer deck (i.e., external to the pressure hull). After discussions with Ernst Heinkel, the firm's chief designer, the Navy specified that a U-boat aircraft would have a top speed of 93 mph and an endurance of 1½ hours.

On 30 April 1917, the German Navy ordered six submarine-launched aircraft from Hansa-Brandenburg: three of the aforementioned floatplanes and three diminutive, biplane flying boats. The Navy also ordered three monoplane flying boats from Junkers; that contract was cancelled before construction began. The Zeppelin company, with Claude Dornier the head designer, proposed building an all-metal aircraft for that role, but the Navy placed no orders.

Priority was given to Hansa-Brandenburg's tiny flying boat—designated W 20—because it had the smallest stowage space requirements. With a pusher propeller and a high-mounted upper wing, the W 20 was an oddly shaped craft. The wings, tail, engine, and fuel tank could be quickly removed, allowing the aircraft to be stored in a pressure-tight hangar with a diameter of 6 feet, 7 inches and length of 19 feet, 8 inches that was mounted forward of the U-boat's conning tower. Heinkel claimed that the small aircraft could be fully assembled or disassembled in about two minutes; that claim was wildly optimistic, even under ideal conditions, much less the wet and rolling deck of a submarine.

The prototype Hansa-Brandenburg W 20 floatplane. This photo probably was taken just before flight tests on Lake Plau in the fall of 1917, during which the aircraft crashed and was heavily damaged. Subsequent W 20s had additional struts between the wings to strengthen the delicate airframe. (AUTHORS' COLLECTION)

Perhaps in an effort to lighten the aircraft or to reduce the assembly time, the first W 20 had a cantilever lower wing, which was found to have insufficient structural rigidity. The few struts connecting the upper wing and tailplane to the fuselage did little to reinforce the flimsy airframe. As a consequence, the prototype crashed into Plau Lake on its maiden flight in the fall of 1917. The aircraft was heavily damaged, although it was repairable. The second and third W 20s had larger wings with struts between them. The damaged prototype was rebuilt to that standard. Once flight testing began the W 20's performance was underwhelming, particularly its sluggish rate of climb. All three W 20s were delivered to the Navy by June 1918.

On 2 June 1917, the U-boat Inspectorate approved plans to install hangars on the nearly complete *U-153* and *U-154*. But the shipyard pointed out that the hangar might upset the submarine's stability. The Inspectorate subsequently confirmed that the hangar would indeed make the submarine top-heavy and that project was abandoned.

The contract for three Hansa-Brandenburg floatplanes was cancelled. The Navy did retain the three W 20s, advising Hansa-Brandenburg that "the probability may arise for the Navy to have to resort to these aircraft."[20] By March 1918, the Navy had entirely given up on the W 20 for service on submarines and ordered Hansa-Brandenburg to convert the three W 20s into conventional seaplanes.[21] They were quickly placed in storage at the Hage seaplane depot on the North Sea coast.

FOLLOW-ON GERMAN EFFORTS

Despite the U-boat Inspectorate's reluctance to build an underwater seaplane carrier, many naval aviators and U-boat commanders continued to support the concept. On 10 January 1918, the Inspectorate received a letter from the Seaplane Testing Command advocating the development of a floatplane for use on board submarines. The missive pointed out that several submarine officers, including Lothar von Arnauld, desired a reconnaissance aircraft on their U-boats.

The case for an aircraft-carrying submarine was bolstered by the return of the auxiliary cruiser *Wolf* to Germany on 23 February 1918. Disguised as an innocent merchant ship, the *Wolf* was heavily armed with guns, torpedoes, and mines. She left Kiel on 30 November 1916, for the Indian Ocean and South Pacific. In those remote waters she captured or sank 14 Allied ships and claimed another 13 sunk by her mines. The *Wolf*'s highly successful cruise had lasted 451 days, and she had sailed 64,000 miles.

The *Wolf* was the first German ship to carry a seaplane. Hidden below decks with its wings removed was a Friedrichshafen FF 33e floatplane, nicknamed the *Wölfchen* (Wolf Cub). Although not perfectly suited to the rigors of shipboard use, the *Wölfchen* proved invaluable to the raider. The *Wölfchen* often would force the merchant ships it found to surrender by bombing them—or threatening to—and dropping a letter demanding surrender. On one occasion the aircraft landed alongside the American sailing schooner *Winslow* and the two aviators compelled the ship's surrender with their pistols. The *Wolf* captured at least four merchant ships with the aircraft's assistance, *making the* Wölfchen *responsible for more Allied shipping losses than the entirety of the rest of German naval aviation.*[22]

The German Navy learned a great deal about shipboard aircraft from the *Wolf*'s cruise. Assembly took up to eight hours because the bracing wires required rigging for every flight.[23] The floatplane's wood swelled and rotted when damp, the canvas ripped, and struts bent when the seaplane was being handled. The only way to keep the aircraft flying was to have a plethora of spare parts, not a desirable feature for a space-limited submarine. In fact, the *Wölfchen* only flew as long as it did because the *Wolf* captured a merchant ship with a load of raw silk that was used to skin the aircraft after the original canvas had deteriorated.[24] Thus, the Navy required that future submarine-launched aircraft be built from corrosion-resistant metals.

On 15 June 1918, the Navy ordered monoplane floatplanes of three designs for submarine operation: three aircraft from Luft Fahrzeug Gesellschaft (LFG), three from Hansa-Brandenburg, and five from Zeppelin.[25] All would have the 110-horsepower Obersel rotary engine and would be constructed entirely of duralumin. When disassembled, the wings, fuselage, floats, empennage, struts, and propellers would be stored in five watertight cylinders under the U-boat's upper deck; the cylinders were 28 inches in diameter; they could withstand the pressure to a depth of 200 feet. The aircraft's engine, fuel tank, and instrument panel detached from the airframe as a single unit and would be stowed in the submarine's forward escape trunk.[26]

The U-boat selected for the initial aircraft trials of these aircraft was the *U-139*, the lead boat of the Project 46 cruiser submarines. It probably was no coincidence that her prospective commanding officer was Lothar von Arnauld— one of the most vocal advocates in the German Navy for aircraft-carrying submarines.

The Project 46 U-boats were among the largest and most capable submarine designs of the war, armed with two 5.9-inch (150-mm) guns and six 21-inch (533-mm) torpedo tubes. Only three units—the *U-139*, *U-140*, and *U-141*—were completed before the end of the war.

The improved Project 46a (*U-142* class) was 23 feet longer to accommodate more powerful engines for greater surface speed and range. The Navy ordered nine of those cruiser submarines. Because of their impressive performance, the Project 46 and 46a U-boats would heavily influence the subsequent designs of cruiser-type submarines later built by the United States, Japan, Britain, and France.

The German Navy considered even more ambitious U-boat designs near the end of the war. The Project 47 *Panzerkreuzer* (Armored Cruiser) was a 3,800-ton submarine protected by armor plating above the waterline and armed with four 5.9-inch guns. That design was scrapped in favor of the less expensive Project 46a.

More impressive was the Project 50 *Tauchschiff* (Diving Ship) that would be about the same displacement as the Project 47 with four 6,000-horsepower steam turbines placed in a 410-foot-long hull to reach 25 knots on the surface. With four 5.9-inch guns and ten torpedo tubes, the *Tauchschiff* would have been the most impressive submarine of World War I.[27] A single *Tauchschiff*— the *UD-1*—was ordered, although her keel was not laid down before the end of the war.[28] Those and further planned U-boat cruisers most likely would have carried floatplanes.

Tests using mockups of the floatplanes on board the *U-139* were scheduled for early July 1918, but the hatch of her forward escape trunk would have to be enlarged to fit the aircraft's engine. Instead, the recently launched Project 46a submarine *U-144* was modified. In September, Hansa-Brandenburg and LFG sent wooden mockups of their aircraft to the Germania shipyard, where they were assembled, disassembled, and stowed on board the *U-144*.

LFG was the only company to complete any of the planned aircraft before the armistice ended the war on 11 November 1918. Zeppelin's contract for five

The LFG V 19 floatplane intended for use on board Germany's large cruiser submarines. The wings, floats, fuselage, and engine were to be stored in watertight cylinders beneath the submarine's superstructure deck. This photo was taken after the war when the sole V 19 prototype was offered for sale as a sport aircraft. (AUTHORS' COLLECTION)

floatplanes had been cancelled in August, and Hansa-Brandenburg failed to deliver any of its three planes. The single LFG aircraft—designated the Roland V 19—was one of the world's first all-metal aircraft.[29] Its assembly time was reduced by connecting the control column to the ailerons and elevators with rods instead of wires that would need to be rigged and properly tensioned. A hoisting point on the forward fuselage would allow a crane mounted on the U-boat's radio mast to swing the aircraft over the side for the water takeoff.

According to the aircraft's designer, Gotthard Baatz, assembly of the aircraft would take about 30 minutes and disassembly would take 15 minutes.[30] A single prototype V 19 was completed about the time of the armistice, and it was placed in storage.[31] No German aircraft-carrying submarines entered service during the war. Of the nine Project 46a submarines laid down, only the *U-142* was commissioned—one day before the armistice ending World War I.

PANIC ON THE EAST COAST

Despite the failure of the German Navy to produce an operational underwater aircraft carrier, rumors of the existence of such submarines had a significant impact on the Allies. As early as July 1917, British intelligence reported that the German Navy was developing a submarine-launched seaplane. On 20 July, Allied intelligence intercepted a secret attachment to the German Navy's daily order titled Designation of U-boat Aircraft that read:

"In the correspondence with aircraft firms the name U-boat aircraft appears frequently. In order to keep this new type secret, a cover name has to be used. The chosen name is a reversal of the earlier designation U-boat aircraft. From now on, Bu aircraft."[32]

Rumors of the German submarine-launched aircraft began to circulate in the United States. In May 1918, U-boats began operating off the East Coast to prey on American coastal shipping. Fear of aerial attack began to appear in the press.[33] On 2 June, the front page of *The Washington Post* newspaper featured illustrations of a submarine-launched aircraft flying over New York City with skyscrapers engulfed in flames. The article began:

> Nothing would so please the fatuous German sense of humor and so assuage their truculent egotism as to be able to send some of von Tirpitz's new supersubmarines across the Atlantic this summer to bomb American coast cities with gas shells and lyddite grenades loosed from airplanes that might be launched a hundred or more miles off New York, Boston or Charleston from the decks of U-boats, or possibly fabricated hydro-airplanes assembled on the surface of the sea alongside the transatlantic "unterseebooten."[34]

Newspapers were not alone in stoking the alarm of the American public: Famed Arctic explorer Rear Admiral Robert Peary, as well as Alan R. Hawley,

A speculative illustration of a U-boat launching a seaplane that was published in the 2 June 1918 issue of *The Washington Post*. The German submarine aircraft program caused a short-lived panic on the U.S. East Coast in the summer of 1918, resulting in blackouts of New York City. (WASHINGTON POST)

president of the Aero Club of America, publicly speculated that German submarines could launch seaplanes to bomb American cities. As a result of the growing concern over aircraft-carrying submarines, the War Department recommended blackouts for East Coast cities. From 4 to 17 June, New York City enforced a partial blackout, as did several coastal cities in New Jersey.[35] Air raid sirens were installed and fire-fighting regulations were established.

Although most New Yorkers appear to have viewed the possibility of air attack as remote, widespread panic was triggered twice in July during air raid siren tests.[36] U-boats did operate close to the city in the summer of 1918, with the cruiser submarine *U-151* sailing near enough to see the glow of Broadway's lights. But neither she nor any other German submarine carried an aircraft across the Atlantic during the war. Erroneous rumors of seaplanes operating from U-boats continued even after the end of the conflict.

Thus, by the end of the World War I both the Allies and Germany had experimented with submarine-launched aircraft. All involved realized that aircraft could be invaluable for searching out targets—and threats—for submarines, which at the time operated almost always on the surface and had severely limited search capabilities. Although a mature design had not come to fruition during the war, the promise of the aircraft-carrying submarine was recognized by the world's major navies. Between the world wars, the U.S., British, French, Italian, Polish, Soviet, and Japanese navies continued the efforts that the German Navy had begun during World War I.

CHAPTER 2

Between the Wars— United States

During World War I the Allies were fully aware that Germany was developing aircraft to be launched from submarines. New York City had even been blacked out for fear of submarine-launched air attacks. Still, when the Allies gained access to German aviation facilities after the war, the submarine-launched aircraft efforts initially escaped their notice.

Allied inspectors touring the Hage seaplane depot on the North Sea coast did not realize the significance of the three Hansa-Brandenburg W 20 flying boats in storage there. The Luft Fahrzeug Gesellschaft (LFG) V 19 was kept secret by the Germans in violation of the 1919 Treaty of Versailles that prohibited Germany from possessing military aircraft.[1]

The veil of secrecy lifted as the German government subsequently relaxed control over classified wartime activities. German submarine and aircraft designers began publishing accounts of their wartime projects in the hope of attracting foreign customers to buy or license their designs.

In 1920, Hansa-Brandenburg designer Ernst Rothenburg provided the U.S. Navy with an inside perspective on the program, although he appears to have overstated the progress that had been made before the end of the war.[2] As a result of that and other overly optimistic accounts from German engineers and naval officers, U.S. Navy submariner-turned-aviator Commander Kenneth Whiting testified before a congressional committee in 1921 that "the Germans at the end of the war had perfected aircraft to put on submarines. . . . We have reports that the Germans had gotten out three planes for use on the large submarines."[3] That misconception was further reinforced when, in 1922, the designer of the LFG V 19, Gotthard Baatz, published a detailed description of that aircraft in a German technical journal.[4] The V 19 subsequently was reassembled, photographed, and offered for sale as a sport plane or an easily transportable aircraft for polar expeditions.[5]

From those revelations, it appeared that developing an aircraft-carrying submarine would be a straightforward exercise. Many U.S. Navy officers and civilian engineers already held German submarine designers in high regard with most U.S. designs of the 1920s being patterned on the Project 42 and Project 46a U-boats and propelled by copies of German MAN diesel engines.[6] The combination of overly optimistic reports and an attitude of "Germanophilia" may have blinded some U.S. naval officers to the difficulties of developing an aircraft for submarines.

Another major factor in the U.S. Navy's early enthusiasm for aircraft-carrying submarines was the creation of the Bureau of Aeronautics (BuAer) in 1921 under the leadership of Rear Admiral William A. Moffett. That technical bureau had responsibilities for aircraft design, a duty previously relegated to the Bureau of Construction and Repair, which primarily handled ship design, construction, and maintenance. Aircraft carriers were central to Moffett's plan to grow U.S. naval aviation, but he also envisioned that seaplanes would be carried by battleships, cruisers, destroyers, submarines, and auxiliary tenders, both for scouting and to supplement the strike capability of aircraft carriers.[7] Among its other responsibilities, BuAer was charged with determining "by trial the practicability and desirability of operating planes from destroyers and submarines."[8] As a result, most U.S. submarine designs of the early 1920s included some capability to carry aircraft.

SUBMERSIBLE BATTLE CRUISERS

After World War I the U.S. Navy turned its attention to the Pacific and to its chief rival in that region: Japan. At that time the U.S. Navy's undersea fleet consisted mostly of small, short-range submarines. The newest and most numerous were the 48 S-class submarines. Completed from 1920 to 1925 in several series, they displaced from 1,062 to 1,458 tons submerged and measured 219 to 267 feet in length.

Operating from forward bases available at Guam, Manila, and Pearl Harbor, the S-boats had neither the range to reach the Sea of Japan nor the speed to operate with the surface fleet. The Navy thus sought to develop long-range "cruiser" submarines with sufficient speed to operate with the battle fleet; there also was interest in submarine minelayers.

The Bureau of Construction and Repair, then headed by the noted naval architect Rear Admiral David W. Taylor, entertained a few radical designs in the early 1920s as advanced submarines were being considered: Lieutenant Commander Francis S. Craven proposed a "submersible battle cruiser"—a gigantic, steam-powered submarine fitted with several gun turrets.

The surface battle cruisers of that era were about the same size and as heavily armed as battleships, but sacrificed armor protection for higher speeds. One of the primary roles of the battle cruiser was as a fleet scout. In theory, the battle cruiser could use her heavy guns to break through the screen of destroyers and cruisers protecting the enemy battle fleet and then use speed to turn tail if she encountered the enemy battleships' guns.

Craven argued that a *submersible battle cruiser* would have a better chance of survival than a surface battle cruiser: his proposed design, armed with four or six 12-inch (305-mm) guns, would be able to attain 25 knots on the surface with a range of 20,000 miles at ten knots (battleships of that era had a maximum speed of 21 knots). An armored deck and hull would protect the submarine from gunfire from enemy cruisers and destroyers.

To accommodate the armor, gun turrets, and steam propulsion plant, Craven's submarine would be enormous. Because a single, large-diameter pressure hull could not easily be made strong enough to survive planned diving depths, Craven suggested constructing the submarine with several smaller diameter pressure hulls arranged in parallel and wrapped in a streamlined, free-flooding outer hull. That arrangement also would serve to isolate the heat of the boilers of the submarine's steam propulsion plant from the crew compartments.

In August 1920, the bureau's version of Craven's concept had a 20,000-ton surface displacement, was 625 feet long, and would be armed with two 12-inch, twin gun turrets, and have 14 torpedo tubes. Inside two of the five pressure hulls were the boilers and turbines for the 52,000-horsepower steam plant— significantly more horsepower than in contemporary battleships. Submerged performance was 50 n.miles at three knots using two 2,000-horsepower electric motors; two 2,000-horsepower diesels were provided for charging batteries. The lead ship was estimated to cost $25 million, which was slightly more than the cost of a battleship.[9]

On 5 October 1920, Admiral Taylor ordered a further study based on Craven's concept. In addition to his pioneering work in naval architecture, Taylor was keenly interested in the new field of aeronautics.[10] He thus required that the submarine design concepts have accommodation for scout seaplanes stored in 16-foot-diameter hangars. Drawn up that month, the study's five design options had surface displacements between 8,750 and 18,500 tons and were between 400 and 550 feet in length.

TABLE 2.1
Submersible Battle Cruiser Designs

	Aug. 1920	Type No. 1	Type No. 2	Type No. 3	Type No. 4	Type No. 5	Type No. 6
Displacement							
surface (tons)	20,000	10,000	13,500	13,500	8,750	18,500	21,500
submerged (tons)							27,573
Length	625 ft. (190.5 m)	400 ft. (121.9 m)	490 ft. (149.4 m)	425 ft. (129.5 m)	550 ft. (167.6 m)	500 ft. (152.4 m)	490 ft. (149.4 m)
Beam	72 ft. 10 in. (22.2 m)	48 ft. (14.6 m)	60 ft. (18.3 m)	60 ft. (18.3 m)	42 ft. (12.8 m)	72 ft. (21.9 m)	67 ft. (20.4 m)
Draft	30 ft. (9.1 m)	33 ft. 3 in. (10.2 m)	29 ft. (8.8 m)	26 ft. (7.9 m)	27 ft. (8.2 m)	29 ft. (8.8 m)	30 ft. 5 in. (9.3 m)
Diesel engines	2	4	8	4		—	6
total shp	4,000	5,600	8,000	4,400	13,250	—	18,000
Steam turbines	—	—	—	—		—	—
total shp	52,500	—	—	—	—	26,000	—
Electric motors	2	4	4	2			2
total shp	2,000	5,600	8,800	4,400	13,250	8,800	18,000
Shafts	2	2	2	2	2	2	2
Speed							
surface (knots)	25	14	14.5	11.75	18	20	17
Range (nm/kn)							
surfaced	20,000/10	16,000/10	20,000/10	18,000/10	9,000/10	11,500/10	10,000/10
submerged	150/3						
Test depth		400 ft. (133 m)					
Torpedo tubes	10 21-in. bow	6 21-in. bow	6 21-in. bow	6 21-in. bow	6 21-in. bow	6 21-in. bow	6 21-in. bow
	4 21-in. stern	2 21-in. stern	2 21-in. stern	2 21-in. stern	2 21-in. stern	2 21-in. stern	2 21-in. stern
Guns	4 12-in.	8 8-in.	8 8-in.	4 8-in.	8 8-in.	8 8-in.	8 8-in.
	4 4-in.	2 4-in.	2 4-in.	2 4-in.	2 4-in.	2 4-in.	10 4-in.
Aircraft	—	4	4	6	3	8	4

Design No. 1 would have mounted eight 8-inch (203-mm) guns in three turrets with little armor plating. The submarine would carry four aircraft in deck-mounted hangars and would have a catapult aft of the conning tower. Design No. 2 would have the same armament with heavier armor and with four aircraft stored in vertical, tube-like hangars forward of the turrets and conning tower. Design No. 3 would have half the number of guns of the previous designs, but was armored against both gunfire and torpedoes; six aircraft would be stored inside of the hull with elevators to move them to the outer deck.

Design No. 4 would be the longest, fastest, and lightest of the submarines, having only one 8-inch twin turret facing aft. To ensure a slender hull for high surface speed there was only a single pressure hull with a figure-eight cross-section. Three aircraft would be stored in the upper half of the pressure hull and could be moved up to the outer deck by an elevator.

Designs No. 1 through 4 had diesel-electric propulsion; design No. 5 would use steam turbines on the surface and electric motors when submerged. That design was the largest of the five concepts at 18,500 tons surface displacement and also the fastest at 20 knots on the surface. Eight aircraft would be stored inside of the pressure hulls, lifted to the deck by elevator. A final variant combining the characteristics of the previous five concepts—design No. 6—was drawn up in February 1921. An even larger submersible battle cruiser, it would displace 21,500 tons on the surface and be armed with eight 8-inch guns. Four aircraft would be carried in the upper pressure hull and would be launched via catapult.[11]

Although those designs later would seem bizarre, their plans and characteristics were widely circulated within the Navy. Sketches of designs No. 1 through 4 were incorporated into one of the bureau's "Spring Styles" booklets. Named after the contemporary ladies' fashion catalogs, those publications were used to illustrate potential ship designs for the Navy leadership. The Navy's General Board—the senior advisory body responsible for determining naval policy and ship characteristics—was the primary audience for the Spring Styles sketches.

In the spring of 1922, Admiral Taylor and the Bureau of Construction and Repair resumed work on a "realistic" cruiser submarine, and the submersible battle cruiser concept was dropped. "It was unquestionably too much of a jump to go from present submarines of about 2,000 tons displacement to large vessels of 10,000 to 20,000 tons displacement," commented a General Board report.[12] Even had the Navy decided to go ahead with those enormous submarines, the craft would have run afoul of the 10,000-ton limit imposed by the Washington Naval Treaty of 1922.[13] Nevertheless, the requirement for onboard scout seaplanes was retained for smaller cruiser submarines.

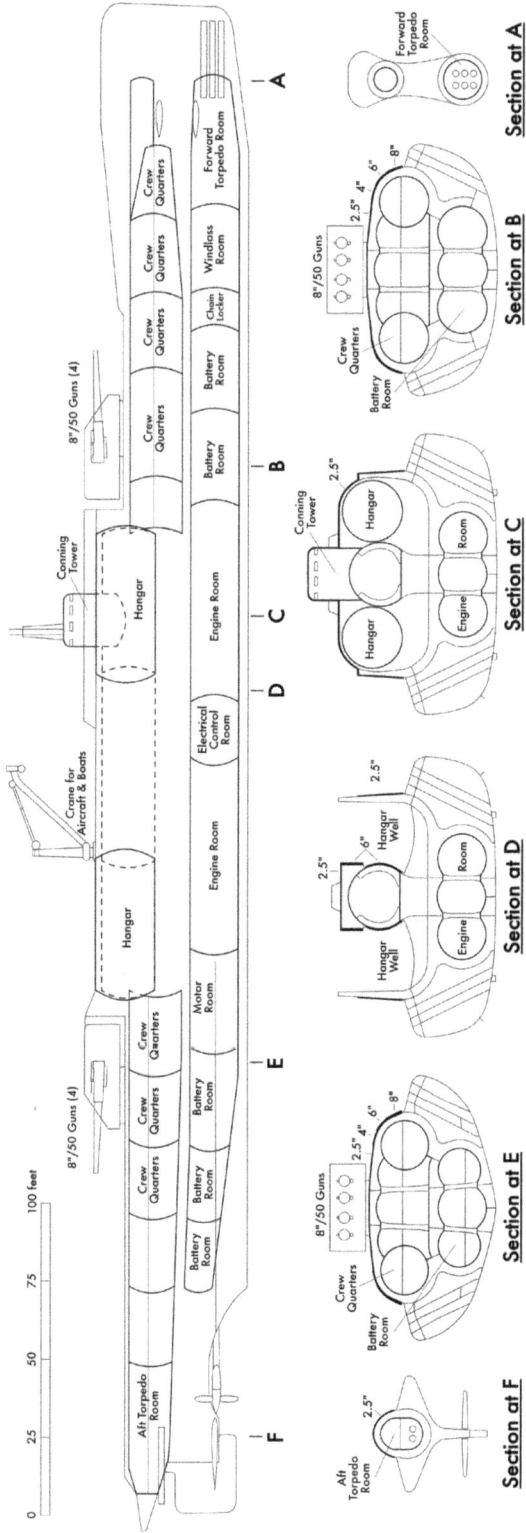

Section at A

Forward Torpedo Room

Section at B

8"/50 Guns

2.5" | 4" | 6" | 8"

Crew Quarters

Battery Room

Section at C

Conning Tower

2.5"

Hangar

Room

Engine

Section at D

2.5"

6" Hangar Wall

Hangar Well

Engine

Room

2.5"

Section at E

8"/50 Guns

2.5" | 4" | 6" | 8"

Crew Quarters

Battery Room

Section at F

Aft Torpedo Room

2.5"

Crew Quarters

Crew Quarters

Crew Quarters

Crew Quarters

Forward Torpedo Room

Windlass Room

Chain Locker

Battery Room

Battery Room

Engine Room

8"/50 Guns (4)

Conning Tower

Hangar

Crane for Aircraft & Boats

Engine Room

Electrical Control Room

Hangar

8"/50 Guns (4)

Crew Quarters

Crew Quarters

Motor Room

Battery Room

Battery Room

Battery Room

Aft Torpedo Room

A B C D E F

0   25   50   75   100 feet

The Bureau of Construction and Repair's design No. 6 for a submersible battle cruiser. The thicknesses of the armor plating are indicated in the section views.

(©JACOB GUNNARSON)

AIRCRAFT DEVELOPMENT

In the fall of 1921, as the naval architects at the Bureau of Construction and Repair were sketching the future of the U.S. Navy submarine force, the aeronautical engineers at the Bureau of Aeronautics began work on a submarine-launched floatplane. Designing the aircraft—designated design No. 4—was one of the first tasks of the new bureau. Design No. 4 was a 1,000-pound, single-seat biplane.[14] BuAer simultaneously was developing a floatplane for destroyers as design No. 2.

In May 1922, the two projects were consolidated into design No. 20, which closely resembled the Army's Sperry Messenger biplane. Detachable struts replaced wire bracing on the wings to speed the aircraft's assembly and disassembly. Able to stay aloft for two hours, design No. 20 was to carry either a radio or forward-firing machine gun for self-defense. When disassembled it could be stowed in a hangar 5 feet, 9 inches in diameter and 22 feet, 9 inches long.

BuAer awarded contracts for six aircraft each to the Cox-Klemin Aircraft Corporation and the Glenn L. Martin Company.[15] The Cox-Klemin XS-1 had a traditional wood airframe, while the Martin MS-1 was of more advanced duralumin construction. Both aircraft designs were skinned with fabric. By acquiring the same aircraft design built using different materials, BuAer was able to directly compare the two methods of construction. The MS-1 first took to the air on 24 April 1923, and the XS-1 followed on 17 May. Although initially intended also for use on destroyers, the aircraft were evaluated only on a submarine.[16]

The Martin MS-1 during flight tests on Lake Erie in April 1923. The MS-1 and the similar Cox-Klemin XS-1 were inspired by the Army's Sperry Messenger. (AUTHORS' COLLECTION)

RENEWED GERMAN EFFORTS

While BuAer was developing submarine-carried seaplanes, the U.S. Navy also sought an aircraft design from Germany.[17] Many German aeronautical engineers were out of work because of the Allied-imposed moratorium on military aircraft construction. Ernst Heinkel, designer of the Hansa-Brandenburg W 20, applied his mechanical talents elsewhere—making a living by repairing automobiles. On a warm spring evening in 1921, a familiar face appeared at his garden gate: Friedrich Christiansen, a naval aviator and fighter ace who had test flown some of Heinkel's aircraft during the war.[18]

Christiansen had recently become technical director of a small seaplane company owned by Karl Caspar, another former naval aviator. Caspar had established the company in 1921 in Travemünde on the Baltic coast. Over glasses of schnapps, they discussed Christiansen's plan to resume building military aircraft despite the ban imposed by the Allies. While it would not be possible to construct aircraft for the German government, he pointed out that neutral countries such as Norway and Sweden were willing to buy aircraft from German manufacturers. Even the United States and Japan—on the Allied side in World War I and thus ostensibly enforcers of the construction ban—were prepared to turn a blind eye to the illicit German aviation industry if they could acquire advanced aircraft from German designers.

Christiansen told Heinkel that his experience designing the Hansa-Brandenburg W 20 could be valuable at Caspar:

> We already have a contract—the Yankees asked me about the submarine aircraft you designed during the war. They are very keen on it. Keen indeed, I say. I think they badly need something like it. Even the American naval attaché in Berlin supports it. . . . I also know a few Japanese. They received less aviation technology [as reparations from the war]. They don't buy from the Americans or the English because they don't have good relations with them. So they buy from us. Listen, I'll make a bet with you. If the Americans buy a submarine aircraft, the Japanese will too.[19]

Heinkel was persuaded to join Caspar as chief designer and he quickly began designing a submarine-launched aircraft—the Caspar-Heinkel U 1. The single-seat U 1 had a loaded weight of 1,124 pounds and could reach 90 mph with its 60-horsepower Siemens radial engine. Its disassembly process was innovative, requiring no tools except for a wrench to remove the propeller. The cantilever wings had no interplane struts or wires, which speeded assembly and, in flight, reduced drag. Heinkel later recounted,

> For the first time, I built a self-supporting biplane without any struts or any bracing. The two wings were hung on the fuselage and clamped down with a central

lock. Nevertheless, they were attached so securely and firmly that eleven fat men could stand on them at the same time. Eleven fat men were hard to come by. But Köhler [a colleague at Caspar] was able to round them up. The floats were attached with hook-shaped fittings and could be easily removed.[20]

The U 1 could be assembled and disassembled in about 90 seconds by a trained team of six men.[21] Undoubtedly that time would be much longer on the wet and rolling deck of a submarine. Still, the disassembly process was quick and simple. The flip of a single lever separated both biplane wings from the fuselage, and flipping a lever in the tail allowed the horizontal sta-bilizers to fold up against the rudder. The floats, fuselage, and wings were placed on dollies that were wheeled into a pressure-tight hangar some 5 feet, 7 inches in diameter, and 24 feet, 4 inches long.[22] The speed and skill with which Ernst Heinkel had designed the Caspar-Heinkel U 1 would serve to further reinforce the belief within the U.S. Navy that Germany had per-fected submarine aircraft.

In the spring of 1922 the U.S. Navy ordered two U 1s for $41,500.[23] And Christiansen won his bet to Heinkel: Two weeks after they completed the first U 1 for the U.S. Navy, the Japanese Navy contacted Caspar, asking to buy two of the aircraft—no matter the price![24]

Although they were building the floatplanes under contracts from two Al-lied countries, Heinkel and others at Caspar were wary of the Allied inspectors

The Caspar-Heinkel U 1 floatplane during trials at the Anacostia naval air station in Wash-ington, D.C., probably in early 1923. The U 1 was an innovative design that was highly influential to the submarine aircraft programs of several nations. (U.S. NAVY)

who might not look so fondly on their illicit aircraft projects. Heinkel was tipped off ahead of time by Japanese officials, who were party to the inspection committees, allowing him to hide the aircraft among the dunes behind his factory before the inspectors arrived! The U 1 project was also entangled in subterfuge: the documents and drawings delivered with the aircraft bore the name Svenska Aero instead of Caspar-Werke. Heinkel had set up the "cover" company in Sweden specifically to avoid the German military aircraft ban.[25]

Caspar built a third U 1, and in 1923 successfully applied for the aircraft to be officially exempted from the ban on German aircraft construction because the Allied Control Commission did not view the small, unarmed aircraft as having military capabilities. That U 1 was shown at exhibitions and was offered for sale as a sport aircraft.[26] During a test flight at Travemünde in October 1923, the aircraft entered a spin and hit the water hard. The pilot was able to swim to shore, but the U 1 was destroyed on impact.[27]

The U.S. Navy received its U 1s at the Anacostia naval air station in Washington, D.C., in September 1922, and flight tests began in January 1923. That June one of the aircraft took part in a parade for "Shrine Week," a convention of the Shriners society in Washington. Carried on the back of a truck, it caught on a tree overhanging the street and was completely wrecked and afterward usable only as a source of spare parts.

Flight tests with the remaining U 1 were concluded in late 1923, without the aircraft ever having operated from a submarine.[28] As Admiral Moffett explained, "The German plane we didn't use, because, although we could break it down faster, we didn't consider the plane safe to fly; it took a very skilled pilot to fly it, and handle it, and even then it was not all right."[29] Part of the problem was the U 1's insufficient structural strength, perhaps caused by its strutless, cantilevered wings.[30]

Although the Caspar-Heinkel U 1 would never fly from a submarine, it would strongly influence the aircraft-carrying submarine programs of the United States, France, and Japan.

A CHANGE IN APPROACH

The strategic picture in the Pacific area changed significantly as a result of the Washington Naval Treaty, signed in February 1922 in Washington, D.C. The treaty halted the development of U.S. and Japanese naval bases in the western Pacific, effectively preventing Guam or the Philippines from being used effectively as forward bases for American submarines. Rather, U.S. submarines would be based at Pearl Harbor, considerably farther from Japanese home waters. The only restrictions placed on submarines by the treaty were a maximum gun caliber of eight inches (203 mm) and a maximum standard (surface) displacement of 10,000 tons.

For the U.S. Navy's leadership, the consequences of the Washington treaty highlighted its need for large, cruiser submarines that would have the range and speed to cross the Pacific as well as serving as scouts for the battle fleet. Those cruiser submarines would carry seaplanes to enhance their scouting ability.

Design efforts on the "practical" cruiser submarine had begun with General Board specifications in 1919 that called for a "long radius submarine" along the lines of the German Project 46a U-boat. The Bureau of Construction and Repair began preliminary design work on the cruiser submarine in February 1922.

The new submarine design was given a substantially larger hangar than required for the MS-1, XS-1, or U 1—initially nine feet in diameter, and later expanded to 11 feet, the largest possible size that did not significantly disrupt the submarine's design.[31] The larger hangar size would allow the aircraft to be stowed with floats attached, speeding launching and recovery time. It also would accommodate larger seaplane designs that could perform better on the open sea. Most previous designs had the hangar aft of the conning tower; BuAer proposed placing it forward of the conning tower with a catapult firing over the bow. The decision whether to include a catapult in the design was put off for a later date.[32]

In April 1923, it was decided to build three large submarines: a minelayer, the V-4 (hull number SF 7), and two cruiser submarines, the V-5 (SF 8) and V-6 (SF 9).[33] (Those submarines later were renamed and redesignated; see table 2.2.)

Although the V-4 would have a completely different stern arrangement to accommodate mine chutes, her characteristics would be almost identical to the two cruiser submarines. They were by a great margin the largest submarines built to that time by the U.S. Navy: the V-4 was 381 feet long and displaced 4,164 tons submerged, and the V-5 and V-6 were 371 feet long and 3,960 tons submerged. Some consideration was given to fitting the V-5 and V-6 with an eight-inch (203-mm) gun. That weapon would have dangerously impacted their stability; thus all three submarines were armed with two six-inch (152-mm)

Table 2.2
V-4 and V-5-class Submarines*

Original Name (Designation)	Name after 1931 (Designation)	Commissioned
V-4 (SF 7)	Argonaut (SM 1)	2 April 1928
V-5 (SF 8)	Narwhal (SS 167)	15 May 1930
V-6 (SF 9)	Nautilus (SS 168)	1 July 1930

*SF = Fleet Submarine
SM = Submarine Minelayer

deck guns in addition to their torpedo tubes.[34] With those submarine designs being developed, all that remained was to develop a suitable aircraft.

SUBMARINE TRIALS, 1923

With the large submarine projects underway, the Navy required a submarine on which to test its new aircraft. In February 1922, BuAer completed a preliminary design for a hangar to be mounted on an S-class submarine. The S-1 (SS 105) was selected for the modification because she was due for an overhaul, providing an opportunity for the hangar installation.[35] The hangar—or "airplane tank"—was installed in the fall of 1922 at the Portsmouth Navy Yard in Kittery, Maine.[36] The addition of the hangar would noticeably reduce the S-1's underwater speed and maneuverability.[37]

On 15 October 1923, the modified S-1 arrived at the Hampton Roads naval base in Virginia. Aviation personnel from the Langley (CV 1), the Navy's first aircraft carrier, came on board to support the trials. The following day a Martin MS-1 was stowed in the S-1's hangar. The floatplane proved to be slightly too large, and the airframe had to be "trimmed" with a knife to fit into the hangar. Subsequently, disassembling and stowing the aircraft, intended to take only a few minutes, took an agonizing three hours![38]

On the morning of 24 October, the MS-1 was extracted from the hangar and assembled for a photo opportunity. Again, what should have been a quick process stretched to more than two hours as the aircraft proved difficult to assemble. In the early afternoon the S-1 got underway and sailed out into the harbor with the aircraft on her deck. She dived and the plane floated off and took to the air, piloted by Lieutenant Commander Virgil C. Griffin, the Langley's executive officer. A few minutes later the submarine surfaced and the floatplane came down on the water and was brought back on board. The process was repeated twice on 27 October, although the MS-1 did not take off on those two occasions.

From even those brief trials it was apparent that the MS-1 had a flawed design, particularly in the time it took to assemble and disassemble the aircraft. It also was underpowered: fitted with a radio and with half a tank of fuel the MS-1 was too heavy to lift off the water.[39] The Naval Aircraft Factory in Philadelphia made improvements to a Cox-Klemin XS-1—redesignated XS-2—to speed its assembly; still, it would be two years before it could be ready to be flight tested. To boost the aircraft's performance it was fitted with an experimental Kinney 5RA five-cylinder radial engine, which developed about 20 more horsepower than the original Lawrence L-4 three-cylinder. However, during flight tests in the spring of 1926 the Kinney threw a connecting rod, and the original engine was reinstalled in the aircraft.[40] As a result, the XS-2

The *S-1* with a Martin MS-1 floatplane on her aft deck during the initial trials at Hampton Roads naval base on 24 October 1924. The submarine's cylindrical hangar is visible between the aircraft and the conning tower. (U.S. NAVY)

was hampered by the same lack of power that plagued the MS-1 and could not bear the additional weight of a radio or machine gun.

BuAer also embarked on design studies of submarine-launched flying boats, which had the potential for better performance and easier stowage. However, those designs would not come to fruition until the end of the decade.

The *S-1* at Hampton Roads submerging her stern, allowing the MS-1 to be recovered. Ten minutes before this photo was taken the *S-1* had fully submerged underneath the floatplane, allowing it to float off and take to the air. (U.S. NAVY)

DESIGN DECISIONS

After the S-1 trials at Hampton Roads the Bureau of Construction and Repair moved ahead with the design for aircraft-carrying minelayer and cruiser submarines. But on 8 September 1924, the Navy's General Board recommended that the V-4 not be equipped with an aircraft, primarily because of the excessive time required to assemble the MS-1. The board also pointed out that the hangar would decrease submerged maneuverability, make the submarine a larger target when on the surface, and pose a flooding risk if an exploding depth charge sprung the hangar door. Also of great concern was the submarine's inability to submerge while in the process of launching or recovering the floatplane.

Those issues led the General Board to conclude that the V-4 should not be fitted to carry an aircraft. However, it did recommend retaining the hangars of the cruiser submarines V-5 and V-6 in the hope that an improved aircraft could be developed. The General Board still labored under misconceptions about the success of the German U-boat aircraft program: "In light of the fact that the Germans had carried planes on submarines, the . . . failure [of the MS-1] merely serves as a warning that the accomplishment of the scheme demands the actual existence of a suitable plane both in its necessary characteristics as well as its adaptability for the peculiar purpose for which it is intended."[41]

The hangar was deleted from the V-4 design when the submarine was laid down the following year. The hangar on the V-5 and V-6 design survived only a short time longer. The General Board's view was summarized in a report of 13 May 1925:

> Up to the present time no plane suitable for use on submarines has been produced, and until such a plane is actually available, the General Board considers it inadvisable to handicap a submarine by providing a tank [for the airplane] that may never be other than a menace to operation and safety. . . .
> The Board can not view without serious misgiving the possibility of accidentally adding 60 tons of water (the content of the proposed tank) through leakage caused by an imperfectly secured joint or by the effects of a depth bomb.
>
> In view of all of the above, the Board recommends that no further consideration be given to the plan of providing submarines V-5 and V-6 with airplanes.[42]

The V-4, V-5, and V-6 were good designs for their time, although sluggish underwater and troubled by their unreliable and underpowered diesel engines. Later they would be fitted for refueling seaplanes and also would be employed in the troop transport role during World War II (see Chapter 10).

Opinion within BuAer and the fleet on the subject of aircraft-carrying submarines was divided. The concept was discussed at length during hearings in the fall of 1924 in front of the Eberle Board, convened to determine the future of U.S. naval aviation.[43] The following exchange between Captain Alfred W. Johnson, the assistant chief of BuAer, and Secretary of the Navy Curtis D. Wilbur was typical of the often-contentious deliberations:

> *Johnson.* If I were a commanding officer of a submarine, I wouldn't want an airplane around me. . . . I think we have a habit in the Navy of putting too many things on everything. . . . I think it is futile to waste our effort to get planes aboard submarines when the submarine itself is endangered by the equipment.
>
> *Wilbur.* We are building a Navy for a first-class power. Whether it is justifiable to make sacrifices necessary in submarine construction to put airplanes on it in order to have her with the fleet is a consideration.[44]

Not all involved were as pessimistic as Johnson. His superior, Rear Admiral Moffett, remained a driving force for putting aircraft on submarines and was confident in the success of the improved aircraft designs that the bureau was developing.[45]

War games held at the Naval War College bolstered the case for aircraft-carrying submarines in the U.S. Navy and also foreshadowed Japan's use of them in the Pacific. Having played for the Orange (Japanese) side in the war games, Captain M. G. Cook recounted:

> I happened to be designated as Orange Air Force Commander and they permitted me to equip a certain number of the Orange submarines with planes under rules which they obtained from the Bureau of Aeronautics. They made the rules as difficult as they could to make sure there would be nothing impossible done. . . . The umpires would not allow the planes to fly off except in smooth water and the water was never smooth. There was so many islands in the Hawaiian Islands, the Marshalls, Carolines and the Philippines that it was almost always possible for one of these Orange submarines to get in the lee of one of the islands, in which case it flew off its plane and obtained an enormous amount of information which could not have been obtained in any other way and it looked as if, on the face of it, that it would be of immense value for a submarine, employed in scouting, to have an airplane. Only once was the submarine forced to dive and lose her plane. The area out there in the Pacific is so great and the distances so great, that the submarine has a great many places to go in hiding where she can employ her planes.[46]

Thus, despite the skepticism of many naval officers and the decision to not provide the V-4, V-5, and V-6 with hangars, enough promise remained to continue trials of aircraft operating from submarines.

SUBMARINE TRIALS, 1926–1927

Aircraft trials with the *S-1* resumed in 1926. The submarine, now commanded by Lieutenant Charles (Swede) Momsen, was moored at the Philadelphia Navy Yard from 11 to 15 May while BuAer specialists test-fitted the newly overhauled XS-2 into her hangar. Once they were satisfied, the *S-1* submerged next to the pier, enabling the XS-2 to float off and be flown back to the nearby Naval Aircraft Factory for additional work.

On 20 July, at New London, the *S-1* received the XS-2 for the second round of trials. Two days later the *S-1* sailed a few hundred yards down the Thames River and submerged to float off the XS-2. No flight was undertaken.

A more significant test was carried out on 28 July: At 1005 the *S-1* submerged in Long Island Sound and surfaced five minutes later for sailors to extract the XS-2 from the hangar. After being assembled on the submarine's deck, the XS-2 was launched and undertook a brief flight. After it alighted on the water Momsen trimmed down the *S-1*'s stern and took the floatplane on board. The XS-2 was stowed in the submarine's hangar and the submarine dived.[47] *That was the first full cycle of seaplane launching ever conducted by a submarine of any nation.*

Similar seaplane operations were conducted with the *S-1* on six occasions during the rest of July and in August and September, all on the Thames River

The Cox-Klemin XS-2 taxiing on the water in 1926. The XS-2 was overhauled by the Naval Aircraft Factory in Philadelphia to reduce assembly time compared to the original MS-1 and XS-1 design. (U.S. NAVY)

or just beyond its mouth in Long Island Sound. (The XS-2 was never operated in the open sea.)

When not participating in aircraft trials, the S-1 operated from New London as a training craft for the submarine school, sailing with new officers to practice torpedo attacks in Long Island Sound. The final XS-2 flight from the submarine in 1926 was from Gloucester harbor in Massachusetts on 27 October. By that time the S-1's crew had become proficient at launching and recovering the floatplane; aircraft assembly time had been reduced to only nine minutes. It took 12 minutes from running submerged at a depth of 40 feet for the S-1 to surface and for the XS-2 to float off and begin its takeoff run. Recovering the aircraft and submerging back to 40 feet took 13 minutes.[48] On 14 December, the XS-2 was shipped back to Philadelphia.[49]

The third and final round of aircraft trials with the S-1 began in the summer of 1927. On 6 June, Lieutenant Frank R. Whitmore reported on board as the submarine's aviation officer, and the XS-2 again was placed inside the S-1's hangar. Later that month Momsen was relieved as commanding officer by Lieutenant Graeme Bannerman. Whitmore became the submarine's executive officer, also serving as the submarine's aviation, torpedo, and commissary officer.

On 4 July 1927, the S-1 launched her floatplane during an Independence Day exhibition in Greenport harbor on Long Island. Later that month the S-1 was conducting practice torpedo attacks off Block Island in Long Island Sound with the submarine S-22 (SS 127) when one of her practice torpedoes, designed to surface after its test run, went missing. After spending the night of 20 July anchored in a cove on Block Island, the next day the S-1 sent her floatplane aloft to search for the errant torpedo. By noon the aircraft had located the surfaced exercise torpedo. Bannerman was sufficiently impressed that he recommended that in peacetime the recovery of practice torpedoes be the primary role of submarine-launched aircraft. Only those two flights are recorded in the S-1's logbook for 1927, although Bannerman stated that the aircraft flew a total of 15 hours during that year.

On 1 August, Bannerman wrote to the Chief of Naval Operations recommending that the aircraft trials be concluded. As with the MS-1, even with its fuel tank only half full, the XS-2 struggled to lift off the water. The lack of power precluded carrying a radio, which was essential for a scouting aircraft. The aircraft could not be used at all "except under conditions of a smooth sea without ground swells."[50]

The aircraft trials with the S-1 finally concluded on 25 August, when the XS-2 floated off the submarine's stern to be returned to the Naval Aircraft Factory. The General Board subsequently concluded "that the disadvantages of carrying an airplane on submarines so far outweigh the advantages that it is not desirable to continue further expenditure on these experiments at this time."[51]

The *S-1*'s hangar was removed at New London in November 1927. It was repurposed by Lieutenant Momsen, who had begun working at the Bureau of Construction and Repair after he left the *S-1*. With Lieutenant Commander Allen R. McCann, Momsen converted the hangar into a prototype diving bell to rescue crewmen from sunken submarines. That concept was developed into the McCann submarine rescue chamber that was adopted by the U.S. Navy.[52]

Despite the failure of BuAer's early efforts to develop a successful submarine-launched scout aircraft, many in the bureau's leadership remained hopeful that a better seaplane could be developed. Even though the MS-1 and XS-2 had not been satisfactory, they had demonstrated that developing a submarine-launched aircraft was feasible.

THE LOENING XSL

In parallel with the development of the MS-1 and XS-1/XS-2, BuAer investigated flying boats for submarines. Once it was clear that the floatplanes had significant shortcomings, the pace of flying boat development quickened.[53] The bureau anticipated that a flying boat, which would have more buoyancy than a floatplane for a given weight, would be able to operate in rougher seas. The new design would be a monoplane to simplify assembly and disassembly, and it would have a more powerful engine, further improving performance.

In early 1924 the BuAer produced design No. 28, a flying boat with an engine mounted above the hull in a pusher configuration. To be assembled for flight in less than five minutes, design No. 28 would have folding wings, a removable tail, and an engine that would swing down into the hull.[54] Another iteration with a tractor propeller—design No. 42—was sketched in the following year.[55]

The final result of that line of development was design No. 87—a single-seat, monoplane flying boat. Like design No. 28, it had a high-mounted engine with a pusher propeller that folded back into the fuselage. The wings could be removed and stowed alongside the aircraft's hull, resulting in a compact "package" that was easily stowed in a hangar eight feet in diameter and 23½ feet long.[56] The aircraft would have an all-aluminum hull and fabric-covered wood wings.[57]

About 1929 BuAer solicited proposals from several companies to build design No. 87 and in June 1930, chose the Grover Loening Aircraft Company to construct a single prototype, designated XSL-1.[58] Loening, the firm's president and chief engineer, was taught to fly by Orville Wright and was the first person to hold a degree in aeronautical engineering from an American university. During World War I he had designed two tiny monoplanes—the M-2 Kitten and M-3 Cat—for use on battleships and destroyers. Although not used beyond an experimental role, they were the smallest manned aircraft ever flown by the U.S. Navy and the service's first with air-cooled, radial engines.[59]

The Loening XSL-1 flying boat during flight trials in Queens, New York. (ALAN REDDIG)

The XSL-1 first flew on 4 February 1931, from the East River in Queens, New York.[60] Loening had made a few improvements to BuAer's design, including a folding tail section. The horizontal stabilizers folded down against the vertical stabilizer, and the whole tail assembly hinged forward over the hull, speeding disassembly compared to the original removable tail.[61] About 50 percent heavier and larger in length and wingspan than the XS-2, the XSL-1 was also more powerful with its Warner Scarab radial engine, which gave it almost double the horsepower of the older floatplane.

The prototype XSL-1 was almost lost in a bizarre accident before it was delivered to the Navy. After preliminary flight tests in Queens, the Navy planned to fly the aircraft via Philadelphia to Anacostia. However, the Delaware River iced over the day before the flight, denying the XSL-1 the ability to come down on the water at Philadelphia. Accordingly, the aircraft was transported by truck. Shortly after leaving Queens the truck was accidentally backed up through a barricade and into an open pit where a subway line was being built. The folded-up aircraft slid up against the truck's closed rear doors. The truck was towed out of its precarious position with the aircraft only lightly damaged. The aircraft was returned to the Loening factory for repairs, after which it safely reached Anacostia—by truck.[62]

Navy trials began at Anacostia on the Potomac River on 2 March and concluded on 18 April. The BuAer inspectors determined that the XSL-1 was "a distinct improvement, from the standpoint of service use, of any submarine plane heretofore tested." It could be stowed in seven minutes and made ready for flight in 20 minutes. However, the aircraft exhibited a worrying flight characteristic at low speed: a sudden loss of control and lift when approaching a stall. That highly undesirable trait probably stemmed from a combination of factors, namely disrupted airflow over the wings caused by the struts bracing the wing and engine and blanking of the tail surfaces by the wing at high angles of attack. As a result, the trial board was unable to recommend the XSL-1 for service use. But the board reasoned that if its dangerous stall behavior could be corrected the aircraft could operate on the open sea "a fair percentage of the time," a substantial advance from the XS-2, which never operated outside of Long Island Sound.[63]

In an effort to better understand the XSL-1's aerodynamic troubles, it was shipped in October to Langley Field in Virginia for evaluation. It was one of the first aircraft tested in the new 30-by-60-foot wind tunnel of the National Advisory Committee for Aeronautics. (That wind tunnel later would test the hull form of the revolutionary submarine *Albacore*/AGSS 569, and the aerodynamics of the Mercury spacecraft, the F-16 fighter, and the Space Shuttle.)

In January 1932, the XSL-1 was shipped back to the Loening factory to remedy its poor low-speed handling and to quicken assembly time. A more powerful Menasco Buccaneer inline six-cylinder engine replaced the original radial engine. The new engine also was mounted low enough that it could be kept in place during stowage. The aerodynamically troublesome struts bracing the wing were replaced by wires, further simplifying assembly. The overhauled aircraft was completed by Loening in May 1933, and redesignated XSL-2.

The XSL-2 was not the only design that BuAer was considering at that time. Amphibions Inc. (formerly Ireland Aircraft) submitted a design to the Navy for a flying boat to meet the same specifications as Loening's. With nearly identical overall dimensions and weight as the XSL, the Amphibions aircraft had a dramatically swept-back wing with large ailerons forming the wingtips. The cockpit was in the extreme nose of the aircraft, and the tail was canted upward relative to the hull similar to the firm's other designs. While model tests were carried out by BuAer in May 1933, the Navy did not order a prototype and Amphibions ceased operations that year.[64]

After being modified by Loening, the performance of the XSL-2 apparently was significantly improved, but not enough to win over Navy support outside of BuAer. For most senior naval officers the question of whether or not submarines should carry aircraft was likely settled several years earlier with the underwhelming results from the S-1 trials. The ability to carry an aircraft did not factor into the characteristics of any U.S. submarine designs beyond the V-6 and the subject was never again broached in the deliberations of the General Board.[65]

The Loening XSL-2 at Anacostia in May 1933 demonstrating how it would be folded up for stowage on board a submarine. The wheels were removable and would not have been installed when stowed on board a submarine. (U.S. NAVY)

As fleet scouts, airships overshadowed submarines during the early 1930s. The Navy's two largest airships—the *Akron* (ZRS-4) and *Macon* (ZRS-5)— each could carry five Curtiss F9C Sparrowhawk fighters. Those biplanes could be launched and recovered by the airships in flight, extending the airships' scouting range and providing protection. Aircraft seemed to be more naturally paired with airships than with submarines.

By 1930 the submarine-aircraft program was purely a BuAer project. Even before the XSL-1 had flown the Bureau of Construction and Repair appeared reluctant to embark on another round of trials. Although Rear Admiral George Rock, the chief of the bureau, promised that a submarine would eventually be allocated to test the XSL, no funding for such an experiment was forthcoming.[66] After completing flight tests in October 1933, the XSL-2 was put into storage at the Naval Aircraft Factory and stricken from service in February 1934—without ever having flown from a submarine.[67]

The U.S. Navy was the first and initially most enthusiastic proponent of aircraft-carrying submarines after World War I. The motivation to develop such craft stemmed from the perceived German mastery of the concept during the war and the energy injected into U.S. naval aviation by the new Bureau of Aeronautics and its chief, Admiral Moffett. Blinded by an overreliance on misleading accounts by German designers, the Navy did not fully anticipate the difficulty inherent in engineering an aircraft both small enough to fit inside of a submarine and also with good characteristics as a seaplane. Moreover, the aircraft's performance had to be exceptional to overcome the reluctance of submariners to make sacrifices to their stealth and resilience to potential battle damage.

Only after disappointing trials of the Martin MS-1 and Cox-Klemin XS-2 on board the submarine S-1 did the challenges become fully apparent. The bureau's subsequent design—the Loening XSL flying boat—improved on nearly all aspects of the previous floatplanes, but it came too late. The rest of the Navy had moved on, and the submarine-aircraft program ceased in about 1934. The U.S. Navy would not again consider aircraft-carrying submarines until after World War II.

Nevertheless, the U.S. Navy's aircraft-carrying submarine program was highly influential abroad. Photos of the aircraft and the trials on board the S-1 were widely circulated in newspapers. The American efforts' publicity helped spur the navies of Japan, Britain, and France to pursue the concept and informed the design decisions of their own aircraft-carrying submarine programs.

CHAPTER 3

Between the Wars—Europe

All of the significant European naval powers—except for disarmed Germany—experimented with aircraft-carrying submarines between the world wars, although none produced truly operational capabilities. The British and French navies—the largest in Europe—led in the development of aircraft-carrying submarines, with Italy, Poland, and the Soviet Union undertaking some efforts in that field. Despite the progress and innovation achieved by several nations, only France's *Surcouf* was in service with an aircraft when war again erupted in Europe in September 1939.

ROYAL NAVY EXPERIMENTS

The Royal Navy's only operational aircraft-carrying submarine had its roots in an unusual World War I submarine program. Admiral of the Fleet Sir John Fisher, the head of the Royal Navy early in the war and the "father" of the modern battleship and battle cruiser, advocated building a "submarine dreadnought" with a single 12-inch (305-mm) battleship gun as its primary armament.[1] Compared to the unreliable torpedoes then in service, the massive shells fired by the gun could reach targets at far greater ranges. And many more of the comparatively inexpensive shells could be carried than torpedoes.[2]

In the fall of 1915, Commodore Sidney Hall, the commander of Britain's undersea fleet, submitted a proposal to build the submarine dreadnoughts—the M class. Four of the large, steam-powered K-class submarines that had not yet been laid down were reordered as M-class submarines. Construction began in August 1916 on the first of the class, the *M-1*.[3] The 296-foot-long submarines had a surface displacement of 1,600 tons; submerged they were 1,950 tons.[4] They had conventional diesel propulsion in place of the troublesome boilers and steam turbines of the K class.[5]

The submarines were designed around the Mark IX 12-inch/40-caliber gun, enclosed in a fairing forward of the conning tower. The gun weighed 50.5 tons and had a range of 32,700 yards (16 n.miles). It could be elevated from 20 to –5 degrees and trained 10 degrees to port or starboard. The guns were mounted in several classes of British and Italian battleships.

An M-class submarine usually would fire the 12-inch gun with decks awash, although it could be fired with the submarine submerged if the gun was at maximum elevation for shore bombardment.[6] The gun's breech was not accessible when submerged, and thus the submarine would have to surface to reload. Diving time was 90 seconds.[7]

While the 12-inch gun enclosure was free-flooding, the gun breech was watertight and a hydraulically actuated tampion covered the muzzle, preventing water from flooding the barrel when submerged. Those measures were essential, as the submarines' crews discovered: The M-3's barrel flooded when the tampion was opened before the muzzle had breached the surface. When the gun was then fired, eight feet of the forward barrel was blown off.

During another exercise the officer responsible for aiming the M-1's gun was distracted by thoughts of a young woman he planned to dance with that evening and he neglected to notice that the tampion still sealed the muzzle. When the gun was fired the tampion went flying off, trailing behind it the strengthening wire that was wound around the inner part of the barrel. Embedding itself in the shallow seafloor, the tampion securely anchored the

The three British M-class submarines were armed with 12-inch guns, the largest ever fitted to a submarine. The *M-1* is shown here in a striking camouflage paint scheme.
(IMPERIAL WAR MUSEUM)

submarine. Embarrassingly, no tool on board the submarine could quickly cut the wire, and it took several hours for the M-1 to free herself.[8] The destroyed guns were exchanged for the shorter, Mark VIII 12-inch/35-caliber guns taken from obsolete Majestic-class battleships.[9]

The M-class submarines were highly controversial within the Royal Navy. Although Admiral Fisher had initially championed the design, he and others began to panic: What if Germany learned of the M class? They feared that if the German Navy built its own big gun–armed submarines they would devastate the Royal Navy. As a result, the submarines then under construction were covered in tarpaulins, the drawings hidden, and work on the M-1 ceased for a full year.[10]

The M-1 was placed in commission in April 1918, but did not see action in the war. The M-2 and M-3 were commissioned in 1920; the uncompleted M-4 was scrapped shortly after she was launched in 1919. In service the M-class submarines handled well at sea despite the mass of the heavy gun high up on the hull. However, their low reserve buoyancy made for a "wet ride" when on the surface in heavy seas.

After the brief experiments with the E-22 in 1916, the Royal Navy had abandoned the concept of the aircraft-carrying submarine, in part because submarines at that time were too small to accommodate a seaplane hangar. In 1921 the Anglo-Japanese alliance dissolved, resulting in the Royal Navy shifting its focus toward Japan as a future adversary. That event prompted the development of the "overseas patrol" submarine, a large, long-range craft, to operate against Japan. Operating independently in the vast expanse of the Pacific, the submarine's effectiveness in seeking out targets would be greatly enhanced if it could carry a scouting aircraft. Renewed interest in aircraft-carrying submarines by Britain also may have been motivated by the Admiralty obtaining documents detailing the German experiments with aircraft-carrying submarines during World War I.[11]

In the summer of 1923, Captain Max Horton, former commanding officer of the M-1, wrote to the Rear Admiral (Submarines) with a proposal to convert an M-class submarine into an experimental underwater carrier as a prototype for future designs:

> The more the probable conditions of a possible future war are studied, the more obvious it becomes that greatly increased reliance, in comparison with the last war, must be placed on submarines and aircraft for early information of the enemy's movements.
>
> The practical combination implied by a submarine carrying aircraft has vast possibilities. The submarine, with its inherent advantages of great endurance and power of acting unsupported far from its base, is perfected where its greatest defect lay, viz. in lack of vision.

I am strongly of the opinion that the time has come when experiments should be pushed on with the least delay in the direction indicated.

For this purpose, an "M" class submarine presents advantages which can only be described as peculiarly fortunate.

It is well known that this type of submarine has superior diving qualities to any other type approaching the same size. It is sure, therefore, that experiments with one of this class will be based on a proved foundation.[12]

Horton proposed removing the 12-inch gun and storing the seaplane inside of the pressure hull in the space previously occupied by the gun's ammunition magazine, which held up to 50 rounds of 12-inch ammunition (weighing some 29 tons). A box-like, non-watertight compartment installed forward of the conning tower would enable the aircraft to be assembled for flight while shielded from waves. The compartment would flood when the submarine submerged. A few weeks later he proposed an alternative arrangement in which the aircraft would be housed in a watertight hangar installed aft of the conning tower.[13] Horton's proposal was forwarded to the Admiralty.

Ultimately, in September 1923, a compromise of the two designs was selected with the aircraft to be stored in a boxy, watertight hangar forward of the conning tower. A catapult track stretching from the hangar to the bow would launch the seaplane into the air.

Some consideration was given to instead equipping a K-class submarine with a seaplane. Various schemes were proposed, with the disassembled aircraft stored in either a single large cylinder or in three smaller cylinders. Without a catapult, the aircraft would be launched by submerging the submarine. That concept took inspiration from the U.S. Navy's efforts with the *S-1*, and the British suspected that the Japanese were adopting similar designs.[14] In the end the Royal Navy would undertake only the conversion of a single M-class submarine.

In late 1924, as the design of the aircraft and carrying submarine still were materializing, the Naval Staff established a list of requirements for the overseas patrol submarine. The *Oberon*, the prototype for the new design, had been laid down that year. Among the design features desired for that submarine was the ability to carry a scouting aircraft.

When the Naval Staff circulated the requirements among submarine officers, their opinions greatly varied on the question of an aircraft. Some were enthusiastic: "An aeroplane is essential. A man-lifting kite would also be useful." Others were more measured: "Provision desirable although the size of the submarine may be increased to a degree, which reduces the number of submarines for which money is available. However they will individually perform more service if carrying an aircraft." And some officers dismissed the concept outright: "Aircraft impracticable except for freak submarine, freak aircraft under freak weather conditions."[15] The Naval Staff concluded that new submarines should not be provided with aircraft until the concept could be tested on an M-class submarine.

In 1924 the M-2 suffered an accident with her gun and thus was selected for the conversion to a submarine aircraft carrier.[16] Her 12-inch gun was removed in December 1924, and she was put into reserve awaiting availability of an aircraft. (There is a misconception that the M-2's gun was removed to comply with the Washington Naval Treaty of 1922. However, the M-class submarines, having been laid down before the treaty took effect, were exempt from its restrictions.)

There was some discussion of providing the submarine with a wheeled aircraft instead of a flying boat or floatplane, which would have better performance, but would have to be ditched at sea after one flight unless it was able to land ashore.[17] Finally, a two-seat floatplane with folding wings was chosen for the program. The Air Ministry laid out the design requirements as aircraft Specification 16/24, which required an endurance of at least 1½ hours and a radio to communicate with the submarine.[18]

Specification 16/24 was circulated among aircraft manufacturers in late 1924. The submission by George Parnall's company met the Navy's requirements. Harold Bolas, chief designer for the company, thus produced the Parnall Peto.[19] Although constructed mainly from traditional wood and canvas, the biplane had a stainless-steel rudder and struts to better hold up at sea.[20] The wings folded back as one unit, allowing for quick assembly and disassembly. The first prototype took to the air on 4 June 1925. A second Peto followed in January 1926.[21]

THE PETO TRIALS

In the fall of 1925, after successful flights of the prototype Peto, the decision was reached to proceed with the M-2 conversion to a submarine aircraft carrier. In August 1927, she emerged from the Chatham dockyards with a boxy hangar forward replacing her 12-inch gun mount. Forward of the hangar was a 51-foot-long catapult, that could be powered by either compressed air or cordite.[22] A crane atop the hangar would hoist the aircraft on board after returning from flight.

The M-2's aircraft launching sequence was significantly advanced over previous efforts. When still submerged, a ten-man team would enter the hangar and begin cranking the aircraft's engine, warming its oil with hot air, and otherwise preparing it for flight.[23] As soon as the submarine broke the surface, the hangar door would swing down to become part of the catapult track. Up to a foot of water could rush into the hangar and the seamen wore waders to keep

The Parnall Peto floatplane is extracted from the *M-2*'s hangar during an exercise. The launching procedure began as soon as the submarine broached the surface.

dry. A 16-inch-high coaming around the hangar's access hatch prevented the submarine from flooding under such conditions.[24]

The Peto was wheeled out of the hangar, connected to the catapult, and its wings were unfolded. The submarine then would head into the wind at full speed and launch the aircraft.[25] It took 12 minutes from surfacing to catapulting the Peto, and 11 minutes to take the aircraft back on board, store it, and submerge.[26]

The M-2 took aboard her first Peto on 7 July 1928, and initial sea trials were completed by October of that year.[27] Over the next two years, the M-2 operated the Peto at every opportunity and cruised with the fleet on two occasions. The submarine and aircraft worked well together, but sea conditions placed significant restraints on aircraft operations. The catapult was only a few feet above water, preventing launching in seas rougher than sea state three. The Peto could not safely alight on the water except in calm seas. Launching and recovery times were longer than desired.[28]

On 11 February 1930, the aircraft came down hard at sea off Gibraltar, sustaining significant damage. The second Peto fared little better, crashing on 29 June near the seaside resort town of Lee-on-the-Solent. In flight the aircraft began to steadily lose altitude, possibly due to the heft of one of the two-man crew—who was rumored to be the heaviest man in the Fleet Air Arm! The aircraft was headed toward a row of bathhouses on the beach. The pilot managed to avoid all but the last one. The Peto demolished the bathhouse with one of its floats, leaving a prominent citizen of the town standing in a pile of rubble clothed only in a bath towel.[29]

Those two accidents left the M-2 temporarily without an aircraft, precluding her involvement in Atlantic Fleet exercises in the fall. Both aircraft eventually were repaired. The Peto damaged at Gibraltar was rebuilt by Parnall with a more powerful Armstrong Siddeley Mongoose IIIC engine and redesigned floats.[30] The rebuilt aircraft was embarked in the M-2 in the winter of 1930.

The M-2 sailed from England to Gibraltar in January 1931, to conduct exercises with the Atlantic Fleet. There she experimented with a technique to recover the Peto in rough seas, similar to that used by cruisers with their scouting aircraft. Just before the Peto set down on the water, the submarine made a sharp turn perpendicular to the wind and waves. The aircraft flew over the bow of the M-2 and alighted on the calm circle of water created by the submarine's maneuver. But that technique had little effect in large swells, and on one occasion the Peto was forced to fly back to Gibraltar due to rough seas around the M-2.

From 5 January to 21 February 1931, the Peto flew from the M-2 a total of 28 times, ten of them reconnaissance flights, which ranged up to almost 30 miles from the submarine in search of possible targets. The Peto was effective, reporting back sightings of the "enemy" fleet and itself was only detected three times. In an exercise against the submarine tender *Lucia* the M-2 was able to achieve a torpedo firing position based on the Peto's reports.[31]

As the M-2 continued her trials with the Peto, the Admiralty solicited the opinions of senior naval officers on aircraft-carrying submarines. Except for the Commander-in-Chief, Mediterranean Fleet, who was entirely against any additional effort to experiment with the concept, the other officers expressed interest in continuing the development of aircraft operating from submarines, albeit

The Peto being fired into the air by the M-2's catapult. (AUTHORS' COLLECTION)

with some reservations. They came to many of the same conclusions as had the U.S. Navy a few years earlier: If mounted on an overseas patrol submarine, the M-2's bulky hangar would increase its silhouette and vulnerability to gunfire and depth charges. Thus, a smaller hangar and smaller aircraft were desired.[32]

Not only would the aircraft have to be smaller than the Peto; it would have to have greater endurance—at least three hours—with a good rate of climb and a higher ceiling to get above the clouds to avoid being sighted. As a potential solution to those conflicting requirements, the Commander-in-Chief, Atlantic Fleet suggested "a miniature flying boat with swiveling monoplane wings"—exactly what the U.S. Navy was developing in the Loening XSL.[33]

Part of the Royal Navy's motivation for continuing to develop aircraft-carrying submarines in spite of the lukewarm attitude of its senior officers was simply to stay abreast of other navies. Captain John Cunningham, the Director of Plans, opined that although he was against outfitting more submarines to carry aircraft, "On the other hand, it appears that while we should not set the pace, we should at least not lag behind other nations in the solution of the technical problems involved."[34]

Regardless of the outcome of the debates over the future aircraft-carrying submarines in the Royal Navy, the M-2's service life was coming to an end. Only 12 years old, she was scheduled to be placed in reserve in March 1932, and then scrapped.

Catastrophe struck before she could be retired: On 26 January 1932, the M-2 was conducting launching trials with the Peto in West Bay off Portland, England. She radioed at 1011 that she was about to dive. A few hours later a local boat captain reported that he had seen a large submarine diving stern-first. When the Navy located the sunken M-2 a week later she was resting on the bottom in 110 feet of water. All 60 men on board had perished.

The hangar door and the hatch to the pressure hull inside of the hangar both were found to be open. The bodies of two members of the aircraft handling team were found inside of the hangar, indicating that the submarine had been surfacing. The most likely cause of her sinking was the unintentional opening of vents in the after main ballast tanks. As those ballast tanks lost air, the stern submerged and water surged over the coaming of the hangar's access hatch. The submarine then sank, stern-first.[35]

Several attempts to salvage the submarine were made, and on one attempt the M-2 was only 18 feet from the surface when heavy seas sent her back to the bottom—where she still remains. The Peto was recovered from the wreck in March 1932—and discarded.

The sinking of the M-2 did not end British investigations into aircraft-carrying submarines. It was determined that one way to improve a future submarine-launched aircraft was to make it a single seater that would have a smaller size and greater endurance. To test that concept, the surviving Peto was fitted with an extra fuel tank in the observer's cockpit, increasing flight time to about 2½ hours. The pilot could not easily operate a wireless telegraph when flying, thus a radio for voice communication was installed.[36] Plans were drafted for the modified Peto to test the new communications equipment with the submarine *Rainbow*. Difficulty obtaining the proper radio led the Admiralty to cease all trials with the Peto in October 1932.[37]

Still, Royal Navy studies of aircraft-carrying submarines continued for at least a few more months. In June 1933, the Director of Naval Construction sketched a modification to the overseas patrol submarine *Oberon* that would allow her to carry a Peto. Patterned after the U.S. Navy's *S-1*, the hangar would be installed aft of the conning tower, albeit without a catapult. A crane mounted atop the hangar would enable launching and recovering the floatplane.[38]

However, by that time, interest in aircraft-carrying submarines in the Royal Navy had waned. Aeronautical technology could not produce an acceptable seaplane, one with both excellent performance and compact dimensions, and operating the Peto made the surfaced submarine a more easily sighted and vulnerable target. The Royal Navy's exploration of aircraft-carrying submarines ended in July 1933.[39]

THE FRENCH *SURCOUF*

France was an early leader in submarine development, launching the *Plongeur*— the first submarine to be propelled by an engine instead of human muscle—in 1863. Inspired by that impressive submarine, author Jules Verne created the fearsome *Nautilus* for his seminal 1870 novel *Twenty Thousand Leagues Under the Sea*, which thrust the submarine into the public consciousness. And in 1888, the French Navy launched the *Gynmote*—one of the first submarines with electric propulsion, torpedo tubes, and a periscope.

Despite those early advances, by 1900 the French submarine force lagged behind the other major naval powers because of poor shipyard construction practices, lack of reliable engines, and a misplaced emphasis on small submarines for harbor defense. The production of new submarines was halted at the outbreak of World War I as the nation's priorities were focused on ground fighting on the Western Front.[40]

As the French Navy began to reassess its submarine force in the aftermath of the war, its focus turned to large, ocean-going types armed with large-caliber guns. The Normand shipyard in Le Havre sketched a design for a huge submarine displacing over 7,000 tons submerged and measuring 393 feet long.[41] One version would be armed with six 12-inch guns in two turrets located fore and

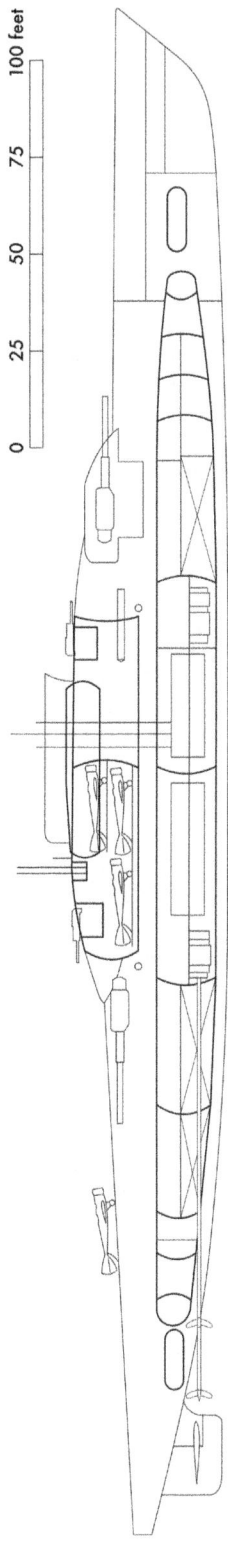

The Normand shipyard's 1921 design for an aircraft-carrying submarine. The shafts appear to have tandem propellers. The small circles forward and aft of the hangar are torpedo tubes. (©JACOB GUNNARSON)

0   25   50   75   100 feet

aft of the conning tower. The other variant would have a forward turret with several 9.5-inch (240-mm) guns and a hangar for four aircraft in the after superstructure. Two additional 9.5-inch guns were emplaced to either side of the ramp leading from the hangar to the stern. Those designs were not seriously considered by the French Navy.[42]

More practical designs were inspired by the German *U-139*, acquired by France after the war. Two types of cruiser submarines based on the *U-139* were contemplated: a high-speed "squadron" submarine to operate with the battle fleet and a long-range "bombardment" submarine for attacking coastal targets. The bombardment submarine designs—designated Projects H, I, and J—would have a 7.5-inch (190-mm), 9.5-inch, or 12-inch gun, respectively, in a turret forward of the conning tower.[43] Those designs were swiftly abandoned because the Washington Naval Treaty limited new-construction submarines to mounting 8-inch (203-mm) or smaller guns.

Instead, the French Navy decided to build a heavily armed cruiser submarine for commerce raiding based on the bombardment submarine designs—Project Q. It would be armed with two 8-inch guns and carry a scouting aircraft. Such an impressive craft had broad support: Retired Vice Admiral Émile Guépratte, a member of the National Assembly, praised the concept: "The submersible cruiser combined with the seaplane will together become a mighty aerial corsair, and . . . will destroy the surface fleets, becoming the undisputed kings of the sea."[44]

In 1925 the Project Q5 design variant was selected for construction, and in July 1927, the first submarine of the planned class—the *Surcouf*—was laid down at the Cherbourg naval shipyard.[45] The Navy initially planned to build four Project Q5 submarines, a number quickly reduced to two units.[46]

The prospect of a submarine intended primarily for commerce raiding alarmed the British, who already were wary of France's intentions regarding submarine warfare. Several years earlier, during the Washington Naval Conference of

The *Surcouf* at high speed in the early 1930s. A group of sailors stands atop the aircraft hangar faired into the after end of the conning tower. (AUTHORS' COLLECTION)

1921–1922, the British had accused the French of preparing a submarine campaign against their merchant fleet just as Germany had carried out during World War I. Britain lobbied at the Washington conference for submarines to be forbidden as a military weapon. British fears were not assuaged by France's refusal to sign a resolution to prohibit the use of submarines against merchant ships.

Eight years later, at the London Naval Conference of 1930, Britain again proposed eliminating the submarine as a weapon of war.[47] And, again, that extreme concept came to naught. However, stricter limits on submarine displacement and armament did threaten the *Surcouf* and her planned sister ship. French Navy Minister Georges Leygues successfully fought to have the *Surcouf* specifically exempted from the treaty restrictions in return for supporting imitations on future submarines: Each of the treaty signatories could build or retain three submarines with a standard displacement limit of 2,800 tons and a maximum gun caliber of 6.1-inches (155-mm).[48] Their remaining submarines were required to be smaller than 2,000 tons with guns no larger than 5.1-inch (130-mm). That compromise prevented the construction of additional Project Q5 submarines, leaving the *Surcouf* as a unique prototype.

When she was launched on 18 November 1929, the *Surcouf* was the largest and most impressive submarine built to that time by any nation. She displaced 3,304 tons on the surface and 4,318 tons submerged, with a length of 361 feet. Forward of her conning tower she mounted two 8-inch guns in a massive, watertight turret.[49] Like the earlier British M-class submarines, the muzzles of the guns were sealed by electrically actuated tampions. Although the *Surcouf*'s guns could be reloaded while submerged, the turret could not be rotated to bear on a target until the submarine had surfaced. In addition to her guns, the *Surcouf* had the heavy torpedo armament of four 21-inch (550-mm) tubes in the bow and two external, rotating "turrets," each with one 21-inch tube and two 15.7-inch (400-mm) tubes. (All French submarines built between the wars had such torpedo devices to enable firing a torpedo salvo in any direction.)[50]

As she was intended to be a commerce raider, the *Surcouf* had a cell to hold 40 prisoners and a motor launch to carry a boarding party. In typical French fashion she also had a "wine cellar" that could store 1,375 gallons in barrels to provide each crewman with a daily ration of a liter of wine during a 90-day patrol.[51]

The *Surcouf*'s aircraft would aid in both searching for targets and increasing the effective range of her guns by directing fire on distant targets. A binocular range finder was mounted on top of the gun turret, and if the periscopes were fully extended the guns could be aimed at targets 8.5 n.miles distant. A rickety "crow's nest" could be mounted to the periscope to extend vision fractionally farther. The only way to fully exploit the 21-n.mile range of the *Surcouf*'s guns was with an aircraft directing their fire.

A litany of mechanical problems had to be solved before the *Surcouf* entered active service. The blast from her guns deformed the conning tower structure. In heavy seas the submarine could roll as much as 25 degrees on the surface, but the turret's traverse jammed if the *Surcouf*'s roll exceeded 8 degrees.[52]

More seriously, the riveted outer hull was put under considerable stress at sea, and the ballast and fuel tanks frequently developed leaks. The *Surcouf*'s propulsion and steering systems experienced numerous faults.[53] On her maiden voyage to Dakar and Casablanca, the interior of the submarine was unbearably hot because of inadequate ventilation, a major issue for a submarine intended to operate in France's colonies in the tropics. By the time that she was commissioned in 1934, some of those problems had been solved, but at a price: At 87 million francs the *Surcouf*'s cost had doubled from the initial estimates, and not all of her issues had been corrected.[54]

THE FRENCH FLOATPLANES

The *Surcouf*'s floatplane had been in development for 12 years when the submarine was placed in service. The French Navy's interest in aircraft on board submarines was piqued by the U.S. Navy's purchase of the Caspar-Heinkel U 1. In October 1923, the Central Aeronautical Service drew up a set of requirements for a submarine-launched seaplane inspired by the U 1: It was required to have two crewmen, a two-hour endurance, a ceiling of 9,800 feet, a speed of 81 mph, and the ability to fit in a hangar 6 feet, 7 inches in diameter and 29 feet, 6 inches in length. The firms of Marcel Besson and Maurice Pecheron both responded with designs; Besson's was selected.[55]

The Besson aircraft was a twin-float monoplane designated MB 35. Its design was influenced by the Hansa-Brandenburg W 29, designed during World War I by Ernst Heinkel, and incorporated quick-detach fittings for the wings and floats similar to those on Heinkel's U 1. The pilot and observer sat side by side in a cramped, open cockpit. The MB 35 first flew in February 1926. Besson also presented the MB 35 to the civilian market. The compact aircraft could fit into a box with wheels for easy transport, leading Besson to christen it as the "*Passe-Partout*" (Go-Anywhere), a reference to the globetrotting character of the same name from Jules Verne's novel *Around the World in Eighty Days*.[56]

During the development of the MB 35, the *Surcouf* was under construction and unavailable for trials, thus the submarines *Souffleur* and *Phoque* carried out rudimentary launch and recovery experiments in 1928. In the calm waters of Bizerte Lake in Tunisia, the two submarines practiced floating off and surfacing underneath a seaplane. A CAMS flying boat was used for those trials as the first MB 35 was not yet available.[57]

Six MB 35s were built through 1929. Although intended specifically for the *Surcouf* and her planned sister ships, some consideration was given to modifying

The French Navy acquired several Besson MB 35 floatplanes intended for use on board the submarine *Surcouf*. Ultimately only going to sea on board cruisers, the MB 35 design evolved into the similar MB 41 that was carried by the *Surcouf*. (AUTHORS' COLLECTION)

the new *Requin*-class patrol submarines with hangars to house the aircraft, motivated in part by the U.S. experiments with the *S-1*. Ultimately the *Requin*-class submarines were judged too small to accommodate the floatplane. As the *Surcouf* still was under construction, the MB 35s were embarked on cruisers.[58]

The aircraft held up to the conditions on deck during long overseas cruises despite its mostly wood and fabric construction. However, the MB 35's structure was fragile and required extremely calm seas to operate. Trials on board cruisers were concluded in May 1929, and the six aircraft were put into storage or scrapped.

The decision was reached that a more robust aircraft than the MB 35 was needed for the *Surcouf*. In May 1931, the Minister of the Navy solicited designs from Besson (then owned by ANF Les Mureaux) and the Gourdou-Leseurre aircraft companies. The Besson design—the MB 41, an improved MB 35—was selected.[59] The new design was slightly larger and heavier than the MB 35, with tandem cockpits instead of the earlier side-by-side seating. To increase the airframe's rigidity, the undercarriage was changed to a large center float and two small, stabilizing wing floats.

The prototype MB 41 flew in August 1932. On 19 July 1933, the aircraft was conducting takeoff tests at Saint-Raphaël on the French Rivera. Although the sea was relatively calm, the 2½-foot waves caused the floatplane to flip over on takeoff, injuring the pilot and killing the observer. The MB 41 was a total loss. The Navy ordered a second prototype, designated MB 411, with a single seat, a more powerful engine, and improved floats. It flew in June 1935. An additional, large fuel tank in the center float gave the MB 411 an impressive endurance of nearly seven hours.[60]

The *Surcouf* received the MB 411 at Brest in November 1935, and it first flew from the submarine during the *Surcouf*'s visit to the Caribbean island of Guadeloupe in December. When the submarine returned to France, the aircraft was fitted with a second cockpit, a larger rudder and stabilizer fins, and a streamlined engine cowling. A second MB 411 with those features was delivered in July 1938.[61]

The floatplane rested on top of a dolly inside of the *Surcouf*'s hangar, located aft of the conning tower. Once it was pushed out of the hangar, a folding crane stowed in the hangar was wheeled out and used to lift the aircraft for the fitting of the wings and floats. The aircraft then was launched by the crane lowering it to the water or by submerging the stern of the submarine. Assembly and launching took up to 30 minutes in calm seas. On several occasions the *Surcouf* used her floatplane to refine her long-range gunnery. However, the MB 411 was fragile and could operate only with calm water. A catapult was considered for launching in rough seas, but the MB 411's airframe was not sufficiently robust to survive that acceleration.

The French Navy began design studies for a successor for the *Surcouf* in 1936— Project W. Due to the restrictions of the London naval treaty it would have a scaled-down hull displacing 2,250 tons on the surface and 3,500 tons submerged.[62] Its armament correspondingly was reduced to either a triple 6.1-inch or twin 5.1-inch gun turret.

AND A HELICOPTER?

For the new submarine design, and also to replace the *Surcouf*'s MB 411, the Navy initiated development of a submarine-launched helicopter. A rotary-wing aircraft could solve many of the previous aircraft problems by being able to take off and land vertically from the submarine's deck without touching the water. The Navy solicited aeronautical engineer René Dorand to design a helicopter for the *Surcouf*.

Dorand had teamed with aviation pioneer Louis Breguet in 1931 to develop experimental helicopters. In 1935, Dorand and Breguet built the Gyroplane Laboratorie, the world's first operational helicopter. The use of coaxial, contra-rotating rotors eliminated torque on the fuselage and allowed the designers to do away with a tail assembly and rotor. Dorand left Breguet in 1938 to found his own firm, the French Gyroplane Company. He immediately began work on the G 20 helicopter that was intended for Project W and the *Surcouf* as well as for operation from land and surface ships.[63]

The futuristic G 20 was an extraordinarily advanced helicopter for its time. It was elegantly streamlined with a bullet-shaped fuselage accommodating two or three men, who would sit behind a panoramic "greenhouse" canopy. At the rear of the finely tapered fuselage a butterfly tail controlled the helicopter at high speeds. Two 240-horsepower engines powered the coaxial, contra-rotating rotors. Dorand's attention to streamlining resulted in an estimated top speed of more than 150 mph.

The prototype G 20 was under construction when Germany invaded France in May 1940, and remained at Chambéry in the foothills of the French Alps for the duration of the conflict. The project was revived after the war with the prototype completed in 1947. Ground tests were conducted, but more advanced helicopters had been developed during the war in both the United States and Germany. The G 20 never flew and the *Surcouf* went to war with her Besson floatplane, albeit with neither seeing combat before the submarine's loss.

THE ITALIAN TRIALS

While the *Surcouf* was under development, the Italian Navy began work on a similar, big-gun cruiser submarine also carrying a scout seaplane. In October 1924, the Ministry of Aeronautics ordered two Dornier Do A *Libelle II* (Dragonfly) flying boats for submarine trials.[64] They were built by Italy's Mechanical Engineering Company, which constructed Dornier seaplanes under license.

Although the diminutive, two-seat flying boat was intended to be a civilian sport seaplane, it was ideal for submarine operations because of its all-metal construction and folding parasol wing. The firm made several modifications to the Dornier design, including making the wing removable and tail folding. Two such aircraft were completed by 1926.

For trials, the *Andrea Provana*, an *Agostino Barbarigo*-class submarine, was fitted with a mockup hangar that was steel-framed with a canvas covering. The trials were to be limited to surface operations as the makeshift hangar was not watertight. The submarine was fitted with a track from the hangar to the stern so that the *Libelle* could be wheeled out on a dolly. On 23 December 1927, the *Provana* sailed into the La Spezia harbor with the *Libelle* on board. After the aircraft was extracted from the faux hangar and assembled on the dolly, the submarine flooded her after ballast tanks, submerging the stern. The flying boat slid down the track and floated off the dolly. For recovery the aircraft was maneuvered over the dolly by swimmers and the submarine fully surfaced to seat the *Libelle* on the dolly. Launching and recovery each took about 15 minutes.

Although those limited trials were successful, the captain of the *Provana* identified several problems: The launch and recovery would be very difficult in heavy seas, especially given the reliance on divers for the recovery. He also criticized the *Libelle*'s flight endurance of only one hour and advocated for a larger, fully waterproof aircraft so that the proposed watertight hangar would not be needed.[65]

As the *Libelle* was being evaluated, Italy's first cruiser submarine—the *Ettore Fieramosca*—was approaching completion. The diminutive flying boat obviously was not suitable for use on board a submarine, thus the Navy put out a request for floatplanes purpose-built for use on board submarines.

Two single-seat monoplanes with removable wings were designed to that 1927 requirement: the Piaggio P.8 and Macchi M.53. The two aircraft were similar: both were powered by the 75-horsepower ADC Cirrus II engine, had wood floats and fuselage, duralumin wings and empennage, and mounted a single Vickers .303-inch machine gun firing through the propeller arc. Both designs also had a camera holding 24 photographic plates for reconnaissance.[66] Comparable in dimensions and performance, the primary difference between the two aircraft was that the Macchi had an unusually thick, low-mounted wing whereas the Piaggio had a thin, parasol wing.

When the *Ettore Fieramosca* slid down the building ways on 15 April 1929, her hangar sat exposed on the deck aft of the conning tower, not yet covered by a streamlined fairwater. At less than 2,000 tons submerged displacement and 270 feet long, the *Fieramosca* was about one-half the size of the *Surcouf*. The Italian submarine mounted a 4.7-inch (120-mm) deck gun and carried 24 mines in two stern chutes in addition to six 21-inch torpedo tubes: four in the bow and two externally mounted in the stern. (Earlier design iterations had provided a single 8-inch gun.)

The Macchi M.53 prototype had flown in October 1928, and the Piaggio P.8 prototype would take to the air in November 1929.[67] The Piaggio, because of its greater ease of assembly and superior visibility from the cockpit, was judged the winner.[68] However, the submarine aircraft program was abruptly cancelled due to concerns about the *Fieramosca*'s stability with the hangar installation.

When the *Fieramosca* entered service in April 1930, her hangar had been removed and her stern mine chutes had been replaced with four 21-inch torpedo tubes.[69] The submarine experienced a thoroughly disappointing career in the Spanish Civil War (1936–1939) and the early years of World War II. Even without her hangar, 8-inch gun, or mines, she still was unstable and in 1940 was relegated to a training role.[70]

Between the world wars the Italian Navy contemplated another design for an aircraft-carrying submarine: In 1926 engineer Roberto Galeazzi submitted a design to the Navy for a remarkably large cruiser displacing 5,200 tons submerged and 400 feet in length. The "oceanic colonial" submarine would have a heavy

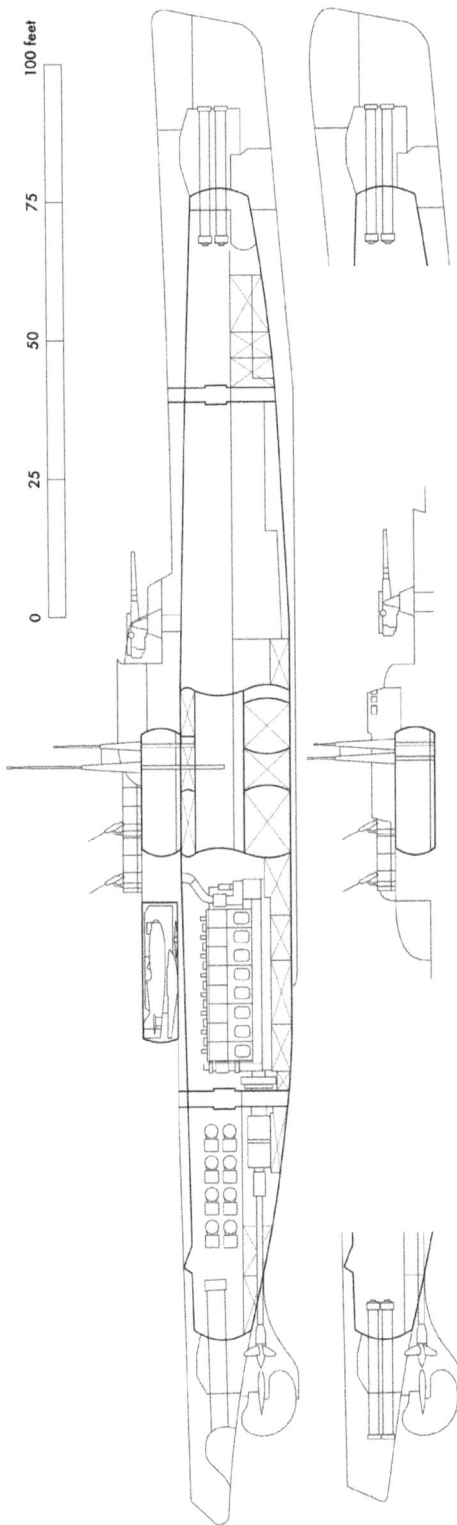

The original design for the *Ettore Fieramosca* had an aircraft hangar and two stern mine chutes. The drawings show how her design was altered before she was commissioned: the mine chutes were replaced by four 21-inch torpedo tubes, the hangar and gun fairing were removed, and the bow buoyancy tank was enlarged in a vain effort to increase stability. (©JACOB GUNNARSON)

0   25   50   75   100 feet

TABLE 3.1
Galeazzi's Oceanic Colonial Submarine

Displacement	
surface	3,800 tons
submerged	5,275 tons
Length	400 ft. 3 in. (122 m)
Beam	34 ft. 5 in. (10.5 m)
Draft	19 ft. 4 in. (5.9 m)
Diesel engines	2
total shp	12,000
Steam turbine generators	2
total hp	5,364
Electric motors	2
total shp	5,000
Shafts	2
Speed	
surface	24 knots
submerged	9.5 knots
Range (nm/kn)	
surfaced	12,700/10
submerged	80/4
Test depth	492 ft. (150 m)
Torpedo Tubes	4 21-in. bow 4 21-in. amidships
Torpedoes	20
Guns	4 6-in. (152-mm) 2 3-in. (76-mm) 2 1.6-in. (40-mm)
Complement	114
Aircraft	1

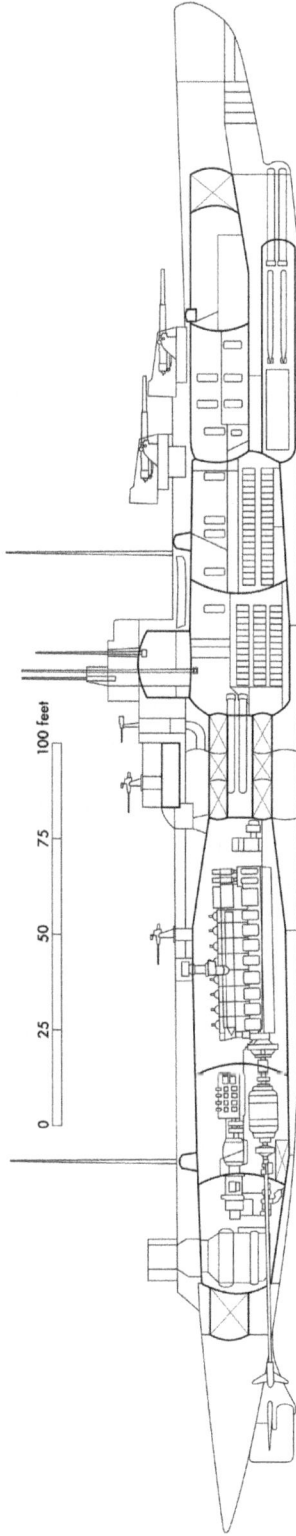

Roberto Galeazzi's 1926 "oceanic colonial" design. The pressure hull was subdivided into several smaller hulls to improve strength. Propulsion was provided by a combination of diesel engines, electric motors, and steam turbine-generators. (©JACOB GUNNARSON)

100 feet

0   25   50   75

armament of four 6-inch (152-mm) guns mounted in two turrets and eight 21-inch torpedo tubes—four bow tubes and four mounted amidships firing aft. It would carry a seaplane in a hangar aft of the conning tower to scout for targets and to refine the submarine's gunnery.

The submarine's hull was subdivided into several smaller (and thus stronger) pressure hulls, which Galeazzi claimed would result in a test depth of nearly 500 feet, an impressive figure for the time. The convoluted internal pressure hull structure was wrapped in a hydrodynamically shaped outer hull.

Equally innovative was the power plant: Two 6,000-horsepower diesel engines would drive the submarine on the surface for economical cruising, providing a range of 16,500 n.miles at ten knots. For bursts of high speed, a boiler and two steam turbine-generator sets could additionally power the two 2,500-horsepower electric motors for a total of 17,000 shaft horsepower and a maximum surface speed of 24 knots. If the steam plant were used immediately before the submarine submerged, the intense heat of the boiler would quickly diffuse into the interior of the submarine; thus Galeazzi placed it at the stern in an insulated compartment where the heat could dissipate into the surrounding ballast tanks. Underwater the submarine was driven by electric motors.

Despite the proposed submarine's potential, the Navy rejected Galeazzi's design. While the ambitious design had superlative characteristics, it would require a long and costly development effort. The complex propulsion plant and unique hull structure would have been challenging to design and construct, especially when considering the difficulties that even the relatively conventional *Ettore Fieramosca* had encountered.[71]

THE SOVIET EFFORTS

The Soviet Union that emerged from the Communist revolution of 1917 had few operational warships. Thirty-two of the 52 pre-revolutionary submarines were lost during the subsequent Russian civil war, and those that remained were in a poor state of repair.[72] Planned economic reforms brought the promise of rebuilding the foundering Soviet Navy, and in 1924 the Revolutionary Military Council laid out a plan for the Soviet Air Force. Significantly, among the new aircraft types put forward for future development was a small, submarine-launched reconnaissance seaplane.[73]

Work on such an aircraft eventually began in 1931 under Igor V. Chetverikov, head of the naval aircraft department of the Central Design Bureau. The designer was only 22 years old; his senior position had been achieved because of the arrest of many of his superiors by the NKVD secret police. Chetverikov's SPL (*Samolet dlya Podvodnykh Lodok*—Aircraft for Submarines) would be a flying boat similar to the American Loening XSL. Development of the aircraft was stalled by the Navy's reaction to the sinking of the British submarine *M-2* and Chetverikov's departure from the Central Design Bureau.

Subsequently, Chetverikov acquired a position with the department of Hydroplane and Aerosled Construction (OSGA) of the Civil Air Fleet Research Institute. He then was able to secure funding for two prototype aircraft from an unlikely source—the Chief Directorate of the Northern Sea Route, which required an ice-reconnaissance aircraft for its Arctic expedition ships.

The first prototype aircraft—designated OSGA-101—had retractable landing gear to facilitate taking off from ice. At the request of the Soviet Navy, the second prototype—the SPL—was smaller and was to fit into a submarine hangar. The SPL had wood wings and hull, and a duralumin tail section skinned with canvas. Like the U.S. Navy's XSL, the wings folded back against the sides of the fuselage; the top-mounted engine swung down between the booms supporting the tail. The aircraft was to be readied for flight from its storage configuration in five minutes. The two-seat cockpit could accommodate the pilot and observer sitting side by side.[74] If the pilot flew the aircraft solo, the SPL could match the French MB 411's exceptional seven-hour endurance.

The Soviet Navy planned to embark the SPL on their newest submarine design—the Type K Series XIV. The Type K was the Soviet Navy's first long-range, cruiser submarine, intended to be a commerce raider, minelayer, and fleet scout. The design, begun in 1934, featured a hangar aft of the conning tower for the SPL.[75]

Meanwhile, Chetverikov's prototypes flew: The OSGA-101 for the first time in May 1934, and the SPL in early 1935. The SPL performed well in trials and was able to take off and land in waves up to 2½ feet. At the conclusion of flight testing, it was planned to embark that aircraft on a submarine fitted with a hangar for further trials on the Black Sea.

Despite the SPL's promise, the Soviet Navy chose to remove the seaplane hangar from the Type K submarine design. The hangar would have reduced the craft's submerged speed from 10 to 8½ knots and significantly increased the displacement.[76] Eleven submarines of that class were completed from 1939 to 1944 and were the largest submarines in Soviet service during World War II.

In 1937 there was a proposal to build an improved submarine variant—the Type KE Series XIV-*bis*—with more powerful diesel engines and a hangar for an SPL floatplane. But again it was determined that the hangar would increase displacement and impair stability; that design never came to fruition. In 1939 the Navy yet again proposed to build an improved Type K submarine—the Type KU—with increased performance and an aircraft hangar, but that design work was abandoned when Germany invaded the Soviet Union in June 1941.

The SPL prototype was given to a paramilitary sporting organization after being exhibited at an international air show in Milan.[77] The OSGA-101 prototype was never embarked in a ship as intended for ice reconnaissance.

The Soviet Navy also briefly entertained concepts for enormous submarines armed with large-caliber guns and carrying seaplanes. In 1935, Sergei A.

Bazilevskiy—a lead designer at the TsKBS-2 submarine design bureau—circu-lated his designs for submersible battleships, aircraft carriers, and cruisers.[78] In his view, the Soviet Union had developed sufficiently advanced weapons, air-craft, and machinery to make a submarine-only fleet feasible.

The "submersible battleship" would be feasible due to the Soviet devel-opment of recoilless guns. Those weapons were considerably lighter than traditional shipboard artillery, allowing a submarine to be armed with large-

TABLE 3.2
Design Proposals by S. A. Bazilevskiy

	Submarine Cruiser	Submarine Battleship	Submarine Aircraft Carrier
Displacement			
surface	6,400 tons	6,900 tons	7,500 tons
submerged	8,640 tons	9,315 tons	10,125 tons
Length	607 ft. 11 in. (185 m)	607 ft. 11 in. (185 m)	639 ft. 9 in. (195 m)
Beam	42 ft. 8 in. (13 m)	44 ft. 3 in. (13.5 m)	44 ft. 11 in. (13.7 m)
Draft	18 ft. 1 in. (5.5 m)	18 ft. 1 in. (5.5 m)	19 ft. (5.8 m)
Diesel engines	2	2	2
total shp	2,000	2,000	2,000
Steam turbines			
total shp	70,000	35,000	80,000
Electric motors	2	2	2
total shp	8,000	4,400	9,000
Shafts	2	2	2
Speed			
surface	30 knots	24 knots	30 knots
submerged	11 knots	11 knots	9 knots
Range (nm/kn)			
surfaced	20,000/14	20,000/14	20,000/14
submerged	200/3	125/3	180/3
Test depth	492 ft. (150 m)	492 ft. (150 m)	492 ft. (150 m)
Torpedo Tubes	10 21-in. bow 4 21-in. stern 6 21-in. external	8 21-in. bow 4 21-in. stern	6 21-in. bow 4 21-in. stern
Guns	6 5.9-in. (150-mm) 7 1.7-in. (45-mm)	3 11.8-in. (300-mm) 4 3.9-in. (100-mm)	4 3.9-in. (100-mm)
Aircraft	1 scout	3 scouts	12 fighters 3 bombers

caliber guns. In addition to a heavy gun armament, Bazilevskiy's designs would have an incredible torpedo armament: 20 tubes and 120 torpedoes in the "submersible cruiser." His submarines could match the 30-knot speed of conventional cruisers and aircraft carriers by using high-pressure boilers and steam turbines that would develop up to 80,000 shaft horsepower on the surface. For lower surface speeds and for submerged operation the submarines would have traditional diesel engines and electric motors.

All of the Bazilevskiy designs were to operate aircraft: the submersible cruiser and battleship would have one and three SPLs, respectively, and the "submersible aircraft carrier" would embark *12 fighters and 4 bombers*. His designs measured between 600 and 640 feet in length and would displace between 8,600 and 10,000 tons submerged.[79]

In part due to his designs' titanic size and the unrealistic figures for the power of their steam plants, Bazilevskiy's vision for an all-submarine fleet never came to fruition. The Soviet Navy would not again seriously consider an aircraft-carrying submarine until after World War II.

OTHER EUROPEAN INTERESTS

The Polish Navy also considered developing an aircraft-carrying submarine.[80] In 1929, engineer Jerzy Nikol began design work on a flying boat for shipboard use. Similar in configuration to the American XSL and Soviet SPL, the Nikol A-2 had wings that could be quickly detached and were buoyant so that the aircraft would float even with damaged hull and floats.

In 1934, the Swedish Navy commissioned the light cruiser *Gotland*, which could embark six British-built Hawker Osprey floatplanes. The concept of a seaplane cruiser caught the attention of the Polish Navy's leadership and plans were developed to fit its newest ships—the minelayer *Gryf* and submarine *Orzeł*—with aircraft.

The *Orzeł* was intended for operations within the Baltic with the heavy armament of eight 21-inch torpedo tubes plus several small deck guns, and a 20-knot surface speed. Submarines employed in the shallow waters of the Baltic typically had a surface displacement of about 600 tons or less and were capable of only short operations before needing to be resupplied. As Poland's naval bases could be vulnerable to attack in time of war, the 1,110-ton *Orzeł* was designed to operate independently for at least 30 days without replenishment. The Polish Navy outsourced much of the design of the *Orzeł* and her sister ship *Sęp* to a Dutch design firm and the submarines were to be constructed in Dutch shipyards.[81]

As originally designed, the *Orzeł* was to have a hangar faired into her conning tower for a Nikol A-2 that would be floated out with the submarine's deck awash. An alternative design had the submarine carrying a small motor torpedo boat to seek out targets over the horizon and in waters too shallow for the submarine. However, it was determined that the hangar for either craft could upset stability and would prevent the installation of a swiveling torpedo launcher in the after superstructure. Thus, the seaplane and torpedo boat were eliminated in the early stages of the submarine's design.

In early 1939, the *Orzeł* and *Sęp* were placed in commission and the Nikol A-2 took to the skies for the first time. Both submarines were operational when Germany invaded Poland on 1 September 1939. The *Sęp* was interned in Sweden for the duration of the war; the *Orzeł* escaped from the Baltic and operated in combat with the Royal Navy. She was lost off Norway in May 1940, probably sunk by a British or German mine. The prototype Nikol A-2 was captured by the Germans shortly after their invasion of Poland.[82]

The Royal Netherlands Navy carried out a single test of a submarine-launched aircraft in 1935. Two K XIV-class submarines and several Fokker C.VIIW floatplanes intended for service on board cruisers were based in the Dutch East Indies. On 29 June 1935, one aircraft was placed on the deck of the submarine K XV, positioned forward of the conning tower. Like the German experiment with the *U-12* some 20 years earlier, it appears to have been an impromptu trial with no modification made to the aircraft or to the submarine. The test apparently was a one-off demonstration rather than a serious effort to develop an aircraft-carrying submarine.

THE END OF INTEREST

Most of the major navies experimented with or at least considered aircraft-carrying submarines between the world wars. The Soviet Union, Italy, and Poland abandoned their projects before they could come to fruition, but the United States, Britain, and France each modified or constructed an aircraft-carrying submarine and acquired a handful of suitable aircraft. Despite the progress and innovation achieved with those efforts, only France's *Surcouf* was in service with an aircraft when World War II erupted in Europe in 1939. The *Surcouf*'s aircraft was not highly regarded and was seldom flown. The submarine saw no combat before being lost—to unknown causes—in 1942.

Several factors contributed to the abandonment of aircraft-carrying submarines in Europe and the United States. Only relatively large submarines were capable of carrying aircraft, and only they had the range to operate independently in remote seas where aerial reconnaissance would be especially useful. The restrictions in the number and size of submarines were dictated by the 1930 and 1933 London naval treaties that limited the construction of large submarines. Moreover, the economies of the major powers were not able to construct large and expensive, specialized submarines in peacetime. Europe was still reeling from the economic devastation of World War I, and although the United States was prospering in the 1920s, its economy came crashing down in 1929.

Despite the early enthusiasm for aircraft-carrying submarines, the ability to carry aircraft always was of secondary importance. The United States, Soviet Union, and Poland drafted designs for cruiser submarines with hangars, but their naval leadership decided that the penalties to stability, silhouette, speed, and displacement were prohibitive. The Italian Navy went so far as to actually launch the *Ettore Fieramosca* with a hangar installed before coming to the same decision.

Beyond design difficulties, operating aircraft raised potential operational problems. The requirement to be on the surface with crewmen on deck to launch and recover the aircraft left the submarine exposed to enemy attack. And there was the question of the vulnerability of flooding if there was enemy damage to the hangar door.

If improved aircraft could have been developed, the benefits of carrying it might have outweighed the problems. Certainly the limitations of 1920s aeronautical technology made it difficult to design a robust aircraft that could fit in a small hangar while having suitable airborne performance. Still, so few submarine-suitable aircraft were built that designers had little opportunity to iterate and improve on designs.

Some navies did make small advances in suitable aircraft: the American XS-2 and XSL-2 were improvements of existing aircraft, and the British Petos received revised floats, wings, and engines. The French iterated more with their successive development of the MB 35, MB 41, and MB 411. Still, those were relatively minor improvements.

Accordingly, several European navies experimented with aircraft-carrying submarines only because others were doing so. Britain, Italy, France, and the Soviet Union—as well as Japan—all appear to have initiated their submarine aircraft programs either in response the U.S. Navy's purchase of the Caspar-Heinkel U 1 in 1922 or the highly publicized demonstrations of the Martin MS-1 and Cox-Klemin XS-2 on board the submarine *S-1*.

The fear of falling behind in naval technology—behind both the United States and other European nations—was a motivating factor beyond the operational need for aircraft-carrying submarines. That anxiety greatly dissipated after the *M-2* was lost and the U.S. Navy abandoned its efforts in the early 1930s. Japan's highly successful program was kept quiet and did not rekindle those fears.

With few large submarines and little coherent concept for their use beyond patrolling in distant waters, the U.S. and European navies concluded that the inherent design challenges for both the aircraft and the submarine outweighed the potential advantages. Only the Imperial Japanese Navy had a vision for the operational use of aircraft-carrying submarines and devoted sufficient time and funds toward developing a series of successively more innovative and capable aircraft. Eventually those efforts resulted in the large-scale employment of undersea aircraft carriers.

CHAPTER 4

Europe at War

The French *Surcouf* was the only European aircraft-carrying submarine in commission when war erupted in September 1939. A month earlier she had made a visit to Dakar on the western coast of Africa. Then, because of the deteriorating situation in Europe, she was ordered to the French Antilles. The French Navy intended to operate the *Surcouf* in the Caribbean until it was decided how she could best be employed in the war. However, the submarine required repairs to her diesel generators and electric motors, thus the Navy ordered her back to France after war was declared on 3 September.

En route to the port of Brest, the *Surcouf* helped to escort the British-French convoy KJ-2 across the Atlantic in late September. A week after leaving the Caribbean, the convoy was sighted by a floatplane from the German "pocket battleship" *Deutschland*, which set a course to intercept the convoy. On the night of 9 October, a lookout on the *Deutschland* sighted the *Surcouf* on the surface and the battleship turned away, most likely saving the convoy from destruction by the 11-inch (283-mm) guns of the German warship.[1]

The *Surcouf* began an extensive refit after reaching Brest. Her temperamental diesels and electric motors were disassembled and rebuilt, her batteries replaced, and the cracks in her ballast tanks welded. Repairs took on a frantic pace when Germany invaded France in May 1940. By June the German forces were drawing close to Brest.

The *Surcouf* would have to sail with the repairs unfinished. Her commanding officer, *Capitaine de corvette* Paul Martin, wanted to sail to Casablanca, but the submarine's mechanical problems forced him to sail the shorter distance to England. On 18 June her MB 411 floatplane returned to Brest from the seaplane base across the bay, and the *Surcouf* set off across the English Channel with the aircraft stowed in her hangar.

The submarine's stern diving planes were jammed and she could only run on electric power, resulting in an agonizingly slow maximum speed of four knots for the crossing. A day later the engineers were able to fix the stern planes; her port diesel engine was fired up and she proceeded into Penzance harbor on the British coast, escorted by Royal Navy ships and aircraft. A suspicious radio message was sent from French Navy headquarters ordering the *Surcouf* back to Brest. Deducing that it was a German ploy, Martin continued on to Plymouth, England.

Despite France being allied with Britain, Martin ordered the *Surcouf*'s officers to be wary of possible attempts by the British to seize their submarine. His fears were realized when the British initiated Operation Catapult in an effort to keep French ships from falling into the hands of the Germans. The Royal Navy blockaded the African ports of Dakar, Alexandria, and Mers El Kébir, where French ships were anchored, and issued an ultimatum demanding that French commanders either fight the Germans, sail out of reach of the war, or scuttle their ships. That ultimatum also applied to French ships in British ports.

Few French captains, including Martin, were receptive to the British demands. In the early hours of 3 July a British boarding party boarded the *Surcouf*. The French fought back—with guns. During the brief struggle two British officers, a British sailor, and a French warrant officer were killed.[2] Still, the *Surcouf* avoided the grim fate of the French warships at Mers El Kébir and Dakar, which suffered heavy casualties before they were captured by the British.

At Plymouth the giant submarine was formally handed over to the Free French Navy and placed under the command of *Capitaine de corvette* Pierre Ortoli. The Free French forces, led by the charismatic General Charles de Gaulle, would serve alongside British (and later American) forces fighting the Germans.

From July until November 1940, the *Surcouf* lay in Plymouth harbor while the British and Free French pondered her fate. The submarine's designed purpose of commerce raiding was not relevant to the current war situation. Some French officers advocated concentrating their efforts on rearming the other French submarines in British ports instead of employing their scant resources and manpower on the ungainly *Surcouf*. Still, many were eager to see the *Surcouf* sail again given her iconic status and repairs finally were resumed in November. Although the Free French Navy ostensibly operated the submarine, the Royal Navy would decide where and how she would be employed.

The *Surcouf*'s repairs were finished by January 1941, and she was assigned to escort transatlantic convoys to and from Halifax. Sailing from Holy Loch, Scotland, on 19 February, her first voyage as a convoy escort was miserable. Rolling up to 35 degrees in the rough North Atlantic, acid spilled from her batteries, causing a fire that filled the submarine with toxic fumes. Escorting another convoy back to England, she was twice mistaken for a U-boat. The first case of mistaken identity was quickly resolved, but during the second event a British aircraft attempted to strafe the submarine. The aircraft missed its target.

In May 1941, the British decided that the *Surcouf* would undertake a mission better suited to her capabilities: She would attempt to destroy German oilers steaming southwest of the Azores that were replenishing commerce-raiding battleships and cruisers. When the *Surcouf* departed England on 14 May, she sailed without her floatplane, which had been damaged in a German bombing raid on Plymouth.

The *Surcouf* would never again operate an aircraft. The aircraft and its crew were transferred to the Royal Navy at Poole. Nicknamed the "Petrel" by the British, the MB 411 was notoriously difficult to fly. On her first flight in Britain the Petrel required a two-mile takeoff run before lifting off the water. After its engine was retuned and the wings and floats were re-rigged, the aircraft's performance improved. The Petrel's performance still was unsatisfactory and a plan to embark it on the British Q-ship *Fidelity* was cancelled.[3]

When the *Surcouf* reached her operating area off the Azores, the German battleship *Bismarck* and heavy cruiser *Prinz Eugen* were battling with British warships in the North Atlantic. The *Bismarck* was sunk on 27 May, but the *Prinz Eugen* eluded the British, sailing south to rendezvous with the German oiler *Esso Hamburg* on 28 May, several hundred miles north of the *Surcouf*'s position The submarine turned north to intercept the oiler and came within 50 n.miles of the German ship, which escaped detection. It was a cloudless day and the *Surcouf*'s floatplane likely would have found the German ship—had it been on board.[4] The decision to leave the MB 411 behind had cost the *Surcouf* the only potential target of her brief service.

With only one day of fuel remaining, the *Surcouf* arrived at Bermuda on 10 June. Her crew was exhausted and electrical issues had cropped up during her 4,000-n.mile voyage. Still, from 30 June to 20 July, she embarked on another unsuccessful search for German oilers. In the year since departing Brest, the *Surcouf* had sailed 25,000 n.miles. She departed Bermuda for a refit at the Portsmouth Navy Yard in Kittery, Maine.

The *Surcouf* after her refit at the Portsmouth Navy Yard in Kittery, Maine. (U.S. NAVY)

Navy yard workers fabricated new parts from scratch as all of the submarine's spare parts were in German-occupied France. They labored day and night to overhaul her engines, repair her steering gear, replace her batteries and electric cables, fix her fire-control system, and seal her leaking ballast tanks.

Meanwhile, the *Surcouf*'s crew had an opportunity to relax and was sent in shifts to a rest camp in the New Hampshire countryside. Despite that respite, crew morale was low and attrition was high. Throughout her service with the Free French Navy, a steady stream of replacement sailors was necessary to keep the *Surcouf* operating. On 29 October, after three months in the shipyard, the submarine departed Portsmouth under a new commanding officer, *Capitaine de frégate* Georges Blaison. She sailed for the submarine base at New London, Connecticut, to conduct trials. A minor collision with a U.S. submarine on 21 November caused leaks in her ballast tanks, which required further repairs at New London.

Subsequently sailing to Bermuda and then returning north to Halifax, the *Surcouf* was ordered by Free France headquarters to take part in an operation to liberate Saint Pierre and Miquelon. Those two small islands off the coast of Newfoundland with some 3,500 inhabitants had been under the control of the German puppet state of Vichy France since 1940. On Christmas Eve 1941, the islands were liberated without bloodshed by sailors from the *Surcouf* and three French corvettes.

U.S. and British officials were incensed: The islands had no strategic value and through special agreements with the United States and the Free French government their status quo was respected, with the proviso that they have no contacts with the Axis. General Charles de Gaulle, commanding Free French forces, had not informed President Franklin Roosevelt or British Prime Minister Winston Churchill in advance of the operation, and the use of military force in North America by a European entity was anathema to both Allied leaders.[5] But the strain on the Allied relationship with the Free French quickly passed.

Following the U.S. entry into the European War after the Japanese attack on Pearl Harbor in December 1941, the Royal Navy ordered the *Surcouf* to the Pacific. She was to sail via the Panama Canal to Tahiti and then on to Sydney, Australia. Departing Halifax on 2 February 1942, she arrived in Bermuda on 6 February, again with a litany of mechanical issues. It was estimated that repairs would take three months. The Royal Navy decided that she should continue in her current condition. The *Surcouf* departed Bermuda on 12 February bound for the Panama Canal and on into the Pacific. The Royal Navy broadcast a notice to Allied ASW forces in the Caribbean establishing a "moving haven" 120 miles ahead and behind and 15 miles to either side of the *Surcouf*'s estimated positions.[6] The submarine would be under radio silence during the voyage.

The *Surcouf* failed to appear at the Panama Canal when expected on 19 February. At 2230 on the previous night, lookouts on board the *Thompson Lykes*, an American cargo ship sailing from Panama to Cuba, sighted a light off their starboard bow. With her own lights extinguished as a precaution against U-boat attack, the *Thompson Lykes* swung to port. Then the light was dead ahead. She collided with the unidentified craft, which exploded in a sheet of fire. The merchant ship's lookouts barely made out the silhouette of the ship, which one described as looking like a submarine.

As the stricken craft sank, it exploded, violently shaking the *Thompson Lykes*. The lookouts briefly heard calls for help in English from men in the water, but no bodies or wreckage were found after the sun rose—only an oil slick. Because the steamer was a civilian vessel, her crew had not been informed of the *Surcouf*'s passage to Panama.

After the *Surcouf* failed to arrive at Panama the favored interpretation of the U.S. Navy was that she had collided with the *Thompson Lykes*. However, the *Surcouf*'s planned track would have put her at least 20 n.miles away from the merchant ship at the time of the collision. It was possible that the submarine deviated from her planned course due to the currents or navigational error, although Captain Blaison probably would have been loath to leave the protection of the "moving haven."

Upon reaching Cuba, the *Thompson Lykes* was drydocked to inspect the damage. Although her bow was slightly deformed, there was no major damage, which would have been surprising if she had collided with the *Surcouf*. The cargo ship was only 1,400 tons larger than the submarine, and British ships had suffered far more damage in collisions with smaller German U-boats.

Another possibility is that the *Surcouf* was sunk by U.S. Army bombers of the 6th Bombardment Group. On the morning of 19 February, three bombers—one B-18 and two A-17s—were ordered to attack a submarine that was detected north of their airfield at Rio Hato, Panama. The aircraft reported finding a "very large submarine" and dropped eight 100-pound bombs. One pilot reported hitting the craft and watching it submerge. The pilots apparently had not been briefed that an Allied submarine would be in the area. However, the precise location of the attack is unknown and may have been outside of the *Surcouf*'s expected route.[7]

Later, a U.S. Navy sailor at the submarine base in Panama recalled hearing that Army aircraft bombed the *Surcouf* near the Gulf of San Blas, about 70 miles west of the northern entrance to the Panama Canal. After the war he worked at San Blas Point and was told by local people that they had buried men from the *Surcouf* who had washed up after the bombing.[8]

No submarine wreckage has ever been located, nor has there been an archaeological examination of the cemetery on San Blas point.

Several conspiracy theories also have been concocted about the *Surcouf*'s disappearance, typically involving a defection to the Axis by her crew or her *deliberate sinking by the U.S. or British forces.*[9] It was certainly true that the Royal Navy was at times less than fond of the *Surcouf*. But that occasional disdain stemmed primarily from her poor material condition and her questionable value as a warship.

Claims of the *Surcouf* crew's treachery or demise in waters outside of the Caribbean were not supported by any evidence. Given the *Surcouf*'s long history of mechanical troubles, it seems just as likely that she sank without any outside intervention. The fate of Europe's most impressive underwater aircraft carrier will remain a mystery until her wreckage is found.

THE TYPE XI U-BOAT CRUISER

Germany had not experimented with submarine-launched aircraft since the early 1920s, although the development of German military aircraft and submarines had secretly continued in violation of the 1919 Treaty of Versailles. In 1937 *Generaladmiral* Erich Raeder, then head of the German Navy, put forth his Z-Plan to rebuild Germany's fleet to rival that of Great Britain. Raeder hoped that war could be forestalled until the plan's shipbuilding was completed—about 1946. The plan, which primarily focused on capital warships, included nine Type XI cruiser submarines.

The Type XI would be the largest submarine yet built in Germany, displacing 3,930 tons submerged. Like the successful U-boat cruisers of World War I, the Type XI would be a commerce raider with a long range to divert enemy forces away from the main battle in the North Atlantic. With a surface range of 15,800 n.miles at 12 knots, the Type XI would be able to operate off the coasts of North and South America and western Africa, areas with a significant amount of unescorted Allied shipping. The submarine could patrol as far north as the White Sea in the Soviet Arctic to attack Soviet sea lanes and to protect German shipping bringing ore from Norway.[10]

To propel the submarine to 23 knots on the surface, the designers crammed eight diesel engines into the hull for a total of 17,600 shaft horsepower, a figure greater than early U.S. nuclear-propelled submarines. The machinery was arranged in two engine rooms, each with four diesel engines abreast, constructed with an unusual cross-section resembling a sideways "figure-eight."

The main armament would be four 5-inch (127-mm) guns in twin mounts and six 21-inch torpedo tubes. The conning tower would be armored against five-inch shell impacts and the hull would be protected by attacking enemy ships with decks awash. It was estimated that incoming shells would lose most of their energy passing through the water above the submarine's hull, greatly reducing their destructive potential.[11]

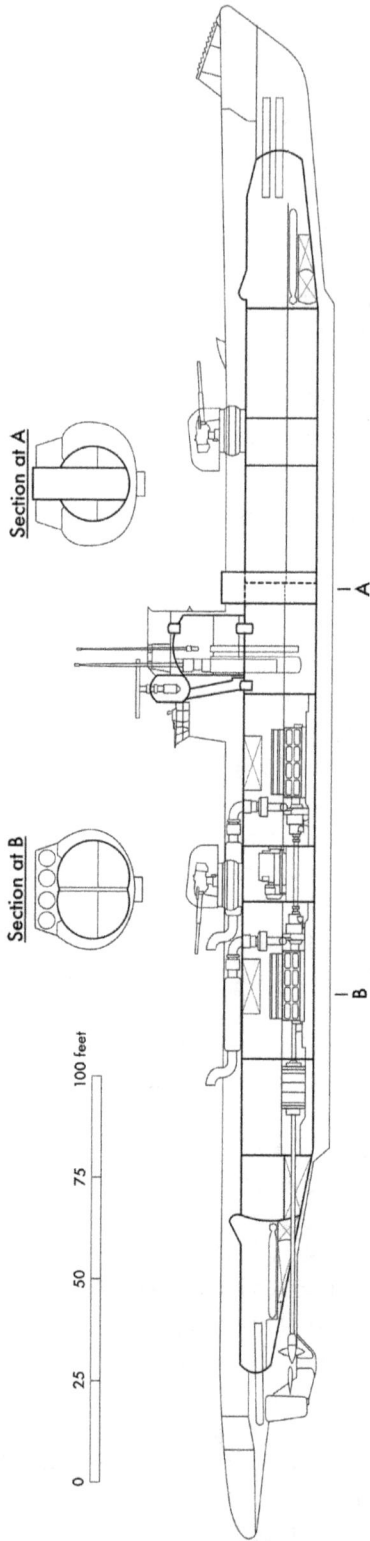

Section at A

Section at B

0   25   50   75   100 feet

A

B

The German Type XI cruiser submarine. (©JACOB GUNNARSON)

Like the *Surcouf*, the Type XI was to carry a seaplane to search out targets and to provide targeting for her guns. Arado Flugzeugwerke designed the Ar 231 floatplane—nicknamed *U-bootsaugen* (Submarine's Eyes)—for the Type XI. Its parasol wing had a unique shape and folding mechanism with the left side of the wing being slightly higher than the right side, allowing the wing sections to overlap when folded back over the fuselage. The plane's twin floats folded up against the fuselage so that the entire aircraft could be stowed as a single unit.

The Type XI had a novel hangar configuration—a vertical cylinder, 7 feet, 5 inches in diameter and 24 feet, 7 inches high, mostly inside of the pressure hull, between the conning tower and the forward gun mount. To launch the Ar 231, the folded-up aircraft would be extracted from the hangar with a collapsible crane and unfolded on the deck. The gun mounts left no space on the deck for a catapult; hence, the aircraft would be launched by the crane hoisting it over the side for a water takeoff.[12]

The final version of Raeder's Z-Plan for a major naval expansion was approved by Adolf Hitler in early 1938, with nine Type XI U-boats scheduled to be delivered from September 1939 to June 1945. However, their design was complex, particularly in the unusual configuration of the machinery spaces. Design difficulties slowed their construction schedule, with the first four submarines not ordered until January 1939—the *U-112* through *U-115*—to be built at the AG Weser shipyard in Bremen.

The Z-Plan fell apart when Britain declared war on Germany on 3 September 1939, resulting in the cancellation of most of the large surface ships then planned with priority shifting to U-boat construction. The complexities inherent in the Type XI design delayed construction too long, and *Konteradmiral* Karl Dönitz, then commander of the German submarine force, favored the smaller Type VII and IX U-boats that could be more easily built in greater numbers. He put the Type XI program on hold and cancelled the orders for the first four submarines, which had not yet been laid down.

Development of the Ar 231 floatplane continued with the first of six completed in 1940. Two were embarked on the armed merchant ship *Stier*, but they were found to be unfit for open-ocean service: The aircraft were difficult to operate in rough weather, handled poorly on water and in the air, and could not take off with a full load of fuel.[13] Instead, the German Navy would pursue rotary-wing aircraft for use on board submarines.

U-BOAT HELICOPTERS AND AUTOGYROS

While the German Navy was unsuccessful in developing submarine-carried, fixed-wing aircraft, there was success in developing a rotary-wing aircraft for submarines. Germany was an early leader in helicopter development, with

Henrich Focke building the world's first practical helicopter—the Fw 61—in 1936.[14] Further advances were made by Anton Flettner Flugzeugbau, which produced the Fl 184 autogyro and the Fl 185 helicopter. An autogyro has an engine with a propeller like a conventional aircraft to provide forward thrust and has a free-spinning, helicopter-like rotor instead of fixed wings to provide lift, thus enabling short takeoff and landing under some circumstances.

In 1938, Flettner introduced the innovative Fl 265, the first *synchrocopter*— a helicopter with two contra-rotating, intermeshing rotors, mounted obliquely to ensure that the blades would not collide. The rotors produced no net torque on the craft, alleviating the need for a tail rotor, thus reducing the length of the aircraft and simplifying storage on board a surface ship or U-boat.[15] That configuration was inherently stable and relatively easy to fly.

The German Navy began to take an interest in Flettner's helicopters in 1939. Although the *Luftwaffe* and not the Navy operated German naval aircraft, the Navy still had a key role in the development and operational use of shipboard aircraft.

After being shown a film showcasing the Fl 265 in October 1939, the Naval War Staff proposed an improved version of that helicopter for service on the Type XI U-boat. It would have similar requirements to the Ar 231: three-hour endurance, a 106-mph maximum speed, and the ability to carry a radio. A helicopter offered several significant advantages over the Ar 231, primarily the ability to take off and land vertically from the deck of a U-boat in sea conditions that would wreck the fragile fixed-wing aircraft. Also, it would be easier to stow on board the submarine. The Navy also required helicopters for use on board surface ships.[16]

Work soon began on an improved version of the Fl 265—the Fl 282 *Kolibri* (Hummingbird). Flight testing began in the fall of 1941, with trials on board the ships *Greif* and *Drache* the following year.

The submarine variant—designated Fl 282 U—could be stored in the Type XI U-boat hangar with the pilot's seat and rotor blades removed. In mid-1942 an order for as many as 120 Fl 282 U helicopters was envisioned. Fl 282 V9, one of 23 prototypes, was built without a tail section as part of the Fl 282 U program.[17] That modification was possible because of the inherent stability of the intermeshing-rotor design. By the time V9 had flown in early 1943, the program had been cancelled in favor of the Focke Achgelis Fa 330 towed autogyro (see below). Development of the helicopter was slow and construction of its intended carrier—the Type XI U-boat—had finally been abandoned. No production Fl 282 Us were built.

While Flettner was developing rotary-wing craft, Henrich Focke was making strides toward his own helicopters for the Germany military. In 1933 he had

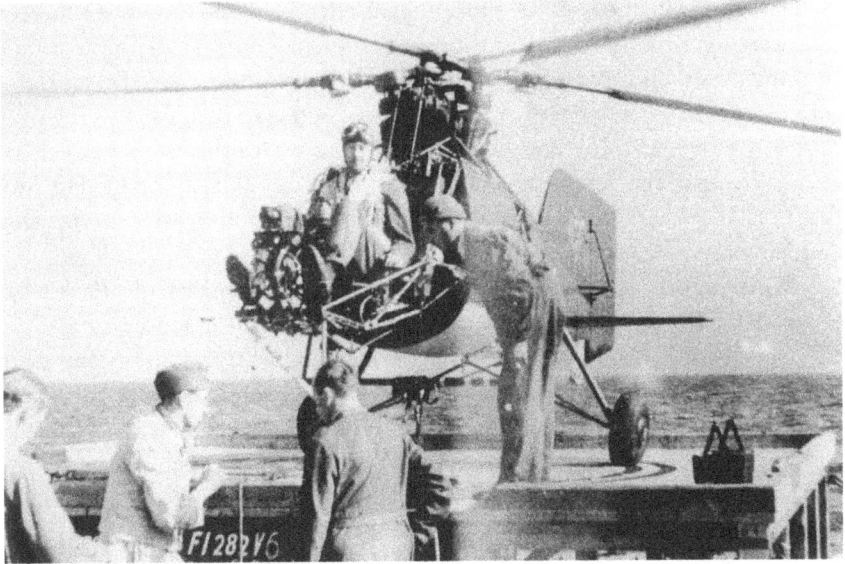

The Fl 282 V6 prototype during flight tests in September 1942 on board the aircraft rescue ship *Greif*. (AUTHORS' COLLECTION)

been ousted as head of his own firm—Focke-Wulf—by the company's board of directors. In 1937, with test pilot Gerd Achgelis, he founded Focke Achgelis & Co., a firm specializing in rotary-wing aircraft, most notably the Fa 223 *Drache* (Dragon), the only German helicopter other than the Fl 282 to see operational service in World War II.

In late 1941, Carl Bode, the test pilot at Focke Achgelis, visited the *Luftwaffe* testing grounds in Rechlin where the Fl 282 was to be evaluated.[18] Bode recalled,

> The head of helicopter development was a good friend of mine. . . . When I entered his room, he sat disheartened in front of the test results for the Flettner 282 helicopter. Dejectedly he slid the documents to me across the table, telling me that the size and flight performance of the helicopter, although improved over the Flettner 265, were not suitable for use on board submarines.
>
> These thoughts occupied me during the trip home. At the Focke company, I immediately called for a meeting between Professor Focke, the division heads, and myself, and asked them if the company could bridge this gap with a small helicopter.
>
> Our discussions resulted in the conclusion that a one-man helicopter would need at least 60 horsepower. However, the effort and development time seemed prohibitive, and eventually someone, I think our chief constructor Dr. Klages, came to the idea that the 60-horsepower requirement could be avoided by building an *unpowered autogyro, towed with a cable* [emphasis added].[19]

Flying high above the U-boat, the autogyro pilot would be able to see targets that were over the horizon and thus unseen by lookouts on the submarine's conning tower. Shortly after that meeting, the Air Ministry gave Focke Achgelis a contract to design and produce a towed autogyro that also was referred to as a "rotary kite." The company worked closely with the U-boat designers at AG Weser in Bremen to design an aircraft that could be accommodated in the Type IX U-boat, the largest combat submarine then in service with the German Navy.

Work proceeded quickly on the autogyro, designated Fa 330 *Bachstelze* (Wagtail).[20] It was a simple aircraft—essentially a chair mounted beneath a three-blade rotor; the "fuselage" was a 2½-inch diameter, 10½-foot-long steel tube that was attached to the pilot's seat at one end and to the stabilizers and rudder at the other end. The three-blade rotor had steel spars with wood ribs and was skinned with doped linen. A folding vertical tube behind the pilot's seat formed the rotor mast. The tail consisted of two fixed, horizontal stabilizers and a rudder.[21]

The pilot could control pitch and roll by changing the tilt of the rotor with the control stick; foot pedals controlled the rudder, which could steer the aircraft 30 degrees to either side around the tow point on the submarine. The pilot's instrument panel contained an altimeter, tachometer, and airspeed indicator. To communicate with the submarine, the pilot wore a telephone headset connected through a wire embedded in the steel tow-cable, although the

The prototype Fa 330 during trials on board the Type IXC submarine *U-523* in August 1942.
(SMITHSONIAN)

telephone reportedly was unreliable because of saltwater corrosion. The pilot
was provided with binoculars. A small platform was added to the after railing of
the submarine's conning tower to launch and recover the aircraft along with a
pneumatic winch for the tow cable.

To prepare the *Bachstelze*, the stabilizers and rudder were affixed to the fuselage tube, and the rotor blades were fastened to the rotor mast. Normally up
to eight minutes were required to assemble and five minutes to disassemble the
aircraft, times that could be significantly bettered by a well-trained crew.[22] To
launch the *Bachstelze*, the submarine would head into the wind at full speed; sustained flight required the combined wind speed and submarine speed to be at least
19 knots. The crew had to take care to stay clear of the Fa 330's rotors—a sailor
on the U-847 purportedly was decapitated when he got close to the blades.[23]

Once aloft, the Fa 330's altitude usually was limited by the wind speed.
At the maximum airspeed of 50 mph, the highest achievable altitude was 720
feet. At that height the pilot's horizon was 33 miles, far greater than the ap-
proximately six miles for lookouts on the U-boat's bridge.[24] The masts of merchant ships or their smoke trails often could be seen above the horizon at even
greater distances by a *Bachstelze* pilot.

If the submarine had to submerge while the Fa 330 was still aloft, the pilot
could jettison the rotor, which automatically pulled the cord of a parachute attached to the rotor mast. The remainder of the aircraft—including the pilot—
would descend on the parachute into the sea, where he was "free to drown in a
conventional manner," in the words of a British report.[25] In theory, the submarine would later surface and recover the aviator.

Focke Achgelis also considered powered variants of the autogyro, finding
that it was impossible to reengineer the Fa 330 to mount an engine. A new
design—the Fa 336—was drawn up featuring a 60-horsepower engine and a tail
rotor. Work was begun on three prototypes before that project was cancelled in
March 1944.[26]

DEVELOPING THE FA 330

The first Fa 330 prototype was ready for initial testing at the Chalais-Meudon
wind tunnel outside of Paris by May 1942. The first open-air flight, with Bode
at the controls, came in early June on board the aircraft rescue ship *Greif* in the
Baltic, followed by further trials on the auxiliary cruiser *Komet* in late July.[27]

In early August, Bode took flight from the Type IXC submarine *U-523* in
Gdansk Bay.[28] Flying the tiny aircraft at sea was a unique if unnerving experience for Bode:

> Before the first flight to 200 meters towed behind a U-boat, I had serious
> concerns about the psychological strain on the pilot. Therefore I trained

beforehand in an open-cockpit glider. That was no help, however, because the view of the glider's wings in my peripheral vision gave me a feeling of security. In the free-flying *Bachstelze* with a view clear through the spinning rotor, it was like sitting in a stool placed in thin air, as far as the eye could see just water and the tiny U-boat below, and the feeling was quite horrible at first. But you get used to it, and the pilots that followed me told me that they drew spiritual support from the fact that someone else had already overcome his fears before them.[29]

In October 1942, Bode tested the rotor jettison mechanism while being towed behind a torpedo boat. The aircraft was skimming the waves at an altitude of just three feet, and he had instructed that the tow rope remain attached for the test so he and the Fa 330 could be pulled out of the sea. When the autogyro hit the water its stabilizers dug in, plunging the craft deep below the surface. Fortunately for Bode the jerk of the parachute opening snapped the tow rope, allowing him to escape the sinking autogyro, suffering only an injured knee.[30]

On 9 September 1942, Admirals Erich Raeder and Karl Dönitz and other senior officers met with Hitler in the Reich Chancellery in Berlin to discuss the U-boat war. Among the topics discussed was the Fa 330. Hitler initially was confused about what powered the autogyro, believing that electric power was sent

Test pilot Carl Bode about to take off in the Fa 330 during trials on board the *U-523*.
(AUTHORS' COLLECTION)

up through the tow cable. The German leader was informed that the Fa 330 was unpowered, and Dönitz assured him that the wind-tunnel tests were promising.[31]

The Fa 330 subsequently was approved for large-scale production at the Focke Achgelis factory in Hoykenkamp, which began in January 1943.[32] In addition to the Fa 330s for U-boats, the Naval War Staff intended to equip surface ships with the autogyro, leading to a substantial production run. At one time as many as 488 aircraft were on order with that figure scaled back to 250 by December 1943.[33]

The *Luftwaffe* unit *Ausbildungskommando* (Training Unit) 330 was formed to train sailors to fly the unusual aircraft. The simplicity of the Fa 330 design allowed enlisted submariners to be trained as pilots relatively quickly. The sailors first learned to fly gliders under the supervision of *Luftwaffe* pilots. They then were taken to the Chalais-Meudon wind tunnel to initially pilot the Fa 330 under controlled conditions. Next, using Fa 330s fitted with wheels, the sailors practiced for two months being towed behind a truck on the autobahn near Bautzen. That was followed by their being towed behind torpedo boats off the coast of the Netherlands. Finally, a brief training session on board a surface ship or U-boat in the Baltic prepared them for duty on board a submarine. After some six months of training across German-occupied Europe the now-qualified pilots were ready for service.[34] Typically each U-boat would have three pilots on board.

THE TYPE IXD2 U-BOAT

While almost all of their fellow submariners would be sailing into the grim battleground of the North Atlantic, the Fa 330 pilots were destined for the tropics. The U-boats faced increasingly capable Allied anti-submarine forces in the Atlantic as the war progressed, and their losses rose dramatically in early 1943. A submarine operating the Fa 330 would be especially vulnerable in the North Atlantic as it had to remain on the surface for the duration of the flight and for recovery.

Admiral Dönitz had considered operating U-boats in the Indian Ocean from the beginning of the war, although severing the supply lines in the Atlantic between America and Britain always took precedence. When the U-boat situation in the North Atlantic began to deteriorate in 1942, Dönitz sent five submarines around the Cape of Good Hope into the Indian Ocean, where they sunk 24 Allied merchant ships in November.[35] Those submarines operating in the Indian Ocean returned to bases in France at the end of their patrols.

In May 1943, the U-boats suffered unsustainable losses in the North Atlantic and Dönitz was forced to withdraw submarines from those waters. He then deployed more submarines into the Indian Ocean, where some Allied merchant ships still sailed without escorts. Dönitz hoped that a successful

U-boat campaign in the Indian Ocean would cause significant Allied anti-submarine forces to be redirected from the Atlantic, where the U-boats could again attack those vital supply lines.[36]

Initially most of the Indian Ocean U-boats transited to and from bases in France; later in the war some operated out of the Japanese bases at Penang in Malaya and Singapore. The latter U-boat operations and several Japanese submarine transits to France were among the few examples of collaboration between the German and Japanese armed forces during World War II.

Fifty-seven U-boats operated in the Indian Ocean during the war, mainly long-range Type IXC/40s and Type IXD2s.[37] The Type IXD U-boats were born out of the cancellation of the Type XI aircraft-carrying cruiser submarines. Admiral Dönitz initially proposed building a redesigned and scaled-down Type XI or the smaller Type XII fleet submarine design. However, given the cost and time necessary to put those designs into production, the requirement for a cruiser U-boat would be fulfilled by enlarging the existing Type IXC design into the Type IXD1 and IXD2.[38]

Thirty-five feet longer and two feet broader than the Type IXC, the two new variants were externally identical, differing primarily in their machinery: The Type IXD1 was designed for high surface speed with six 1,500-horsepower Daimler diesels instead of the two standard 2,200-horsepower MAN diesels, thus powering them to almost 21 knots.[39]

The Type IXD2—designed for very-long-range operations—had two MAN diesels and two 580-horsepower auxiliary diesel generators. Those submarines had a 32,000-n.mile surface range at nine knots, sufficient for operations more than halfway around the world from the German U-boat bases in France.[40] With extra crew accommodations and their longer range and larger size, the Type IXD2s became the exclusive carriers of the Fa 330 *Bachstelze*.

Two stowage cylinders, two feet in diameter and 11 feet, 9 inches tall, were mounted vertically in the antiaircraft gun platform aft of the conning tower. The starboard cylinder housed the fuselage, parachute, and instrument panel; the port cylinder housed the rotor blades and the tail surfaces. A smaller cylinder mounted between the two contained the winch and cable. A second disassembled Fa 330 was stowed inside of the submarine.[41]

Beginning in January 1943, all new Type IXD2 U-boats were completed with Fa 330 stowage cylinders and most of the older boats had them retrofitted.[42] All of those U-boats were built at the AG Weser shipyard in Bremen—a few miles north of the Fa 330 factory.

BACHSTELZE OPERATIONS

The lead Type IXD2 submarine—the *U-177*—was the first U-boat to undertake a war patrol with the Fa 330. She was modified in early 1943 to carry additional antiaircraft guns as well as the autogyro. Joining the crew were three enlisted sailors trained to fly the Fa 330. Also on board was *Unteroffizier* Kurt Weiden, a *Luftwaffe* instructor from *Ausbildungskommando* 330, assigned to report directly to U-boat headquarters on the autogyro operations.

The *U-177* was under the command of *Kapitänleutnant* Robert Gysae, a seasoned U-boat captain and recipient of the Knight's Cross award for six earlier patrols in the North Atlantic.[43] The *U-177* departed Bordeaux for the Indian Ocean on 1 April 1943. Once the submarine was south of the Azores, the Fa 330 typically flew twice a day for about 15 minutes each time, primarily for training.

Gysae regularly radioed information about the performance of the autogyro to U-boat headquarters. Among the problems were flooding of the stowage cylinders, lubrication issues with the winch, poor training of the enlisted pilots, and lax maintenance. However, he also noted that the "*Stelze* was used successfully up to sea state 4, medium high swell, where [use of] a floatplane would not be possible."[44]

British intelligence was reading Gysae's radio messages as cryptographers at the Bletchley Park codebreaking center could intercept and decrypt many of the messages between U-boat command and submarines at sea. On 30 April 1943, analysts deduced that the *U-177* was carrying an aircraft or glider, and

The Fa 330 flying above a Type IXD2 U-boat, possibly the *U-177*. The men are standing to either side of the landing platform and two stowage tubes on the upper level of the antiaircraft gun platform. (AUTHORS' COLLECTION)

a week later confirmed that the U-boat was equipped with "a manlifting kite probably with rotor blades."[45]

While the *U-177* was on patrol, the *U-849*, a newly completed Type IXD2, was testing the Fa 330 in the Baltic to experiment with possible tactics for the autogyro.[46] U-boat command radioed the *U-177* with the results of those tests, recommending that the submarine sail at an angle to the wind, allowing the pilot to see in a "blind spot" to the rear of the submarine.

The *U-177* sank the first ship of the patrol on 29 July, 400 n.miles south of Madagascar. Later that day the Fa 330 sighted a ship that was able to evade the submarine because of poor visibility. Gysae, perhaps in a sour mood, wrote in the *U-177*'s log: "Although the enemy might be 20 miles away in the worst case, nothing found with the *Bachstelze* (this demonstrates the limited possibilities for use of the *Bachstelze*)."[47] Despite Gysae's disappointment in the aircraft, his patrol was going well. The *U-177* had already sunk five Allied merchant ships totaling nearly 34,000 tons; subsequently, Hitler would award Gysae with Oak Leaves for his Knight's Cross.[48]

Around noon on 5 August, the Fa 330 again caught sight of a merchant ship, the Greek freighter *Efthalia Mari*. The *U-177* maneuvered ahead of her, submerged at twilight, and sunk her with two torpedoes some 100 miles off the coast of Madagascar. Three days later, the Fa 330 sighted another freighter; however, the pursuit was halted when a fire broke out in the submarine's engine room, destroying the rotor blades of the second Fa 330 stored on board. The U-boat resumed the chase. Again the merchant ship was lost in the low visibility.

That month the Fa 330 was flown up to four times a day. After the submarine returned around the Cape of Good Hope and entered the South Atlantic, the aircraft was not flown again. The *U-177* reached Bordeaux on 1 October. During the 184-day patrol the Fa 330 flew 182 times, totaling 60½ flight hours.[49] Other Type IXD2 boats would use their Fa 330s in the Indian Ocean. Still, the *Efthalia Mari* remained the only ship definitively confirmed to have been sunk with the autogyro's direct assistance.

SUBSEQUENT OPERATIONS

Only one use of an Fa 330 was recorded in the North Atlantic: In June 1944, the *U-862* was sailing south from Narvik, Norway, to Penang in Malaya. Four pilots were on board, including the ship's physician, Dr. Jobst Schaefer. The autogyro served as the U-boat's eyes when the submarine traversed a seemingly endless fog bank:

> Like a veil it laid itself upon the sea and the boat. It was not more than five to six meters thick. The onboard aircraft, the "*Bachstelze*," was fetched from

the upper part of the conning tower and made ready. . . . The *Bachstelze* was brought to five to seven meters high in order to get itself above the hazy sea. The pilot called out, "Here comes a freighter," and there was only the mast of the ship for him to see. One can imagine the terror of the merchant marine sailor when suddenly a man appeared floating above the mist. . . . So it went for several days through the fog.[50]

The *U-862*'s commander, *Korvettenkapitän* Heinrich Timm, believed that flying the Fa 330 made his submarine vulnerable to air attack. After the *U-862* arrived in Penang in October, Timm bartered two Fa 330s, his and one previously discarded by the *U-196*, for a Japanese Aichi E13A (Jake) floatplane. Operating from Penang harbor, the Aichi patrolled the waters off the port, replacing a German Arado Ar 196 floatplane at the base that had been destroyed in a fire.[51]

The *U-861* was among the last U-boats to fly the Fa 330 while on a patrol. Off the east coast of Madagascar in late August 1944, the autogyro was sent aloft and the pilot reported an object on the horizon. After drawing closer, the "ship" was revealed, primarily through its lack of movement, to be an island.[52]

Allied anti-submarine efforts in the Indian Ocean increased as the war continued, pushing German submarine commanders to be more cautious when on the surface. Although it only took a few minutes to assemble and launch the Fa 330, the submarine was essentially defenseless when on the surface and many commanders believed that once aloft the aircraft could be easily seen by the enemy. That belief was unfounded: the Fa 330 could see ships much farther than they could see it. However, the aircraft was vulnerable to detection by the radars of Allied warships and aircraft. Further, U-boats were beginning to use snorkels to provide air for their diesels while submerged, minimizing their time on the surface.

Also, the Fa 330 was fragile: During a test flight before the *U-177*'s third patrol, a gust of wind caught the autogyro and sent it crashing to the deck, wrecking the aircraft.[53] By mid-1944 the Fa 330 was being phased out. Some U-boats had their stowage tubes welded shut. The training of new pilots was halted in June 1944, and in July the Fa 330 production was officially suspended with low-rate production continuing until the end of the war. Ultimately about 200 machines were built, most of which never were embarked on a submarine.[54]

BACHSTELZE ABROAD

The *U-177*—on her third war patrol—was attacked and sunk by a U.S. Navy PB4Y-1 Liberator bomber some 500 miles off the coast of Brazil on 6 February 1944. Fourteen crewmen survived, including two of the three Fa 330 pilots who were on board the U-boat. Interrogated by U.S. Navy officers, they revealed detailed information about the Fa 330.

The U-177's commander on that third patrol, Korvettenkapitän Heinz Buchholz, had never launched the Fa 330 although he had three pilots on board. Allied intelligence was already aware of the autogyro's existence from interrogations of other U-boat survivors and decrypted radio messages. However, that apparently was the first time the Allies learned in detail how the aircraft operated.[55]

In May 1944, the U-852 was damaged by a British bomber and forced aground on the coast of Somalia.[56] The submarine was heavily damaged by scuttling charges, but the British were able to recover her Fa 330 and it was delivered to the British Air Ministry for examination.[57] Engineers eventually flew it and were impressed by the German designers' ingenuity and attention to detail.[58]

When the Soviet Navy learned of the aircraft's existence, it requested an evaluation from the Central Aerodynamic Institute. Mikhail Mil', the institute's authority on autogyros, sketched a design for a Soviet version of the Fa 330. His concept was larger and heavier than the German autogyro, with a semi-enclosed cockpit. The Soviets never captured an Fa 330, and Mil's design was not pursued.[59]

After Germany was defeated, a considerable number of Fa 330s were found on board surrendered U-boats and unassembled in crates ashore. The United States and Britain tested their examples extensively, towing them behind automobiles and motorboats.[60]

After the war, the French Navy was still developing the Dorand G 20 helicopter that had originally been intended for the Surcouf and was keenly interested in the German autogyro. The French Navy's autogyro expert, Lieutenant Jacques Châtel, first took flight in the Fa 330 from an airfield near Toulon in July 1945. He then traveled to Paris to fly the craft under the supervision of Henrich Focke in the Chalais-Meudon wind tunnel. Further tests were conducted with a speedboat. The speedboat was not particularly fast, and at one point he dipped to just two inches above the water, narrowly avoiding Carl Bode's harrowing experience several years earlier.

Subsequently, during a period of two weeks Châtel successfully flew the Fa 330 several times from the submarine Casabianca in the Mediterranean. When the submarine pulled into port, his makeshift launch platform was the center of attention:

> One Sunday we were moored at Cannes, and on Sundays the public can visit the warships. There was this kitchen table that was bolted securely to the submarine, so people were asking us, "Is this table for the crew's dinner?"

And we told them: "Don't tell anyone, because it's secret, but it's an airfield." Nobody believed us.

Châtel had flown the Fa 330 from off of a kitchen table ashore and at sea.

In September 1946, experiments were carried out on the *Casabianca* to measure the Fa 330's radar reflectivity. A Vickers Wellington bomber fitted with anti-submarine radar made several passes over the *Casabianca*, with and without the autogyro being towed aloft. As suspected, the Fa 330's radar signature made the submarine easily detectable.

Despite that result, Châtel was enthusiastic about the future of submarine autogyros. He proposed fitting a motorcycle engine to the Fa 330, thus transforming it into a helicopter. Recognizing that a significant limitation of the craft was the danger to the pilot if the submarine had to submerge, he also recommended the development of an unmanned autogyro, fitted with a television camera or radar. His proposals fell on deaf ears: the French Navy conducted no further trials with autogyros or helicopters on board submarines.[61]

By the end of World War II, only Japan operated aircraft-carrying submarines. France's *Surcouf*, in an almost constant state of disrepair, had never operated her aircraft during the war. Even if she had not been lost, she would have contributed little to the Allied war efforts with her aircraft likely remaining ashore. Despite France's lengthy development of the Besson submarine-launched floatplanes, the *Surcouf*'s MB 411 was unsuitable as an operational aircraft.

Germany had much greater success with development of the Fa 330 *Bachstelze* towed autogyro. Despite major advancements in helicopters and autogyros by the United States and France during World War II, only Germany developed operational rotary-wing aircraft for submarines. Like the floatplanes developed by the Japanese for use on board submarines, the Fa 330 was a simple and effective aircraft, easily accommodated in the limited space of a submarine.

But like the Japanese aircraft, the Fa 330 was rendered obsolete by the devastating effectiveness of Allied anti-submarine forces in 1944–1945. As Allied ships and aircraft equipped with radar drove the U-boats underwater, operation of the towed autogyro became increasingly dangerous. Even before it became useless, the Fa 330 was only sparingly used. It appears that the majority of total operational flights occurred on the *U-177*'s initial trials of the aircraft, and that it seldom was flown by subsequent U-boat captains, who were wary of the risk posed by its operation. Only one merchant ship is known to have been sunk with the direct assistance of an Fa 330.

CHAPTER 5

Japan Prepares for War

While many naval officers in Europe and the United States regarded the combination of aircraft and submarines with skepticism, the concept found early and ardent supporters in the Imperial Japanese Navy. Before the Japanese attack on Pearl Harbor on 7 December 1941, the prevailing concept of a Pacific conflict to most Japanese and American admirals was one of a great, decisive battle in the western Pacific between the Japanese and U.S. fleets.

The Japanese envisioned that the U.S. fleet would come steaming westward across the Pacific toward Japan, suffering losses en route to Japanese submarine attacks. The diminished American armada would then be decisively crushed by the Japanese fleet, supported by land-based aircraft.[1] The submarines to support the Japanese fleet action would need to be large to achieve the range and speed necessary to search out and attack the American warships steaming toward Japan. The Japanese submarines would be the first to sight the American fleet, and thus would need every possible advantage to extend their range of vision.[2] The obvious solution was for the submarines to have their own reconnaissance aircraft.

On the other side of the Pacific Ocean, the U.S. Navy had considered aircraft-carrying cruiser submarines for the same reason as had the Japanese. However, the U.S. Navy could not develop a satisfactory aircraft and only a few large cruiser submarines were built, in part due to the London Naval Treaty of 1930 limiting the construction of most submarines to 2,000 tons surface displacement and restricting the total displacement of all submarines for each navy.[3] Instead, the United States would pursue smaller "fleet" submarines that were able to achieve the range and speed of cruiser submarines, but with a lower displacement, permitting more units to be built under the treaty restrictions.

Thus, Japan was the only nation to continue the significant development of aircraft-carrying submarines through the 1930s. The Japanese Navy built cruiser submarines, which they named with the first letter of the Japanese syllabary—I—to signify their premier status.[4] The highly capable and formidable I-boats would comprise the majority of Japan's submarine fleet by the beginning of World War II in the Pacific. Looking toward a future war in the Pacific with their perception of the impending conflict, the Japanese naval leadership closely followed American and European developments in submarine-carried aircraft.

THE FIRST PROTOTYPES

After World War I the Japanese Navy was allocated seven German U-boats as war prizes, and a delegation was sent to Germany to acquire information on submarine construction. Subsequently, Japanese shipyards employed German engineers as consultants, and several senior naval architects, including Hans Techel, head of submarine construction at the Germania shipyard, and Professor Oswald Flamm, who provided extensive technical documentation on U-boats to the Japanese.

Apparently Flamm also disclosed to the Japanese the efforts of German aircraft manufacturers to develop a scout aircraft for submarines and recommended that the Japanese Navy purchase Caspar-Heinkel floatplanes for trials.[5] The Japanese Army and Navy also acquired numerous aircraft and technical assistance from France and Britain in the immediate post–World War I period.

In November 1922, the Japanese Navy took delivery of two Caspar-Heinkel U 1 floatplanes from that firm. The U 1s were carefully studied and reverse-engineered at Kugisho—the Naval Air Technical Arsenal—at Yokosuka, the Japanese counterpart to the U.S. Navy's Bureau of Aeronautics and Naval Aircraft Factory.[6]

Construction of an indigenous copy began in 1925, designated the Kugisho No. 1. That aircraft was similar to the U 1 with a higher upper wing, metal-clad forward fuselage and floats, and a more powerful, 80-horsepower French Le Rhône engine.

The prototype No. 1 was completed in 1927, by which time the submarine I-21 was available for trials. The first of the *Kiraisen* (mine submarine) Type—built from plans of the German Project 45 submarine—the I-21 had a hangar 5 feet, 7 inches in diameter and 24 feet, 3 inches in length that was installed behind the conning tower with a crane to help assemble the aircraft. Launching was accomplished by submerging the stern for the aircraft to float off. The Kugisho No. 1 was tested for 18 months with the I-21.[7] Although simulated submarine launchings on land had taken only 16 minutes, at sea it took 40 minutes from surfacing to floating off the aircraft. The Navy leadership deemed that time unacceptable.

Observing the success of the Royal Navy's M-2, Kugisho began work on the significantly larger No. 2 aircraft, resembling a single-seat Parnall Peto.[8]

Japan's first submarine-launched aircraft, the Kugisho No. 1. The diminutive floatplane was based on the Caspar-Heinkel U 1, which the Japanese Navy had purchased for examination. (AUTHORS' COLLECTION)

The narrow hangar of the *I-21* dictated that the wings of the No. 2 be detachable instead of folding. The aircraft's rudder was positioned mostly beneath the fuselage to decrease the aircraft's height for stowage. The prototype, completed in May 1929, was fitted with the Armstrong Siddeley Mongoose, the same engine as the Peto, built under license by Mitsubishi.[9]

The *I-21* sea trials began in late 1929 with the submarine having been refitted with a wider hangar. She was joined by the *I-51*, the first of Japan's I-boats and the prototype of the *Kaidai* (Large Navy) Type submarines.[10] With a maximum surface speed of 20 knots, the *I-51* was chosen to test the No. 2 floatplane because she was close in performance to the specialized, aircraft-carrying submarines then being developed. That submarine was fitted with small hangars located on either side of the conning tower.[11] Opening onto the aft deck, one of the hangars held the aircraft's wings and the other held the fuselage.

In 1931, the Navy Aviation Bureau issued the *6-Shi* requirement for a second, improved prototype aircraft. The result was the No. 2 Modified, which had improved struts, floats, and fuselage with a more powerful engine. Trials of the No. 2 Modified on board the *I-21* and *I-51* continued until September 1931. The Navy's leadership deemed the trials a success and in January 1932, decided to acquire production aircraft as the E6Y1 Type 91.[12] The Kawanishi aircraft firm was directed to produce eight aircraft.[13] The E6Y1 was the first

The *I-51*, first of the large *Kaidai* Type submarines, shortly after she was completed in 1924. She later was fitted with hangars to either side of her conning tower to test submarine-aircraft operations. (U.S. NAVY)

The Kugisho No. 2 Modified was the prototype for the Japanese Navy's first series production submarine-launched aircraft, the E6Y1. The markings indicate that it was assigned to the submarine *I-5* when the photo was taken. (AUTHORS' COLLECTION)

Japanese aircraft to be fitted with a high-frequency radio to enable communications with submarines.

The *I-21* had her aircraft-handing gear removed after the preliminary trials while the *I-51* continued to test the new aircraft. In 1933, a prototype pneumatic catapult was fitted on the *I-51*, behind her hangars.[14] The aft-firing catapult required the submarine to run at full reverse speed into the wind to launch the aircraft. Although the submarine was slower and less controllable moving astern than forward, the arrangement worked well enough that it was retained for subsequent classes. With a successful prototype submarine and limited aircraft production underway, the Japanese Navy was ready to produce specialized aircraft-carrying submarines.

NEW SUBMARINES AND AIRCRAFT

Beginning in the mid-1920s, the large I-boats were developed in two parallel series: The *Kaidai* Type was a heavily armed torpedo-attack submarine and the *Junsen* (Cruiser Submarine) Type was a long-range scout, the ideal platform for submarine-launched aircraft.

The *Junsen* Type was a virtual copy of the German Type 46a U-boat.[15] The first four *Junsen* 1 series submarines were completed before the trials of Kugisho's No. 1 and No. 2 floatplanes and did not have aviation features. The *I-5* was laid down in 1929 as a *Junsen* 1 Modified with two hangars half-recessed into the after superstructure. She was completed in 1932 and was fitted with a catapult the following year.[16]

The two hangars were positioned perilously close to the waterline to minimize the impact on the submarine's stability if they flooded and thus it proved difficult to extract the aircraft at sea. Accordingly, an improved design—the *Junsen* 2—was ordered with the *I-6* the sole submarine built to that design. She had a wider deck with hangars that could be retracted into the superstructure

The *I-5* was the Japanese Navy's first purpose-built submarine aircraft carrier. Her hangars were mounted in the side of the superstructure, aft of the conning tower, a position ultimately found to be too close to the waterline. (AUTHORS' COLLECTION)

after the seaplane was stowed to reduce underwater drag and improve stability. She also had more powerful engines and a refined hull form, raising her surface speed to 21 knots.[17]

In early 1934 the Navy Aviation Bureau issued the 9-Shi requirement for a two-seat floatplane that could fit the hangars of the I-5 and I-6. In response, the Watanabe aircraft firm designed the E9W, a floatplane with twice the horsepower and a more robust structure than the E6Y1, and with double the range of the contemporary Parnall Peto.[18] The rear-seat observer had a 7.7-mm machine gun, making it the first submarine-launched aircraft with defensive armament. However, to reduce weight the machine gun normally was not installed.

The first of four prototype aircraft was completed in February 1935, with sea trials on the I-5 and I-6 following. Although the E9W was a major improvement over previous submarine-launched aircraft, the requirement to fit into existing submarine hangars significantly constrained the design as the wings and floats had to be detached and stored in a separate hangar from the fuselage. Struts and wires had to be affixed and tensioned while preparing the aircraft for launching. As a result, the time from surfacing to aircraft launching was between 20 and 40 minutes. Additionally, the hangar size constraints resulted in a fuselage that was too short to keep the aircraft longitudinally stable in flight. Watanabe unsuccessfully attempted to improve stability by extending the vertical stabilizer and the rudder below the fuselage, as in the E6Y1. The problem eventually was corrected with a taller rudder and stabilizer.[19]

The Watanabe E9W Slim was a considerably larger and more capable aircraft than its predecessors. The aircraft pictured was assigned to the submarine I-6. The Slim saw service in World War II. (AUTHORS' COLLECTION)

The four E9W prototype aircraft were flight tested until July 1936, with the aircraft approved for production as the E9W1 Type 96.[20] It earned the nickname *Geta* because its floats resembled the traditional Japanese wooden sandals (and later was given the Allied codename "Slim").[21] Thirty-two E9W1 production aircraft were built from 1936 to 1939, making it the world's first submarine-launched aircraft to be produced in significant numbers.

At about the same time the first series-produced, aircraft-carrying submarines of the *Junsen 3* Type were entering into service. The *Junsen 3* had a more refined design than the one-off *Junsen 1* Modified and *Junsen 2*, having more powerful diesel engines and a hull of stronger steel. Like the previous designs, those craft had twin aircraft hangars fitted aft of their conning tower. The *I-7* was completed in 1937, and the *I-8* followed a year later with an improved catapult.[22] In addition to their role as scouts for the battle fleet, they also were fitted with extra radio equipment to act as submarine squadron flagships.[23]

The *I-7* and *I-8* were the largest and in many respects the best-performing Japanese undersea craft prior to World War II. They displaced 2,525 tons surfaced, 3,583 tons submerged, and were 358½ feet in length; they were armed with six bow torpedo tubes and a 5.5-inch gun mount.[24]

Japan's four operational aircraft-carrying submarines saw their first wartime service during the Sino-Japanese War that began in July 1937. The Japanese Navy blockaded much of the coast of China during that conflict with their submarines on patrol in the South China Sea. The E6Y1 aircraft from the *I-5* and *I-6* performed reconnaissance during the battle for Shanghai from August to November 1937, and the newly commissioned *I-7* and *I-8* undertook patrols later in the conflict with the new E9W1 floatplane. The *I-5* and *I-6* had their aircraft equipment removed in mid-1940 because their aviation arrangements were too cumbersome and improved submarines were entering service.

The *I-8* about to launch an E9W1 Slim floatplane in 1941. The submarine's twin hangars could be retracted into the superstructure. (KURE MARITIME MUSEUM)

THE KUGISHO E14Y

Just as the E9W1/Slim was entering service, the Navy Aviation Bureau issued the 12-*Shi* specification for its successor. The new aircraft was to have a range of at least 600 n.miles and an assembly time at sea of less than ten minutes. A single large hangar, 6 feet in diameter and 28 feet in length, was planned for future submarines to house the aircraft. Kugisho and Watanabe competed to develop the aircraft design: Watanabe's E14W floatplane submission was a more powerful version of the E9W1 biplane, while Kugisho's E14Y was a totally new, low-wing monoplane design.

The Kugisho team concentrated on reducing weight, shipboard assembly time, and water landing speed. To reduce weight the aircraft's fuselage was made of thin-wall, high-strength steel tubes, skinned with duralumin on the forward fuselage, and with wood and canvas covering the rear fuselage. The wings, tail, and floats were metal-framed, covered with canvas and plywood. A sliding canopy enclosed the two-man cockpit, unlike the open-cockpit Watanabe aircraft. And the E14Y was the first submarine-launched aircraft to carry bombs: two 66-pound bombs could be fitted on optional wing racks.

The first E14Y prototype was completed in late 1938 and tested on board the *I-7*. However, it was 220 pounds over the weight limit imposed by the existing submarine catapult. Thus, the aircraft's fuel tanks could only be partially filled, limiting range to a still impressive 300 n.miles.

The aircraft also was found to be longitudinally unstable in flight, again due to the short fuselage limited by hangar length. Although the Watanabe E14W was based on a proven design, the troubled E14Y was chosen as the winner of the trials because it promised significantly better performance. As

The E14Y Glen prototype undergoing flight trials. Production aircraft had a removable fin added to the vertical stabilizer to improve stability, among other small aerodynamic improvements. (AUTHORS' COLLECTION)

with the earlier E6Y1, Kugisho was not capable of producing the E14Y in large numbers; thus production was allocated to Watanabe.

The new submarine catapult—installed on the *I-8*—was strengthened and equipped with an optional gunpowder booster, increasing its maximum aircraft weight capacity. The Watanabe designers were able to shave 176 pounds from the airframe of the second E14Y prototype, solving the previous weight issue. To remedy the stability problem, the aircraft's wing root was redesigned and a detachable extension to the vertical stabilizer and a fin under the tail were added. After the Navy was satisfied by those improvements, the aircraft was accepted as the E14Y1 Type 0 on 17 December 1940 (later it was given the Allied codename "Glen").[25]

Ten preproduction aircraft followed, but series production did not begin until April 1942, after World War II had begun.[26] The preproduction aircraft would see operational service in 1942. Although they could be disassembled and stored in the two separate hangars on the *Junsen* 3 submarines, the aircraft was intended to be used with the new, single-hangar submarines then under construction and rarely, if ever, flew from the twin-hangar submarines after their trials.[27]

SUBMARINES FOR WAR

About the time that the 12-*Shi* specification was issued and the E14Y1 design began, the Third Naval Replenishment Plan—the Japanese Navy's shipbuilding program for 1937–1941—was being implemented. That plan called for 13 cruiser submarines, most with aircraft capabilities.[28] The *Junsen* 3 Type served as the starting point for those submarine designs that would develop into three classes: Type A, B, and C. The Type A and B were scout submarines with a single, bulbous hangar faired into the leading edge of their conning tower fairwater to house a single floatplane.

The Type A also was a squadron flagship submarine with additional radio equipment and was slightly larger than the near-identical Type B.[29] On both classes a catapult ran from the hangar to the bow, enabling the submarine to use forward speed to assist takeoffs instead of having to run in reverse. The Type C was a large, torpedo-attack submarine of a similar design, but without aircraft facilities. All of those submarines had exceptional speed and endurance— a maximum of 23½ knots on the surface and a cross-Pacific surface range of up to 16,000 n.miles at 16 knots. Displacing between 3,561 and 4,150 tons submerged, they were only a few hundred tons shy of the French *Surcouf*.

Launching an E14Y1 Glen floatplane under ideal conditions took less than 25 minutes from the submarine surfacing, and could be undertaken at night as the components critical to assembly were coated with phosphorescent paint. The dome-shaped hangar door opened to the port side, and the aircraft

The *I-15* at high speed on sea trials in Hiroshima Bay on 15 September 1940. The Type A and B submarines had a single hangar faired into the leading edge of the conning tower. (AUTHORS' COLLECTION)

fuselage was extracted on a dolly. With the aircraft lifted off the deck by a folding crane, the wings and propeller were attached and the horizontal stabilizers folded down, after which the floats were attached under the fuselage. The record-setting assembly time was just over six minutes, although at sea it often took longer. While the engine was run up for five minutes, the submarine would head into the wind, the pilot and observer would board the aircraft, and it would be catapulted into the air.

At the conclusion of the flight, after alighting on the water off the starboard side of the submarine, the observer would remove the hoisting cables from a container inside of the cockpit and hook them to the crane. The aircraft then would be lifted onto the deck, disassembled, stowed in the hangar, and the submarine would dive.[30]

Efforts by other countries to develop aircraft-carrying submarines had only produced single units and of those only the British *M-2* and French *Surcouf* had entered operational service. On the eve of the Pacific War, in late 1941 the Japanese Navy had 11 aircraft-carrying submarines in service with at least 40 floatplanes available for them. Additional submarines were under construction.

In a continual cycle of development beginning in 1922, the Japanese had honed their underwater aircraft carriers into state-of-the-art weapons. Beyond their ability to carry reconnaissance aircraft, those were among the most capable and potent submarines of World War II, and they would play a role in the first blows of the Pacific War.

CHAPTER 6

War in the Pacific—Part 1

Submarines of the Imperial Japanese Navy's Sixth Fleet began departing their bases in mid-November 1941, in preparation for the opening blows of the Pacific war. The Sixth Fleet's 30 submarines included all 11 aircraft-carrying submarines, six of which had floatplanes embarked: the *I-7*, *I-8*, *I-9*, *I-10*, *I-19*, and *I-25*.[1] Only the Watanabe E9W1 (Slim) floatplanes were carried as the more advanced Kugisho E14Y1 (Glen) aircraft were not yet operational.

While most of those submarines and the carrier striking force had sailed toward Hawaii for the surprise attack planned for 7 December, the *I-10* and *I-26* reconnoitered other islands: The *I-10* was sent on a southerly course across the Pacific, arriving off Fiji in late November, where she launched her floatplane to scout Suva Bay. The airmen radioed that they did not sight any Allied warships. Still, the aircraft failed to return to the *I-10*. After three days of searching, the *I-10* departed for American Samoa, where she sighted the U.S. heavy cruiser *Astoria* (CA 34) on 5 December. The I-boat then took up station southeast of Oahu, ready to intercept American ships fleeing from the air attack on Pearl Harbor.

Meanwhile, the *I-26*—without an aircraft—had her hangar crammed with food in preparation for a long cruise into the North Pacific. She made periscope observations of Attu, Kiska, Adak, and Dutch Harbor in Alaska's Aleutian Islands before heading to a location 750 n.miles northwest of Seattle, Washington. There the *I-26* sighted and began stalking the American-flag steamer *Cynthia Olson* on 6 December, holding off an attack until the war began the following day. (At 0800 Hawaiian time on 7 December the *I-26* sank the merchant ship with her deck gun.)

In company with the carrier striking force approaching Pearl Harbor, the *I-19*, *I-21*, and *I-23* scouted ahead of the carriers to give warning of U.S.

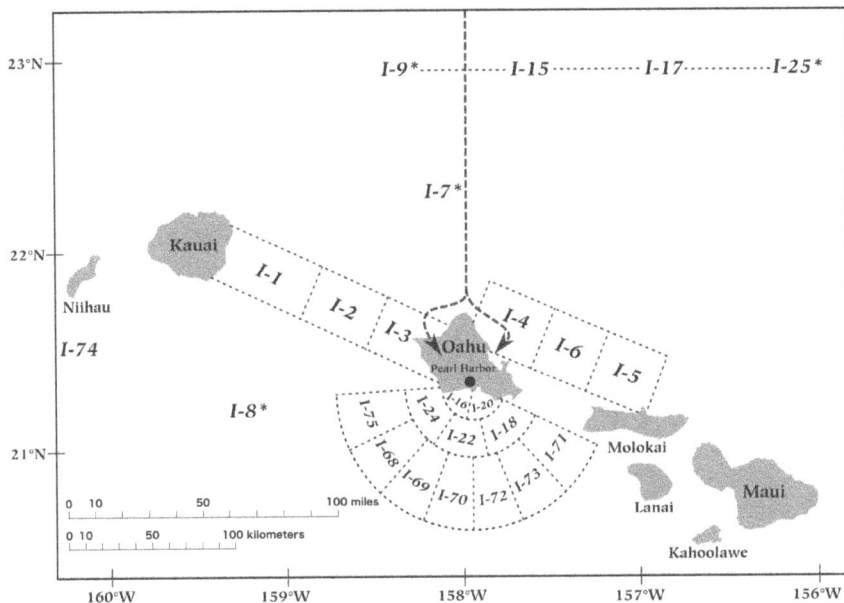

Japanese submarines around Hawaii on the morning of 7 December 1941. Submarines with embarked aircraft are denoted with asterisks. The dashed arrows indicate the path of the carrier aircraft toward Oahu. Adapted from Figure 4 in *Senshi Sosho*, Volume 98. (©JACOB GUNNARSON)

warships and to rescue downed airmen. The remainder of the Japanese submarine fleet took up positions surrounding Oahu (see map).

The *I-9*, *I-15*, *I-17*, and *I-25* formed a patrol line north of Oahu, further screening the carriers from a counterattack. Only the *I-25* planned to launch her aircraft on the day of the attack: a reconnaissance flight over Pearl Harbor would survey the damage after the carrier strike. As the submarine had plowed through heavy seas on the surface en route to Hawaii, the crew heard thumps emanating from the hangar. When the hangar hatch was opened, they found that the floatplane had not been properly secured and was damaged beyond repair.[2]

In addition to the submarine scouting forces, the Special Attack Unit of five Type C submarines, each carrying a two-man midget submarine, took up positions close to the entrance to Pearl Harbor; those were the *I-16*, *I-18*, *I-20*, *I-22*, and *I-24*.[3] In the early morning hours of Sunday, 7 December, their midget submarines were released off the coast of Oahu to penetrate the harbor and add their torpedoes—two per submarine—to the carnage inflicted by the air attack. Several other submarines were arrayed around the Hawaiian Islands, tasked with reconnaissance and recovering downed airmen.[4]

The carrier air attack on Pearl Harbor commenced at 0755 on 7 December, plunging the United States into war with Japan. The massive damage inflicted on the U.S. Pacific Fleet at anchor in Pearl Harbor, the large number of Army and Navy aircraft destroyed on Oahu airfields, and the human casualties all were caused by aircraft from the six Japanese carriers. The six midget submarines—one of which gained entry into the harbor—inflicted no damage in the attack. All six were either sunk or abandoned, with one being made a "prize" by the Americans when that craft ran aground.

The large Japanese submarine force saw little action on 7 December and in the days immediately after. When the *I-6* sighted the aircraft carrier *Enterprise* (CV 6) on 10 December, returning to Pearl Harbor from delivering Marine fighters to Wake Island, several Japanese submarines converged at high speed toward the carrier's reported position. Of those responding, the *I-70* was sunk by a bomb from one of the carrier's SBD Dauntless dive bombers, becoming the first Axis warship to be sunk by the United States in the war.[5]

On 16 December the *I-7* launched her E9W1 Slim floatplane to survey the damage at Pearl Harbor. The airmen counted four battleships (three of which were sunk or damaged), five cruisers, and other ships. The aircraft encountered no opposition. In fear of the submarine being caught on the surface while recovering the floatplane, immediately after returning to the submarine the aircraft was abandoned and scuttled. The *I-7* dived as soon as the two fliers were on board.[6]

Following the successful carrier strike on Pearl Harbor, Vice Admiral Mitsumi Shimizu, commander of the Sixth Fleet, ordered the Type A and Type B submarines to begin patrols off of the West Coast of the United States to attack both naval and merchant shipping. Those nine submarines took up positions close to the coast, from the Strait of Juan de Fuca—on the border of the United States and Canada—down to San Diego. No blackout measures had been implemented along the American coast, and the submarines had some success sinking merchant ships. However, they were hampered by a directive to only expend one torpedo per ship. When a torpedo missed or failed to detonate, the submarine could either abandon the attack or use her deck guns to attack the merchant ship. In total, they sank only two steamers and damaged another two, facing little resistance from U.S. anti-submarine forces. At no point did any of the submarines use their aircraft to search for targets.

On 16 December, Admiral Shimizu ordered the submarines to shell American coastal targets with their deck guns on Christmas Day. The order was countermanded by Admiral Osami Nagano, the chief of the Naval General Staff, because he feared retaliatory attacks against Japanese coastal cities.[7] In late December all of the submarines turned back toward their base at Kwajalein in the Marshall Islands.

On 4 January 1942, the *I-19* launched another reconnaissance flight over Pearl Harbor. Her catapult was inoperative, thus her Slim floatplane was hoisted over the side for a water takeoff. As the aircraft dangled from the crane the submarine was sighted by a U.S. patrol boat, which thought she was an American submarine and attempted to contact the *I-19* with a signal light. Quickly releasing the floatplane to take off, the *I-19* dived. Evading the patrol boat after an hour of pursuit, the submarine surfaced and recovered the floatplane when it returned from its mission. The airmen reported that one carrier, five cruisers, and several other warships were in Pearl Harbor.

The results of the Japanese submarine force's first combat operation of the war were underwhelming. However, the two flights that surveyed the aftermath of the Pearl Harbor attack were successful and confirmed that aircraft-carrying submarines could be effective reconnaissance platforms.

ATTACKING AMERICA

The first attack on the mainland United States during the war occurred on 23 February 1942. In the evening twilight, the *I-17* surfaced off the coast of Santa Barbara, California. Aiming her deck guns at the Ellwood oil refinery, the fire from her single 5.5-inch (140-mm) gun destroyed a few buildings along the waterfront. The attack caused little damage to the refinery but had far-reaching psychological impact.[8]

The panic induced by the *I-17*'s shelling had put the entire West Coast on alert, and on the following night an errant weather balloon detected by Army radar was enough to convince the air defense command that a large force of Japanese bombers was descending upon Los Angeles. During the ensuing "Battle of Los Angeles" an intense barrage of antiaircraft fire lit up the skies over the city. Many of the shells fired at the imagined Japanese bombers exploded when they fell to the ground, having failed to detonate in the air. The only casualties were due to heart attacks and automobile crashes provoked by the gunfire.

In the American press various theories were advanced to explain the origin of the mysterious attack on the refinery, including the supposed existence of a secret Japanese air base in the Mexican desert. *Some newspapers suggested that the aircraft might have been launched from Japanese submarines!*

And there were reports—erroneous or fabricated—of signaling between the *I-17* and Japanese agents on the shore. That notion fueled paranoia about Americans of Japanese ancestry and contributed to the subsequent internment of more than 100,000 innocent Japanese American citizens during the war.

SOUTH PACIFIC RECONAISSANCE

In early 1942, Japanese military leaders drew up plans to attack the Australian cities of Darwin and Sydney, and Port Moresby in New Guinea in an effort to isolate Australia from the Allies. Darwin and Port Moresby were to be attacked by land- and carrier-based aircraft, with the latter city then assaulted by landing forces. Sydney, a major Allied naval base, would be attacked by midget submarines.

The I-25, under the command of Lieutenant Commander Meiji Tagami, was chosen to undertake the initial reconnaissance of Australia and New Zealand with an E14Y1 Glen floatplane, being the first submarine to embark the new aircraft during the war. The Glen was piloted by Warrant Flying Officer Nobuo Fujita, a veteran naval aviator. Originally attached to the I-23, Fujita and his Slim floatplane were transferred to the I-25 before that submarine had departed Japan for Hawaii in November 1941. Petty Officer 2nd Class Shoji Okuda was in the Glen's rear seat as radio operator.

After a few days of exercises with the new floatplane, the I-25 departed Kwajalein for Sydney on 8 February 1942. When she arrived offshore on 14 February, the lights of Sydney, a city not yet accustomed to blackouts, greeted the I-25. The submarine took up a position 100 miles south of the city to avoid being discovered while launching the floatplane. Initially rough seas postponed the flight. By 16 February the waters were calm and Tagami decided to launch the aircraft the following morning. The aircraft would take one hour to reach Sydney, observe the city for another hour, and then return to the submarine.

Radio communications were not permitted between the submarine and aircraft; thus their rendezvous would have to be made visually after sunrise. Fujita decided that if his aircraft were pursued by enemy fighters he would fly in the opposite direction from the I-25 until his fuel tanks ran dry. Then, upon coming down on the water, the two airmen would destroy the aircraft and shoot themselves. Their contingency plan won them the respect of the I-25's crew.[9]

The Glen was taken out of the hangar at 0330 on 17 February and assembled, a process that took about one hour on the dark, rolling deck. Once Fujita and Okuda climbed into the aircraft, the submarine turned into the wind and increased speed to 18 knots as the floatplane shot down the catapult.

Fujita headed toward Sydney at 7,500 feet, descending to 5,000 feet over the city to get below clouds. Large portions of the harbor were lit up in spite of warnings of potential air raids. The airmen were able to observe 23 Allied ships, including several warships and five submarines. Unseen, the aviators departed Sydney at dawn, around 0630, and the aircraft descended to 150 feet for the flight back to the I-25.

Nobuo Fujita (left) and his E14Y1 Glen floatplane at Kure naval base. (AUTHORS' COLLECTION)

When they arrived at the rendezvous point the submarine was not there. A faulty compass had led the aircraft astray. Fujita almost broke radio silence when a yellow smoke signal on the horizon alerted him to the *I-25*'s location.[10] The aircraft alighted on the water next to the submarine; it was disassembled and stowed in the hangar by 0730.

The *I-25*'s next target was Melbourne. Fujita and Okuda launched into overcast skies early on 26 February. They were sighted when they inadvertently flew over an Australian air force base. Two fighters took off to intercept them but lost the Japanese floatplane in the clouds. Fujita then flew over an antiaircraft gun battery, but by the time the guns were given permission to fire, the floatplane was out of range. Again, the loose adherence to blackout conditions allowed Okuda to record the Allied ships in Melbourne's harbor.

The aircraft returned to its mother ship, was recovered without incident, and the *I-25* set sail for Tasmania. On 1 March, the submarine moved into the remote Great Oyster Bay to launch a flight over the port of Hobart. The floatplane returned without sighting any warships and the *I-25* proceeded on to New Zealand.

At 0400 on 7 March, the *I-25* prepared for a reconnaissance flight over the capital of Wellington. Due to heavy swells breaking over the submarine's bow and catapult, Fujita recommended that the aircraft be lowered into the water for takeoff. Suspended precariously from the crane, the Glen began to sway, and one of its wings smashed into the submarine. The flight was aborted. The damage was repaired sufficiently that Fujita was able to overfly Wellington the following day.

On 12 March, after making her way up the coast of the North Island, the *I-25* was depth charged by New Zealand Navy patrol boats. She suffered no damage and was able to elude her attackers.

At 0230 the following morning, Fujita and Okuda were launched on a flight over Auckland, where they sighted four large transport ships. An hour after takeoff, lookouts on the submarine sighted a large steamer heading toward them. The submarine's 5.5-inch deck gun was manned, but the ship passed unaware of the *I-25*'s presence. After the floatplane returned, Tagami decided to pursue the merchant ship that had sailed past them. In the early afternoon the submarine caught up to the large merchant ship, which the *I-25* attacked with four torpedoes after sundown. Tagami claimed that the ship was sunk, although there is no record of such a ship being lost on that date in that area.

The next objective for the *I-25* was a reconnaissance of Fiji and American Samoa. On 16 March, during her journey north from New Zealand, the submarine's bridge watch sighted another large merchant ship under escort by a U.S. heavy cruiser. The submarine was approaching the two ships submerged when the cruiser turned toward the *I-25*'s periscope, prompting Tagami to take the *I-25* deep. No attack occurred, and when the submarine surfaced the two ships were not in sight. Fujita and Okuda were quickly sent into the air to locate them. The aircraft returned to the submarine after 40 minutes without a sighting.

With the *I-25* arriving off Fiji on 19 March, the airmen took to the predawn skies over Suva, the island nation's capital. During the flight, Fujita and Okuda were illuminated by a British cruiser's searchlight. Okuda flashed meaningless Morse code with his signal lamp and the cruiser evidently perceived them as a friendly aircraft and turned off the searchlight.

Fujita had intended to overfly Pago Pago in American Samoa on 23 March; however, heavy seas prevented flight operations. Carrying out the reconnaissance by submarine periscope, Tagami decided to end the patrol and the *I-25* headed for Yokosuka, Japan, via the naval base at Truk. The *I-25*'s two-month patrol, encompassing seven reconnaissance flights, was the most successful to be carried out by an aircraft-carrying submarine. The accomplishment would lead to the submarine and its airmen being selected for a secret and special mission: the first aerial attack on the U.S. mainland.

SCOUTING FOR MIDGET SUBMARINES

In April 1942, two groups of Japanese submarines sailed to carry out midget submarine attacks against Allied naval bases. Unit A—consisting of the *I-10*, *I-16*, *I-18*, *I-20*, and *I-30*—left the Japanese base at Penang, Malaya, for the western Indian Ocean, while the Eastern Unit—consisting of the *I-21*, *I-22*, *I-24*, *I-27*, and *I-29*—departed Japan for Sydney, Australia, previously scouted by the *I-25*.[11] The *I-28* sailed with the latter group, but did not participate in the attack on Sydney. Four submarines carried E14Y1 Glenn floatplanes—the *I-10*, *I-21*, *I-29*, and *I-30*—while the others carried a midget submarine each. Those two-man undersea craft each were armed with two torpedoes.

When the five submarines of Unit A arrived off the eastern coast of Africa, the *I-10* and *I-30* surveyed ports in British and French colonies in search of suitable targets for the midget submarines. On 7 May, the *I-30*'s Glen conducted the first reconnaissance flight of the operation, overflying Aden at the southern tip of the Arabian Peninsula. The next day the aircraft was launched after dark into the skies over Djibouti in French Somaliland. The floatplane came under gunfire from warships in the harbor and turned back for the submarine. On another flight over Zanzibar Island and Dar es Salaam, Tanganyika, the airmen observed only two merchant ships. The *I-30* completed her reconnaissance operation with periscope observations of Mombasa, Kenya, and Diego-Suarez, Madagascar.

The Glen from the *I-10* continued where the *I-30*'s aircraft had left off: Lieutenant (junior grade) Shunshi Araki and Flying Petty Officer 2nd Class Yoshiharu Ito overflew Durban, South Africa, on 20 May, again sighting no potential targets for a midget submarine attack. Their aircraft evidently was detected, and Ito picked up a radio message demanding that they identify themselves. As Okuda had done over Fiji two months earlier, Ito broadcast a gibberish identification message in the hope that it would confuse the enemy. The ploy appeared to have worked, with the floatplane returning safely to the *I-10*.

Their flight over Diego-Suarez on 29 May was more successful. The port, formerly occupied by Vichy France, had been captured by the British three weeks earlier as the first step in a planned invasion of Madagascar. Flying over Diego-Suarez at night, Araki and Ito sighted numerous merchant ships and warships, including the battleship *Ramillies*. The commander of the submarine group ordered a midget submarine attack on Diego-Suarez on the following night.

On the evening of 30 May, two midget submarines detached from the *I-16* and *I-20*; the third midget, carried by the *I-18*, could not launch because of mechanical problems. The two midget submarines entered the harbor undetected. One of their torpedoes struck the *Ramillies* and one hit the tanker *British Loyalty*. The battleship remained afloat, suffering a 30-foot hole in her side. The tanker sank. The two midget submarines and their two-man crews did not return to their "mother" submarines, their fate unknown. The next day the *I-10* sent her Glen aloft to search for them—to no avail.

After the attack on Diego-Suarez, the five I-boats sank several merchant ships off the eastern coast of Africa. While the other submarines departed for

Japan via the naval base at Penang, Malaya, in early July, the *I-30* broke away from the group to proceed around the Cape of Good Hope on a voyage to Europe. On 5 August she entered the German-occupied port of Lorient, France, where the submarine's captain, Commander Shinobu Endo, was decorated by the Germans for the voyage—the first Japanese submarine to reach Europe during the war.

OPERATION YANAGI

The *I-30*'s voyage was the first of several such *Yanagi* (Willow) submarine exchange missions between Germany and Japan. The submarine carried advanced torpedoes and strategic ores, which were passed to the Germans after the submarine reached Lorient.

In turn, the Germans provided a radar detector and an advanced, quad 20-mm antiaircraft gun mount for the submarine. For the return voyage, the *I-30* loaded German radar equipment, torpedoes, bombs, anti-tank weapons, industrial diamonds, and 40 Enigma cipher machines. The *I-30*'s floatplane was left at Lorient as a gift to the Germans.

The submarine departed Lorient on 22 August and arrived at Penang on 9 October. She then was directed to deliver ten of the Enigma machines to Singapore. On the 13th, while departing Singapore, the *I-30* struck a British mine and sank.[12] Thirteen of her crew were killed. Some of her cargo was recovered by divers; most was lost.

Subsequently, the *I-8*, *I-29*, *I-34*, and *I-52* all attempted transits to France. The *I-34* and *I-52* were sunk en route to France; the *I-8* was the only one to survive a round-trip voyage.

Several German and Italian submarines also undertook transits to the Far East. The submarine transits between Japan and Germany were a means of transferring aviation technology and also German technicians, scientists, and engineers. Material sent to Japan in the *I-29* included the rocket engine used by the Me 163 *Komet* fighter-interceptor and the turbojet engine used by the Me 262 *Schwalbe* fighter. The submarine unloaded passengers brought from Europe at Singapore, but not cargo. (Both engines and her other cargo were lost when the submarine was sunk on 26 July 1944, off the Philippines by the U.S. submarine *Sawfish* (SS 276) while en route to Japan; there was one survivor of the sinking.)

The high loss rate of submarines making those inter-Axis voyages was due in large part to Allied codebreaking efforts.[13]

Before the attack on Diego-Suarez in May 1942, while the submarines of Unit A still were sailing across the Indian Ocean toward Africa, the submarines of the Eastern Unit were redirected several times from their original

The *I-8* entering a submarine pen in German-occupied Brest, France on 31 August 1943. The starboard aircraft hangar is visible in its lowered position. (AUTHORS' COLLECTION)

mission to attack Sydney. Those submarines were sent southwest of Guadalcanal in the Solomon Islands to guard against Allied naval action against the forthcoming Japanese attack on Port Moresby, New Guinea, and Tulagi in the Solomons. The submarines then scouted east of the Bonin Islands, seeking the U.S. aircraft carriers that had launched the raid led by Lieutenant Colonel James (Jimmy) Doolittle that had struck Japan on 12 April. They sighted no U.S. warships.

The group then sailed on to Truk in the western Pacific to refuel, and then into the Coral Sea, northeast of Australia. An American task force, centered on the carriers *Lexington* (CV 2) and *Yorktown* (CV 5), was bearing down on the Coral Sea to oppose the Japanese offensive against Port Moresby and Tulagi.

On 2 May, the *I-21* was sighted on the surface and attacked by an SBD Dauntless dive bomber from the *Yorktown*. Although the submarine escaped damage, her lookouts were unable to identify that their attackers were carrier-based aircraft and thus did not alert the Japanese invasion forces that they would be facing an American carrier task force. Two days later the Japanese and American carrier forces clashed in the Coral Sea—the first carrier vs. carrier battle of the Pacific War.

The *I-21* temporarily broke off from the rest of the group to scout Fiji and then Auckland, New Zealand, before rejoining off Sydney. Flying in a dawn

rain shower over Auckland on 24 May, Warrant Flying Officer Susumu Ito piloted the I-21's Glen low over the harbor, so low that the unsuspecting New
Zealanders courteously turned on the airport's runway lights for him!

The Eastern Unit finally arrived off Sydney in mid-May 1942. In preparation for the midget submarine attack, the I-29 launched her Glen over Sydney
on 23 May to follow up the I-25's February observations. Ten Allied warships
were sighted, including a British battleship believed to be the *Warspite*. Although the floatplane was sighted over the harbor and was tracked by radar, it
returned safely to the I-29.

The I-21, returning from the reconnaissance operation off Auckland,
launched a predawn flight over Sydney on 29 May that confirmed that the warships still were in the harbor and recorded the position of anti-submarine nets.
Australian forces observed a small aircraft circling the harbor *with navigation
lights on*, which they initially identified as American. When they realized that
the aircraft was Japanese, the Glen was caught in the beams of brilliant search-
lights. Australian fighters were sent up to intercept the floatplane, but the Glen
was able to elude them and return safely to the I-21.

An E14Y1 Glen is fired off the I-29's catapult. (AUTHORS' COLLECTION)

News of the midget submarine attack on Diego-Suarez had been suppressed and the British did not alert other naval bases to that threat. In addition to sighting the two Japanese floatplanes over Sydney, the Allies intercepted and decoded Japanese reconnaissance reports and messages coordinating the impending attack. However, there was no reaction to that intelligence of a forthcoming attack. Thus, no additional defensive measures were taken to secure Sydney's harbor.

On the evening of 31 May, only hours after the Diego-Suarez attack, three midget submarines launched from the *I-22*, *I-24*, and *I-27* made their way into Sydney harbor. Their attack caught the Australian forces completely by surprise: Two torpedoes were fired at the largest ship in the harbor, the U.S. heavy cruiser *Chicago* (CA 29), that earlier had been misidentified as the battleship *Warspite*; one torpedo missed and one passed under the cruiser and sank the nearby Australian depot ship *Kuttabul*.

Two of the midget submarines were hunted down and sunk. The third escaped from the harbor and sank of unknown causes several miles to the north. The attack was a tactical failure, but coupled with the Diego-Suarez raid Japan had scored major propaganda victories.

After waiting several days for the Sydney harbor midget submarines to return, the "mother" submarines headed north to attack merchant shipping. They sank six merchant ships. In the early hours of the morning of 8 June, the *I-21* and *I-24* bombarded two Australian coastal cities with their 5.5-inch deck guns. Shortly after midnight the *I-24* fired 34 rounds at Newcastle on the coast north of Sydney, and the *I-21* fired on Sydney two hours later. Neither attack caused fatalities, partly because many of their armor-piercing shells failed to detonate. The five submarines returned safely to Kwajalein in mid-June.

BOMBARDING AMERICA

While the Japanese main carrier force steamed toward Midway in late May 1942, for what would become the decisive battle of the Pacific War, a smaller force with two light carriers approached Alaska's Aleutian Islands. The Japanese planned to attack U.S. military installations in the Aleutians with carrier strikes and then land troops on two islands to secure the northern flank of their empire.

The task of scouting those remote islands fell to six Type A and B submarines, three of which—the *I-9*, *I-19*, and *I-25*—embarked Glen floatplanes. The three others—the *I-15*, *I-17*, and *I-26*—had empty hangars in the event that one of the three aircraft-carrying submarines was not able to recover her aircraft.

The *I-9*'s Glen made the first reconnaissance flight over the islands of Kiska and Amchitka in the western part of the island chain on 24 May. There

Two E14Y1 Glen floatplanes in formation over Kure naval base in late 1943 or 1944. All Glens were based at Kure when not assigned to a particular submarine. (AUTHORS' COLLECTION)

had been previous reports of a U.S. airfield on Amchitka and troops on Kiska, but the Glen's crew sighted neither and recommended Reynard Cove on Kiska for a future troop landing. Two days later another flight by the *I-9*'s Glen revealed the presence of American troops on Adak Island.

Rough seas prevented the *I-25* from launching her Glen that same day for a reconnaissance flight over Dutch Harbor, the major port in the Aleutians. That evening the *I-19* was preparing to launch her Glen northwest of Dutch Harbor when lookouts sighted an American destroyer. The submarine immediately dived, wrecking the aircraft.

On 27 May, the *I-25* again attempted a reconnaissance flight over Dutch Harbor. While the aircraft was being readied for flight, the lookouts sighted an American cruiser. The attempt at an immediate launch failed because of a catapult malfunction. The *I-25* readied her deck gun to engage the larger and considerably more powerful warship, but the cruiser passed within a mile without sighting the submarine. The catapult was repaired, and Nobuo Fujita's Glen was successfully launched.

Over Dutch Harbor he and Okuda observed several cruisers, destroyers, and transports. After the aircraft was recovered, the *I-25* again had a close call with two American destroyers, which also failed to sight her.

Those submarines provided valuable information for the approaching light carriers, which launched aircraft to bomb Dutch Harbor on 3 June, one day before the start of the Battle of Midway some 1,800 miles to the south. Japanese troop landings on Kiska and Attu began several days later, and some of the submarines remained in the Aleutians area for several weeks of further reconnaissance. The I-9 launched a final Glen flight over the naval air station on Kodiak Island on 15 June.

The I-25 and I-26 continued eastward for patrols off the coast of British Columbia, Washington, and Oregon. A few days after departing from the Aleutians, the I-25 sighted a U.S. cruiser and a transport that slipped out of sight into the fog. In an effort to regain the contact, the submarine launched her floatplane, but Fujita was unable to find the ships because of the poor visibility. That was one of the few occasions on which a Japanese submarine-launched aircraft was employed for its originally intended purpose: to scout for enemy warships and merchant targets.

On 18 June, the I-25 and I-26 were ordered to bombard coastal targets in western Canada and the United States in the hope of further stoking the alarm and confusion that were caused by the I-17's shelling of the Ellwood oil refinery in February 1942. After sinking a freighter off British Columbia on 7 June, the I-26's captain, Commander Minoru Yokota, decided to shell the Estevan Point lighthouse on the coast of Vancouver Island. On the night of 20 June, the submarine's 5.5-inch deck gun fired more than 20 rounds—none of which struck the lighthouse. That was the first attack on Canadian soil in more than 70 years and made newspaper headlines in Canada and the United States.[14]

Resources for the coastal defense of British Columbia were dispatched and the Canadian government stepped up military conscription following the shelling. There were conspiracy theories about the shelling, including that it was done by an American submarine or that the Canadian government staged the attack to bolster the case for conscription. Those theories finally were put to rest by the discovery of an unexploded Japanese shell near the lighthouse—in 1973![15]

Lieutenant Commander Tagami chose a more ambitious target for the I-25: a U.S. submarine base near Astoria, Oregon, on the south bank of the Columbia River.[16] The Civil War–era Fort Stevens stood guarding the mouth of the river, bristling with a formidable array of artillery and having a remote-controlled minefield. The guns, while impressive, were antiques and had a fairly short range—less than 15,000 yards. Thus, the I-25 was able to remain 20,000 yards offshore and shell the fort with impunity on the night of 21 June. She avoided the minefield by sailing among a group of fishing boats.[17]

The attack caught Fort Stevens by total surprise and the defenders did not fire a shot in return. Ironically, the inability of the American guns to engage the submarine made it nearly impossible for the Japanese to accurately target the fort; there were no muzzle flashes at which to aim. The I-25 fired 17 rounds, causing little damage, and she departed for Japan immediately after the attack.[18] That was the only attack on a military installation in the contiguous United States during the war.

CHAPTER 7

War in the Pacific—Part 2

On 7 December 1941, Nobuo Fujita stood watch in the submarine *I-25's* control room. The veteran aviator wished that he could be flying over Pearl Harbor to survey the devastation inflicted on the American fleet. He was unable to do so because his E9W1 Slim floatplane was damaged, having been improperly secured inside of the submarine's hangar. He listened to the reports of the sonar operator, who could detect the ominous rumbles of distant explosions emanating from Oahu. With little to do on board the *I-25*, Fujita began to draw up a plan for the offensive use of submarine-launched floatplanes.

With other members of the crew, he discussed attaching small bombs to the aircraft and flying ahead of the submarine in search of ships to attack. Lieutenant Tatsuo Tsukudo, the *I-25's* executive officer, suggested bombing the Panama Canal as well as U.S. naval bases and aircraft factories on the West Coast. Although Fujita thought the plan of attacking the mainland United States was a fantasy, Tsukudo encouraged him to develop such a plan and to put it in writing. The executive officer subsequently forwarded Fujita's proposal to Navy headquarters.[1]

When the *I-25* returned to Yokosuka from the Fort Stevens attack in July 1942, Fujita was summoned to a meeting at Navy headquarters in Tokyo. He was told that his proposal to attack the mainland United States was approved and that the *I-25* would undertake the mission. It was explained to Fujita that his plane would carry incendiary bombs to start massive forest fires in Oregon. It was known that wildfires, especially in the dry period at the end of summer, could burn out of control, damaging towns and causing panic.[2]

That intelligence was accurate: A few months earlier a senior Oregon civil defense official had stated that "fire is the greatest danger we will have to face" and "an airplane from a large Japanese submarine could spread many phosphorus sheets throughout the forests."[3] Beyond causing hysteria, the

Warrant Flying Officer
Nobuo Fujita.
(AUTHORS' COLLECTION)

Japanese hoped that the raid would increase the resources devoted to defending the West Coast, thereby diverting ships and aircraft from the fighting in the South Pacific.

Fujita had been in Yokosuka on 18 April when a bomb from one of "Jimmy" Doolittle's B-25 Mitchell bombers had slammed into the submarine tender Ryuho, then undergoing conversion to an aircraft carrier.[4] The Doolittle raid had been the first aerial attack to be made against the Japanese home islands, and Fujita hoped to "return the favor" by making the first air attack on the contiguous United States. Tagami—promoted to commander—was briefed, and the I-25 departed Yokosuka on 15 August for the coast of the United States.

Fujita's E14Y Glen aircraft was specially camouflaged for the raid with the bright red Hinomaru roundels and all identifying markings being painted over and thus barely visible.[5] A rack for a 148-pound incendiary bomb was fitted under each wing; upon release each bomb would spew 520 white-hot thermite pellets over a small area. Six such bombs were loaded on board the I-25, sufficient for three attacks.

A Glen floatplane is readied for flight on board the *I-29*. The white outlines around the red *Hinomaru* insignia on each wing have been painted over in a dark color to reduce the aircraft's visibility. Fujita's Glen was altered similarly. (AUTHORS' COLLECTION)

When the *I-25* arrived off of the coast of Oregon coast on 7 September it was raining heavily and the sea was too rough to launch the floatplane.[6] The weather cleared on the 9th and Fujita and Okuda prepared for an early morning flight. Fujita placed his will, a few strands of hair, and some nail clippings in a box for his family in the event that he was killed on the mission.[7] He brought his family's 400-year-old *katana* sword with him into the cockpit. At 0535 the floatplane was catapulted off the *I-25*, then about ten miles offshore of the small town of Brookings, Oregon.

Fujita overflew Brookings and continued on to the low mountains of the Siskiyou National Forest.[8] At 0634 a Forest Service station on Mount Emily reported an unidentified aircraft.[9] The two lookouts there initially assumed that it was a U.S. aircraft. As they observed the circling floatplane, Okuda released one of the bombs, which exploded in a brilliant white flash and engulfed the trees below in flames. He dropped the second bomb five miles away, after which the Japanese aviators flew back to the *I-25*. On the return flight, Fujita sighted two steamers heading north. Warned via radio by Fujita, the *I-25* proceeded north-northeast to stay out of sight of the merchant ships.

After the floatplane came down on the water and was stowed on board, the *I-25* submerged. *Fujita and Okuda had carried out history's first aerial attack on the contiguous United States.*[10]

The *I-29's* Glen climbs after being launched by the submarine's catapult. Most of Fujita's flights began in the predawn darkness. (AUTHORS' COLLECTION)

The submarine then attempted to intercept the two steamers that Fujita had sighted.[11] As the *I-25* maneuvered into an attack position, a U.S. Army Air Forces A-29 Hudson twin-engine bomber patrolling the area sighted and bore down on the submarine. The *I-25* dived, narrowly avoiding the detonation of several depth charges, which did cause minor fuel leaks that later were visible on the surface.

Meanwhile, damp soil and foliage had quenched the conflagration ignited by Fujita's bombs.[12] By the following day, the U.S. Army, Federal Bureau of Investigation (FBI), and civil defense agencies had been informed of the bombing. Army examiners found Japanese writing on bomb fragments. FBI agents searched remote lakes in the area in the unlikely event that the Japanese were using them as secret seaplane bases. Still, to most persons involved in the investigation it was obvious that the attack was carried out by an aircraft launched from a submarine.[13]

The bombing did not cause the panic that the Japanese had intended. News of the attack was the topic of animated discussions, not hysteria. The story became front-page news in newspapers across the country after the Army released a statement on 14 September about the bombing.[14] The story, like the incendiary bombs themselves, quickly fizzled.

Four incendiary bombs remained on board the *I-25*, and Tagami and Fujita decided to undertake a second raid. On the early morning of 29 September, the floatplane was catapulted off the submarine and flew toward Cape Blanco, about 55 miles north of Brookings.[15] The blackout on the West Coast did not impair navigation as Fujita and Okuda used the still-illuminated Cape Blanco lighthouse as a landmark. At 0522, when the floatplane was about ten miles inland, Okuda released the two incendiary bombs.

Hearing the aircraft in the predawn darkness, Forest Service lookouts at a nearby station saw the brilliant explosions.[16] Correctly suspecting that his aircraft might be heard, Fujita cut the Glen's engine and glided out to sea. After passing over the coast, he restarted the engine and began searching for the I-25. The submarine could not be found. To reestablish his position, Fujita flew back to the Cape Blanco lighthouse and again searched for the I-25. He found the submarine after sighting an oil slick on the water, probably the result of the air attack on the I-25 several weeks earlier.[17]

Again, the forest fire was quickly extinguished by the damp foliage.[18] The U.S. government kept news of the second bombing a secret until June 1943.

Tagami and Fujita planned a third attack with the last two bombs, but their plan was stymied by rain and rough seas.[19] For the remainder of her patrol, the I-25 hunted merchant ships, sinking two in October. Those were the final ships to be sunk off the U.S. coast by Japanese submarines. The I-25 then began the long voyage back to Japan.

While sailing westward on 11 October, lookouts on I-25's bridge reported two warships that soon were identified as American submarines. Despite the heavy seas, Tagami fired the I-25's last torpedo, which struck and sank one of the submarines.

The targets were in fact the Soviet submarines L-15 and L-16. They were being transferred from the Pacific to the Northern Fleet in the Russian Arctic via the Panama Canal. When sighted by the I-25, they were en route from Vladivostok via Dutch Harbor to San Francisco. The L-16 was sunk by the I-25's torpedo with the loss of her entire crew. The L-15 fired her deck gun at the I-25's periscopes to no avail and then resumed the voyage to San Francisco. Japan and the Soviet Union were not at war at the time. The Soviets—ever wary of their American allies—long entertained the possibility that a U.S. submarine had sunk the L-16.

Although Fujita's attacks on Oregon were historically significant, they had no impact on the war.[20] Because the bombings were in a remote area and did not cause major forest fires or casualties, they were treated by the press more as curiosities than as serious attacks. The earlier coastal shellings by the I-17, I-25, and I-26 had a greater impact on the public because they were closer to populated areas. Still, the I-25 proved that attacks on the United States with submarine-launched aircraft were feasible. At that time the Japanese were planning far more ambitious submarine-launched air attacks on the United States (see Chapter 8).

MORE FLOATPLANE OPERATIONS

The Japanese Navy planned several operations against the U.S. staging areas in the South Pacific and used aircraft-carrying submarines to gauge the strength of the defenses and of the composition of the U.S. fleet in the region. From June 1942 to August 1943, ten Japanese submarines launched 19 flights to reconnoiter Fiji, New Caledonia, the New Hebrides, and the Santa Cruz Islands. Those areas served as staging locations for the planned U.S. invasion of the Solomon Islands, and Allied warships were repaired and resupplied in their harbors.

The first American offensive of the war had begun on 7 August 1942, when U.S. Marines landed on Guadalcanal in the Solomons. The Santa Cruz Islands, a few hundred miles east the Solomons, were ideal for basing U.S. long-range reconnaissance aircraft to monitor Japanese naval operations in the South Pacific area. In early 1942, the U.S. Navy based a squadron of PBY Catalina flying boats at Nendo Island in the Santa Cruz Islands. The Japanese sent submarines to investigate reports of the new base.

On 28 August, the *I-19* sent her Glen on a flight over Nendo finding six PBYs and a destroyer in the main harbor. Three days later the submarine shelled the seaplane base with her 5.5-inch gun—causing no damage. She was relieved by the *I-31*, which arrived off the island on 11 September, and catapulted her Glen on a dawn reconnaissance flight. The Japanese airmen sighted floating PBYs and two seaplane tenders. After sneaking into the bay submerged during the day, the *I-31* surfaced after sunset and readied her 5.5-inch deck gun. Although under return gunfire from the seaplane tenders, the submarine's fire struck two of the PBYs. But after firing only ten rounds her deck gun jammed and the *I-31* submerged and retreated out of the bay. Following those two attacks, the U.S. Navy transferred the flying boats and their tenders to Espiritu Santo in the New Hebrides, 300 miles farther south.

In October 1942, the *I-21* and *I-7* launched aircraft over Espiritu Santo in the New Hebrides in preparation for a planned Japanese amphibious landing.[21] The *I-7*'s Slim floatplane was damaged after the first flight, and she was relieved on station by the *I-9* carrying a Glen. Those flights determined that the U.S. defenses were too strong for the planned assault. In addition to reconnaissance in support of planned operations in the Solomons area, aircraft-carrying submarines in 1943 also scouted major Allied harbors including Diego-Suarez, Sydney, and Mombasa.

In a photo-reconnaissance flight over the coast of New South Wales, Australia, on 19 February 1943, the *I-21*'s Glen's observer used a hand-held camera.

BACK TO PEARL HARBOR

Two submarine-launched reconnaissance flights were made over Pearl Harbor in late 1943. The *I-36* launched her Glen after sunset on 16 October, but the aircraft was detected shortly after reaching the harbor. The aircraft's observer transmitted a single dash—the signal for the submarine to recover the float-plane—and the *I-36* raced toward the rendezvous area. The submarine received a garbled radio message stating that the floatplane had sighted 4 carriers, 4 bat-tleships, 5 cruisers, and 17 destroyers. The aircraft's radio then went silent.

The *I-36* searched in vain for the missing floatplane for several hours, flashing her running lights and signal lamp—a risky action considering the proximity to Pearl Harbor. The aircraft was not found and the *I-36* returned to Kwajalein.

The *I-19* launched the final Japanese flight over Pearl Harbor on 17 No-vember, which revealed that only a single battleship and one aircraft carrier were in port at that time. Due to patrolling U.S. aircraft in the area, the float-plane was scuttled immediately after coming down next to the submarine be-cause of the time that it would take to recover the aircraft.

In 1943 the Glen floatplanes were approved to carry a 138-pound bomb under each wing, up from the earlier 66-pound limit. However, an aircraft carrying bombs could not come down on the water with the bombs still attached; if not used against targets, the bombs would have to be jettisoned.

The *I-37* embarked three 138-pound bombs with her Glen at Penang on the Malaysian peninsula for a patrol off the Chagos Archipelago and Diego Garcia in the Indian Ocean. Despite the Glen being approved for the wing bomb racks, the mechanics at Penang disagreed with the engineers in Japan and decided that the wings were not strong enough; instead they installed a single bomb rack under the fuselage.

At sea on 3 March 1943, the *I-37* launched her floatplane with a bomb in the hope of finding a ship to attack. No ships were sighted and the bomb was jettisoned before the aircraft returned to the submarine.[22] On 30 March 1944, the *I-8* launched her E9W1 Slim floatplane in the same area. The aircraft sighted the British armed merchant *City of Adelaide* and guided the submarine toward the ship. The merchant ship was damaged by a torpedo from the *I-8* and then was sunk with the submarine's 5.5-inch deck gun. That was the only known occasion of a Japanese aircraft successfully vectoring a submarine to attack a ship.

In early 1944, the Japanese Navy began preparations for Operation *Yu-Go*, a strike against American aircraft carriers anchored at Majuro coral atoll in the Marshall Islands. The U.S. warships would be attacked by an armada of battleships, cruisers, carrier- and land-based aircraft, and submarines.[23] In the afternoon of 22 April, the *I-36*'s Glen made the first reconnaissance flight over Majuro, sighting 11 aircraft carriers and three battleships at anchor.

After the flight the airmen were unable to locate their submarine, and came down on the water, hoping that the submarine would find them. At dawn on the 23rd the *I-36* located the Glen and scuttled the aircraft after taking aboard the two fliers. Despite those successful reconnaissance flights, Operation *Yu-Go* was not carried out due to technical problems with the torpedo-armed assault craft that were intended to penetrate the anchorage.[24]

NEW AIRCRAFT AND SUBMARINES

The Kugisho E14Y1 Glen was regarded as an excellent aircraft by both pilots and submariners, although its slow speed was a major limitation. The Navy Aviation Bureau issued the *16-Shi* specification in late 1941 for an improved floatplane aircraft with greater cruising speed and ceiling. An order was placed with Watanabe for the design and production of the E14Y2, a thoroughly reworked variant with a more powerful engine producing 510 horsepower compared to the E14Y1's 340 horsepower unit. Among the other modifications to the design were a streamlined fuselage and strengthened wing struts.

At least one prototype was flight tested. Still, the E14Y2 never entered production as Watanabe already was having difficulty producing the Glen. During the entire E14Y1 production run from April 1942 to September 1943, the company was able to deliver only 126 of the 254 aircraft that the Navy had ordered.[25] Specifications for a new aircraft to replace the Glen—the *18-Shi* and *19-Shi* requirements—were issued in 1943 and 1944, respectively, but were never fulfilled as most submarine-launched aircraft were being phased out.

In that period several additional Type A and B submarines were being completed in Japanese shipyards. As Japan faced severe shortages of high-quality metal alloys, the submarine designers were forced to make changes to submarine hulls and propulsion machinery. The Type B Mod. 1 had slightly less powerful diesel engines and pressure hulls constructed from medium steel instead of high-strength "Ducol" steel. By using thicker hull plating, the designers could retain the 330-foot test depth of earlier submarines while using the more readily available, albeit weaker, medium steel.

The Type A and B submarines achieved their exceptional 23½-knot surface speed with two enormous Kanmoto diesel engines, each producing 6,200 horsepower. Their unusual "double-acting" design resulted in a powerful engine, although inherent design complexities led to difficulties in both manufacturing and maintenance. Those engines frequently suffered overheated pistons and cracked cylinder heads due to the rigors of wartime use and inexperienced crews.[26]

Those mechanical problems were remedied with the Type A Mod. 1 and Type B Mod. 2 submarines. They were fitted with smaller and more conventional diesels that, although developing only 2,250 horsepower each, were more reliable, simpler to manufacture, and more fuel-efficient. The submarines' electric motors also were simplified, dropping their power from 1,000 horsepower each to 600 horsepower. Those changes cost the undersea craft almost six knots on the surface and about 1½ knots submerged. However, the decreased weight of the new diesels—about half that of the previous model—allowed the submarines to carry more fuel, extending their surface range at 16 knots from 16,000 n.miles to 22,000 n.miles.[27]

The cost in material and manpower for those large submarines forced the Navy to cancel many Type A and B variants in favor of smaller and more economical submarines: Of 21 Type B Mod. 2 submarines planned, only three were completed; one Type A Mod. 1 was completed, with the other four reordered as Type A Mod. 2 submarines, which each could carry two *Seiran* attack aircraft (see Chapter 8). With the exception of the Type A Mod. 2, none of the improved variants of the Type A and B submarines ever embarked an aircraft although they retained the same hangar and catapult as the earlier designs.

In September 1942, in response to the disastrous warship losses at the battle of Midway in June, the Japanese Navy drew up an ambitious shipbuilding program that called for the construction of more than 400 ships.[28] Among those were two highly modified variants of the Type A and B submarines, designated S48 and S49A.[29] The most significant change in those craft was that the hangar and catapult would be moved aft of the conning tower, exchanging positions with the deck gun. The S48 would remain a flagship submarine like the Type A while the S49A would add two bow torpedo tubes and a minelaying capability to the Type B design. Three S48 and 18 S49A submarines were ordered. All would be cancelled in 1943 in favor of more conventional and economical submarine designs.

As those new submarine classes came into service, the Japanese were facing increasingly capable and numerous American anti-submarine forces. The Japanese were slow to adopt radar and radar-warning devices to submarines, and the radars that did go into service were primitive compared to available American and British sets. Surfaced submarines, especially those forced to stay on the surface to launch and recover aircraft, were increasingly vulnerable to Allied warships and aircraft fitted with state-of-the-art radar.

An E14Y Glen from the *I-10* performed the last recorded reconnaissance flight of a Japanese submarine-launched aircraft on 12 June 1944, over the U.S. ships anchored at Majuro in the Marshall Islands. That aircraft capsized upon coming down on the water after the mission and was lost. The *I-39* embarked a Glen at Truk on 21 November 1944, for scouting the Gilbert Islands, but she was sunk by a U.S. destroyer five days later, before she could carry out the reconnaissance.

By late 1944, all Slim and Glen floatplanes were removed from submarines and were assigned to land bases, most to air stations in Japan. Three Glens had been used to patrol off the submarine base at Penang, Malaya, starting in April 1943. The German Navy contributed two Arado Ar 196 floatplanes, painted in Japanese markings, to the defense on Penang and apparently also flew the Glens. (At least one Glen was used by the Indonesian Air Force after the float-planes from Penang were transferred to Jakarta in December 1944.)

Seventeen of the 138 Glens survived the war; none survive today.

NEW MISSIONS

Without floatplanes, Japan's aircraft-carrying submarines were assigned new missions: Starting with the Guadalcanal campaign of August 1942, many large Japanese submarines delivered supplies to troops on isolated and beleaguered islands. Those submarines were especially valuable for the supply missions, being able to carry more than 50 tons of supplies in their watertight hangars.[30] Their contribution to the Guadalcanal campaign was small, but those subma-rines would play a more significant role in the Aleutians campaign.

The I-9 and I-21, in addition to four other I-boats and nine smaller RO-series submarines, were tasked in the spring and summer of 1943 with supplying and, if necessary, evacuating troops from the Aleutian islands of Attu and Kiska. The submarines landed 125 tons of supplies and evacuated 820 men from those islands. The Japanese troops on Kiska were evacuated entirely by submarine.[31]

The submariners detested supply missions, believing that their capabil-ities were being squandered. Their submarines had been designed for long-range scouting and attack. Morale dropped significantly as a result of these supply and evacuation missions. The Japanese continued the use of dedicated cargo submarines and towed submersible containers to transport supplies as the war continued.

Among the more interesting uses for the aircraft-carrying submarines was as a carrier for the Type 4 *Katsu* landing vehicle—tracked amphibious vehi-cles that could be armed with two torpedoes. Those vehicles originally were intended to be used as troop and cargo craft; they were reconfigured to carry two torpedoes each. When released from a surfaced submarine off an anchor-age harboring U.S. Navy warships, they were to "swim" and then drive over the shallow reef and reenter the water to fire their torpedoes at the unsuspect-ing anchored ships. The Type 4 landing vehicle was watertight, enabling the mother submarine to submerge with the landing craft lashed to her deck. Four landing vehicles could be carried on the deck of a Type B or C submarine.

However, vehicle trials with the I-36 in May 1944 were not promising. The engine compartments of the landing craft frequently flooded, the craft

As Japan's prospects in the Pacific waned, its submarines were put to increasingly desperate and unusual use. Here the *I-36* embarks two Type 4 landing vehicles, which were intended to attack American ships in anchorages. (AUTHORS' COLLECTION)

were slow and noisy, and they had trouble gaining traction on exposed reefs.[32] The Type 4 landing vehicles were intended to be used in Operation *Yu-Go* to assault the U.S. anchorage at Majuro, but their numerous technical problems prevented the craft from seeing combat.

A CHANGE IN STRATEGY

As U.S. forces swept through the central and southwest Pacific in 1944 and Japan's defeat seemed inevitable, the Japanese increasingly resorted to suicide tactics, euphemized as "special attacks." The *kaitens* (meaning "return to heaven") were the underwater counterpart to the *kamikaze* aircraft—large manned torpedoes for suicide missions. The Type A, B, and C submarines were well suited for *kaiten* operations because of their long range and large decks. Many aircraft-carrying submarines had their hangars and catapults removed to accommodate *kaitens*. Ultimately, the *kaitens* were totally ineffective. In nine attempts to use them against American warships they sank only the destroyer escort *Underhill* (DE 682) and the fleet oiler *Mississinewa* (AO 59).

As fast, long-range submarines armed with the highly effective Type 95 torpedo, the Type *Junsen* 3, A, and B boats were formidable attack craft. In addition to sinking a few dozen merchant ships, they scored some impressive warship kills. On 25 September 1942, several weeks after a launching a reconnaissance flight over Graciosa Bay in the Santa Cruz Islands, the *I-19* sighted a U.S. Navy task force escorting reinforcements heading for Guadalcanal.

The *I-19* then fired the single most effective torpedo salvo of the Pacific war: From a spread of six 21-inch torpedoes, three struck the carrier *Wasp* (CV 7), and one each hit the battleship *North Carolina* (BB 55) and the destroyer *O'Brien* (DD 415). The torpedoes sank the *Wasp*, damaged the *North Carolina*, and mortally wounded the *O'Brien*. The captain of the *I-19*, Commander Takakazu Kinashi, later was personally awarded the Iron Cross 2nd Class by Hitler in Berlin.[33]

Two months later, on 13 November 1942, the *I-26* sank the antiaircraft cruiser *Juneau* (CL 52) during the Guadalcanal campaign, claiming the lives of all but ten of her crew. Those lost included the five Sullivan brothers, who had insisted on serving in the same warship.

On 30 July 1945, the heavy cruiser *Indianapolis* (CA 35), steaming toward the Philippines after delivering atomic bomb components to the island of Tinian, was sunk by two torpedoes from the *I-58*. At the time the *I-58* was carrying six *kaitens*. However, her commanding officer, Lieutenant Commander Mochitsura Hashimoto, decided that the cruiser was an easy target for a conventional torpedo attack; 879 Americans were lost in the *Indianapolis* sinking.

By the end of the war in August 1945, U.S. Navy anti-submarine forces had eliminated almost all of the Japanese submarine fleet. Of the 35 Type *Junsen* 3, A, and B submarines that had entered service, only three—the *I-14*, *I-36*, and *I-58*—survived the war. Despite their intended use as fleet scouts, Japan's aircraft-carrying submarines almost exclusively preformed reconnaissance of land installations. Of the 65 recorded flights, on only four occasions were floatplanes catapulted into the air in search of ships for the submarine to attack (see Appendix C).

In most situations the Watanabe E9W1 Slim and Kugisho E14Y1 Glen aircraft had performed well. The two floatplanes held up remarkably well at sea under wartime rigors for such compact and light aircraft that were intended to be "semi-disposable." They also were well suited for covert reconnaissance.

On only two flights did the aircraft fail to return, and on the majority of flights the aircraft appear to have flown completely unnoticed by their targets. And when they were detected by the enemy, more often than not their diminutive size and ingenious use of subterfuge by the airmen—flashing meaningless Morse code or leaving navigation lights on—confused Allied forces, at least briefly, into believing they were friendly aircraft. Only a few flights encountered Allied antiaircraft guns or fighters. The aircrafts' success can also be attributed to their operation over cities and harbors, far from the main thrust of the war, where the threat of Japanese air raids was low and the air defenses were lax.

Still, the overall contribution of aircraft-carrying submarines to the war was minor. The midget submarine assaults on Diego-Suarez and Sydney may not have been possible without the reconnaissance flights provided by Japanese submarines. However, those attacks were not especially successful and had only a meager psychological and propaganda impact. Similarly, Fujita's bombing missions over Oregon failed to achieve their goal of setting alight the forests of the American northwest, and ultimately its propaganda value was overshadowed by the shelling of Canadian and American coastal targets by Japanese submarines.

Perhaps the most significant use of Japan's aircraft-carrying submarines was the reconnaissance in direct support of major naval operations. They provided the first Japanese glimpse of the devastation inflicted on the U.S. Pacific Fleet at Pearl Harbor. In the Aleutians they provided valuable intelligence for air attacks and troop landings. During the Solomons campaign and the later stages of the war they monitored the harbors and anchorages used by the Allies as staging areas and repair depots. However, aircraft-carrying submarines were not employed as effectively as they could have been, which was symptomatic of the Japanese submarine fleet as a whole.

A postwar U.S. Navy report summarized:

> Hampered by shortages of all kinds, assigned to a minor role with its forces dispersed in a losing war against a well-equipped enemy, the Japanese submarine force should be given credit for effort. However, in addition to its handicaps, there were several shortcomings of its own which prevented a creditable performance. Among these shortcomings were vacillating polices in building, false economy in withholding submarines for future use, failure to correct known mistakes, confusion of tactical command, poor communications, and a lack of individual caliber in many of the commanding officers. Briefly, in no particular could it be said that the Japanese submarine force excelled, while examples are many of its deficiency in strategical, tactical, research and personnel performance.[34]

In retrospect, it is easy to conceive of ways in which aircraft-carrying submarines could have had a greater impact on the Pacific War. If they had operated effectively off the U.S. West Coast, the aircraft-carrying submarines could have severely disrupted American merchant shipping just as the German U-boats had done off the East Coast in Operation Drumbeat. Such attacks may have caused significant alarm among civilians and diverted anti-submarine resources. But the few West Coast submarine patrols that were undertaken resulted in only a handful of merchant ships being sunk.

When Admiral Isoroku Yamamoto, the Commander-in-Chief of the Combined Fleet, devised the plan to attack Midway Island in June 1942, to lure the U.S. fleet into combat, he was echoing the long-held Japanese strategy of the decisive naval battle. It was precisely for this ultimate clash of fleets that the Imperial Navy's aircraft-carrying submarines were designed: they would be the forwardmost scouts of the Japanese Navy.

Still, when the order of battle for the Midway operation was drawn up, the picket line positioned between Midway and Pearl Harbor was composed of older *Kaidai* Type submarines, none carrying aircraft. The aircraft-carrying submarines were instead assigned to the attack on the Aleutians. Such "misuse" of those submarines' impressive capabilities was characteristic of the Japanese submarine force.

The aircraft-carrying submarines could have been used more effectively as a "terror weapon": Consider the widespread panic that could have followed if Fujita had dropped his bombs on downtown Los Angeles or San Francisco instead of on a remote forest. The Japanese did recognize that nefarious potential use for underwater carriers early on in the war and did embark on a program to build such terror weapons—the *Sentoku* Type submarine and *Seiran* light bomber—and even considered employing them to wage biological warfare.

CHAPTER 8

The Ultimate
Underwater Carriers

Following the air and midget submarine attacks on Pearl Harbor on 7 December 1941, Admiral Isoroku Yamamoto began to envision the next dramatic strike against the United States. On board his flagship, the battleship *Nagato* moored in Tokyo Bay, Yamamoto discussed with his senior officers the possibility of constructing a massive aircraft-carrying submarine to bomb America: "If we send a submarine aircraft carrier to the U.S. mainland and drop bombs like rain over their major cities, the American people will surely lose their will to fight."[1]

Yamamoto was well aware of the power of naval aviation. In 1924, he had become the head of the Navy's flight school at Kasumigaura, despite not being a pilot himself. In the 1930s he commanded the First Carrier Division and, subsequently, became director of the Aeronautical Department of the Navy Ministry.

The admiral was an avid gambler and, as one of his staff officers recalled, "In all games Yamamoto loved to take chances just as he did in naval strategy."[2] As with the Pearl Harbor attack, his plan for a submarine carrier strike was for a daring surprise attack that would have psychological impact in addition to accomplishing strategic objectives. Bombers emblazoned with the rising sun striking New York City, or possibly even the capital city of Washington, D.C., would be the ultimate expression of Yamamoto's audacity.

A submarine large enough to carry *several* attack aircraft had not previously been considered by any navy. Yamamoto turned to his senior staff officer, Captain Kameto Kuroshima, to determine the feasibility of such a craft. Kuroshima was an unusual officer, prone to highly inventive if occasionally outlandish ideas. Yamamoto appreciated his eccentric ingenuity.

The *Sentoku* Type submarines were the largest and most impressive undersea craft built during WWII. The hangar, mounted amidships, could house three *Seiran* attack aircraft. Here the *I-401* is pictured in Tokyo Bay after the end of the war. (U.S. NAVY)

Kuroshima presented Yamamoto's vision for the underwater carriers to the Naval General Staff on 13 January 1942, less than one month after Yamamoto's conference on board the *Nagato*. The concept was approved and passed to the Bureau of Naval Construction. In charge of the preliminary design were the experienced submarine constructor Captain Ariki Katayama and the Naval General Staff's submarine officer, Lieutenant Commander Tatsunosuke Ariizumi.[3]

The result of their combined effort was a submarine about the size of a destroyer, dwarfing even the large Type A and B cruiser submarines. Each submarine would carry two bombers each carrying a torpedo or a 1,764-pound bomb. The submarine carrier, with a range of 40,000 n.miles on the surface, could strike from anywhere in the world's oceans and return to Japan without refueling. The design—designated the *Sentoku* (Special Submarine) Type—was finalized in May 1942, a remarkably brief time for developing such an ambitious project. The first unit, the *I-400*, was laid down at the Kure shipyard on 18 January 1943.[4] A total of 18 of the giant aircraft-carrying submarines were planned.

DESIGNING THE AIRCRAFT

The Aichi Aircraft Company was selected on 15 May 1942 to design and build the *Sentoku* submarine's "special attack bomber." The original 17-*shi* specification called for a catapult-launched aircraft without floats or other undercarriage.[5] The design team, led by Toshio Ozaki, coordinated with the submarine designers to ensure that the aircraft and submarine would be a highly effective combination.

At that time Aichi was producing the D4Y *Suisei* dive bomber (Allied codename Judy). The *Suisei* had outstanding aerodynamic characteristics and was among the fastest dive bombers of the war. Studies into modifying the D4Y for submarine operation were unsuccessful due to the aircraft's large size, forcing the Aichi designers to develop an entirely new aircraft.

One of the M6A1 *Seiran* prototypes at the Aichi factory in 1944. (TETSUKUNI WATANABE)

The result was the Aichi M6A1 *Seiran* (Clear Sky Storm). Originally the floatplane was called the *Nanzan* (Southern Mountain) with the land-based, wheeled trainer named the *Seiran*. After February 1944, both aircraft were referred to as the *Seiran*.[6]

At almost three times the weight of the E14Y Glen, the *Seiran* would be the largest aircraft ever to operate from a submarine. It retained the D4Y's sleek lines as well as its Aichi Atsuta V12 engine, a copy of the German Daimler-Benz DB 601A built under license in Japan. While most Japanese naval aircraft used radial engines, the water-cooled Atsuta offered less drag and its length ensured that the propeller arc would safely clear the nose of a torpedo carried beneath the fuselage.[7] Another advantage of the Atsuta was that hot water could be circulated inside of the engine when the aircraft was in the submarine's hangar, alleviating the need to warm up the engine when on the catapult preparing to be launched.

The *Seiran* was one of the few aircraft that was both a dive bomber and torpedo bomber: it could carry a single, 1,764-pound armor-piercing bomb— one of the largest in the Navy's arsenal—or an 1,808-pound, 18-inch-diameter torpedo. For dive bombing, the wing flaps would rotate 90 degrees to serve as dive brakes.[8] A forward-firing 7.7-mm machine gun was considered but was eliminated as it would have little value on a bomb-laden attack aircraft. The rear seat observer had a 13-mm machine gun in a flexible mount.

For training and missions with a small bombload the *Seiran* was launched with floats installed. A small fin was attached to the upper rudder to counteract the destabilizing aerodynamic effect of the floats. The weight and drag of the floats greatly reduced the aircraft's payload and limited its maximum speed and range.[9] Thus, to carry a torpedo or its maximum bombload, the *Seiran* was to be launched without floats. Returning from their mission, the airmen would ditch the aircraft alongside the submarine and be taken on board.

The first *Seiran* prototype was flown on 8 December 1943, by Lieutenant Tadashi Funada, an experienced seaplane test pilot. Three land-based aircraft were constructed with retractable landing gear to train pilots to fly without floats.[10] Eight prototypes, including the three land-based trainers, were built before series production began in October 1944. Including prototypes, *Seiran* production would total 28 aircraft through July 1945.[11]

The *Seiran* had comparable if not superior performance to conventional naval aircraft. Ensign Kazuo Takahashi—the former pilot of the *I-37*'s Glen—claimed that without floats it was as capable in every respect as the famed A6M Zero (Zeke) fighter despite being larger and heavier.[12] He also praised the aircraft's stability and controllability during water operations. Funada further extolled that the aircraft's "responsive controllability" as "unforgettable" and called the aircraft "a masterpiece."[13]

The *Seiran* was officially accepted by the Navy on 24 November 1944.[14]

The Japanese Navy did its utmost to keep the *Seiran* aircraft and the *Sentoku* submarine concealed from U.S. intelligence. The construction of the *Sentoku* submarines was given the Navy's highest security classification. The Allies knew that the *Seiran* was a submarine-launched aircraft but had no knowledge of its true purpose.[15]

Still, the giant undersea craft could not be concealed entirely from U.S. intelligence efforts. During the American invasion of Saipan in the Mariana Islands in the summer of 1944, the U.S. troops captured shipbuilding documents that listed the *Sentoku* submarines then under construction.[16] Based on those documents and other sources, the U.S. Navy eventually determined that those submarines were "very large." However, the Japanese were able to hide the submarines' mission. A U.S. naval intelligence manual in June 1945 classified them as "cruiser transport submarines," that "may be used long-range supply and transport operations. It is believed that a scout observation plane is carried for reconnaissance patrol."[17]

SUBMARINE-LAUNCHED *KAMIKAZES*

While the *Seiran* floatplanes and *Sentoku* Type submarines were being constructed, the Japanese Navy developed a bizarre suicide aircraft to fend off the American naval forces approaching the home islands. Conceived in the summer of 1944, the Kugisho MXY7 *Ohka* (Cherry Blossom) was a manned flying bomb.[18] It was small and torpedo-shaped, with an explosive-filled nose section and rocket propulsion. Constructed of wood and noncritical metals, the *Ohka* was intended as a mass-produced anti-ship weapon. It was one of the few aircraft ever designed specifically as a *kamikaze*—suicide—weapon.[19]

Between September 1944 and March 1945, more than 750 of the initial variant—the *Ohka* Model 11—were produced.[20] The Model 11 could be carried under a G4M2 Betty twin-engine bomber. Once released, the *Ohka* would glide toward an American warship and the pilot would ignite three rocket boosters shortly before impacting the target ship, accelerating the aircraft to 400 mph to help evade defending fighters. Compared to conventional aircraft used for *kamikaze* missions, the small size and high speed of the *Ohka* would make it a difficult target for both defending fighters and shipboard antiaircraft guns.

The first *Okha* combat mission was against U.S. ships during the invasion of Okinawa. The first success was achieved on 1 April 1945, when *Okhas* damaged the battleship *West Virginia* (BB 48) and several transports. The first and only ship sunk by the suicide aircraft was the destroyer *Mannert L. Abele* (DD 733), which was hit by two *Okhas* off Okinawa on 12 April.

The *Ohka* Model 11 was followed by the longer-range Model 22, powered by a motorjet—a jet turbine driven by a four-cylinder gasoline engine. The Model 33 was a further improvement, powered by a Ne-20 turbojet. The greater ranges provided by those engines enabled those *Ohkas* to be released farther from the target to reduce the losses of the carrying aircraft. Only some 50 of the Model 22 were built, and the Model 33 soon was cancelled due to the slow development of its planned carrier aircraft, the Nakajima G8N1 *Renzan* bomber.[21]

Instead, a new *Ohka* model was developed—*specifically to be launched from submarines*. The Model 43A that evolved from the Model 33 was intended to be carried by the *Sentoku* submarines. With the exceptional range of the *Sentoku* submarine, *Ohka* attacks could be carried out against naval *and land targets* far behind the battle fronts and possibly launched against the American homeland. Six of the suicide aircraft could fit inside the *Sentoku* submarine's hangar.[22]

The Model 43A was powered by a turbojet and was larger than previous models, being 26¾ feet long with folding wings. It had fittings for launching from a submarine catapult. The 43B variant was modified for launching from catapults to be installed in caves along the coast of Japan to help repel an American invasion of the home islands.[23]

Design work on the Model 43A started in March 1945, and production was assigned to the Aichi firm, which by that time was modifying existing fighters into *kamikaze* aircraft rather than building new aircraft. The Aichi factories, heavily damaged by U.S. bombings, could produce only a half-assembled mockup of the Model 43B by the end of the war.[24] Even if the

Model 43A suicide aircraft were produced there probably would not have been submarines to launch them as the dwindling number of Japanese submarines were being employed to carry midget submarines or "human torpedoes" to attack U.S. warships.

By the end of the war 852 *Ohkas* of all models had been produced.[25]

THE INNOVATIVE *I-400*

The *Sentoku* submarines were remarkable, not only for their impressive size, but also for their unique design. To accommodate eight bow torpedo tubes while retaining a deep and narrow bow to cut through the waves when on the surface to launch aircraft, the first compartment of the pressure hull was divided into two torpedo rooms, *one above the other* with a vertical figure-eight cross-section; 20 torpedoes were carried.[26]

Aft of the torpedo rooms the pressure hull section transitioned to a wide, horizontal figure-eight, partitioned down the center by a watertight bulkhead.[27] The wide amidships hull allowed for double the power plant of previous aircraft-carrying submarines: two engine rooms, each with two diesel engines coupled to a propeller shaft for a total of 9,000 horsepower delivered to the two shafts. The *I-51*—first of Japan's I-boats—had used a similar configuration (see Chapter 5). The *Sentoku*'s wide beam also increased the craft's surface stability, making it a steadier platform for preparing and launching aircraft. The after end of the stern compartment was the only portion of the pressure hull to have a conventional, circular cross-section.

Topside, the hangar dominated the superstructure. For the first time on a Japanese submarine the hangar was accessible to the crew while submerged and was fitted with water and oil preheaters to prepare the aircraft for flight while still in the hangar. One pair of floats was stored above the *Seiran* at the after end of the hangar; the two other pairs were in watertight cylinders flanking the hangar.

The deck above the hangar bristled with nine 25-mm antiaircraft guns plus an additional 25-mm gun behind the bridge. The submarines also mounted a 5.5-inch deck gun aft of the hangar. The conning tower and bridge were offset to the port side in an attempt to reduce the submarine's silhouette when on the surface by not positioning them atop the hangar. Beneath the hangar, inside the starboard side of the hull, were an aircraft engine overhaul station and a weapons magazine that could hold 4 aircraft torpedoes and 15 bombs.[28]

The *Sentoku* submarines were fitted with German-developed sonar- and radar-absorbing coatings. The coatings cost one knot of speed and sloughed off the side of the submarine after a few months, but Japanese sources claimed that it reduced the noise emitted from the submarine's hull by 15 decibels.[29] (Based on their lack of effectiveness in postwar U.S. Navy testing, it appeared that the coatings mainly served to attract algae growth!)

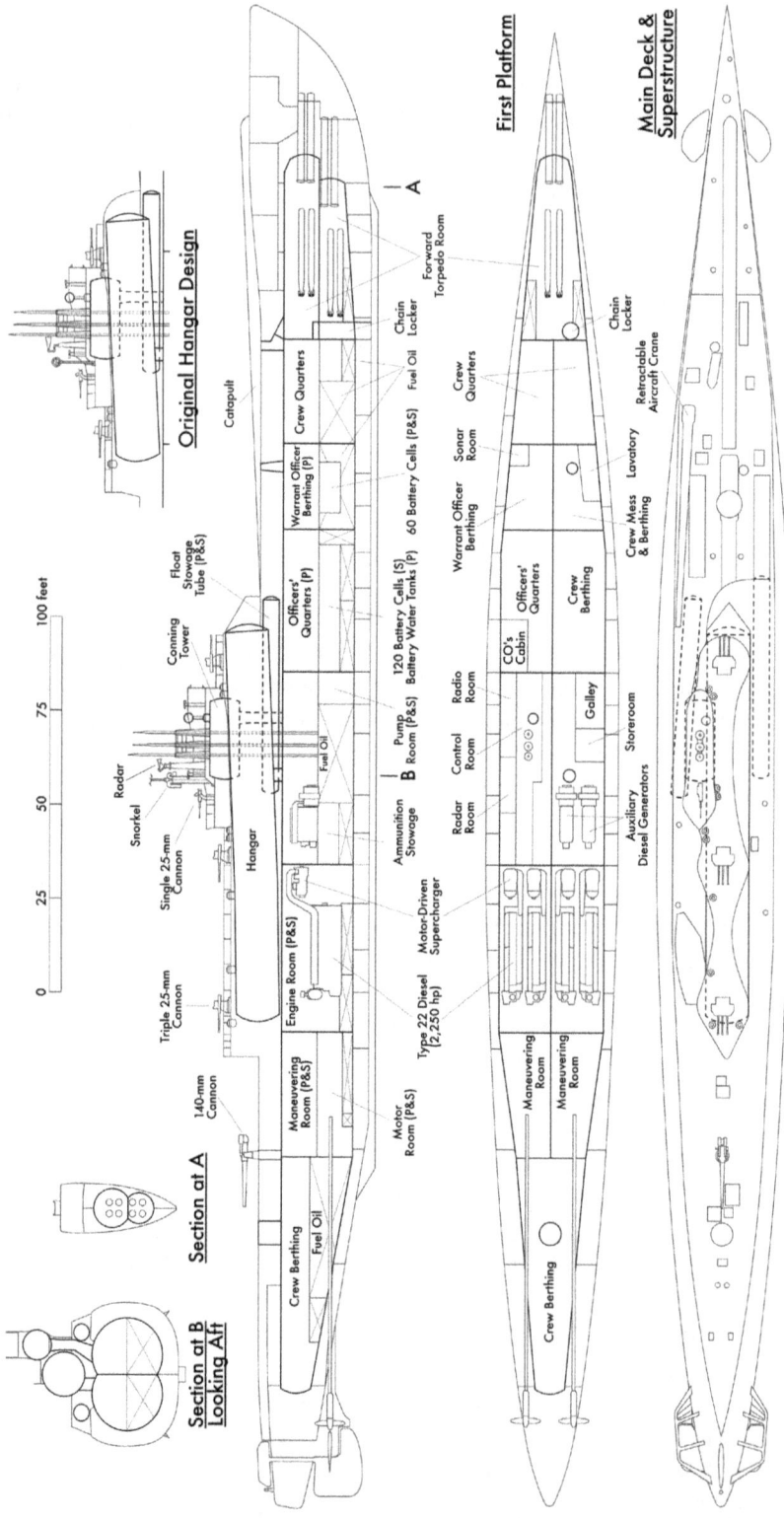

Original Hangar Design

First Platform

Main Deck & Superstructure

Section at A

Section at B
Looking Aft

0 25 50 75 100 feet

The Japanese *Sentoku* Type submarine (P = Port, S = Starboard). (©JACOB GUNNARSON)

Like many late-war Japanese undersea craft, the *Sentoku* submarines were fitted with snorkels, although the devices were significantly less advanced than contemporary German designs. Instead of feeding air to the powerful main diesels when submerged, the snorkel supplied two 536-horsepower auxiliary diesel generators that charged the batteries and provided current to the electric motors.[30] The submarines were fitted with air and surface search radars; they were significantly less effective than contemporary U.S. submarine radars.[31]

Despite their capacious hulls, the submarines provided few comforts for their crews. Initially designed for a complement of 145 men, the operational submarines were typically manned by more than 200 men.[32] For example, at sea the *I-401*'s crew consisted of 21 officers, 174 enlisted men, 6 pilots, and 3 aircraft technicians—a total of 204 men. Many of the crew slept on mats on the deck. The submarines' air-conditioning plants could not keep up with the tropical Pacific waters, forcing men to work shirtless, or when in the engine room to labor clad in only loincloths. The humidity was stifling, and the hangar had to be kept dry with desiccants to avoid damaging the *Seirans'* electronics.[33] The submarine's two "heads" (toilets) were simply holes cut in the tops of the sanitary tanks.

However, in contrast to the other sections of the submarine, the deck of the stern room, where most of the crew slept, had varnished wood flooring. Before entering, the crew would remove their shoes to walk on the dance-floor-like decking.[34]

On the surface their towering superstructures often caught the wind and pushed the huge submarines off course, although their large size made for smooth sailing through rough seas. Their size and high silhouette made the submarines easily detectable visually or by radar. Submerged, the drag from the conning tower—offset to port—required the helmsmen to steer to starboard. The bow and stern planes were undersized for such a large submarine, making depth control difficult unless the submarine was expertly trimmed.[35] The last was not an ideal characteristic for a 400-foot-long submarine that could quickly exceed its test depth of 328 feet if the dive angle were too steep.

The aircraft launching procedure of the *Sentoku* Type submarine was considerably improved over previous Japanese aircraft-carrying submarines. Once surfaced, the vault-like hangar door would be swung open. The *Seirans* rested on dollies that easily could be wheeled out of the hangar. Then the crew attached a hydraulic line from inside of the hangar to the aircraft's wing root and the wings quickly and automatically unfolded. A few turns of a hand crank locked the wings into place, and the tail stabilizers and rudder tip were unfolded and locked. The floats were rolled out of the pressure-tight containers under the deck and attached under the wings with quick-connect fittings.

U.S. Navy submariners inspect the bank vault–like hangar door on the *I-400*. (U.S. NAVY)

Inside the hangar the dolly was configured to keep the aircraft as low as possible; when on the catapult the dolly tilted upward to provide the *Seiran* with a better angle of attack for takeoff.[36] Once the dolly was attached to the catapult the pilot would start the engine and the aircraft would be catapulted off the submarine by compressed air.[37] All three aircraft could be launched within about 30 minutes of the submarine surfacing.

CONSTRUCTION CHALLENGES

Despite its swift progress, the *Sentoku* program quickly found detractors. Commander Shojiro Iura, a Naval General Staff officer who had briefed Fujita before his Oregon raids, questioned the need for such expensive submarines. The *Sentoku* submarines were conceived as an offensive weapon, but after the disastrous defeat at Midway in June 1942, Japan was fighting an increasingly defensive war with U.S. naval and air forces continuing to move closer to the Japanese home islands.

Iura advocated reducing the number of *Sentoku* submarines to two units and employing them to attack U.S. ships. He was countered by submarine constructor Captain Katayama, who pointed out that the materials for four *Sentoku* submarines already were on order.[38]

Greater threats to the project emerged after the aircraft carrying Admiral Yamamoto was shot down by U.S. fighters in the Solomon Islands in April 1943. The death of the Combined Fleet commander emboldened opponents within the Naval General Staff to again raise their objections to his ambitious submarine program. Chief among those detractors was Vice Admiral Shigeyoshi Miwa, a submariner who oversaw shipbuilding programs for the Naval General Staff. Thus, the planned number of *Sentoku* submarines was reduced from 18 to 10—still a significant program.[39]

At the time Japan was facing severe shortages of critical materials, which had already forced the Navy to install less powerful diesel engines and electric motors in submarines, and to construct their hulls with weaker grades of steel. Would the ability to conduct one or two terror attacks against the continental United States be worth sacrificing the resources needed for weapons critical to the defense of Japan?

Some of Admiral Yamamoto's acolytes remained, including Captain Kuroshima. Just as Yamamoto had asked him to investigate the *Sentoku* program's feasibility, Kuroshima assigned his staff officer—Lieutenant Commander Yasuo Fujimori—to determine the best method of moving forward with the aircraft-carrying submarine program. Fujimori realized that submarine production had to be consolidated as nearly a dozen types were under construction in mid-1943. To conserve resources and to speed production, he advocated concentrating on producing only three types:

- *Sentoku* Type aircraft-carrying submarines
- Type D cargo submarines
- *Sentaka* Type high-speed torpedo attack submarines

Fujimori also advocated for the *Sentoku* submarines' targets to be changed from American cities to the Panama Canal. Although air raids on New York or Washington possibly could cause panic, the canal was a far more significant strategic target. Every day more warships, troop ships, and even submarines passed through the canal from the Atlantic to the Pacific and the war against Japan. Passage through the canal was so crucial that the newest U.S. battleships were being built with beams only a few feet narrower than the width of the locks to avoid the long voyage around South America.[40]

Armed with Fujimori's plan, Captain Kuroshima was able to convince Admiral Miwa that the *Sentoku* program was necessary. To compensate for the limited number of submarines, Fujimori recommended lengthening the hangar

The *I-14*, one of the two completed Type A Mod. 2 submarines, comes alongside the *I-400* in Tokyo Bay after the end of the war. (U.S. NAVY)

to nearly 100 feet to accommodate a third aircraft, bringing the submerged displacement from 5,760 tons up to 6,560 tons.[41]

Fujimori persuaded Captain Katayama to complete the *I-400* at the Kure yard by the end of 1943, and the *I-401* and *I-402* at the Sasebo yard by the end of 1944.[42] To bolster the *Sentoku* submarine fleet, four Type A Mod. 1 submarines still on the building ways were modified to each carry two *Seiran* aircraft. Redesignated Type A Mod. 2, their outer hulls were widened 7 feet and their submerged displacement increased by 600 tons.[43] Six new-construction Type A Mod. 2 submarines were ordered in addition to the four already under construction, although they would be cancelled shortly after being ordered.[44]

Because of their advanced design and the small production planned, each M6A1 *Sieran* aircraft was hand built at the Aichi factory in Nagoya. Many of the workers were girls from a local high school, which had suspended classes to enable students to help in the war effort.[45] With Japan facing major shortages of almost all materials, Aichi was forced to make the *Seirans'* instrument panels and bombsights from wood instead of metal. Those difficulties, in addition to issues with the Atsuta engines, limited production to about one aircraft per month.

Compounding those difficulties, Nagoya came under attack by both nature and U.S. air forces. An earthquake rocked Nagoya on 7 December 1944, warping the jigs used to fabricate the *Seiran* wings. On 13 January 1945, another

THE ULTIMATE UNDERWATER CARRIERS 133

quake struck the city, damaging the *Seiran* production building. From December 1944 until the end of the war in August 1945, U.S. B-29 Superfortress bombers struck the city of Nagoya 56 times. The aircraft factory was not destroyed, although production was greatly slowed.[46]

Wartime shortages and the air raids also disrupted construction of the submarines. Only the *I-400* and *I-401* were completed as underwater aircraft carriers, in late 1944 and early 1945, respectively. The *I-402* was converted on the building ways to a submarine tanker for transporting desperately needed oil from the East Indies to Japan. She was completed in late July 1945, but did not become operational. Two additional *Sentoku* submarines—the *I-404* and *I-405*—were mostly complete when construction was halted in March 1945. Of the four planned Type A Mod. 2 aircraft-carrying submarines, only the *I-13* and *I-14* were completed; the *I-1* and *I-15* were never finished.

TARGET: PANAMA CANAL

The plan for the Panama Canal attack was drawn up in December 1944, with four submarines planned for the strike: the *I-400*, *I-401*, *I-13*, and *I-14*; their *Seiran* aircraft were organized into the 631st Air Group. The unit was under the command of now-Captain Ariizumi, one of the original architects of the *Sentoku* program. After his service with the Naval General Staff, Ariizumi commanded the aircraft-carrying submarine *I-8*. Under his command, the survivors of several ships torpedoed by the *I-8* were brutally massacred.[47] The British nicknamed him "The Butcher."

The captains of the *I-400* and *I-14*, Commanders Toshio Kusaka and Tsuruzo Shimizu, respectively, had also killed survivors of sinkings during their previous submarine commands. The skippers of the *I-13* and *I-401*, Commander Katsuo Ohashi and Lieutenant Commander Nobukiyo Nambu, respectively, later were judged innocent of such war crimes. Nambu had been the executive officer of the *I-17* when that submarine bombarded the Ellwood refinery in California.

The earthquakes affecting the Aichi factory in Nagoya meant that no *Seiran* aircraft were available for training when the 631st Air Group was formed. Instead, the airmen had to train with Aichi E16A *Zuiun* reconnaissance floatplanes (Allied codename Paul).

Because few of the flyers were combat veterans and most lacked dive-bombing training, the absence of the *Seirans* made their training difficult. By January 1945, the air group had five *Seiran* and six Paul floatplanes. The unit had no permanent base and flew from sandy beaches on the Inland Sea to avoid the U.S air attacks on major airfields. The *Seirans* were carefully hosed down to prevent saltwater corrosion; still, sand often fouled their engines and

Aichi built three *Seiran*s with landing gear to train pilots to fly without floats. The aircraft pictured is *Seiran* no. 6, which was tested in the United States after the war. (AUTHOR'S COLLECTION)

wing-folding mechanisms. The training itself was dangerous—two Pauls and one *Seiran* crashed in training flights, killing five men.

U.S. air strikes and the relentless sinking of merchant ships by U.S submarines severely affected Japanese submarine operations. The *Sentoku's* intended 40,000-n.mile range was reduced to 37,500 n.miles because of the poor quality of available fuel oil, which by the end of the war was in part synthesized from liquefied coal and soybeans. The aviation gasoline for the *Seirans* had to be cut with alcohol and turpentine.

Even those fuels were in short supply. The Kure naval base had only enough diesel fuel available for a single *Sentoku* submarine. Captain Ariizumi decided to sail the *I-401* to Dalian, China, to load fuel. A mock smokestack was installed on the submarine for a surface transit in an attempt to make the submarine less conspicuous to U.S. submarines and aircraft.

American B-29 bombers had mined the Inland Sea and the *I-401* struck a mine on 11 April 1945, one day after setting out for China. While the damage was minor, one of her fuel tanks developed a leak and the *I-400* sailed in her place. Her "costume" was more elaborate—crates were stacked on top of the catapult and dummy gun turrets in an attempt to disguise her as a destroyer. The *I-400* emerged from the Inland Sea unscathed and successfully completed her fueling operation.[48] In late May 1945, the *I-13* and *I-14* were sent to Chinkai in Korea, to fill their fuel tanks.

During the training for the Panama Canal attack, the Japanese Navy also considered a far more nefarious mission for the *Sentoku* submarines. In December 1944, Vice Admiral Jisaburo Ozawa, the deputy chief of the Naval

General Staff, conceived of a plan to attack the U.S. West Coast with *biological weapons* dropped from *Seirans*—Operation PX (also called Operation Cherry Blossoms at Night).

Although the Japanese Navy had its own biological warfare division, the Naval General Staff enlisted the help of Japanese Army specialists. The Army had considerable experience in that field, having purposely infected American and Chinese prisoners of war for several years with virulent diseases during weapon trials, and having employed biological weapons in China.[49]

The joint Army-Navy Operation PX plan was finalized in March 1945. Fleas carrying the bubonic plague would be dropped on American West Coast cities by submarine-launched aircraft. Operation PX abruptly was vetoed on 26 March by General Yoshijiro Umezu, the chief of the Army General Staff, who opposed it on ethical grounds: "Germ warfare against the United States would escalate to war against all humanity."[50] Lacking support from the Army, the operation was cancelled and planning continued for the "conventional" air attack on the Panama Canal.

The Japanese naval leadership knew that the Panama Canal would be heavily defended, although information from an interrogated American prisoner previously stationed there suggested that the defenses had been substantially scaled back from the early years of the war. A Japanese engineer who had worked on the canal provided documents detailing its layout and construction. While the locks on the Pacific side appeared on first inspection to be more vulnerable, emergency measures could bring damage there under control. However, the Gatun locks on the Atlantic side would be unable to stop the outflow of water if damaged, and that was estimated to stop shipping through the canal for six months.

The plan for the canal attack envisioned four aircraft-carrying submarines to sail from Japan to a location off the coast of Ecuador, about 200 miles south of Panama City.[51] According to the original plan, spaced 50 miles apart, the four submarines would launch their aircraft at 0300 on a moonlit night—eight armed with bombs and two with torpedoes. But none of the airmen except Takahashi were proficient in torpedo attacks; thus it was decided that all ten aircraft would carry bombs. The pilots would be given hormone injections to enhance their night vision.

Once assembled on the submarines and launched, the aircraft would fly at low altitude across Colombia and then turn south to strike the canal locks. Upon returning to the submarines the airmen would ditch their *Seirans* alongside and be taken aboard the submarines.

Takahashi in particular had problems with the plan: He thought it would be extremely difficult to get the aircraft into formation at night, especially since the submarines would be widely separated. Also, he noticed that the *Seirans* were being fitted with bomb racks without release mechanisms. Confronting the executive officer of the 631st Air Group, Lieutenant Commander Masayoshi Fukunaga, he learned that it had been decided in April to forgo conventional bombing and to use the *Seirans* as suicide aircraft against the canal locks. Takahashi did not voice a protest about the suicide mission, although he wondered why a *kamikaze* attack was necessary given that the canal locks were large, static targets, unlike moving U.S. warships that were the primary targets of suicide attacks.[52] The Naval General Staff decided that only suicide attacks would ensure that the bombs hit their targets in view of the lack of skill of most of the pilots.

Training for the mission began on the night of 6 June, when all of the submarines and aircraft had assembled in Maizuru Bay on the western coast of Japan. A wooden model of the canal locks had been built and was towed into the bay for practice attacks. During that training session two of the *Seirans* crashed, killing four additional airmen. Training was concluded on 19 June 1945, by which time the pilots felt confident in formation flying and making the attack run on the canal locks.

OPERATION *ARASHI*

When training for the Panama Canal attack had been completed, the target had again changed. The intense bombings by U.S. B-29 Superfortress bombers were devastating many of Japan's major cities and industrial facilities. On the night of 9/10 March 1945, B-29s dropped cluster and incendiary bombs on Tokyo that produced a massive conflagration with an estimated 100,000 people dying in that attack—more deaths than in either of the later atomic bombings of Hiroshima and Nagasaki. Many submarine officers wanted to strike San Francisco or Los Angeles with their *Seirans* in retribution for that Tokyo strike. That proposal was rejected by Navy headquarters.

The Panama Canal mission was cancelled. The more pressing danger was the threat of American aircraft carriers striking the Japanese home islands, adding to the carnage inflicted by the land-based Army Air Forces bombers. Further, to defend the homeland against the later American invasion threat, the Japanese high command initiated Operation *Ketsugo* (Decisive). The operation's first step was to use submarine-launched aircraft to attack forward bases where the U.S. invasion forces were being assembled.[53]

The foremost staging area for U.S. carrier task forces was Ulithi, an atoll in the Caroline Islands, 1,700 miles south of Japan. The coral atoll encircled a 200-square-mile lagoon and within that vast anchorage were scores of U.S. warships, literally as far as the eye could see. At its peak, Ulithi harbored more than 600 U.S. naval ships. Warships in the lagoon had previously been attacked without success by *kaiten* manned torpedoes in November 1944, and by *kamikaze* aircraft in March 1945. The Naval General Staff ordered a submarine-launched air attack on the Ulithi anchorage.

Operation *Arashi* (Storm) would begin with the *I-13* and *I-14* each carrying two disassembled Nakajima C6N *Saiun* (Allied codename Myrt) reconnaissance aircraft to Truk, 850 miles east of Ulithi. The four aircraft would be assembled, and taking off from land, would reconnoiter the anchorage.[54] Based on their reports, the *I-400* and *I-401* would launch their six *Seirans* on suicide attacks on the American ships on 17 August. Each *Seiran* would attempt to smash into an aircraft carrier. Then all four submarines would head to Singapore where they would refuel and take on replacement *Seirans* for subsequent attacks.

In recognition of their coming sacrifice, the 631st Air Group was given the honorific name Divine Dragon Special Attack Unit. A few days before the submarines sailed from Maizuru, the aircraft were covered in silver paint and U.S. insignia were painted on the *Seirans'* wings instead of the Japanese red *Hinomaru*. Takahashi and the other airmen were concerned, believing that since thousands of their comrades had died flying under the emblem of the rising sun, it was cowardly and dishonorable to use the deceptive U.S. markings. It also was a war crime.[55]

Lieutenant Commander Fukunaga, who had earlier failed to tell the airmen that they would be embarking on a suicide mission in the canal attack, was behind the repainting scheme. "The intense desire to succeed in the slim-chance attack overrode the shame of the acknowledgedly 'cowardly' tactic," in the words of the *Seiran* air group commander, Lieutenant Atsushi Asamura.[56] The false markings apparently were kept secret from other Japanese Navy personnel.

The *I-13*, carrying the two reconnaissance aircraft, sailed from Ominato in northern Japan on 11 July for Truk. The *I-14* remained in Ominato undergoing repairs to a propeller shaft bearing when U.S. carrier aircraft attacked. Again delayed to repair minor damage sustained during that attack, the *I-14* departed on 14 July.[57] The *I-400* and *I-401* sailed for Ominato on 20 July for provisioning. There the submarines were loaded with so much food that some passageways were nearly impassable. Also on board was an enormous quantity of sake to be consumed at Singapore after the first attack mission. The two aircraft-carrying submarines would take a circuitous route to Ulithi to avoid U.S. forces, first sailing southeast to rendezvous off Ponape in the Carolines and then sailing 1,300 miles westward to Ulithi.

The *I-14* reached Truk safely, although she was depth-charged by U.S. forces during her journey. Forced down by U.S. destroyers for 35 hours and with depleted batteries and air reserves, the submarine still managed to evade her attackers.[58] The *I-13* was not as fortunate: On 16 July, she was sighted on the surface by a TBM Avenger from the escort carrier *Anzio* (CVE 57). Struck with five-inch rockets when she was submerging, the submarine left an oil slick. More Avengers followed up the attack with sonobuoys, depth charges, and a Mark 24 homing torpedo. The I-13 finally was sunk by a hedgehog mortar barrage from the destroyer escort *Lawrence C. Taylor* (DE 415).[59]

The I-400 and I-401 sailed for Ulithi on 23 July; Captain Ariizumi sailed in the I-401. The two submarines were to proceed independently to reduce the probability of both being attacked and sunk. A few hours after leaving Ominato, the I-401 dived when she came under fire from a trigger-happy Japanese coastal gun battery. Although not suffering damage, the submarine remained submerged the following day.

From 28 to 30 July the submarines faced another menace—a tropical storm that thrashed the ungainly submarines. The I-400 was able to ride out the storm underwater, but the I-401 was hit harder. A week later wires—possibly loosened during the storm—sparked an electrical fire, forcing the I-400 to surface in sight of American ships. After crash-diving the fire was quickly extinguished, but the submarine was filled with smoke. Broaching just her conning tower, the submarine was vulnerable while ventilating and making repairs. But she remained undetected.

A week after the storm the I-401 was greeted by an ominous sight: A vast armada of U.S. warships steaming toward Japan. To avoid detection, Ariizumi decided to detour east of the Marshall Islands and to change the location of the submarine rendezvous point. The I-400 never received the I-401's message of the change of plans, and her captain never stopped at Ponape, instead reaching the attack point south of Ulithi on 13 August. The I-401 had been considerably slowed by her detour and waited for the I-400 off Ponape; the I-400 waited for her sister ship off Ulithi.[60]

TOTAL DEFEAT

The Pacific War ended on 15 August 1945. The submariners responded with disbelief to the message of surrender broadcast by the emperor. However, the Sixth Fleet had not transmitted any order to cease combat operations, and both submarine crews remained committed to the strike on U.S. warships at Ulithi. The I-401 immediately left the rendezvous point off Ponape for Ulithi. In the absence of radio communications, the submarines planned to attack independently.

On the evening of 16 August, the Sixth Fleet broadcast orders cancelling all combat activities. Further messages specifically terminated Operation *Arashi* and ordered the submarines to return to Japan. Both the I-400 and I-401 were hours away from launching their *Seirans* when they received those transmissions.[61] With some reluctance, particularly on the part of Captain Ariizumi,

The *I-400* (left) and *I-14* (right) tied up next to the submarine tender *Proteus* (AS 19) in Tokyo Bay. (U.S. NAVY)

the officers in both submarines agreed to sail home and surrender. They dumped their *Seirans* into the sea as the falsely marked aircraft might be used to try their crews for war crimes. Their bombs also were cast overboard, and the submarines' torpedoes were disarmed and launched.

The *I-14* and *I-400* surrendered to the U.S. destroyers *Murray* (DD 567) and *Dashiell* (DD 659) northeast of Tokyo Bay on 27 August. The *I-401* surrendered to the U.S. submarine *Segundo* (SS 398) south of Tokyo Bay two days later. Captain Ariizumi committed suicide after the *I-401* surrendered to avoid prosecution for his war crimes when he was on board the *I-8*.

The Japanese crews were in relatively good spirits and were helpful to the U.S. Navy personnel who came on board their submarines. In Tokyo Bay the three submarines moored alongside the submarine tender *Proteus* (AS 19) along with 12 American submarines. On 2 September, Vice Admiral Charles Lockwood, the commander of U.S. submarines in the Pacific, ordered his personal, three-star flag to be flown from the *I-400* during the formal Japanese surrender ceremonies on board the nearby battleship *Missouri* (BB 63).

The three aircraft-carrying submarines sailed from Sasebo for Pearl Harbor on 11 December 1945. Their American prize crews had been trained by the

Japanese sailors, but a great deal of improvisation was needed on the 3,400-n. mile journey. Upon arrival at Pearl Harbor on 6 January 1946, the submarines were carefully examined, and the *I-400* was drydocked for a detailed inspection.[62] Their overall design impressed the Americans, but their construction indicated poor workmanship and many of their systems were needlessly complex:

> This submarine, as in other modern types inspected, is a combination of good and bad shipbuilding, meticulous detail and complicated design, simplicity in main propulsion, carelessness in upkeep, radical departures from previous practice, and utilization of the oldest forms of mechanical advantage in operating gear.[63]

In Japan the Americans found several *Seirans* at the Aichi factory. Two were brought back to the United States for inspection: one land-based, wheeled trainer and one with floats.[64]

The U.S. Navy gave some thought to converting the three submarines to carry cargo and to be used operationally. The modifications would have cost an estimated $750,000 per submarine, not including replacement American batteries.[65] And the Soviet Union demanded that some of the submarines be handed over to their experts for examination. The United States wished to minimize the knowledge the Soviets could gain from captured Axis weapons; thus it was decided to scuttle all surrendered Japanese submarines—those at Pearl Harbor as well as others in Japanese ports. In late May and early June 1946, the *I-14*, *I-400*, and *I-401* were unceremoniously used as practice torpedo targets for American submarines.[66] The most impressive submarine aircraft carriers ever built sank into the dark abyss off Oahu.

The *Sentoku* submarines were among the most remarkable undersea craft ever constructed. Their enormous size would not be eclipsed until 1958, when the U.S. nuclear-propelled, radar picket submarine *Triton* (SSRN 586) was launched; the Japanese *Sentoku* submarine carriers were the largest nonnuclear submarines to be constructed.

Most significantly, those Japanese submarines were the first undersea craft intended for strategic attacks against an enemy's homeland. Their cruising range gave them the ability to strike from oceans anywhere on the globe. In those respects they presaged the development of the strategic cruise missile and ballistic missile submarines of the nuclear era.

CHAPTER 9

Underwater Tankers—Part 1

Only submarines of large displacement and with dedicated equipment could effectively serve as underwater aircraft carriers. Their aircraft had to be as small and as light as possible at the expense of performance and durability. The complexity of operating aircraft from submarines dissuaded most navies from pursuing the concept beyond initial experiments.

However, it soon was determined that submarines could covertly refuel and rearm seaplanes at sea in remote areas with few if any modifications to the submarines. That concept had considerable appeal to military planners, especially as the performance and weapons load of seaplanes improved over time. Japan, Germany, the United States, and the Soviet Union all experimented with employing submarines to provide stealthy and mobile seaplane support capabilities.

EARLY SOVIET EFFORTS

The Soviet Union probably was the first country to consider refueling seaplanes from submarines. On 20 May 1934, the deputy chief of the Soviet Navy, Ivan M. Ludri, approved plans to retrofit Type SHCH Series V submarines to serve as seaplane tankers. The Type SHCH boats were medium-size submarines of 700 tons submerged displacement and made up a large portion of the Soviet submarine force.

The dozen Series V boats were an improved version of the previous Type SHCH design, the Series III.[1] Their conversion consisted of modifying one of their main ballast tanks in the outer hull to store 2,000 gallons of aviation gasoline, enough to refuel three Tupolev R-6A/ANT-7 floatplanes or seven Beriev MBR-4 flying boats. Two 79-foot hoses would be streamed from folding booms on the submarine's stern. When rigged out the booms would be supported by floats; when not in use the booms folded forward, against the hull. Forced out of the storage tank with compressed air, gasoline could be delivered at a rate of up to 80 gallons per minute to the aircraft. Lubricating oil would be supplied to the aircraft in 4¼-gallon cans; 30 cans would be carried. Intended for use only in special operations, the refueling equipment was intended to be easily installed and removed.[2]

The refueling system remained only a concept and, apparently, was never provided to submarines.

THE SECOND STRIKE ON PEARL HARBOR

The Japanese Navy was another early proponent of the submarine-seaplane refueling concept. In the late 1930s several *Kiraisen* Type minelaying submarines were fitted with aviation gasoline tanks, including the *I-121* (formerly the *I-21*), which was the first Japanese submarine to carry an aircraft (see Chapter 5).

Before World War II, the *I-122* carried out a test refueling of a Kawanishi H6K four-engine flying boat (Allied codename Mavis).[3] Subsequently, the Navy initiated designs for the purpose-built *Senho* (Supply Submarine) Type, but did not begin construction of the submarines until 1943.

As Japanese submarines were preparing to sail for Hawaii in November 1941, in support of the carrier attack on Pearl Harbor on 7 December, the *I-23* transferred her floatplane to the *I-25* and was fitted with a tank for aviation gasoline aft of her conning tower to refuel seaplanes. Her seaplane refueling capability was not used during the attack on Pearl Harbor, but she and three other, similarly fitted submarines would take part in a second attack on Hawaii.

A few days after the 7 December attack, Commander Tatsukichi Miyo of the Naval General Staff pondered potential missions for the Navy's new

The *I-122* refuels a Kawanishi H6K Mavis flying boat in 1941, before the start of World War II in the Pacific. (AUTHORS' COLLECTION)

Two Kawanishi H8K1 Emily flying boats were used in the second air attack on Pearl Harbor—Operation K. To enable that long-range strike, the aircraft were refueled by submarines at the remote French Frigate Shoals. (AUTHORS' COLLECTION)

long-range, four-engine flying boat, the Kawanishi H8K1 (Allied codename Emily). One of the most impressive Japanese naval aircraft, the Emily—nick-named the "Flying Porcupine" because of its impressive array of defensive can-non and machine guns—was the fastest and most heavily armed flying boat of the Pacific War.

Commander Miyo realized that the aircraft—with a range of 4,475 miles and a 4,400-pound bomb load—was ideal for a second strike on Pearl Harbor.[4] He presented his plan to the Naval General Staff. Another strike on Pearl Harbor could disrupt the warship salvage and repair efforts at Pearl Harbor and could deliver another psychological shock to the United States. Perhaps the aircraft might hit one of the aircraft carriers that were missed by the first Pearl Harbor attack (none were in port on 7 December 1941).

From a base in the Marshall Islands, Hawaii was at the very limit of the fly-ing boat's range, thus Miyo envisioned the aircraft refueling from submarines in a remote lagoon closer to their target. The plan was enthusiastically accepted by the Naval General Staff in January 1942, and was labeled Operation K—the name derived from the Japanese code designation "AK" for Pearl Harbor.[5]

When the Japanese captured Wake Island from U.S. forces in December 1941, they captured a confidential U.S. Navy publication detailing seaplane landing areas in the Pacific. Based on that information, the French Frigate Shoals were selected for Operation K. That uninhabited atoll, 550 miles north-west of Oahu, had been a popular location for U.S. Navy seaplane exercises before the war, including refuelings of flying boats from submarines (see Chap-ter 10). On 24 January 1942, the *I-22* reported that the French Frigate Shoals were clear of U.S. forces.

The final Operation K plan called for several Emily aircraft to take off from Wotje atoll in the Marshall Islands, loaded with bombs, and fly 1,850 miles to the French Frigate Shoals. There they would be refueled by submarines and take off to strike Pearl Harbor. Relieved of their bomb load, the flying boats could return directly to Wotje. Attacks were planned for 1 March and for 6 March 1942.

Five submarines would take part in Operation K. The I-9, a Type A flagship submarine, would take up station halfway between Wotje and Hawaii to act as a radio navigation beacon and communications relay for the aircraft. The Type B submarines I-15, I-19, and I-26 would refuel the flying boats in the French Frigate Shoals; each was fitted with a 3,000-gallon fuel tank inside of their hangar. If their periscope observation of the Shoals revealed an American presence, the submarines would surface and destroy the enemy with their deck guns. The I-26 would be the backup refueling submarine, remaining outside of the atoll to warn of approaching U.S. forces. If the flying boats needed to refuel or ditch off of Oahu, the I-23 would be on "lifeguard" duty ten miles off Pearl Harbor.

However, as series production of the H8K1 Emily had just begun, only two preproduction aircraft were available for the attack. The submarines departed Kwajalein in early February. The attack was delayed several days because all submarines in the area were redirected to attack the U.S. carrier task force poised to attack the Japanese base at Rabaul in New Guinea. The Japanese submarines continued eastward after the American attack was cancelled due to the loss of the element of surprise.

The I-9 launched her E9W1 Slim floatplane on the night of 23 February for a reconnaissance flight over Pearl Harbor, but the airmen were unable to see through the clouds blanketing Oahu. The wings of the aircraft were damaged during recovery; thus there could be no second attempt to scout Pearl Harbor in advance of Operation K. The I-9 set sail for her radio beacon station. The I-15, I-19, and I-26 arrived at the French Frigate Shoals on 3 March.

Clear skies over the target were critical to the success of the attack as the Emily flying boats would rely on visual landmarks to aim their bombs with the large "Ten-Ten" wharf in Pearl Harbor being their aim point. The Japanese had broken the U.S. Navy's weather code and were able to decipher weather reports from Hawaii. However, a routine change of the weather code on 1 March left the attackers in the dark. Compounding problems, the I-23 had been on station just south of Oahu since early February, but had not been heard from since 24 February and was presumed lost. Thus, the Japanese were left without accurate weather information for Oahu. The weather over the French Frigate Shoals was clear; therefore the attack went ahead.

In the basement headquarters of Station Hypo, the U.S. Pacific Fleet's codebreaking unit at Pearl Harbor, the Americans were able to read portions of the main Japanese naval code. Hypo's analysts were all but certain that

Operation K would be an attack on Pearl Harbor on 4 March, although the exact nature of the operation was puzzling. Hypo had noted an unusual level of coordination between Japanese air and submarine units and the presence of Japanese submarines in the French Frigate Shoals.

Unaware of the existence of the long-range Emily flying boat, the codebreakers were not able to predict how Operation K would unfold. The commandant of the 14th Naval District, responsible for the defense of the Hawaiian Islands, was not informed of the possible impending attack; thus the Navy and Army defenses on Oahu would be caught unaware.[6]

The two Emily aircraft—piloted by Lieutenant Hisao Hashizume and Ensign Shosuke Sasao—took off from Wotje before dawn on 3 March, each laden with four 550-pound bombs. Guided by a radio beacon from the I-9, the flying boats alighted in the shoals just before sunset and retrieved the refueling buoys trailing behind the I-15 and I-19. At 2138 the aircraft took to the air for Pearl Harbor. Hashizume's aircraft incurred minor damage during takeoff, but both planes continued toward Pearl Harbor in the moonlight.

Shortly after midnight on 4 March a U.S. Army radar station on the island of Kauai detected the Japanese aircraft when they were 200 miles from Oahu. Within 30 minutes the defense forces on Oahu were ordered into action: PBY Catalina flying boats were dispatched to search for the Japanese aircraft carriers or seaplane tenders assumed to have launched the attack, and a flight of Army P-40 Warhawk fighters took off to defend Pearl Harbor.

The weather, clear during the evening and early night, turned overcast to the detriment of both attackers and defenders. The two Japanese flying boats passed over the coast of Oahu about 0200—undetected. They became separated because of miscommunications. The clouds, coupled with the blackout, forced the airmen to guess where to release their bombs. Through gaps in the clouds, Hashizume claimed he saw a battleship in drydock and a moored aircraft carrier and cruiser. Despite allegedly seeing those targets, his aircraft bombed the forest on the slopes of Tantalus ridge, nine miles east of Pearl Harbor. Sasao most likely dropped his bombs into the sea.

The only destruction inflicted in the attack were a few broken windows in Honolulu. The defending American fighters never sighted the Japanese attackers. Sasao headed back for Wotje, but Hashizume elected to fly to Jaluit atoll, 240 miles south of Wotje, which had better facilities to repair a hole in his aircraft's hull suffered on takeoff from the French Frigate Shoals.[7]

Because of the delay in launching the first attack and the time needed to repair Hashizume's aircraft, the planned second attack of Operation K was cancelled. Although unsuccessful, Operation K was the longest bombing mission carried out by any nation up to that time.

When the sun rose over Honolulu on 4 March, U.S. Army and Navy airmen began accusing each other of accidentally jettisoning bombs on Tantalus. The codebreakers at Station Hypo knew that the bombs were Japanese. When Captain Edwin Layton, the head of Pacific Fleet intelligence, called up Hypo in the morning, he asked the duty officer, Lieutenant Wilford J. (Jasper) Holmes, if he knew what had occurred the previous night. Holmes recounted,

> I did not, but I could guess that Japanese seaplanes had come in from the Marshall Islands, refueled from submarines at French Frigate Shoal, and then come in to bomb Oahu. "That's right," he replied, "and they copied the idea from Alec Hudson's story 'Rendezvous' in last August's *Saturday Evening Post*."[8]

Holmes had written that story two years earlier under a pen name. In "Rendezvous," American flying boats sortied from Hawaii to a fictional "Moab Atoll" 1,000 miles off the coast of Japan, where they were refueled by submarines. The flying boats then inflicted devastation on an unsuspecting Japanese naval base.[9]

The concept of submarines refueling seaplanes was suggested to Holmes in early 1940 by an editor of the *Saturday Evening Post* magazine. At first Holmes was reluctant to write about the subject as he suspected that the U.S. Navy was conducting such operations. He was correct: the submarine *Nautilus* (SS 168) had refueled flying boats on several occasions at the French Frigate Shoals, a location chosen specifically to keep the operations secret. However, other authors had published books and written stories about the possibility of seaplanes refueling from submarines, and Holmes decided to write the story. Although publication of the story initially was blocked by Navy censors, his two-part "Rendezvous" finally was published in two August 1941 issues of the *Saturday Evening Post*.

Holmes disagreed with Layton that "Rendezvous" had inspired Operation K, thinking that the similarities were simply a coincidence.[10] Given that the Japanese interest in refueling seaplanes using submarines predated the story by several years, Holmes likely was correct.

Not only was Operation K a failure; it provided the U.S. Navy's codebreakers at Station Hypo with a small piece of intelligence that would later influence the course of the Pacific War. The Japanese radio traffic surrounding Operation K contained references to code designators for many of the islands in the Hawaiian region. Subsequently, Hypo's officer-in-charge, Commander Joseph Rochefort, was able to pin down the Japanese designation "AF" for Midway.[11]

Two months later, Station Hypo and other U.S. Navy codebreaking units began to pick up indications of a looming Japanese offensive and hints of a second Operation K. The location of the offensive was unclear: the Japanese might strike in the South Pacific or attempt to attack and invade Oahu. On 13

May 1942, Hypo found the Japanese Navy's target—Midway—when the cryptologists intercepted a message ordering a supply ship to load equipment for the "K Campaign" at AF.[12]

Immediately following Operation K, the Japanese Navy had decided to embark on a repeat mission—Operation K-2—before the forthcoming assault on Midway atoll that was planned for the first week of June 1942. By attacking Midway, the fleet commander, Admiral Isoroku Yamamoto, intended to lure the U.S. fleet into a decisive confrontation.

On 30 May, several days before the planned Midway assault, Operation K-2 would determine which ships were in Pearl Harbor. When those ships sortied in response to the Japanese attack on Midway, two picket lines of submarines would engage the U.S. forces dispatched from Pearl Harbor. Again, two H8K1 Emily flying boats would perform the reconnaissance and bomb Pearl Harbor.

The Type B submarines that had taken part in Operation K already were assigned to reconnoiter the Aleutian Islands; therefore Operation K-2 employed three *Kiraisen* Type minelaying submarines that had been fitted with aviation gasoline tanks—the *I-121*, *I-122*, and *I-123*.[13] The refueling submarines would operate with three *Kaidai 6* Type attack submarines: the *I-171* would take up position east of the Shoals to act as radio beacon for the Emily flying boats, the *I-175* would be on station 80 miles southwest of Oahu to report on the weather, and the *I-174* would patrol 20 miles south of Oahu on "lifeguard" duty if the flying boats were forced to come down in the sea.[14] Once their mission was completed, the latter three submarines would race to the picket lines between Pearl Harbor and Midway to intercept the American fleet.

The refueling submarines departed Kwajalein between 19 and 25 May for the French Frigate Shoals. Arriving at the shoals on 29 May, the *I-123* sighted American patrol boats and seaplane tenders refueling PBY flying boats. The submarine radioed her observations, and it was decided to postpone Operation K-2 by one day to 31 May. On 30 May the *I-123* observed more ships and aircraft in the shoals, which prompted cancellation of the flying boat operation.[15]

Another Japanese failure of prebattle reconnaissance came with the late and scattered assembly of the submarine picket lines. The submarines arrived at the picket lines late due to poor operational planning and maintenance difficulties—taking station between 1 and 4 June instead of the planned 30 May.[16]

Admiral Yamamoto and Vice Admiral Chuichi Nagumo, commander of the Japanese carrier force, were aware of the breakdown of Operation K-2 and of the picket line issues. However, they saw little cause for concern. They believed that if Operation K-2 found Pearl Harbor empty the American carriers must be in the South Pacific, confirming prior intelligence. Conversely, if the carriers were present then complete surprise had been achieved.[17]

That restricted and overly optimistic mindset on the part of Japanese commanders and their staffs would have disastrous consequences. The Japanese commanders did not know that U.S. naval intelligence had broken the Japanese Navy's ciphers and that three U.S. carriers and several submarines would lay in wait for them at Midway.

Several weeks earlier, U.S. naval intelligence had determined that a second Operation K was being planned. Admiral Chester W. Nimitz, commander of the U.S. Pacific Fleet, had sent additional forces to the French Frigate Shoals to reinforce the seaplane tender *Ballard* (AVD 11), which had been stationed there shortly after the first Operation K.[18]

The aircraft carriers *Enterprise* (CV 6) and *Hornet* (CV 8) sailed from Pearl Harbor on 29 May, and the *Yorktown* (CV 5) departed one day later, sailing unseen through the area where the northern submarine picket line would assemble a few days later.[19] Capturing the element of surprise from the Japanese, the American carriers destroyed Nagumo's four-carrier force on 4 June. Although the failure of Operation K-2 ultimately did not contribute to Japan's defeat at Midway, it was symptomatic of the Japanese intelligence failure that did.[20]

No further Japanese attacks similar to Operation K were attempted. However, those submarines modified for refueling seaplanes did have a supporting role in the Guadalcanal campaign following the American landings on the island on 7 August 1942. From 14 September to 8 November, the *I-15*, *I-122*, and *I-26* refueled floatplanes in the Indispensable Strait, the 30-mile-wide body of water between Guadalcanal and Malaita in the Solomon Islands.[21] The submarines, transiting to and from the major base at Rabaul to load on fuel, could covertly supply the seaplanes without the conspicuous presence of a surface ship tender. The Aichi E13A (Allied codename Jake) floatplanes had flown to the strait to search for American warships in the Solomon Islands area while being refueled from the submarines.

The floatplanes had some success in tracking U.S. warships. On 13 October and again three days later, a Jake that was refueled by the *I-15* sighted the carrier *Hornet*. That intelligence contributed to the Battle of the Santa Cruz Islands one week later, the fourth major carrier battle of the war—in which the *Hornet* was sunk.

The *I-26* relieved the *I-15* on 18 October. That morning she refueled two floatplanes, and while one was taking off a U.S. patrol aircraft swooped over them. The second Jake scrambled to take off and the *I-26* crash-dived; she was damaged when her bow was crushed against a reef.

On 22 and 23 October, the *I-26* refueled three Jakes, which located an Allied convoy and the battleship *Washington* (BB 56). Two days later the refueling operations again were interrupted, that time by the appearance of an American B-17 Flying Fortress bomber, which forced the *I-26* to dive. She left the area the next day and was relieved by the *I-122*, which tended the seaplanes from 26 October to 8 November. The *I-122* conducted further floatplane refuelings in the Indispensable Strait in early February 1943. Those apparently were the last such floatplane refueling operations carried out by Japanese submarines.

SPECIALIZED SUBMARINES

Japan's first *Senho* Type purpose-built seaplane-refueling submarine—the *I-351*—was laid down at the Kure shipyard in May 1943. She was similar in size to the early aircraft-carrying types, 364 feet in length and displacing 4,220 tons submerged. The *Senho* Type was designed specifically to support the large H8K Emily flying boats operating in forward areas where neither shore facilities nor surface support ships were available.

The *I-351* could carry 132,000 gallons of aviation gasoline, 60 550-pound bombs or 30 bombs and 15 torpedoes, and 11 tons of fresh water for transfer to seaplanes. Six *Senho* Type submarines were planned; only three were laid down with only the *I-351* entering service. Her sister ship—the *I-352*—was 90 percent complete when a U.S. B-29 Superfortress bombing raid sank the submarine at Kure in June 1945.[22]

The *Senho* Type submarine *I-351* in drydock. Designed to resupply flying boats with gasoline and munitions, six submarines of this type were planned, but only the *I-351* was completed. (AUTHORS' COLLECTION)

The *I-351* never refueled seaplanes. Like many of the Japanese Navy's large submarines, near the end of the war she was employed for critical cargo and fuel transportation. Her first voyage, in May 1945, brought aircraft parts, ammunition, and clothing from Kure to Singapore. She returned to Sasebo in early June with a load of aviation gasoline that was needed for *kamikaze* operations. She sailed again for Singapore in late June and began her return journey back to Japan on 11 July carrying 43 aviators and, presumably, more aviation fuel.

Shortly before midnight on 14–15 July, in the South China Sea, the U.S. submarine *Blower* (SS 325) made a radar detection of the surfaced *I-351*. Submerging after detecting radar emissions from the Japanese submarine, the *Blower* fired two torpedoes, both of which struck their target—but did not detonate. The *I-351* dived and the *Blower* radioed the contact information to the nearby submarine *Bluefish* (SS 222). Several hours later the *Bluefish* detected, pursued, torpedoed, and sank the *I-351*. The next morning the *Bluefish* picked up three survivors of the 113 men on board the Japanese submarine.[23]

ARCTIC U-BOAT TANKERS

There was major cooperation between the German Navy's U-boat arm and the *Luftwaffe* in the Arctic theater, despite the rivalry between the German armed services during World War II. Allied convoys to the Soviet Union's Arctic ports delivered crucial war materiel from the United States and Britain to the USSR. Those convoys, sailing north of German-occupied Norway en route to Murmansk and Arkhangel'sk, were lucrative targets for German aircraft, surface ships, and U-boats operating from bases in Norway. The Germans initially achieved success in attacking Allied shipping in the Barents Sea and began venturing farther east into Soviet waters to seek out targets.

In August 1942, the German Navy planned Operation *Wunderland* (Wonderland)—a surface force with the heavy cruiser *Admiral Scheer* sailing from Narvik in northern Norway was to sweep through the Kara Sea. Previously the Germans had hunted only in the Barents Sea, which was kept free of ice by warm ocean currents, but had not ventured past Novaya Zemlya archipelago into the icy Kara Sea. The northern shipping route connecting the Soviet Far East and Northern Fleet bases was thought by the Germans to significantly contribute to the Soviet war effort. In Operation *Wunderland*, the *Admiral Scheer*, three destroyers, and several U-boats were to interdict merchant ships in the Kara Sea.

To provide reconnaissance for *Wunderland*, the Type VIIC submarine *U-255* was teamed with a Blohm & Voss BV 138, an odd-shaped, twin-boom flying boat propelled by three diesel engines. Although officially named the *Seedrache* (Seadragon), the aircraft's bulbous fuselage earned it the nickname *fliegender Holzschuh* (Flying Clog). Its three Junkers Jumo diesel engines had exceptional fuel efficiency, providing the BV 138 with an endurance of 18 hours and a range up to 2,500 miles. Ideal for long-range maritime patrol, the diesel engines also allowed the BV 138 to refuel directly from a U-boat's fuel tanks.

On 4 August 1942, the *U-255*, under the command of *Kapitänleutnant* Reinhart Reche, departed Bergen, Norway, for the remote Svalbard archipelago, where she would meet her BV 138 reconnaissance partner. On 11 August 1942, the U-boat was in position off Svalbard, but even at the height of summer there was too much ice for the flying boat to alight on the water and it returned to a Norwegian base. The following day the *U-255* found an ice-free area near Wilhelm Island, and the BV 138 returned and came down at sea. The *U-255* took the floating BV 138 under tow; lines for diesel and lubricating oil were passed to the flying boat, and the airmen came on board the submarine to eat and sleep.[24]

Due to worsening ice conditions, the *U-255* was ordered to leave Svalbard and head south. On taking off on 16 August, the flying boat's engines almost immediately sputtered and stalled, forcing an emergency landing. With help from the U-boat's engineers, the airmen quickly found the problem: As the submarine consumed diesel fuel, seawater was added into the tanks to compensate for the decreased weight and volume of fuel. The U-boat's piping system

The *U-255* provided fuel, food, mechanics, and relief crewmen for the flying boats. The teaming of U-boats and BV 138s worked well but ultimately provided little useful reconnaissance information in the remote seas of the Soviet Arctic. (BIBLIOTHEK FÜR ZEITGESCHICHTE)

ensured that no seawater was fed into the submarine's own engines, but the BV 138's designers had never anticipated the possibility that the aircraft's fuel tanks would be filled with anything other than pure diesel fuel.

Kapitänleutnant Reche wanted to tow the BV 138 to a sheltered bay to make repairs. He briefly considered carrying the flying boat on the submarine's afterdeck. Taking the flying boat in tow, the tow ropes broke repeatedly and efforts to reaffix them damaged the aircraft's port wing. Meanwhile the aircraft's wing floats slowly filled with water. As the *U-255* neared the calm waters of a secluded bay, the BV 138 capsized. The submarine picked up the airmen from the water and scuttled the flying boat with gunfire. Reche summarized, "working with a BV 138 was an especially challenging navigational and seamanship task which also brought worthwhile technical experience; better preparation of the flying boat operations would have spared its loss."[25]

Operation *Wunderland* went ahead without BV 138 reconnaissance. The German warships achieved little in the Kara Sea, sinking only a few Soviet merchant ships and icebreakers. Poor weather and encroaching ice ended the operation in late August. The *U-255* continued her patrol and shelled a Soviet radio station on Novaya Zemlya, but otherwise had no contact with the enemy.

One year later the German Navy planned Operation *Husar* (Hussar), effectively a repeat of *Wunderland* with the *Admiral Scheer*'s sister ship *Lützow*.[26] The *Lützow*'s involvement was cancelled in July 1943, when problems were discovered with her diesel engines.[27] The German assault on the Kara Sea would be carried out solely by U-boats.

Those submarines would be aided by reconnaissance from a BV 138, which would be replenished by the Type VIIC submarines *U-601* and the *U-255*, the latter now commanded by *Oberleutnant zur See* Erich Harms. Both U-boats carried an extra flight crew so that the seaplane could fly around-the-clock, landing only to refuel and exchange crews. The submarines also carried a *Luftwaffe* officer to coordinate the operation, aircraft mechanics, and meteorologists.[28] The *U-255* would be the primary refueling submarine with the *U-601* her backup.

On 27 July, while searching for a suitable seaplane base on the northern end of the Novaya Zemlya archipelago, the *U-255* encountered a Soviet survey ship, which she sank with her deck gun. Three days later the submarine anchored in a shallow bay off Cape Sporyy Navolok that offered some concealment from passing ships. Camouflage netting was strung over the *U-255*'s conning tower and deck, and Harms found a shallow area where the submarine could lie on the bottom with just the conning tower exposed. Crewmen took shifts manning a makeshift lookout post on a low headland on the south side the bay, scanning the waves for the Soviet ships and aircraft. A Soviet Catalina flying boat flew directly over the *U-255* and failed to sight the concealed submarine.[29]

A BV 138 floats aft of the camouflaged *U-255* in a secluded bay in Novaya Zemlya.
(BIBLIOTHEK FÜR ZEITGESCHICHTE)

The BV 138 arrived at the bay on 4 August after flying 950 miles from its base in Norway. So effective was the U-boat's camouflage that the aircraft flew right over the *U-255* without sighting her until the submarine shot off a signal flare. For the next three days the BV 138 flew daily reconnaissance missions across the Kara Sea, reporting on ice conditions for the rest of the Operation *Husar* warships. The U-boat provided fuel, maintenance, and relief crewmen. But the wind began to pick up from the east, creating low swells and rough water that prevented the BV 138 from taking off until 12 August. The aircraft sighted neither ice nor targets. The *U-255* was resupplied by the *U-601*, which then took up station in a bay on the west coast of Novaya Zemlya.

High waves prevented the BV 138 from taking off to fly back to Norway until 20 August. Two hours after the aircraft departed the bay, the *U-255* and *U-601* picked up an emergency radio message from the flying boat: the BV 138 had made an emergency landing off the west coast of Novaya Zemlya. The *U-601* found the BV 138 eight hours later. Despite high winds and heavy swells, the submarine's crew managed to affix a line to the flying boat—which promptly snapped. The aircraft rode lower in the water as waves washed over it.

Without warning two Soviet bombers appeared overhead. The Soviet aircraft failed to notice the Germans. It became clear that the sinking aircraft could not be saved. After rescuing the aircraft's crew the BV 138 was scuttled.[30]

The *Luftwaffe* attempted to send a replacement BV 138, but bad weather prevented its arrival at Cape Sporyy Navolok until 4 September. Reconnaissance

The *U-255* tows a foundering BV 138 flying boat off the coast of Novaya Zemlya on 20 August 1943. The aircraft subsequently was scuttled by gunfire. (BIBLIOTHEK FÜR ZEITGESCHICHTE)

flights on the next two days revealed only empty sea and fog. On 10 September the flying boat's radar broke, and it returned to Norway; another BV 138 flew out to the *U-255*. Returning from a long reconnaissance flight over the Kara Sea, that flying boat was unable to find the fog-shrouded bay due to a compass error and put down on the open ocean 260 miles to the northwest.

The *U-255* put to sea in search of the aircraft and was joined by the *U-307* and *U-629*. After a day of searching, the *U-307* located the BV 138 and rescued its crew. The *U-255* arrived on the scene and Harms decided to tow the flying boat to nearby Franz Joseph Land. After a few hours it became clear that it was impossible to tow the BV 138, and the *U-255* sank it with gunfire.

On 14 September, the *U-255* received a message ending seaplane operations in the Kara Sea. During Operation *Husar* the U-boats sank only a handful of Soviet merchant ships. Although the BV 138 did provide useful ice reconnaissance, none of the flying boats sighted Soviet ships.

Japan and Germany undertook intensive efforts to employ submarines to refuel and support flying boats, both for bombing attacks and for reconnaissance operations. While the submarines were well operated and the aircraft were well flown, their "coupling" proved to be extremely difficult. Technical issues, rough seas, and bad weather all interfered with those operations. Still, efforts to combine the capabilities of submarines and aircraft would be continued by other navies.

CHAPTER 10

Underwater Tankers—Part 2

As the United States began contemplating a Pacific war against Japan in the aftermath of World War I, the flying boat emerged as an important component of the U.S. Navy's strategy. Long-range flying boats could have a crucial role in patrolling the vast expanse of the Pacific. But some American naval officers foresaw a more decisive role for the big seaplanes: They envisioned a strike force of flying boats laden with torpedoes and bombs that could deliver devastating attacks on the Japanese fleet.

The flying boats could be a flexible strike force if properly supported by seaplane tenders and thus able to shift rapidly to different combat areas. A seaplane striking force could constitute a significant portion of the Navy's offensive aviation capability in view of the limitations placed on aircraft carriers by the Washington Naval Treaty of 1922.

The seaplane striking force never fully materialized between the world wars or during World War II. The U.S. Navy's principal long-range flying boat by the late 1930s was the Consolidated PBY Catalina, an excellent, twin-engine aircraft with a 2,500-mile range and capable of carrying 4,000 pounds of torpedoes, bombs, or depth charges. However, the PBY was slow and vulnerable, and there were not sufficient tenders to support the envisioned seaplane striking force.

With a limited number of seaplane tenders it would be difficult to carry out wide-ranging attacks with flying boats, leading the Bureau of Aeronautics (BuAer) to investigate other types of ships to support the seaplanes. In June 1937, BuAer proposed modifying a submarine to refuel up to six seaplanes during a single patrol. Minor repairs and maintenance could be carried out by submerging underneath the aircraft and lifting it out of the water. The submarine *Nautilus* (SS 168) was selected for modification during her planned overhaul in the winter of 1937–1938 at the Mare Island Navy Yard in California.[1]

The cruiser submarine *Nautilus* (SS 168) was the first U.S. Navy submarine to be modified to refuel seaplanes. One of her main ballast tanks was altered to carry nearly 60 tons of aviation gasoline. (NATIONAL ARCHIVES)

One of the submarine's main ballast tanks was converted to store 19,320 gallons of aviation gasoline, enough to fully refuel a squadron of 12 PBYs.[2]

The *Nautilus*'s new capability was quickly put to the test: During 1938 the U.S. Navy held Fleet Problem XIX, a large-scale exercise off the California coast and the Hawaiian Islands. From 22 March to 2 April, the submarine operated in the French Frigate Shoals in the northwestern Hawaiian Islands, specifically chosen for its remote location so that the refueling operations could be kept secret from foreign observers.[3] The *Nautilus* transferred some of her aviation fuel to the small seaplane tender *Avocet* (AVP 4) and then began refueling PBYs, which searched for the "enemy" fleet in the exercise.[4] Encouraged by that successful refueling operation, in March 1939, the Commander-in-Chief, U.S. Fleet ordered the *Nautilus* to conduct refueling exercises with PBYs on a regular basis.[5] The submarine sailed to the French Frigate Shoals to refuel flying boats in May, August, and October 1939.[6]

In April 1940, the *Nautilus* took part in Fleet Problem XXI, a simulated defense of Hawaii. The submarine was stationed off Johnston Island, a small atoll 820 miles southwest of Pearl Harbor, with the seaplane tender *Swan* (AVP 7). On 19 April, the submarine transferred 5,800 gallons of aviation gasoline to the *Swan*. The next day they were "attacked" by the "enemy" and the *Swan* was "sunk" by opposing aircraft and warships. The appearance of the opposing forces precluded the refueling of flying boats, and the submarine returned to Pearl Harbor.[7]

Although tending to PBYs was a relatively simple operation, the process was time consuming: fully refueling a 12-plane PBY squadron was estimated to take 6½ hours. Still, following a successful exercise at the French Frigate Shoals in October 1940, in which the *Nautilus* refueled an entire PBY squadron, her refueling capability was judged "mature." The commander of the Navy's Scouting Force considered it of "greatest strategic importance" that more submarines be equipped to refuel seaplanes.[8] The large submarines *Argonaut* (SM 1) and

Narwhal (SS 167) were modified to refuel seaplanes. In addition, 24 *Gato* (SS 212)-class fleet submarines were authorized to be built with the capacity for 9,576 gallons of aviation gasoline (SS 217–227, 240–252).[9] They also were fitted with a watertight trunk above their after engine room to store the fueling hoses.

Early Sunday morning on 7 December 1941, four PBY Catalina flying boats lifted off the calm waters of Pearl Harbor. The aircraft set course to the southeast for Lahaina Roads, a sheltered anchorage between the Hawaiian islands of Maui, Molokai, and Lanai. They were to conduct refueling and rearming exercises with a submarine.[10] However, none of the submarines able to refuel seaplanes were available: the *Argonaut* was patrolling near Midway, the *Narwhal* was being overhauled at Pearl Harbor, and the *Nautilus* was in dry dock at Mare Island. The only submarines in Lahaina Roads that morning were Japanese. Thus, the planned exercise must have involved simulated refueling operations without the cooperation of a submarine.

After being notified of the attack on Pearl Harbor, the four PBYs conducted fruitless searches for the Japanese carriers. They then returned to their base on Ford Island, at the center of the still-smoldering naval installation.

Only one instance of a U.S. submarine refueling a flying boat was recorded during all of World War II: The *Argonaut* was converted to a troop-carrying submarine (APS 1) in early 1942, but she retained her aviation fuel tanks.[11] On 16 December 1942, she carried out an experimental refueling of PBYs in Sandwich Lagoon in the New Hebrides.[12] The potential for follow-on refueling operations ended when the *Argonaut* was sunk by Japanese destroyers near Rabaul on 10 January 1943.

The two dozen *Gato*-class submarines completed between 1942 and 1944 with gasoline tanks never refueled seaplanes; their primary mission of sinking Japanese warships and merchant shipping always took precedence. The gasoline lines were blanked off and the tanks were used for diesel fuel.

One of those submarines did make use of her unique capability to store aviation gasoline: In the fall of 1942, U.S. Marines were in a fierce struggle to hold Guadalcanal in the Solomon Islands and their air support, based at the island's Henderson Field, was running low on fuel. Normal tankers were thought to be too vulnerable to Japanese forces to resupply the airfield, thus the submarine *Amberjack* (SS 219) was given the task. On October 22, after cleaning and re-plumbing the tanks, the *Amberjack* was loaded with 9,000 gallons of aviation gasoline. She also carried 15 Army fighter pilots and 200 100-pound bombs. En route to Guadalcanal she was redirected to nearby Tulagi, where she offloaded her cargo on 25 October.[13] None of the 23 other modified fleet submarines carried gasoline during the war and many had their gasoline tanks permanently converted to store diesel fuel.

Two years later, in September 1944, Admiral Nimitz endorsed a proposal for a seaplane-refueling submarine. That proposal did not come to fruition during the war.[14]

POSTWAR DEVELOPMENTS

The PBY Catalina had served the U.S. Navy well during the war. Effective at reconnaissance and attacking enemy island targets and ships, the ungainly flying boat proved invaluable in many theaters of the war. Still, the PBY and other flying boats had inherent limitations in speed, range, and payload compared to land-based bombers, due in large part to their drag-inducing, boat-like hulls and stabilizing floats. However, advances in aircraft design after World War II promised to revolutionize the performance of flying boats.

Research in Germany and the United States in the 1930s and 1940s had determined that flying boats with high length-to-beam ratios had both superior aerodynamic and hydrodynamic properties (most flying boats of the period like the PBY had stubby hulls with relatively small length-to-beam ratios).[15] Flying boats had the potential to equal the performance of their land-based counterparts when coupled with the turbojet engine.

The promise of high-performance seaplanes breathed new life into the concept of a seaplane striking force. Within the U.S. armed forces the newly established Air Force possessed the only means of nuclear weapons delivery with long-range bombers; having that capability in the "nuclear age" threatened to decimate the Navy's budget. The Navy had planned a "super carrier"—the United States (CVA 58)—that would be able to carry nuclear-armed bombers, but that ship was cancelled in 1949, five days after being laid down, due in large part to political opposition from the Air Force. The Navy had to find other means of developing a viable nuclear striking force.

The Navy initially explored three means of nuclear weapons delivery: guided missiles, aircraft launched from aircraft carriers, and a seaplane striking force. All three could involve submarines to varying degrees: Submarines would be the primary launch platform for guided missiles and were considered as submersible carriers for nuclear strike aircraft (see Chapter 12). And submarines as well as surface ships could refuel and rearm a seaplane striking force.

The seaplane striking force was particularly attractive in the atomic age. Flying boats could use the world's oceans as airfields—a vast and invulnerable base from which to strike the Soviet Union. Also, refueling submarines could be covertly located near the Soviet coasts to extend the range of seaplane strike aircraft to attack targets beyond the range of land-based bombers.

The U.S. Navy initiated development of a trio of jet-powered flying boats for the seaplane striking force: The Convair P5Y/R3Y Tradewind patrol/transport aircraft, the Convair F2Y Sea Dart fighter, and the Martin P6M Seamaster minelayer/bomber. The Seamaster would serve as the nuclear strike component of the force, with the Sea Dart providing fighter cover over the at-sea bases and the Tradewind transporting men and supplies to those bases.[16] The aircraft were intended to be resupplied by submarines and surface ships and, in the case of the Sea Dart, launched from submarines.

CONVAIR TRADEWIND AND SEA DART

The Convair Tradewind was the U.S. Navy's first jet-propelled flying boat. In June 1946, Convair—the merger of the Consolidated and Vultee firms—received a Navy contract to build two prototype turboprop flying boats for the maritime patrol and anti-submarine roles. Designated P5Y, the four-engine aircraft was developed using data from the Blohm & Voss BV 222 *Wiking* (Viking) obtained from Germany after World War II. Despite problems with its turboprop engines, the P5Y had exceptional hydrodynamic characteristics due to its slender hull and achieved a speed of 354 miles per hour, a previously unimaginable figure for a flying boat. (The maximum speed of the Navy's newest flying boat at the time—the Martin P5M Marlin—was 269 mph.)

Only two XP5Y-1 prototypes were built before the Navy shifted its focus for the design to a transport aircraft. Convair modified the P5Y design into the slightly larger R3Y-1 Tradewind, which could carry 90 troops; an "assault

Convair's R3Y-1 Tradewind was the cargo and troop-carrying component of the Seaplane Striking Force. (U.S. NAVY)

transport" variant—the R3Y-2—had cargo space and a hinged bow for loading vehicles. Eleven transport Tradewinds were built: five R3Y-1s and six R3Y-2s, with the latter subsequently being converted to in-flight tankers. The Tradewinds were envisioned to provide logistical support to the flying boat bases afloat as well as amphibious operations.[17]

The fighter component of the seaplane striking force stemmed from a 1946 contract issued by the Bureau of Aeronautics to Convair to study advanced seaplane design concepts. Convair began by modifying its XB-46 turbojet bomber design by blending the fuselage into the wings. The engines were moved from wing-mounted pods to a position buried within the widened hull. The broad, flat hull created a large planning surface, which had less aerodynamic drag than the deep hulls of traditional flying boats. Retractable "spray dams" on the bottom of the hull aided takeoff performance while minimizing drag when airborne.[18] Because of its resemblance to a ray, the design was christened the Skate. Convair's design evolved through several iterations, Skate 1 through Skate 9.[19]

Stimulated by Convair's promising research, BuAer issued a requirement in 1948 for a turbojet-powered, radar-equipped night fighter able to be refueled and rearmed from surface ships and submarines. Both Convair and Curtiss-Wright submitted design proposals. Curtiss-Wright's design had a single engine and used hydro-skis—retractable skis that lifted the aircraft off the water during takeoff. Hydro-skis permitted takeoff on rougher water than traditional flying boat hulls. Convair submitted its Skate design, which was judged superior to the Curtiss-Wright design in almost every respect.[20]

However, the Navy elected not to procure the Skate, citing budgetary shortfalls. Instead, Convair would continue research on the Skate and other advanced seaplane concepts. Scale models of the Skate underwent extensive testing at the Convair facility on San Diego Bay with all aspects of takeoff, flight, and landing being tested with remote-control models. In 1952, Convair built a ⅒th scale mockup of a fleet-type submarine that could accommodate a Skate in a cradle on the afterdeck, enabling the aircraft to be securely held while being maintained. A small crane could be used to remove the engines for repair or maintenance. No hangar was provided. Ultimately the Skate was considered to have been too large, too expensive, and would have had poor rough-water landing characteristics.[21]

In parallel with the Skate, Convair developed two turbojet seaplanes for the ground-attack role: the subsonic Cudda and supersonic Betta. The Cudda had conventional swept wings instead of the Skate's blended wings, and later iterations had hydro-skis for takeoff and landing. The dart-like Betta had a sharply swept delta wing, resembling Convair's experimental XF-92 interceptor built for the Air Force.[22]

A ¹/₁₀th-scale mockup of the Convair Skate resting on a model fleet submarine. The Skate was intended to be resupplied and serviced by submarines. Its development halted in favor of the supersonic F2Y Sea Dart. (CONVAIR AIRCRAFT CORP)

The Betta's supersonic performance was particularly enticing to BuAer. Most early supersonic aircraft had high landing speeds, required long runways, and were difficult to control at low speeds. As a result, it was considered unlikely that supersonic jets could be operated from carriers. A supersonic seaplane, however, would be able to use water runways of unlimited length.

Convair was awarded a contract in early 1951 to build a prototype of a supersonic seaplane fighter based on the Betta: the F2Y Sea Dart.[23] Using twin Westinghouse J46 afterburning turbojets, the Sea Dart promised a level of performance never before achieved by a seaplane—a supersonic speed of Mach 1.4. At rest the fuselage and wings provided floatation, while during takeoff the aircraft was lifted off the water by twin hydro-skis that extended from the fuselage. Takeoff was possible in waves up to five feet.[24]

The Sea Dart would be armed with four 20-mm cannon or rockets, and the development of lightweight nuclear weapons could have potentially provided a nuclear strike capability. A smaller, single-engine variant of the Sea Dart was designed as a nuclear strike aircraft to operate from submarines (see Chapter 12).

Twelve F2Y-1 Sea Dart aircraft were ordered, but only five prototypes were completed.[25] A fatal crash in 1954 had stalled high-performance tests and the hydro-skis were problematic. While an impressive engineering achievement,

An XF2Y-1 Sea Dart taxiing on hydro-skis. The futuristic-looking Sea Dart was the first seaplane to promise supersonic performance. (U.S. NAVY)

the Sea Dart was hampered by underpowered engines and a fuselage designed before the "area rule" concept, which dramatically reduced supersonic drag. In level flight the Sea Dart was unable to reach Mach 1. Those limitations, compounded by a lack of funding, led to the program's cancellation in 1956. Supersonic carrier-based aircraft, such as the Grumman F11F Tiger and Vought F8U Crusader, were entering service and were more capable in every respect.

Still, Convair continued to develop Sea Dart, producing an improved attack version—the "Tactical F2Y"—with radar, more powerful engines, an area-ruled fuselage, a second seat, and internal stowage for a small nuclear bomb. Along with concepts to convert cruisers and light aircraft carriers to become Sea Dart tenders, Convair proposed converting fleet submarines to resupply the improved Sea Dart. Two Sea Darts would taxi up a ramp on the submarine's stern to refuel and rearm. A turntable fitted in the submarine's deck would rotate the aircraft around to taxi off the stern. The operation was predicted to take just 24 minutes. Despite Convair's efforts, the Navy was no longer interested in supersonic seaplane fighters.[26]

THE MARTIN SEAMASTER

The nucleus of the seaplane striking force envisioned to conduct nuclear strikes on the Soviet Union was the Martin P6M Seamaster. It was one of the most impressive flying boats ever developed.

The Martin Company had a long history of successful flying boat designs, especially the PBM Mariner that operated alongside the PBY Catalina in World War II. The subsequent P5M Marlin was an improved PBM design that incorporated the aero- and hydrodynamics of the German BV 222 with advanced engines for enhanced performance.[27]

The Seamaster originated from a 1951 requirement of the Bureau of Aeronautics for a seaplane minelayer. It was envisioned that squadrons of turbojet seaplanes could mine the approaches to Soviet naval bases, preventing ships and submarines from leaving or returning to rearm.[28] Although ostensibly a minelayer, the aircraft also could have a nuclear strike capability. Both Convair and Martin submitted designs for the aircraft, with Convair proposing an evolved version of its earlier Cudda design. The Martin entry was declared the winner.

The P6M Seamaster had a long, slim hull and four turbojet engines mounted above swept wings. The bomb bay could accommodate up to 30,000 pounds of mines, bombs, or photo-reconnaissance equipment.[29] The Seamaster was intended to operate at sea for up to eight months and, accordingly, it was designed to be refueled, rearmed, and maintained on the water. The bomb bay

The Martin YP6M-1 Seamaster taxiing on the water. Its impressive performance nearly equaled that of contemporary land-based based bombers. (GLENN L. MARTIN MARYLAND AVIATION MUSEUM)

was top-loading to permit rearming while afloat and the four Pratt & Whitney J75 engines could be replaced while at sea.

The Navy required tanker submarines to support the Seamaster in forward areas. The prototype for those craft was the *Guavina* (SSO 362), a war-built fleet submarine that had been converted to a submarine tanker in 1949 (later redesignated AGSS 362 and AOSS 362). She initially was envisioned as a multipurpose tanker, able to supply fuel to amphibious landing beachheads and to other submarines, while also carrying small amounts of jet fuel for refueling aircraft and guided missiles. During the *Guavina*'s 1949 conversion at Mare Island, large fuel bunkers were built up around her amidships ballast tanks for carrying 150,000 gallons of aviation fuel.[30]

In 1954 the *Guavina* entered Philadelphia Naval Shipyard for conversion to a submarine seaplane tender. A large platform—nicknamed the "flight deck"—was added to her stern to store the hoses and buoys needed for refueling operations. She carried out her first experimental refueling of a P5M Marlin at sea off Norfolk in the summer of 1955.

Between 7 and 11 May 1956, the *Guavina* was teamed with four P5Ms off the Florida Keys to demonstrate the concept of a mobile submarine-seaplane base. Rubber floats stored on the submarine's deck served as a floating bridge between the aircraft and submarine to transfer personnel and supplies. By the end of the exercise the airmen and submariners had operated so well together that they could bring the aircraft alongside the *Guavina*, begin simulated maintenance, take on board spare parts and hot food, refuel, and cast off within 45 minutes. A second exercise in the Florida Keys from 16 to 20 July further streamlined operations.[31] The submarine subsequently deployed to the Mediterranean for two months with the seaplane tender *Currituck* (AV 7) to refuel P5M Marlins. During 1957 and 1958 the *Guavina* operated with the flying boats in the Caribbean and Florida Keys.[32]

The *Guavina* (then AGSS 362) refuels a Martin P5M flying boat off Norfolk on 3 March 1955. A group of sailors is clustered around the "flight deck" on her stern for the refueling operation. (U.S. NAVY)

Development of the Seamaster proceeded while the *Guavina* tested her capabilities. The first of two XP6M-1 Seamaster prototype aircraft flew in July 1955. Both crashed. They were followed by six modified YP6M-1 aircraft. The aircraft's development proceeded smoothly, but the future prospects for the Seamaster steadily deteriorated as other Navy projects—especially the Polaris ballistic missile program—competed for funds. The initial 1956 order for 24 production P6M-2 aircraft was reduced to 18 units in 1957 and then cut to only eight aircraft in 1958. Ultimately, only four production aircraft were completed when the Seamaster program was cancelled in August 1959.[33] The completed airframes were scrapped and the *Guavina* was decommissioned in 1959; she was relegated to dockside training duties in Baltimore, Maryland, never having refueled a Seamaster. Subsequently she was scrapped. The Seamaster was the last flying boat developed for the U.S. Navy.

THE NUCLEAR NAVY

Prior to the Seamaster cancellation, the Navy had ambitious plans for future seaplanes and submarines. In 1955, the Bureau of Ships (BuShips) sketched preliminary designs for nuclear-propelled submarine seaplane tenders. Ranging between 4,800 and 7,300 tons submerged, they were to carry between 150,000 and 800,000 gallons of jet fuel and have major maintenance capabilities. The largest design could lift the Seamaster out of the water on its deck to perform maintenance.[34]

Nuclear propulsion also was applied to aircraft designs, with both the Navy and Air Force undertaking projects to develop nuclear-propelled aircraft. Nuclear reactors within the fuselage would heat and expand air, propelling the aircraft without jet fuel and resulting in virtually unlimited range. Martin developed several designs for nuclear flying boats based on an enlarged Seamaster. To support that aircraft, BuShips developed a submarine design designated SSO-N. That submarine would displace 5,500 tons submerged and would be propelled by an S5W nuclear reactor plant. The SSO-N would carry 180,000 gallons of fuel, 60 tons of bombs, and 34 relief aircraft crewmen.[35] The nuclear-propelled aircraft would have limited radiation shielding to minimize weight, hence the flight crews would rotate flying duty to minimize their exposure to radiation.

One of the more interesting concepts developed by BuShips to support nuclear flying boats was a submersible seaplane tender. All aspects of that design were motivated by the danger of the high levels of radiation emanating from the nuclear aircraft while their reactors were operating. The submersible tender would have been some 420 feet long with a surface displacement of 16,600 tons. The wide outer hull wrapped around two parallel pressure hulls containing living quarters and diesel generator rooms to provide electric power. Forward of the twin pressure hulls were shielded rooms for working on the nuclear

TABLE 10.1
Submersible Seaplane Tender

Displacement	
surface	16,600 tons
submerged	23,000 tons
Length	420 ft.
	(128 m)
Beam	76 ft.
	(23.2 m)
Draft	28 ft.
	(8.5 m)
Diesel generators	4
total HP	6,400
Electric motors	2
total SHP	6,400
Shafts	2
Speed	
surface	15 knots
submerged	4 knots
Range (nm/kn)	
surfaced	12,000/12
Test depth	80 ft. (24 m)
Torpedo Tubes	2 21-in. bow
Torpedoes	4
Aircraft Ordnance	30 tons
Aircraft Fuel	100,000 gal.
Complement	114
Aircrew	32

aircraft engines via remote control. Forward of those rooms and aft of the bow torpedo room were three small watertight capsules for storing the highly radio-active spent cores of the aircraft reactors. Protruding above the hull to either side were two heavily shielded "islands" containing the bridge and docking control room. The tender would be able to submerge completely to shallow depths for brief periods and had torpedoes for self-defense.

The tender would proceed on the surface under diesel power to the operating area. After lying in wait for the aircraft at periscope depth, the tender would deballast underneath the aircraft, lifting it between the two island structures. Except for the shielded islands, those portions of the ship that were

Section at B

Section at C

Section at D

100 feet

0 25 50 75

Docking Control

Watertight Hatch

Traveling Bridge Crane

Bridge Crane Rails

Bridge

Watertight Hatch

Docking Guide

Neutron Shield Tanks

Engine Checkout Space

Living Space

Living Space

Machinery Room

Aux. Machinery Room

Engine Handling Room

Control Room for Engine Checkout Space

Living Space

Living Space

Bomb Stowage

Machinery Room

Aux. Machinery Room

Steering Gear Tank

Anchor Windlass Room

Torpedo Room

Nuclear Power Package Stowage

Bridge Crane Rails

Traveling Bridge Crane

Periscope (S)

Bridge (S)

CIC (S)

Fixed Snorkel (P)

Docking Control Room (P)

Telescoping Bridge Crane Support

Nuclear Element Stowage

Engine Handling Room

Engine Checkout Space (P)

Engine Spare Instrument Parts (P) Room (S)

Machinery Room

Motor Room

A B C D

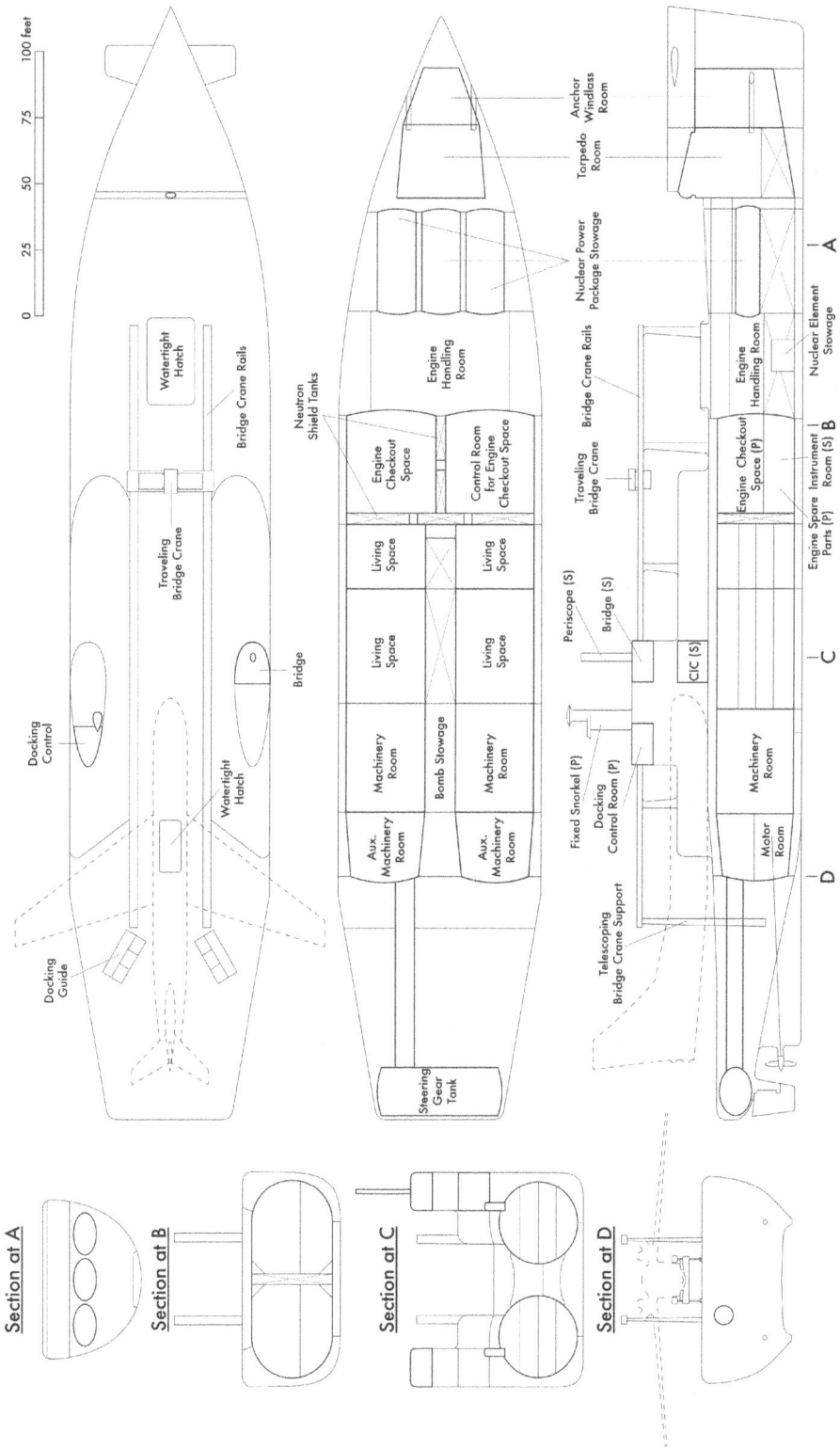

Submersible seaplane tender designed by the Bureau of Ships to resupply nuclear-propelled flying boats (P = Port, S = Starboard). (©JACOB GUNNARSON)

manned remained submerged until the aircraft's reactor was shut down with the water above the hull serving as a radiation shield.[36]

Ultimately neither the Navy nor Air Force produced nuclear-propelled aircraft. No submarine seaplane tenders were built after cancellation of the Seamaster program.

THE SOVIET PROJECTS

The Soviet Union resumed studies into refueling seaplanes from submarines after World War II. In the late 1940s the Tupolev design bureau began work on a new long-range, strategic bomber—the Tu-85—based on the Tu-4 (NATO codename Bull), a modified, Soviet copy of the American B-29 Superfortress. The Tu-85 had insufficient range to reach the United States with internal fuel and would have to be refueled from a tanker aircraft. However, navigating bombers and tankers to meet at precisely the right time and location for aerial refueling over remote areas was beyond the state of the art at that time.

Thus, in 1950 the Tupolev bureau investigated turning the Tu-85 design into a flying boat able to be refueled by submarines. Rendezvousing with submarine tankers in the Atlantic or Pacific would be a substantially easier task than distant aerial refueling. Still, the task of reengineering a four-engine bomber to alight on the open sea was viewed with incredulity by some designers at the bureau, with one remarking, "Nobody needs this work, it's just [Chief Designer] Andrey Nikolayevich's hobby."

The new design—Project 504—was completed in 1953. However, by that time the Tupolev Tu-95 (NATO Bear), a turboprop bomber with intercontinental range, had flown and Project 504 was abandoned.[37]

Far more advanced designs were on the horizon: In 1952, at the Siberian Aviation Research Institute, the Hungarian-born designer Robert Bartini began development of a groundbreaking supersonic strategic bomber. His project—designated A-55—would have a fuselage that blended smoothly into the wing to turn the entire body of the aircraft into an arrowhead-shaped lifting surface. Equipped with retractable skis, the A-55 could take off from water, snow, and even from ice floes in the Soviet Arctic. The aircraft would be refueled by submarines and surface ships and would be capable of striking the mainland United States. However, Bartini's proposal was judged unrealistic and was shelved.[38]

Despite that initial rejection, Bartini's work stoked interest in high-performance seaplanes by the Soviet government. In August 1956 the Council of Ministers set out requirements for a "supersonic long-range naval reconnaissance bomber": a maximum speed of Mach 1.4, a range of 4,800 miles, a payload of 11,000 pounds, and the ability to take off and land in waves up to six feet high. In the reconnaissance role, the aircraft would work in conjunction with submarines, using its powerful radar to relay targeting information on enemy ships. In the strike role, the aircraft would carry an air-launched cruise missile or bombs to attack enemy convoys. The bomber would be refueled from submarines or surface ships. Two refuelings from a submarine would extend the maximum range to about 15,000 miles.[39]

The Beriev and Myasishchev aircraft design bureaus submitted proposals for that advanced seaplane requirement.[40] The Beriev design—the SD-MBR—had a long, slender hull with a compound delta wing and a T-tail. Two NK-10 turbojet engines were mounted in pylons above the wings, and two additional engines were faired into the tail structure. Three large hydro-skis would lift the bomber off the water during takeoff.[41] Myasishchev's M-70 was a broadly similar design with a trapezoidal wing and conventional tail.[42]

The refueling process would be substantially more advanced than that developed by the U.S. Navy for the Seamaster: The submerged tanker submarine would release a buoy with a radio homing device to guide in the aircraft. Once on the water, the aircraft would establish communication with the submarine using an underwater telephone. The submarine would surface, and via a system of cables, winches, and floats, connect a refueling hose to the bomber.[43]

Beriev was preparing to build a prototype SD-MBR when the Soviet government halted the project in September 1957. Although the advanced designs by both design bureaus were considered technically feasible, the Navy and Air Force preferred to rely on more conventional, land-based aircraft.[44]

At about the time that Beriev and Myasishchev were developing their flying boats, Robert Bartini, undeterred by the rejection of his A-55 design, embarked on an even more ambitious project. His A-57 design would be an enormous blended-wing design, 233 feet in length and powered to speeds up to Mach 2.4 by five turbojet engines. Like the A-55, it would be capable of takeoff from ice, snow, or water, and would be refueled by submarines, reducing its reliance on airfields that could be destroyed in the opening stages of a nuclear conflict. The A-57 would carry nuclear weapons in its bomb bay or a large cruise missile mounted atop the fuselage. The missile could be released before the aircraft became vulnerable to interception by American air defenses, increasing the probability of a successful nuclear strike on the United States.

Bartini developed a number of variants of the A-57: a reconnaissance aircraft (R-57), a scaled-down version to strike Europe (Ye-57), and a land-based tactical bomber for use on the front lines of a war in Europe (F-57). Like the Seamaster, ultimately the A-57 was rendered obsolete by the introduction of land-based and submarine-launched ballistic missiles.[45]

While the supersonic seaplanes were being designed, the Soviet Navy and the submarine design bureaus began the development of submarine tankers. Trials with Beriev Be-6 flying boats being refueled from a Project 613 (NATO Whis-key) diesel-electric submarine took place in 1956–1957. There was a proposal to build a dedicated, tanker version of that submarine—Project 613B—to re-fuel the new Beriev Be-10 turbojet flying boat, but it was not pursued.[46] In-stead, purpose-built tanker submarines would be developed.

In 1957, the TsKB-16 submarine design bureau began work on Project 648, a diesel-electric supply submarine that could rearm and replenish other subma-rines.[47] It would carry ten P-5 or P-6 (NATO SS-N-3 Shaddock) cruise missiles or 60 torpedoes, and food, fresh water, and 1,000 tons of aviation or diesel fuel, enabling it to also refuel seaplanes in remote areas.[48] A variant propelled by two nuclear reactors—Project 648M—also was designed.

Project 648 subsequently was redesigned to also carry mines, increasing the complexity of an already ambitious design. That project was cancelled shortly after the first submarine was laid down at Severodvinsk in early 1961. Nuclear submarines were beginning to be built in large numbers at the Severodvinsk yard—the world's largest submarine construction facility—and other Soviet yards, and building the complex Project 648 would slow work on more impor-tant undersea craft.[49]

Project 648 was succeeded by the nuclear-propelled Project 664, which could carry twice the number of torpedoes and missiles. As with the previous design, Project 664 could carry 1,000 tons of aviation fuel that would be de-livered to the aircraft while submerged through a hose that could be streamed from the stern. When employed as a transport submarine, it could carry 350 troops for lengthy periods or 500 troops for a five-day journey.

Meanwhile, the Beriev design bureau created several aircraft designs to be refueled by the Project 648 and 664 submarines. In 1961 it initiated develop-ment of an amphibious aircraft capable of both the anti-submarine and trans-port roles. Powered by four turboprop engines, it could lift up to 44,000 pounds of cargo or a combat payload of 10,000 pounds of torpedoes, depth charges, and sonobuoys. For the cargo mission the aircraft would land on retractable landing gear and unload cargo via a rear ramp. In the following year Beriev produced a substantially larger version of that design with double the load capacity and range and without landing gear.[50]

Construction began on the lead Project 664 submarine at Severodvinsk in 1964, but in May 1965, it was decided to complete the craft at a Leningrad (St. Petersburg) shipyard. Like Project 648 before it, the 10,000-ton, multi-role Project 664 was complex and it was delaying the construction of high-priority ballistic missile submarines. The transfer to Leningrad did not occur and Project 664 was cancelled.[51] Beriev thus ceased work on its anti-subma-rine transport flying boat project. Although the Soviet design bureaus kept drafting concept designs for replenishment and cargo submarines, no further projects were intended to refuel seaplanes.

MANY PROJECTS, FEW SUCCESSES

Japan, Germany, the United States, and the Soviet Union all considered employing submarines to support seaplanes for long-range strikes and reconnaissance. The Japanese exploited that capability to the fullest extent, carrying out a second strike on Pearl Harbor as well as reconnaissance operations during the Solomon Islands campaign.

Germany conducted several seaplane reconnaissance missions in the Soviet Arctic to limited effect and with the loss of several aircraft due to weather conditions.

The United States considered a force of submarine seaplane tenders and tankers for many years, using the *Nautilus* to demonstrate the concept before World War II. After the war the U.S. Navy embarked on a most ambitious plan for a seaplane striking force supported by submarines, envisioning mobile bases for the impressive P6M Seamaster nuclear-capable, turbojet flying boat, as well as the F2Y Sea Dart seaplane fighter and R3Y Tradewind transport flying boat. The submarine tanker *Guavina* demonstrated the efficacy of the concept, but the advent of submarine-launched strategic missiles made the Seamaster obsolete. The Soviet Union never completed construction of similar aircraft and submarines for the same reason.

The concept of the flying boat bomber—supported by surface ships and, especially, by submarines—had come to an end.

CHAPTER 11

Cold War Concepts

The early years of the Cold War (1946–1991) brimmed with the promise of new technologies that had been initiated in World War II. The jet engine, rocket propulsion, nuclear energy, radar, and guided missiles all promised to revolutionize warfare. Thus, in the immediate postwar years there was rapid development in naval and aviation technology, resulting in many innovative submarine and aircraft concepts, and many fantastical designs— including "flying submarines."

SOVIET PROJECTS

The Soviet Union is believed to have designed only one aircraft-carrying submarine during the Cold War: Project 621 was the first in a series of Soviet submarine concepts for large amphibious landing and supply submarines. Project 621 was developed in 1948 by the design bureau TsKB-18 (later named Rubin); it would be 484 feet long with a surface displacement of 5,845 tons.[1] The planned capacity of the submersible landing ship was immense: 745 troops, 10 T-34 tanks, 12 trucks, and 14 towed cannon. A bow ramp would enable vehicles to be unloaded close to the beach. Propulsion would be diesel-electric or a closed-cycle turbine system.

The Project 621 submarines also would carry three Lavochkin La-5 piston-engine fighters in a hangar faired into the front of the conning tower. A catapult would launch the aircraft over the bow. Although turbojet aircraft were in service by that time, they may have been considered too large, heavy, and unproven to operate from a submarine.

That submarine design was never pursued, yet rumors of giant aircraft-carrying Soviet submarines persisted in the West for several years. In 1953 the U.S. Air Force sponsored a RAND Corporation study of potential Soviet attacks on Strategic Air Command (SAC) bases within the United States. That study conjectured that Soviet nuclear-armed jet aircraft launched from submarines could destroy a significant portion of SAC's bombers at their airbases with the launches close to U.S. coasts greatly reducing warning times.[2]

In 1954 the U.S. Central Intelligence Agency (CIA) reported that the Soviet Union had developed a long-range, deep-diving submarine capable of carrying two specially designed aircraft.[3] But those submarines existed only in the minds of Western defense analysts.

Instead, the Soviet Union pursued submarine-launched cruise missiles to strike the United States and other NATO nations. In 1955 the Beriev aircraft design bureau developed the P-10, a 36½-foot long, subsonic cruise missile with wings that folded so that the missile could fit inside a deck-mounted hangar. The B-64, a Project 611 (NATO codename Zulu) torpedo-attack submarine, was converted to carry a single P-10 missile in a hangar aft of her conning tower. The missile would be fired forward, over the conning tower from an elevating ramp on the stern of the submarine.[4]

About 1956, Beriev designed a manned, submarine-launched flying boat designated P-10B. The forward fuselage was sleek with prominent chines, and a delta wing with wingtip floats was mounted above the rear fuselage. Two turbojets installed atop the wing would give the P-10B supersonic performance. Illustrations of the aircraft indicated two air-to-air missiles slung under the wings. Like the P-10 missile, the P-10B would be launched from a submarine with rocket boosters.[5]

Despite their similar designations, the relationship between the P-10 and P-10B is unclear. The aircraft, perhaps 100 feet in length, dwarfed the missile, requiring a substantially larger hangar and carrier submarine. In 1957 the P-10 cruise missile project was cancelled in favor of the superior, Chelomey-designed P-5 missile (NATO Shaddock), which would be carried by both nuclear-propelled and diesel-electric submarines as well as by surface ships. The P-10B design was not developed further.

The Soviet Navy subsequently considered launching miniature helicopters from submarines. During the Cold War both the United States and the Soviet Union experimented with single-seat, ultralight helicopters for the Army observation role. The Kamov design bureau led the Soviet efforts in developing those aircraft—the diminutive Ka-8 and Ka-10 helicopters, nicknamed "aerial motorcycles."

In 1971, Kamov was tasked with building an even smaller helicopter for the Soviet Navy: The aircraft was to fit in a cylindrical storage container no wider than 20 inches to enable it to be launched from a submarine's 21-inch (533-mm) torpedo tubes, dragged ashore by swimmers, and then assembled in less than 15 minutes. The Navy stipulated that the helicopter had to be able to operate from a makeshift base for an extended period without maintenance. The helicopter would be used for special forces operations on an enemy coastline.

The Kamov design was designated Ka-56 and used a 40-horsepower Wankel rotary engine to power a pair of two-blade, coaxial rotors. A Wankel engine was selected because of its compactness, light weight, nearly vibration-free operation, and high reliability with only a handful of moving parts. The landing gear and tail assemblies folded against the rotor mast, and the rotors could be detached to enable storing the helicopter in a container. The Ka-56 was tiny—just 485 pounds fully loaded. The pilot sat recumbent, straddling the rotor mast and engine. It would have a range of 95 miles, a maximum speed of 70 mph, and a maximum altitude of 5,600 feet.

A mockup Ka-56 was built to prove out the design. In tests it could be assembled in just ten minutes by a single person. However, there was little technical expertise in the Soviet Union to design and build Wankel engines, thus a flying prototype was never built.[6]

CIA RECONAISSANCE CRAFT

As the so-called Iron Curtain fell across Europe in the early stages of the Cold War, the United States had little capability to see into the vast expanse of the Soviet Union. Peripheral reconnaissance flights soon were being flown near the borders with communist countries and the Soviet Union, but at significant risk with several aircraft being shot down. Accordingly, the U.S. Navy and Air Force began unmanned, high-altitude balloon projects carrying cameras and other "spy" equipment for scientific objectives as well as for intelligence collection.

Balloons were promising as reconnaissance craft because of their minimal radar signature and their ability to overfly almost any area of the Soviet land mass—provided that the winds cooperated. The starting point for the Navy and Air Force spy balloons was the Navy's Project Skyhook, which used plastic balloons filled with helium or hydrogen to lift cosmic ray detectors and other scientific instruments, some to altitudes above 100,000 feet. The Air Force developed camera-carrying balloons, which culminated in the launching of several hundred Project Genetrix balloons over the Soviet Union in 1956.

In August 1954, the Central Intelligence Agency (CIA) proposed flying a *manned* reconnaissance balloon over the Soviet Union.[7] A manned balloon could overfly a Soviet island or peninsula if it were launched and recovered by a Navy surface ship *or submarine.* Collaborating with the Office of Naval Research (ONR), the CIA developed a balloon that could be launched and recovered by a surfaced submarine.[8]

The craft consisted of a four-by-three-foot canvas gondola carrying a single observer that was suspended beneath a 30-foot-diameter, plastic helium balloon. The gondola was specifically sized to fit through a submarine's 25-inch-diameter hatch. A large-format K-20 camera was mounted on the bottom of the gondola, aimed straight down. Because the balloon might not be carried directly over the target by the winds, a second camera on a trainable mount was fitted to the side of the gondola.[9] The gondola also had a sensor to record Soviet radar signals. Some consideration was given to fitting an antenna for radar imaging of the target, but the weight and size of that system were prohibitive.

The balloon's pilot had a radio homing device to enable the submarine to locate him after the overflight. The gondola had an insulating hood and oxygen for operations above 20,000 feet.

The project's test balloonist was a former Navy blimp pilot, known by the pseudonym "James Parker." He was recruited by the CIA after World War II and became the agency's balloon expert. Parker's first operation was supervising the insertion of agents into Czechoslovakia using balloons launched from West Germany.[10] In 1953, he was involved in a similar operation to insert Finnish agents into the Soviet Union. Launched from a trawler in the Barents Sea, the Finns landed near Murmansk and covertly photographed a Soviet air base. They then hiked to the Finnish border.[11] After staying "behind the lines" on those missions, Parker would be in the gondola for the submarine operations.

Before tests could begin with a submarine the Navy carried out land-based flights to assess the performance of the balloon and its equipment. During March–April 1955, Parker made three successful test flights at a Navy facility near Minneapolis, Minnesota, where Project Skyhook was based. Although the balloon could be visually sighted under some conditions, it was virtually invisible to radar.

At-sea trials off Key West, Florida, from the fleet submarine *Sennet* (SS 408) followed. The *Sennet*'s crew stowed a bank of 60 helium cylinders in the forward torpedo room and made provisions to store the gondola, balloon envelope, and equipment.[12]

All recoverable equipment on the balloon would be protected by waterproof containers upon landing in the water, and Parker was provided with an inflatable life raft. The *Sennet* was aided in tracking and recovering the balloon by the submarine tender *Bushnell* (AS 15), the minesweeper *Albatross* (AMS 1), recovery boats, a blimp, and aircraft. If civilians noticed the balloon over Key West, the Navy would distribute a cover story claiming that the balloon was measuring cosmic rays and testing scientific instruments.[13]

With Parker manning the balloon, three flights were carried out from 26 to 29 April 1955. The flights lasted for two to four hours, carrying the balloon over the Florida Keys for 20 to 90 miles. Aside from some equipment being damaged from accidental seawater immersion, the flights were considered suc-cessful, capturing high-resolution images of Key West.

With the trials completed the CIA moved to use the submarine-launched balloon over Soviet territory. The target was Sakhalin Island, north of Japan. Parker would attempt to photograph Soviet airfields to obtain intelligence on runways and the numbers and type of aircraft. The CIA was also interested in petroleum facilities near the airfields.[14] According to Parker, in the summer of 1955 he was launched from a submarine east of Sakhalin. Drifting over the southern tip of the island, he attempted to photograph Soviet military instal-lations although cloud cover may have obscured the targets. The cameras also suffered malfunctions due to the rapidly changing temperatures during the bal-loon's ascent. Apparently undetected, Parker and the film were recovered by the submarine in the Sea of Japan.[15]

Details of the balloon project beyond the Minneapolis and Key West trials remain classified, although a declassified CIA memo suggests that the operation over Sakhalin occurred prior to 1 July 1955.[16] Another CIA doc-ument alludes to plans for a second overflight: "the project was called off for this fall but they are getting the material and equipment ready for action in the Spring of 1956."[17]

The era of balloon reconnaissance was short-lived. Able to take high-resolu-tion photos while having a small radar signature, balloons were at the mercy of the winds and only islands such as Sakhalin or Soviet offshore ice stations were practical targets. The Air Force's large number of unmanned Project Genetrix balloons were detected by Soviet air defenses and many were shot down by fighter aircraft. Of the balloons that were not intercepted, few returned useful intelligence.[18] Instead, reconnaissance of the Soviet mainland would be suc-cessfully accomplished by the Lockheed U-2 high-altitude spy plane beginning in 1956 and the Corona spy satellite starting in 1959.

The U-2 could reach an altitude of 70,000 feet, above the reach of Soviet air defenses. But even as the first U-2 took to the air, it was clear from Soviet advances in surface-to-air missiles that it would not be untouchable forever. The U-2's successor would have to fly faster and higher and have a reduced radar cross-section.

UNUSUAL SPYCRAFT

In 1958 the CIA and Bureau of Aeronautics initiated the Project Champion program to develop a high-speed, high-altitude reconnaissance aircraft.[19] The requirements were for a single-seat aircraft capable of Mach 2 to 3 flight at an altitude of 150,000 to 200,000 feet with a range of 3,200 miles.[20] It would be powered by either a ramjet or a liquid-fueled rocket. *The aircraft originally was intended to be launched and recovered by a submarine*; launch from a modified bomber or even an enormous balloon also were contemplated. Designed with a buoyant airframe and hydro-skis, the aircraft would come down on the sea to be recovered by a submarine or surface ship.

Under Project Champion, the CIA and BuAer tasked the Convair firm with the preliminary design study of the aircraft. (Convair's portion of the program was labeled Project Hazel.) A wide range of aircraft designs was studied. Most had a slim fuselage with one or two ramjets atop a large, triangular wing. One unusual concept had the pilot sitting inside the center of the ramjet, which was suspended from a triangular parasol wing.

The most novel aspect of Project Champion was the aircraft's construction: Some designs had typical, rigid metal construction; others would be constructed from fiberglass. The nose and ramjet intake would be made from rigid fiberglass, with the wings, fuselage, and even the ramjet body constructed from flexible fiberglass fabric that would be inflated by pressurized gas and kept in shape by an internal rigid fiberglass substructure.[21]

That unusual construction yielded a large, yet light structure and would allow the aircraft to be deflated and packed into a hangar on board a submarine. The nonmetallic airframe would also dramatically reduce the aircraft's radar cross-section. Goodyear Aerospace, a subsidiary of the Goodyear Rubber and Tire Company, was contracted to study structural material for Project Champion, having already built a small aircraft—the Inflatoplane—entirely out of fabric.

Most of the Champion designs were intended to reach a speed of Mach 3, and a rocket-propelled version was projected to reach Mach 8! To reach such high speeds, exotic fuels such as pentaborane and liquid hydrogen were considered along with standard JP-4 jet fuel. The rocket engine was specially designed to minimize the aircraft's infrared signature. That design had rigid, folding wings and could fit into a submarine-mounted hangar 12 feet in diameter.

Convair sketched two carrier submarine designs, both about 350 feet long. One proposal had two angled hangars for ramjet aircraft, which would be brought up to the deck and launched from a vertical rail. The alternate design had four vertical hangars for rocket-propelled aircraft, which would launch from vertical rails after being mated with a rocket booster.

At the same time the CIA was working with the Air Force on a successor to the U-2. Famed aircraft designer Clarence (Kelly) Johnson, head of Lockheed's Skunk Works division, was asked to evaluate Project Champion in August 1958 and found several aspects of the project infeasible.[22] He concluded that the Champion designs, while still facing steep technical challenges, could actually be made lighter by using a traditional metal structure instead of inflatable fiberglass.[23]

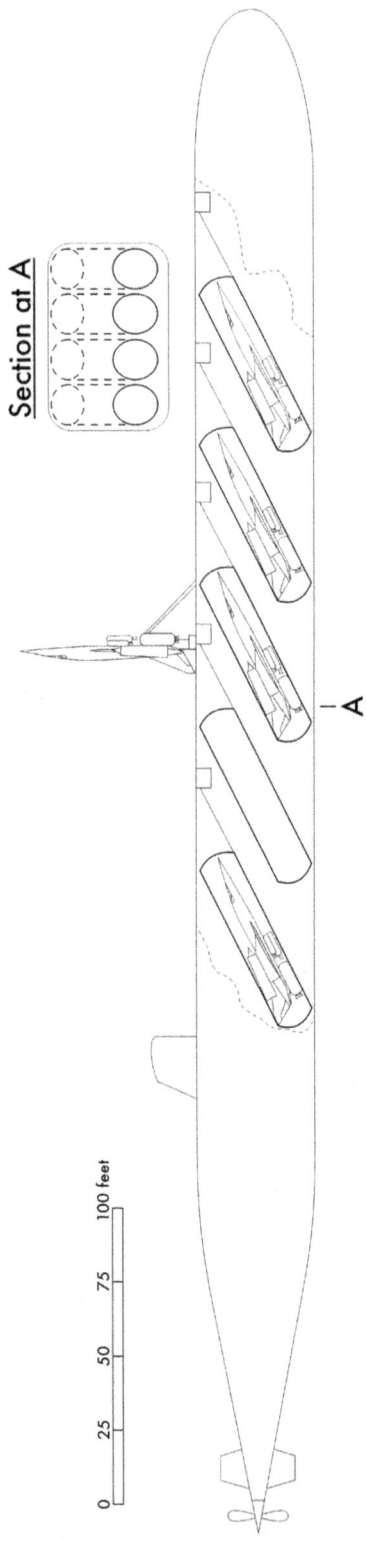

Section at A

Convair studied exotic high-altitude spy aircraft designs for the Navy and CIA under Project Champion. This May 1959 design for a submarine carrier could carry 20 Mach 3 aircraft. (©JACOB GUNNARSON)

As a result of Johnson's recommendations, Convair began designing aircraft with metal structures. Still capable of Mach 3 flight at about 100,000 feet, the designs became more conventional in appearance, most with two ramjets on the tips of a smaller delta wing. Additionally, landing gear could be fitted in place of hydro-skis. The aircraft could be launched from the ground using jet or rocket boosters, from the air by a B-52 Stratofortress bomber, or at sea from a surface ship or surfaced submarine. The submarine carrier would be about 500 feet long and accommodate 20 Champion aircraft. Each aircraft would be stored in an angled silo 64 feet long and 13¼ feet in diameter and would launch from vertical rails.

The Champion program was cancelled in September 1959 and ultimately Johnson's team at the Skunk Works was selected to develop the successor to the U-2 for the CIA.[24] Initially using funds from Project Champion, Johnson developed more conventional Mach 3 spyplane designs that culminated in Project Oxcart. That program produced the highly successful Lockheed A-12, the basis for the SR-71 Blackbird. Both aircraft were capable of speeds exceeding Mach 3 and had a maximum altitude of some 85,000 feet.

FLYING SUBMARINES

One of the most unusual Cold War concepts was a fusion of the aircraft and submarine—the "flying submarine." Such craft were popular in science fiction, and several patents and unbuilt designs were dreamed up in the first half of the 20th Century.[25] Those aircraft are more accurately referred to as "submersible seaplanes" because they were closer in design to aircraft than to submarines. Submarines typically have a density about four times greater than that of a typical aircraft and are thus too heavy for flight. However, an aircraft can be designed to have large parts of its structure flood and become neutrally buoyant like a submarine, although its lightweight fuselage will not enable it to survive the pressure of great depths.

The first serious attempt to design a submersible seaplane was by Boris P. Ushakov, a naval architecture student at the Leningrad Naval Engineering School. In 1934 he devised a manta ray-like craft named the LPL (*Letayushchaya Podvodnaya Lodka*—Flying Submarine). Once aloft, the craft would search for an enemy ship. The LPL would fly ahead of its target, alight on the water, submerge, and lie in wait at the optimum torpedo firing position. Once the enemy ship drew close, the LPL would release the two 18-inch (456-mm) torpedoes slung beneath its wings. In addition to the anti-shipping role, Ushakov envisioned the LPL as a harbor-attack craft, able to fly over minefields and anti-submarine nets to attack ships in port.[26]

Each of the three AM-34 radial engines—one in the nose, two on the wings—would be enclosed in a watertight container. The engine intake and

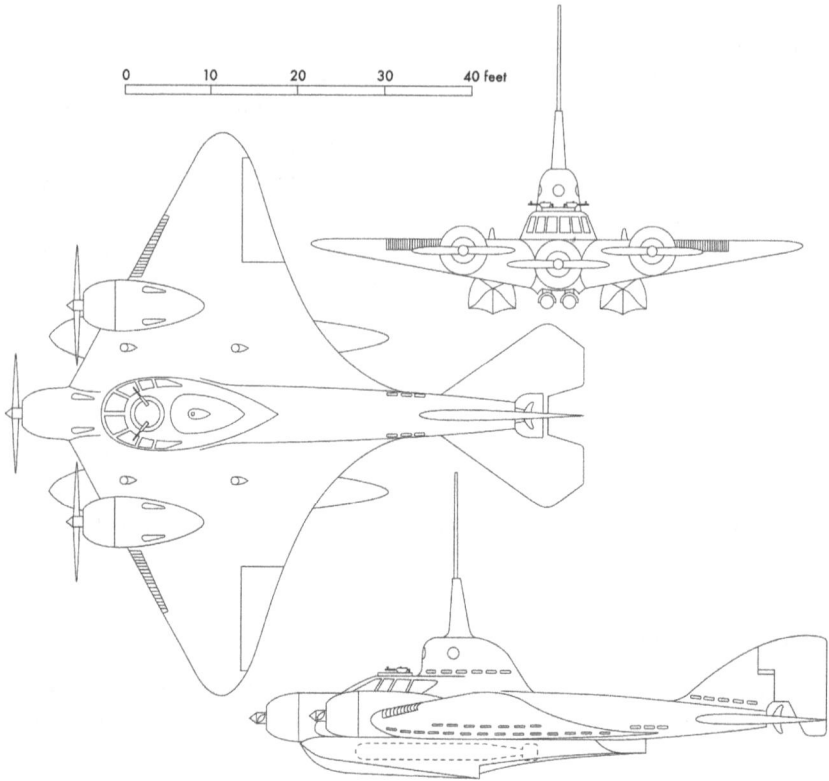

The LPL designed by Boris P. Ushakov was among the first "flying submarines" to be designed. Armed with torpedoes, it combined the high speed of an aircraft with the stealth of a submarine. Note the flood holes in the underside and leading edge of the wings.
(©JACOB GUNNARSON)

exhaust ports penetrating those containers could be sealed for submergence. The rear of the fuselage held the battery compartment and a compartment for the ten-horsepower electric motor that would provide underwater propulsion.

Before submerging, the three-man crew would move from the free-flooding cockpit into a cramped conning tower atop the fuselage, which had a periscope. The remainder of the wings and fuselage were free-flooding. In the air, the LPL would have a maximum speed of 115 mph with a range of 500 miles. Underwater it was capable of three knots for six miles. The LPL would be able to submerge to a depth of 150 feet.

Ushakov presented his design in April 1936, to the Scientific Research Institute of Military Shipbuilding, where he was employed. He received mostly positive reviews, and the institute began feasibility studies in 1937. Among the unknowns of the innovative design were the aerodynamics of the wing, which had sizable flood holes in the leading edge that could potentially disrupt airflow when in flight. Although the institute ultimately abandoned the project, Ush-akov continued to work on it in his free time. He submitted a revised design to the institute in January 1938, but the project was put aside. No physical proto-types or even models appear to have been constructed.[27]

Some interest in the flying submarine concept remained in the Soviet Union. Sergei N. Kovalev—the chief designer of the Soviet Navy's nuclear-propelled ballistic missile submarines—recounted that Soviet leader Ni-kita Khrushchev asked him to develop a flying submarine in the early 1960s. Khrushchev's request was motivated by intelligence indicating that NATO was developing such a craft. Although Kovalev would later dismiss the concept as "nonsense," some design work was carried out. It was intended for the anti-shipping role, with "wolf packs" of flying submarines searching for targets in the air and attacking from beneath the waves. As Kovalev recalled,

> They even drew up something, which floated very poorly and flew even worse. Under water, it would be beaten by craft that swim, and in the air by those that fly. That's how the matter ended.[28]

Three decades later, the Beriev design bureau would attempt to revive the flying submarine concept. Just before the fall of the Soviet Union in 1991, the bureau sketched a design for a submersible seaplane. The craft had a T-tail and engine intakes flush with the top of the slim, flying boat-like hull. The wings would fold back along the hull for rapid submergence.[29] Like the designs before it, the Beriev flying submarine never came to fruition.

The first submersible seaplane to actually be built was the Reid Flying Sub-marine, constructed in 1962 by inventor Donald Reid of New Jersey, assem-bled from spare aircraft parts.[30] However, that craft was barely able to stay airborne and had no watertight crew compartment. The single pilot sat in an open cockpit wearing scuba diving gear. Reid hoped that his design would be adopted by the Navy, but it was never more than a curiosity. At the time the Navy was developing its own submersible seaplane.

The U.S. Navy had developed an interest in submersible seaplanes after World War II. Starting in 1946, Navy laboratories began researching the con-cept, and the Department of Defense contracted the All American Engineer-ing Company to study submersible aircraft in 1955. Famed aircraft designer Jack Northrop also was working on designs for such a craft at that time.[31]

The Navy initially was interested in flying submarines for the anti-submarine role. In the early years of the Cold War, a future "third battle of the Atlantic" was foremost in the minds of many Western naval planners. German U-boats had nearly severed the vital shipping lanes between North America and Britain in both world wars. The massive force of Soviet submarines seemed poised to succeed where the German U-boats had failed, dominating the Atlantic shipping lanes and preventing the flow of troops, weapons, and fuels to western Europe to defeat the Red Army.[32] Thus, the development of anti-submarine weapons was of the highest priority.

A flying submarine promised to be an effective Anti-Submarine Warfare (ASW) craft by combining the best aspects of aircraft and submarines. Able to traverse long distances at high speed in the air, the torpedo-armed craft would have better sonars than a fixed-wing aircraft or helicopter to search for Soviet submarines. The craft could surface and fly to a new patrol area far more rapidly than could a traditional ASW ship or submarine, thus expanding the area covered by anti-submarine forces.[33]

In December 1962, Convair proposed a submersible flying boat for the ASW role to the Navy's Bureau of Naval Weapons (BuWeps)—formed in 1959 by a merger of BuAer and the Bureau of Ordnance.[34] BuWeps sent out design requests to several firms with the following desired characteristic:

air cruise speed	150 to 225 knots
air cruise altitude	1,500 to 2,500 feet
air cruise radius	300 to 500 nautical miles
maximum gross takeoff	less than 30,000 pounds
submerged speed	5 to 10 knots
max submerged depth	25 to 75 feet
submerged range	40 to 50 nautical miles
submerged endurance	4 to 10 hours
payload	500 to 1,500 pounds

All American Engineering, Lockheed, North American, Republic, and several "one-man one-car garage outfits" submitted candidate designs. Ultimately Convair was awarded a contract to study the concept.[35] That firm, having become a division of General Dynamics, worked with submarine designers at Electric Boat, also a General Dynamics division, and found the concept both feasible and practical.

One concept that Convair considered was a dart-like, supersonic seaplane with Vertical Takeoff and Landing (VTOL) characteristics. It would have a turbojet engine in the tail for forward flight and four vertical turbojets for VTOL operation. Another Convair design had thick wings housing two torpedoes. That craft would use wing-mounted lift fans for ground-effect takeoff and landing, which was being studied by Convair for a similar, non-submerging ASW seaplane. An alternative design consisted of a VTOL aircraft carrying a detachable "mini" submarine.[36]

An artist's conception of the Convair Sub-Plane. The subject of an intensive research and design effort, ultimately no prototype was built. (GENERAL DYNAMICS CORP.)

By the end of the study period Convair had settled on the High Density Seaplane or "Sub-Plane," which looked outwardly like a conventional jet flying boat. Except for the crew module, avionics bay, and engine nacelles, the aircraft's structure would be free-flooding. In an emergency situation the crew module could be released while in flight to descend on a parachute or while underwater to float to the surface and serve as a life raft. The maximum operational depth of the craft was to be 100 feet.[37]

Three podded engines would power the aircraft in flight: two turbojets mounted over the wings for takeoff and a turbofan behind the cockpit for sustained flight.[38] Underwater, the Sub-Plane would be propelled by an electric motor mounted under the fuselage, powered by batteries or fuel cells.[39] The control surfaces worked in both the air and water. A single hydro-ski aided the takeoff.

Convair developed an innovative solution for sealing the engines against seawater, which also would decrease buoyancy sufficiently to submerge. After the aircraft had alighted on the water, the engines would be cooled by using the starter motors to spin the hot compressors and turbines. Butterfly valves at each end of the engine nacelles would close to seal the engines. As the craft began to sink beneath the surface the fuel—stored in rubber bladders—would be forced into the engine nacelles as the water pressure compressed the bladders, displacing the air inside of the engines and lowering the buoyancy enough to completely submerge. A simple float valve on each nacelle would allow air to vent while preventing water from flooding into the engines. The Sub-Plane would surface using tanks of high-pressure air like a submarine, and the fuel would drain from the engine nacelles back into the fuel bladders. When the Sub-Plane gained speed, it would lift onto the hydro-ski and water could drain from the fuselage, lightening it enough for takeoff.

As the development of the Sub-Plane progressed, its mission shifted away from ASW toward anti-shipping and special operations. A large volume of Soviet shipping enjoyed safe passage in the Baltic, Black, and Caspian Seas, largely unprotected by escorts. The Sub-Plane would be able to fly to the target area and then submerge to continue its mission underwater like a midget submarine.[40] Beyond an anti-shipping role, missions could include harbor attacks, surveillance, or landing and retrieving saboteurs and spies on foreign shores.

BuWeps deemed Convair's work promising and development continued with model tests in wind tunnels and towing tanks. Not everyone shared that optimism: In congressional hearings in March 1965, Louisiana Senator Allen J. Ellender repeatedly pressed Department of Defense officials about the Sub-Plane. "How did you even spend a thin dime on it?" Ellender exasperatedly asked after being informed that $36,000 had been spent on the project.[41]

The Sub-Plane survived Ellender's ridicule and model testing continued.[42] By 1966, Electric Boat had taken over the design from Convair.[43] Work continued until at least 1969, and although the technical aspects of the Sub-Plane remained promising, the intended mission for the craft was nebulous to many officials as well as to some members of Congress. The project was cancelled in the early 1970s, before a flying/submerging prototype was built.

STILL MORE SUBMARINE AIRCRAFT

The Sub-Plane was not the only submersible aircraft design considered by Convair. In 1960–1961 the company dreamt up a truly bizarre craft: a nuclear-powered submersible ramjet. With its slender fuselage and rear-mounted fins, the craft resembled a rocket. It would measure eight feet in diameter and about 140 feet in length.[44]

Underwater, most of the interior volume would be filled with water except for the crew compartment in the nose. Water would be passed over the hot core of a nuclear reactor in the aft fuselage, which would rapidly turn to steam and shoot out from the ramjet's four nozzles. Convair predicted *a maximum submerged speed of 100 knots.* Pitching up toward the surface at this speed, it would be shot into the air and the nuclear ramjet would begin heating and expanding the air through it, producing enough thrust to boost the craft to over Mach 3.

To alight on the water the craft would be slowed by a set of air breaks near the nose and would use the thrust of the ramjet to gently touch down on the sea, aft-end first. Up to 20,000 pounds of nuclear weapons could be carried.

There are few details about how that unusual craft was intended to be employed. Presumably it would patrol underwater, waiting for the alert to strike the Soviet Union. Because the ramjet used the ambient air and water as propellants it had effectively unlimited submerged and airborne range.

Convair never took the project beyond the earliest conceptual design stage. The concept was novel, but many problems would have inevitably cropped up had the project progressed further. For example, salt would have been deposited inside the reactor core from seawater passing over it, potentially causing catastrophic damage. However, the craft, at least in its air-breathing guise, did resemble the Air Force's Supersonic Low-Altitude Missile (SLAM) that would have been propelled by a nuclear ramjet. Convair's project never came to fruition due to the superiority of intercontinental ballistic missiles.

Another submersible seaplane concept came from an unexpected source: the U.S. Air Force. In the early 1960s it sponsored a RAND Corporation study on seaplanes that could be based underwater to increase their survivability from Soviet nuclear strikes in comparison to land-based aircraft.[45]

RAND considered numerous types of submersible seaplanes including strategic bombers, tactical strike aircraft, anti-submarine patrol aircraft, ballistic missile interceptors, airborne tankers, and reconnaissance aircraft. The two most promising types were the strategic bombers and airborne tankers. The strategic bomber would have a loaded weight of 100,000 pounds, a weapons load of 8,000 pounds, and a 2,000-mile range at high subsonic speeds, with a crew of four. It would be launched off the Soviet coast from a mobile underwater base. The tanker variant would be stationed under the flight path of U.S. land-based strategic bombers, which they would refuel on the bombers' transit to the Soviet Union. The tanker variant would have a loaded weight of 300,000 pounds, one-half of which would be fuel.

RAND envisioned the submersible aircraft operating from submersible barges pushed by nuclear-propelled submarine-tugs. The barges would consist of several parallel pressure hulls housing the aircrew, munitions, and spare parts. Trunks would connect the pressure hulls to the aircraft docked to the upper surface of the barges. The pressure hulls were wrapped in a

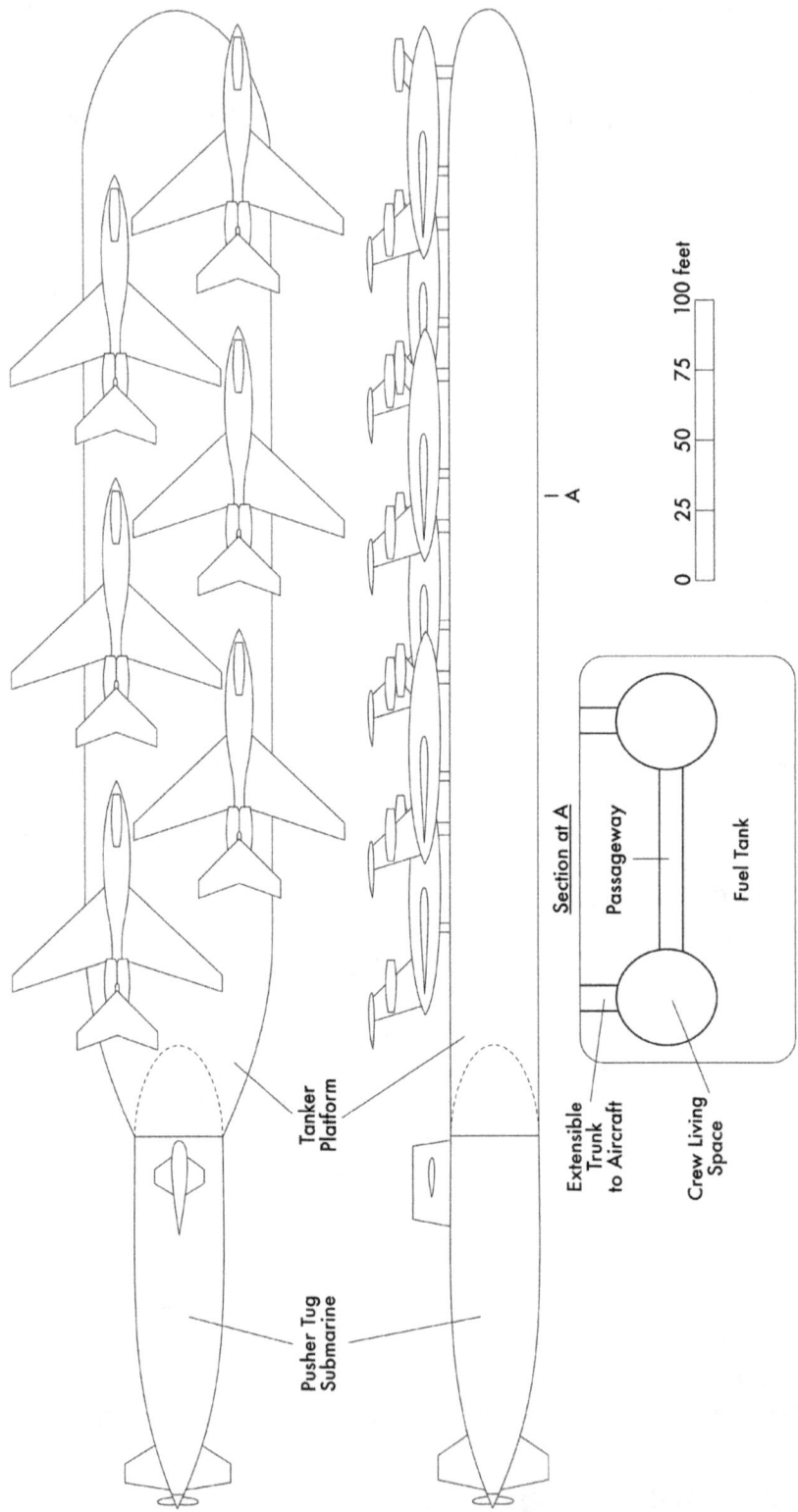

The RAND Corporation concept for submersible aircraft docked to a submersible tanker platform. The platform was pushed by a nuclear-propelled tug submarine.
(©JACOB GUNNARSON)

rectangular outer hull containing ballast and fuel tanks. For propulsion the submarine-tugs would mate to the after end of the barge, its bow nestling in a matching cavity in the barge. The barges and aircraft would be capable of operating at depths to 200 feet.

Two variants of the barge and submarine-tug were designed. One barge, displacing 10,000 tons submerged and measuring 356 feet in length, could carry ten bombers. The submarine-tug would be only 167 feet long and displace 2,655 tons submerged, propelled by a 15,000-horsepower S5W reactor plant. It would be considerably smaller than the contemporary *Skipjack* (SSN 585)-class attack submarines, which had the same reactor, but were 252 feet long and displaced 3,513 tons submerged. The submarine-tug would have no armament, sonar, or fire control equipment.

The other barge design would accommodate six refueling tanker aircraft. To store the large volume of fuel required for in-air refueling operations, the barge would be 405 feet long and displace 16,000 tons submerged. Accordingly, the submarine-tug had to be larger and more powerful: 176 feet long, 3,060 tons submerged displacement, with an 18,500-horsepower nuclear reactor plant. Both barges could be propelled to 16 knots with the aircraft on board.

An alternative concept was to dock a single, smaller aircraft to the deck of a diesel-electric fleet submarine. That would have been a 40,000-pound, single-seat aircraft.

The RAND study never made it beyond those very early concepts.

Thus a large number of innovative concepts for aircraft-carrying submarines and submersible aircraft were investigated in the early years of the Cold War. Except for the CIA's submarine-launched balloon, none of those craft became operational nor even left the designer's sketchbook.

Still, some interest in submersible seaplanes remained in the United States into the 21st Century. In 2008 the Defense Advanced Research Projects Agency (DARPA) solicited proposals for submersible aircraft design studies.[46] The craft was to be used to insert and extract eight special forces troops and their equipment near coastal targets. It would have a range of 1,000-n.miles in the air, 200 n.miles on the surface, and 24 n.miles submerged.

In 2010, the U.S. Navy took DARPA's concept further: The Carderock Division of the Naval Surface Warfare Center devised several submersible seaplane concepts, most having a flying-wing design.[47] Radio-controlled scale models aided in the design process. As Convair had determined nearly half a century earlier, the study found that a submersible aircraft was feasible. But like the Sub-Plane, nothing practical has resulted from those studies.

The concept of flying submarines—or submersible seaplanes—remained for the creators of science fiction and comic books.

CHAPTER 12

The Atomic Age

In the aftermath of Japan's defeat, a mass of U.S. Navy officers and specialists descended upon the country, tasked with examining Japanese naval technology, especially the giant *Sentoku* Type submarines. Over the next year the U.S. Naval Technical Mission to Japan interviewed Japanese officers, sought documents, and examined the surviving remnants of the Japanese fleet. Based on their findings, the mission made the following suggestions for future U.S. submarine designs:

1. Reopening the question of carrying aircraft on submarines.
2. Study the advantages of building other than a single type of sub.
3. Recommending the building of an experimental submarine of each type determined upon. In this connection, consideration should be given to a multipurpose "hangar" capable of holding anything from planes to amphibious tanks.

. . .

6. Close affiliation with the atom-bomb experiments.[1]

The first and third recommendations likely stemmed from the U.S. Navy's inspection of the aircraft-carrying *I-400*, *I-401*, and *I-14*, while the sixth was acknowledgment that the atomic bomb could have radical impact on naval warfare. For the U.S. Navy the prospect of nuclear weapons prompted considerable thought about the potential of submarines as well as aircraft to deliver nuclear weapons on targets in the Soviet Union.

At that time the U.S. Army Air Forces possessed the only means of nuclear weapons delivery and threatened to decimate the Navy's budget and to retain its monopoly on the nation's nuclear arsenal by procuring advanced long-range nuclear bombers.

Soon after the war ended the Navy began planning a new class of carriers to operate nuclear-armed aircraft, led by the carrier *United States*; that ship was laid down in 1949—and cancelled five days later. Subsequently, the Navy sought other means of becoming a viable nuclear-armed service.

Submarines carrying nuclear strike aircraft were one option, although even the advancements in submarine and aircraft technology during the war could not eliminate all of the difficulties inherent in designing and operating aircraft-carrying submarines. Still, the Navy pursued several designs, most of them taking advantage of nuclear propulsion that became available in the 1950s.

Cruise missiles were another avenue for a Navy nuclear striking force. Cruise or guided missiles were developed by Germany and the United States during World War II. The German effort was the V-1 "flying bomb," more than 12,000 of which were launched against England and Allied forces in Europe in the latter part of the war. If fitted with a nuclear warhead and launched from a mobile platform—such as an aircraft, ship, or submarine—the cruise missile could quickly deliver devastating destructive power hundreds or thousands of miles away from its launch point.

The U.S. development of cruise missiles and submarine-launched aircraft in the postwar era were intimately intertwined. Early cruise missile configurations closely resembled aircraft, and the hangars and the catapults used to launch aircraft from submarines easily could be redesigned to launch missiles. In turn, innovations in missile storage and launching influenced the design of advanced aircraft-carrying submarine designs.

TROOP TRANSPORT SUBMARINES

Among all of the innovative concepts in the postwar era, the only submarines to carry manned aircraft after World War II were two converted U.S. Navy fleet submarines: the *Perch* (SSP 313) and *Sealion* (SSP 315). They were converted in 1948 to troop-carrying submarines to land raiders on hostile beachheads or behind enemy lines.[2]

Aft of their conning tower both submarines were fitted with a multipurpose hangar, 36 feet long and 16 feet in diameter that could hold rubber rafts or an LVT-type amphibious tractor, itself carrying a jeep or howitzer as well as troops. In 1948, two decades after commanding the U.S. Navy's aircraft-carrying submarine *S-1*, Rear Admiral Charles Momsen recommended that the Navy's General Board study converting fleet submarines to helicopter carriers.[3] Although no dedicated helicopter-carrying submarines were built, the *Perch* and *Sealion* were able to carry a Bell HTL helicopter, which fit within the hangar assembled with rotor blades folded within the hangar.[4] An electrically heated dipstick could keep the engine oil warm so that the helicopter could be

The hangar installed aft of the conning tower of the *Perch* (ASSP 313) could accommodate an amphibious tractor, inflatable boats, or a Bell HTL helicopter. She and her sister ship *Sealion* were the last submarines capable of carrying manned aircraft. (U.S. NAVY)

quickly rolled out of the hangar and lift off the deck about five minutes after the submarine surfaced.

Despite fears that the hangar could make diving difficult, the only issue encountered was that the submarine would unintentionally broach the surface at periscope depth due to the hydrodynamics of the hangar. The hangar had another novel effect—the submarines listed ten degrees to starboard with the hangar door swung open. Below, two of the submarines' four diesels and all of their torpedo tubes were removed to provide space for 160 Marines and their equipment.

The Marine Corps sought 12 transport submarines to carry a full assault battalion, but only the *Perch* and *Sealion* were converted. The Navy abandoned the concept of carrying an entire Marine battalion and concentrated on employing the submarines in special operations. In October 1950, during the Korean War, the *Perch* landed a team of British commandos in North Korea that successfully destroyed a train tunnel.[5] Both the *Perch* and *Sealion* had their hangars removed in 1956, although they were still able to embark special forces.[6]

In the summer of 1956, the *Sealion* used her expansive after superstructure, originally widened to support the hangar, as a helicopter landing pad. After an initial experiment with helicopters in May off the Little Creek amphibious base in Virginia, the *Sealion* embarked on a more intensive exercise in July: Flying from the air station in North Carolina, eight Sikorsky HRS helicopters shuttled Marines and their weapons and equipment to the submarine sailing off the coast.[7] Landing on the *Sealion*'s deck at five-minute intervals, 28 helicopter flights brought out 55 reconnaissance Marines and their gear. The *Perch* continued to conduct exercises with helicopters off the coast of California during

The *Sealion* (ASSP 315) continued to operate with helicopters to carry Marines ashore after her hangar was removed. This July 1956 photo shows a Sikorsky HRS (H-19) helicopter perched on her enlarged afterdeck. (NATIONAL ARCHIVES)

1958–1959.[8] Although the demonstrations were successful, the *Perch* and *Sealion* apparently never used helicopters operationally with troops.

Both submarines were active during the 1960s. The *Sealion* was deployed to the Caribbean in October 1961, during the Cuban Missile Crisis, ready to land special forces to scout for a potential amphibious assault of the island. During the Vietnam War both submarines landed underwater demolition teams (UDT; predecessors to the Navy's sea-air-land/SEAL teams) in South Vietnam in preparation for amphibious landings.

The *Perch* and *Sealion*, with their ability to carry a Bell HTL helicopter, remain the last submarines of any nation to operate manned aircraft.

"PILOTLESS AIRCRAFT"

The U.S. Navy's advanced cruise missile development began with the German V-1, which was reverse-engineered to produce the LVT-N-2 Loon. The Loon was 27 feet long with a wingspan of 18 feet; its launch weight was 5,020 pounds with a 2,100-pound warhead; the missile flew at about 400 mph.

The Loon program was under the control of the Bureau of Aeronautics as the Navy considered it an unmanned aircraft. At the time, cruise missiles were referred to as "pilotless aircraft."[9] From 1946 to 1953, the Loon missile was tested on board the modified fleet submarines *Carbonero* (SS 337) and *Cusk* (SSG 348). The Loon was launched with JATO rocket boosters from a ramp behind the conning tower and was guided by radio commands from the submarine. In 1947, the *Carbonero* was fitted with a small hangar to store a single Loon.[10]

The only fundamental difference between aircraft-carrying submarines and those early missile submarines was that the latter had no provision to recover their "aircraft." Evidently that similarity was not lost on the Bureau of Ships (BuShips)—the successor to the Bureau of Construction and Repair as the Navy's ship design authority: The *S-1* hangar installation of 1922 was used as reference for the *Carbonero*'s hangar![11]

The next stage of the Navy's cruise missile development was the SSM-N-8 Regulus.[12] Resembling the jet fighters of its day, the missile's fuselage had a similar shape, weight, and size as the North American F-86 Sabre. The Alison J33 turbojet of the Regulus already was flying in several Air Force and Navy aircraft. The missile's folding wings and rudder enabled the missile to be stored in a hangar on board a submarine or surface ship. Test variants of the missile had retractable landing gear so that they could land at airfields and be reused.

In 1952, after two years of land-based test flights, the Regulus was ready for trials on board a submarine. The modified fleet submarine *Tunny* (SSG 282) was provided with a launch ramp and a hangar derived from the amphibious vehicle/helicopter hangar fitted to the *Perch* and *Sealion*.[13] The hangar door opened upward, eliminating the list caused by the earlier side-opening hangar doors. Inside of the hangar a rotating "cage" held two, stacked Regulus missiles. Once the submarine surfaced, the missile was extracted from the hangar, its wings and tail were unfolded, and it was mounted on the launch ramp. The turbojet engine was started and the JATO rockets mounted to either side of the after fuselage propelled the missile into the air. The rocket boosters jettisoned a few seconds after takeoff.[14] After the first Regulus was removed, prepared, and launched, the cage inside the hangar would rotate 180 degrees and the second missile could be extracted. The first launch of a Regulus missile by a submarine was from the *Tunny* on 15 July 1953.[15]

The Regulus entered service in 1955, and the *Tunny* was followed by another fleet submarine conversion—the *Barbero* (SSG 317). Two torpedo attack submarines already under construction were modified on the ways to become guided missile submarines—the *Grayback* (SSG 574) and *Growler* (SSG 577).[16] Those two submarines, each with two 14-foot-diameter bow hangars, could hold four Regulus missiles.

In 1956, a purpose-built SSG on the BuShips drawing boards was redesigned with a nuclear propulsion plant. She was completed in 1960 as the *Halibut* (SSGN 587).[17] Her cavernous bow hangar, 25 feet in diameter and 90 feet

The *Tunny* (SSG 282) preparing to launch a Regulus I cruise missile in November 1956. Her hangar, based on those fitted to the *Perch* and *Sealion*, held two missiles. (U.S. NAVY)

long, was nearly three times the volume of the Japanese *Sentoku* Type submarine hangar and could accommodate five Regulus missiles.

Between 1959 and 1964, the five Regulus submarines conducted 41 nuclear deterrent patrols in the western Pacific, carrying nuclear-armed missiles that were targeted against Soviet installations in the Far East. Normally two diesel-electric SSGs or the *Halibut* SSGN were on station, bringing four or five missiles to the area.

The enlarged, supersonic Regulus II (SSM-N-9) missile was planned to succeed the original Regulus. Test flights were conducted, but the introduction of the Polaris submarine-launched ballistic missile made the Regulus II missile obsolete; it never went to sea. A dozen nuclear-propelled SSGNs were planned as carriers for the Regulus II. In the event, only three were ordered and they were completed as attack submarines (SSN 594–596) of the *Thresher* (SSN 593) design.

The *Tunny* and *Grayback* were converted to amphibious transport submarines (APSS) during the Vietnam War, and the *Halibut* became a unique special operations submarine (SSN 587).[18] The *Halibut* would have a key role in the later, clandestine recovery of the sunken Soviet ballistic missile submarine *K-129*.[19]

The Regulus program directly influenced designs for aircraft-carrying submarines. In late 1952, John Floberg, the Assistant Secretary of the Navy for Air, proposed the rapid conversion of a large number of fleet submarines into submarine aircraft carriers using the existing two-missile Regulus hangar design, designated SSG(V).[20]

In the search for a suitable aircraft for those submarines, the Navy approached Douglas Aircraft and its famed designer Edward Heinemann. He had already been tasked several years earlier by the Office of Naval Research to design a small, submarine-launched aircraft for the anti-submarine role. Heinemann, who preferred to be called an innovator rather than a designer, had an impressive résumé during his career at Douglas: he had designed the SBD Dauntless dive bomber, A-20 Havoc and A-26 Invader light bombers, and the AD Skyraider and A3D Skywarrior attack aircraft.[21]

The result of his design effort was a diminutive flying boat: the Douglas Model 640. With a length of 32 feet, a 25-foot wingspan, and a loaded weight of 7,800 pounds, the Model 640 would have been fitted with folding wings and nose to fit into a Regulus hangar like those on the *Barbero* and *Tunny*. The Westinghouse J34 turbojet (also used by the Regulus I) was fed air from intakes mounted atop the fuselage to keep spray out of the engines; an external fuel tank or bomb could be carried below the fuselage, although the aircraft could not alight on the water with them attached. The aircraft would be launched from a ramp like that used to launch the Regulus and would be propelled into the air by similar JATO rockets. After putting down on the water, the Model 640 would be recovered in a "dock" on the submarine's stern and hoisted on board with a crane.

The Office of Naval Research considered three designs from Heinemann and Douglas. The first was the Model 640, which had already been designed in detail. The second was an A4D Skyhawk fitted with hydro-skis with folding wings, nose, and tail, and other modifications to be launched from a submarine and recovered on water. (The length of the hangar would have to be increased by 4¼ feet to accommodate the modified Skyhawk.)

The third aircraft resembled a scaled-down Skyhawk able to fit in the existing *Tunny* hangar. All three aircraft could launch with an external fuel tank or nuclear bomb carried under the fuselage.

The Bureau of Aeronautics also considered the supersonic Convair F2Y Sea Dart for the SSG(V) (see Chapter 10). If redesigned with folding wings, the Sea Dart could fit inside a hangar with the same diameter as that of the *Tunny*, but 20 feet longer.[22] A similar concept was used in the Bureau of Ships CV/SS design (see below).

None of those proposals were accepted and the Douglas submarine-launched aircraft project was cancelled in 1955. None of the aircraft could alight on the water with external stores; therefore a nuclear weapon would have to be discarded into the sea if it were not delivered, which was deemed unacceptable. Nothing directly resulted from the development of the Model 640, but it did contribute significantly to development of the Skyhawk, which would go on to become a highly successful conventional attack aircraft for the U.S. Navy and for several other air forces and navies, while retaining a nuclear strike capability.[23]

NUCLEAR UNDERWATER CARRIERS

Along with the atom bomb came nuclear propulsion. Submarines propelled by nuclear energy could be independent of the atmosphere, able to travel submerged almost indefinitely at high speeds that previously were measured in hours. The tantalizing promise of nuclear propulsion also enabled the U.S. Navy to contemplate far larger submarines than had previously been considered. Among the many submarine concepts studied by the Navy in the late 1940s and 1950s were several aircraft-carrying submarine designs.

In late 1946, the Bureau of Ships began preliminary design of a "carrier submarine" designed SSV. The concept had been advocated during the yearly Submarine Officer's Conference of senior officers that examined future submarine requirements and programs.[24] The SSV would carry either two North American A2J "Super Savage" turboprop bombers or four McDonnell F2H Banshee turbojet fighters.[25] The Super Savages were able to carry the existing 10,000-pound Mk 3 (Fat Man) atomic bomb, and smaller nuclear weapons were in development for the Banshee.[26]

Unlike previous aircraft-carrying submarines, the SSV was to be a true submersible aircraft carrier to be fitted with a flight deck. Measuring 400 feet by 68 feet, the flight deck would be only slightly smaller than that of a World War II-era escort carrier. Fitted with cavernous hangars and multiple catapults, the submarine would be immense—600 feet long with 24,000 tons surface displacement; a variant with double the aircraft capacity would be 750 feet long and displace 35,000 tons surfaced. A 40,000-horsepower nuclear plant or a closed-cycle power plant would drive the submarine to 18 knots on the surface. The costs and engineering difficulties of such a design were immense. The SSV was not built.

The second design was developed in May 1952, when Secretary of the Navy Dan Kimball asked that BuShips "make a study of a nuclear submarine capable of carrying and operating three fast airplanes." After conferring with BuAer, the BuShips team determined that the best aircraft candidate would be the Convair F2Y Sea Dart.[27] The submarine-launched Sea Dart would have the same overall shape as the standard aircraft, but would be seven feet shorter with only a single turbojet engine. The aircraft's nose and wings would fold up, against the fuselage to fit into the submarine hangar. The Sea Dart would be capable of carrying two 1,000-pound nuclear bombs. Three modified Sea Darts could be carried by the submarine, initially designated CV/SS.

The CV/SS would be powered by a 60,000-horsepower nuclear plant to achieve a submerged speed of 28 knots.[28] It would displace about 7,000 tons submerged and would be 460 feet in length. Within the submarine would be three 15-foot-diameter hangars, each holding a single Sea Dart: hangars No. 1

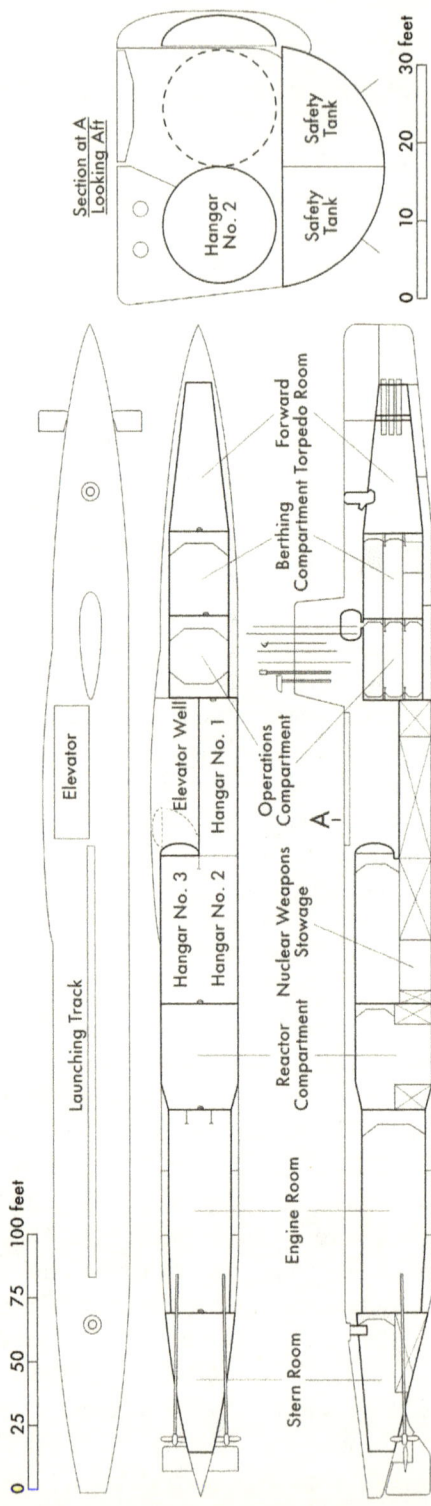

Section at A
Looking Aft

Hangar No. 2

Safety Tank

Safety Tank

Safety Tank

0   10   20   30 feet

Elevator

Launching Track

0   25   50   75   100 feet

Elevator Well

Hangar No. 3

Hangar No. 1

Hangar No. 2

Operations Compartment

Forward Torpedo Room

Berthing Compartment

Reactor Compartment

Nuclear Weapons Stowage

Engine Room

Stern Room

A

The Bureau of Ships CV/SS design. Three modified F2Y Sea Dart fighters/attack aircraft could be carried in amidships hangars. (©JACOB GUNNARSON) and No. 2 were inline, one abaft the other, on the starboard side; hangar No. 3 was on the port side, with a large, hemispherical watertight door at its forward end that opened into the elevator well. The hangars and watertight door were modeled after those on the purpose-built Regulus submarines. The hangars were interconnected to enable the aircraft to be transferred between them, and brought up to the submarine's deck *by elevator*.[29] Once on the submarine's deck, the Sea Darts would taxi down the flat, gently sloping stern into the water. The submarine's superstructure would be wide and flat, with the stern gently sloped downward for the aircraft to taxi in and out of the water. In rough seas the aircraft could use a 170-foot catapult on the afterdeck.

At that time the Navy was building the first nuclear submarine, the *Nautilus* (SSN 571), and was close to laying the keel for the second, the *Seawolf* (SSN 575). For the third nuclear submarine the Chief of Naval Operations ordered studies into a "truly high speed" submarine capable of exceeding the *Nautilus*'s 23-knot submerged speed. That submarine would either have to be very large to accommodate the enlarged reactor plant, or the reactor plant weight would have to be reduced. BuShips entertained several unusual concepts for the project, including placing the reactor in the bow so that only the after bulkhead of the reactor compartment would require heavy lead shielding.[30] Eventually the bureau accepted that the high-speed submarine would be large, an estimated 8,000 to 10,000 tons submerged, double that of the *Nautilus*.[31]

To justify the expense of building such a large aircraft-carrying submarine, the high-speed submarine would need to have a unique mission only possible with such a large displacement. The CV/SS, already a large design, fit that requirement. BuShips proposed building variants of the design capable of carrying guided missiles, or missiles *and* aircraft. In 1955 the design was redesignated CVSSN, and the displacement grew to 9,000 tons submerged. Test depth was increased from 500 to 700 feet, and the reactor plant from 60,000 to 70,000 horsepower.

Ultimately the CVSSN was not built. Instead the Navy chose to build the large, high-speed submarine in the form of the *Triton*, a radar-picket submarine, capable of scanning the skies for aircraft with her large, sail-mounted radar. Commissioned in 1960, she was the world's largest submarine at the time, 447½ feet long with a submerged displacement of 7,780 tons. The *Triton*'s twin-reactor plant allowed her to achieve over 27 knots on the surface and about 23 knots submerged. But her role as a radar picket had already been rendered obsolete by carrier-based radar aircraft. Having never been operationally deployed in that role, she was best known for undertaking the world's first underwater circumnavigation of the globe in 1960. The *Triton* was decommissioned in 1969, becoming the first U.S. nuclear submarine to be taken out of service.

The final BuShips design for an underwater carrier was drawn up in 1957. Like the earlier SSV, that design would have a flight deck. With a length of 500 feet, beam of 120 feet, and displacements of 24,000 tons surfaced and 40,000 tons submerged, the submarine would carry six subsonic attack aircraft.[32] Take-off would be aided by rocket boosters and a ski jump at the bow. The nuclear propulsion plant would be the same as the earlier CVSSN, although the submarine would be much slower owing to its substantially larger displacement. That design was too large to be practical and was not pursued.

PROJECT FLYING CARPET

The Bureau of Aeronautics conceived of a more unusual type of submarine aircraft carrier employing Vertical Takeoff and Landing (VTOL) aircraft. Such aircraft were attractive for use on board ships and submarines because they did not require a takeoff run. Unlike the later British Harrier, which took off and landed with its fuselage oriented horizontally, most early VTOL aircraft of the 1950s did so in a vertical orientation. Although takeoff was straightforward, landing required unorthodox landing gear or a rig to catch the aircraft while it was in a precarious vertical hover.

BuAer's interest in VTOL aircraft began with submarine platforms being considered. In 1947 the bureau began design studies for a turboprop-powered VTOL fighter able to operate from merchant ships in convoys to provide protective air cover without an aircraft carrier. The aircraft would also be able to launch from submarines, with preliminary studies allowing for three aircraft to be operated from a single submarine.[33] As BuAer further developed the concept, the focus shifted away from the submarine role toward the convoy defense role. In 1950 the bureau solicited designs from aircraft manufacturers, resulting in the Lockheed VF and Convair FY Pogo VTOL fighter designs. Those turboprop aircraft, which landed on their rear control surfaces, had poor performance compared to contemporary conventional aircraft and they were difficult to land, in part due to a lack of reaction-control thrusters. The aircraft were flight tested by the Navy in 1954–1955 and the project was cancelled.[34]

A contemporary Air Force project—the Ryan XF-13 Vertijet—was more successful. By using vectored thrust from its turbojet and a reaction control system, it was more controllable than the Navy aircraft and successfully landed several times on a special vertical rig without touching the ground. Although the Air Force cancelled the Vertijet because of a lack of an operational requirement, the innovations it incorporated were not lost on the Navy.

BuAer hoped to increase the performance of a submarine-launched VTOL aircraft by using a turbojet-powered booster—termed the "Flying Carpet"—to lift an aircraft heavily laden with fuel and weapons into the air. As soon as the aircraft was boosted to a sufficient speed, the winged Flying

Carpet vehicle would detach and autonomously circle back to the submarine to recover vertically on the launch rail. After completing its mission the aircraft would return to the submarine and land vertically. The concept was patented by BuAer in 1955, and contracts were issued to Lockheed and Boeing for detailed designs in 1958.[35]

Boeing's design was selected by BuAer. The design of the Flying Carpet was tailored to the specific aircraft but followed a general theme: an airframe almost entirely consisting of two engines with stubby folding wings. Until an advanced VTOL aircraft was developed, the Flying Carpet would boost a Grumman F11F Tiger, which would be heavily modified with thrust-vectoring and a reaction-control system. To fit into existing Regulus submarine hangars, the aircraft would also have wings that folded at the roots and a folding tail assembly. Its corresponding Flying Carpet would be about 25 feet long with a 20-foot wingspan and would be powered by two J65 afterburning turbojets, the same engines in the F11F.[36]

Boeing planned for tests of the aircraft and Flying Carpet on board the Regulus submarine *Grayback*. At that time the *Grayback* was carrying out nuclear deterrence patrols in the Pacific and would not have been available for experimentation. Subsequently it seemed unlikely that either aircraft could have landed on the submarine because of the proximity of the sail and hangars to the small landing area. Tests of that iteration of the Flying Carpet never took flight.

Boeing designed a new Mach 3 aircraft powered by a single turbojet.[37] The aircraft resembled a dart, being 70 feet long with only a 21-foot wingspan. Some 1,500 pounds of its 32,630-pound gross weight was reserved for an unspecified armament. At 36 feet long with a 20½-foot wingspan, its corresponding Flying Carpet booster had two engines.

A larger aircraft required a larger submarine. Boeing's first submarine design—designated AN-1—was essentially a massive, scaled-up *Halibut*, enlarged to nearly 500 feet in length (from 350 feet). Boeing estimated a 16-knot submerged maximum speed from the widely used 15,000 horsepower S5W reactor plant. At 14,700 tons submerged the AN-1 had two large, *Halibut*-like hangars, each housing four aircraft. Before takeoff, the Flying Carpets would be affixed to the underside of the aircraft. After the aircraft had been launched and the Flying Carpets had returned, they would be stored in two smaller hangars to either side of the pressure hull to keep the vertical launchers clear for the aircraft to come back aboard.

Two parallel tracks on the deck would enable the aircraft to be moved to eight launchers spread out across the length of the submarine. Stabilized launchers would have been necessary for flight operations in other than calm seas. All eight aircraft could be launched within nine minutes of

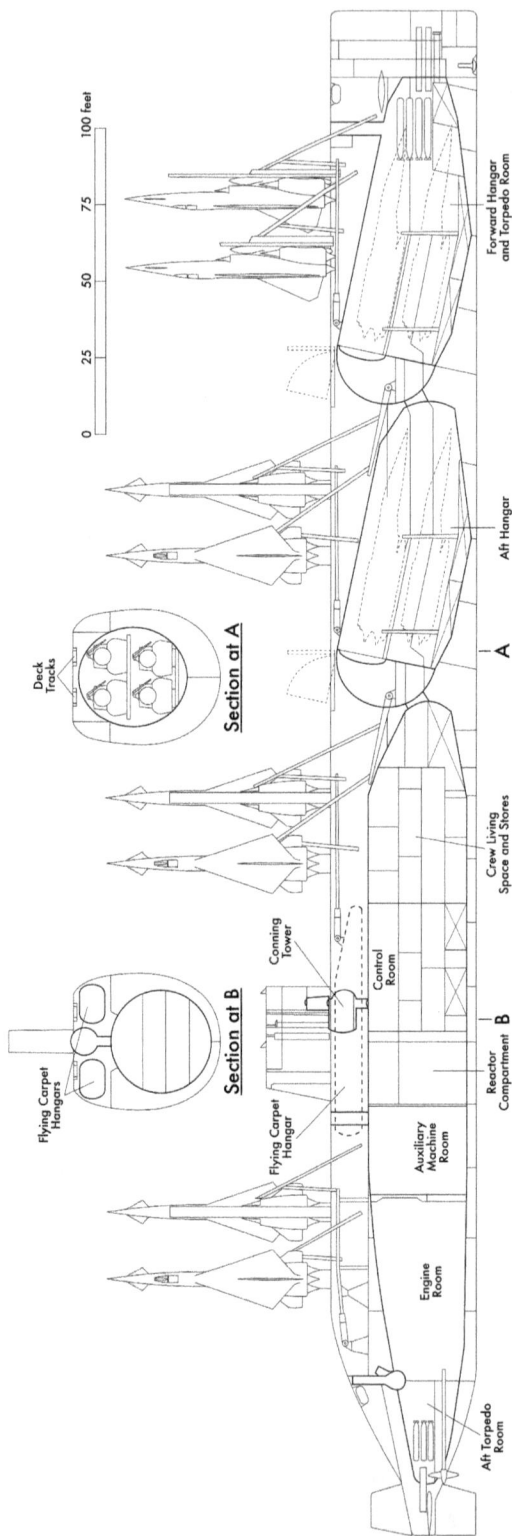

The Boeing AN-1 design developed for Project Flying Carpet. Resembling an enlarged *Halibut*, the enormous submarine would be able to carry eight super-sonic aircraft in two hangars. (©JACOB GUNNARSON)

surfacing—and 18 minutes in rough sea conditions. The submarine would carry enough weapons and fuel for ten missions per aircraft.

The AN-2, the second Boeing design, was similar to the AN-1, but with eight vertical silos, each holding one aircraft that would be raised above the deck by a telescoping launcher. Because the silos were shorter than the hangars on board the AN-1, the Mach 3 aircraft would have to be redesigned with a folding front fuselage. Although that configuration made aircraft handling simpler than with the Regulus-like gear on the AN-1, it introduced complications for landing. The AN-2 did not have separate hangars to store the Flying Carpet boosters after they returned to the submarine. They would have to land vertically on the launch rails. Thus, the returning aircraft would have to carefully hitch themselves to the Flying Carpets already mounted to the launchers.

The AN-1 and AN-2 progressed no further than the preliminary design stage. Beyond the questionable feasibility and utility of these designs, they would have to compete with existing shipbuilding projects. Polaris ballistic missile submarines had national priority, and BuShips may have been resistant to a shipbuilding project developed by BuAer and an aerospace company such as Boeing. Additionally, the projected cost of such a large craft was substantial: $140–150 million per submarine in 1958, compared with $75 million to build the *Nautilus*, $85 million for the *Halibut*, and $100 million for a Polaris ballistic missile submarine.[38]

PROJECT DIPPER

The Bureau of Naval Weapons, the 1959 successor to the Bureau of Aeronautics, initiated a submarine aircraft program intended to develop a submarine capable of launching and recovering aircraft *while submerged*. Project Dipper was begun about 1963 by the Naval Ordnance Laboratory in Corona in California.

A Polaris ballistic missile submarine design was to be adapted to carry 18 VTOL aircraft, each armed with three missiles, presumably with nuclear warheads. The aircraft would be watertight and buoyant to enable them to ascend from the mother submarine:

> In preparation for a mission, the aircraft would be placed, one at a time, in the top compartment [of the submarine] where the wings would be unfolded and locked. The compartment would then be flooded, the hatches opened and the aircraft allowed to rise to the surface controlled by a cable attached to a buoy. It would be released from the buoy, take off, carry out its mission, return to the buoy . . . and be reattached to the buoy and hauled back into the submarine.[39]

The classified program was likely abandoned after preliminary design studies.

PROJECT STRIKE

The final American proposal for an aircraft-carrying submarine came in November 1963, from the Electric Boat division of General Dynamics, builders of U.S. Navy submarines since the *Holland* (SS 1) of 1900. That proposal came in response to Project Strike, a study of manned naval strike aircraft by the Center for Naval Analyses (CNA). The CNA tasked Electric Boat with investigating underwater aircraft bases; however, the vulnerability and logistic challenges of a static base led the company to focus on aircraft-carrying submarines with VTOL aircraft.

Although a submarine aircraft carrier similar in capability to a surface "flat top" would be large and very expensive, Electric Boat considered that the increased stealth of such a craft would eliminate the need for escort ships, concluding "their practical use for naval strike operations by the 1970s appears virtually assured.[40]

VTOL aircraft had significantly advanced in the few years since Boeing's Flying Carpet study. The Hawker Siddeley P.1127—predecessor to the highly successful Harrier aircraft series—had flown in 1960, demonstrating that VTOL aircraft did not have to land in the awkward vertical orientation of the Vertijet and Flying Carpet.

Electric Boat produced 12 submarine carrier designs, designated A through L. All were broadly similar in size and external configuration, except for Design L, which was significantly smaller and only carried ten aircraft. In all but a few variants, Electric Boat's designs had flight decks large enough so that the aircraft could operate in STOL (Short Takeoff and Landing) mode, which would consume less fuel and allow for heavier payloads to be carried. A few designs had vertical or tilted silos for individual aircraft; most had large hangar decks below the flight deck, like a conventional aircraft carrier.

The majority of the design work was focused on Design A, the basic reference design. If built it would be by far the largest submarine ever constructed, dwarfing even the aircraft-carrying "submersible battlecruisers" proposed in the 1920s. At 840 feet long with a 106½-foot beam, the displacement would be around 46,000 tons surfaced and 100,000 tons submerged. The substantial difference between the surfaced and submerged displacements would give the submarine a high freeboard to keep the flight deck dry. Flasks to store enough compressed air to completely drain the ballast tanks would be too heavy; therefore, after surfacing, gas turbines mounted in the two sail structures would use their exhaust to fully blow the ballast tanks. Electric Boat estimated a 20-knot submerged speed with propulsion by two D2G nuclear reactor plants for a total of 60,000-horsepower. Defensive armament consisted of six torpedo tubes and several Mauler surface-to-air missile launchers—then in development by the U.S. Army—in waterproof containers.

Section at A
Looking Aft

0 25 50 75 100 feet

Forward Deck Elevator
Torpedo Room
Forward Aircraft Lock
Aux. Machinery Room
Submarine Personnel
Aviation Personnel
Crew Quarters
Aircraft Repair and Maintenance
Crew Quarters
Hangar Deck
Control Room
Conning Tower
Gas Turbine Chamber
Gas Turbine Exhaust
Crew Quarters
Reactor Compartment
Aft Aircraft Lock
Engine Room
Aux. Machinery Room
Steering Gear
Aft Deck Elevator

Mauler Missile Chamber
Aircraft Lock Compensating Tanks
Forward Aircraft Lock
Elevator
Hangar Deck
A
Aft Aircraft Lock
Aircraft Lock Compensating Tanks
Propulsion Turbines
Steering Gear
Mauler Missile Chambers

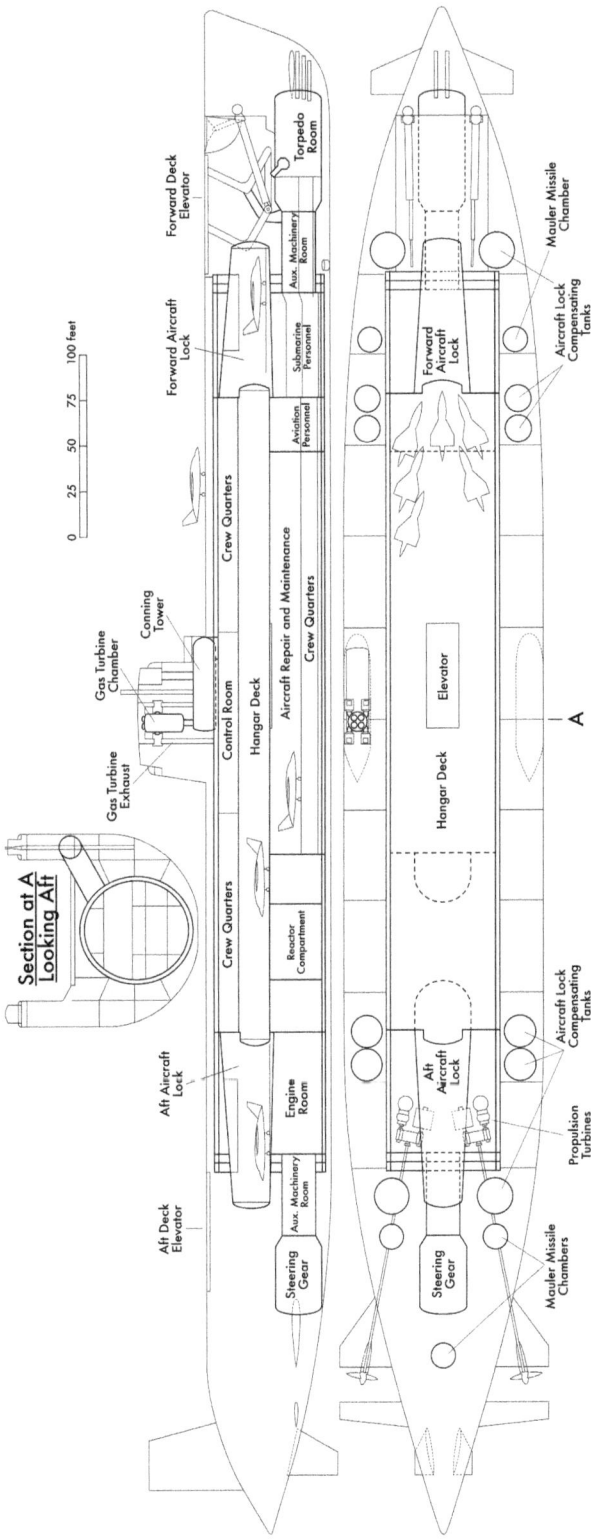

Electric Boat's design for a submersible aircraft carrier developed for Project Strike. (©JACOB GUNNARSON)

TABLE 12.1
Proposed U.S. Navy Aircraft-Carrying Submarines

	BuShips SSV	BuShips CVSSN	BuShips	Boeing AN-1	Electric Boat Design A
Proposed	1948	1952–1955	1957	1958	1963
Displacement					
surface (tons)	25,000	6,700	24,000	9,260	46,000
submerged (tons)	34,000	9,000	40,000	14,700	100,000
Length	600 ft. (183 m)	460 ft. (140 m)	500 ft. (152 m)	498 ft. 6 in. (152 m)	840 ft. (246 m)
Beam	68 ft. (20.7 m)	38 ft. (11.6 m)	120 ft. (36.6 m)	44 ft. 3 in. (13.5 m)	106 ft. 6 in. (32.5 m)
Draft					
Nuclear Reactors	*			1 S5W	2 D2G
Steam Turbines (shp)	40,000	70,000	70,000	2, 15,000	4, 60,000
Shafts		2	2	2	2
Speed					
surface (knots)	18	20	20		
submerged (knots)	15	28	>5	16	20.8
Test depth		700 ft. (213 m)			1,500 ft. (457 m)
Torpedo tubes		6 21-in. bow		4 21-in. bow 2 21-in. stern	6 21-in. bow
Torpedoes		22		20	
Missile Launchers	—	—	—	—	5 MIM-46 Mauler
Complement				163	430
Aircraft	2 A2J or 4 F2H	3 F2Y	6	8	28–42

*Both nuclear and closed-cycle propulsion plants were considered.

Aircraft were to be housed in a large hangar deck within the pressure hull, and there was a smaller deck below it for aircraft maintenance and repair. Possible aircraft were simply listed as the subsonic "small," supersonic "medium," and "large."[41] At maximum capacity the submarine could carry 38 small aircraft, 25 medium aircraft, or 22 small and eight large aircraft. A more typical loadout was to be 28 small aircraft. Aircraft were lifted to the flight deck by two elevators external to the pressure hull. Some 600 tons of ordnance and more than 1,600 tons of jet fuel would be carried. Surfacing, launching a strike force of 20 aircraft, and submerging again was to take only 22½ minutes!

Crew quarters, machinery, and the command centers were crammed into decks above and below the hangar. The pressure hulls would have an unusual structure, consisting of two cylindrical shells with the ring frame stiffeners in the gap between the shells. That design could be made from thinner steel plating than a more traditional hull and the gap between the shells could store jet fuel and water. The high strength of that structure would give the carrier submarine a test depth of 1,500 feet, some 200 feet deeper than the attack and missile submarines being built at that time.

The Electric Boat submarine aircraft carrier—even larger than the ambitious Boeing designs—was never seriously considered by the Navy. Its estimated cost was $271 million, not including the nuclear propulsion plant, compared to about $185 million at that time for a similar-size, conventional aircraft carrier. The submarine also was far too large for construction in any contemporary submarine shipyard including, ironically, Electric Boat's Groton, Connecticut yard. No U.S. VTOL aircraft were in development at the time; hence, the Navy would either have to initiate development of its own or wait for the British to complete development of the Harrier, which became operational in 1969. The proven success of ballistic missile submarines and large aircraft carriers made aircraft-carrying submarines superfluous.

The first decades of the Cold War saw rapid technological progress, both above and below the waves. The U.S. Navy showed considerable interest in developing submarines to carry nuclear-armed aircraft, with designs being drawn up and solicited by the Office of Naval Research, Bureau of Ships, and Bureau of Aeronautics/Naval Weapons. In addition to those official proposals, a number of private individuals advocated for the development of such submarines.[12]

Like many of the unusual and interesting submarine and aircraft designs of the postwar era, none of the ambitious submarine aircraft carriers came to fruition. Still, those unbuilt designs showed that interest in underwater aircraft carriers did not end with the sinking of the I-400 in 1946.

CHAPTER 13

Sailing into the Future

Aircraft-carrying submarines were the union of two of the most significant weapons of the 20th Century. Naval and aeronautical engineers and designers devised a great number of interesting and innovative aircraft and submarine designs in pursuit of that concept. However, the practical implementation of those designs almost always failed to provide an operational capability.

Aircraft-carrying submarines had two primary roles: reconnaissance and striking land targets. In the strike role, they were succeeded by guided (cruise) missile submarines and then by ballistic missile submarines. The replacement of a pilot with an electronic control system in guided missiles reduced the size of the missile compared to manned aircraft, and nuclear warheads vastly increased their destructive potential. Further, missiles could be launched with simplified systems compared to manned aircraft and did not need to be recovered after the mission.

SUBMARINE-LAUNCHED DRONES

Drones or Unmanned Aerial Vehicles (UAV) date to World War I, although effective reconnaissance drones did not fly until the Cold War era. The U.S. Navy's interest in submarine-launched drones began in the early 1990s. When the Soviet Union collapsed at the end of 1991, it left the submarine force without a capable sea-going adversary. Thus, the U.S. Navy placed greater emphasis on submarines supporting special forces in coastal waters.

Submarine technology advanced profoundly during the Cold War, with highly sensitive passive sonar replacing the periscope as the submarine's primary sensor. However, for reconnaissance missions requiring the periscope, the submarine's range of vision was almost as limited as it had been early in the 20th Century. Just as the earlier submarine-launched floatplanes served as long-range "eyes," UAVs could provide the submarine with the means of ob-serving the progress of operations ashore.

Trials initially focused on submarines taking over control of UAVs that were already airborne as dedicated, submarine-launched UAVs had not yet been developed. The U.S. nuclear-propelled submarine *Chicago* (SSN 721) was provided with a modified BRD-7 electronics mast with drone control consoles installed in her torpedo room. In a June, 1996, exercise off San Diego, the *Chicago* used a General Atomics RQ-1 Predator UAV to locate a simulated enemy missile launch site ashore. With the drone circling overhead to ensure that the area was clear, the submarine surfaced and launched a special forces team to "destroy" the missile site. During the two-day mission the *Chicago* used the Predator to guide the troops to the missile site, which was then destroyed with a simulated air strike.[1]

Launching a drone from a submerged submarine became a significant challenge. However, the U.S. Navy's Harpoon and Tomahawk cruise missiles, launched from standard, 21-inch-diameter submarine torpedo tubes, pro-vided a starting point. Drones could use the same encapsulation technology as the missiles, but reduced in size to be launched out of a submarine's three-inch- or six-inch-diameter launchers normally used to eject flares or acoustic countermeasure devices. Larger drones could be launched from the submarine's ten-inch-diameter trash disposal chute or the 21-inch torpedo tubes.

The first U.S. Navy drone to use cruise missile launching technology was the Northrop Grumman–developed Sea Ferret, which began development in 1991. It was intended to be launched using either a modified Harpoon capsule or six-inch countermeasure canister. The Sea Ferret was to be propelled by a turbojet with a range of about 375 miles. Although primarily a reconnaissance drone, it could be armed with a 20-pound warhead to serve as an attack missile.

In December 1996, the submarine *Asheville* (SSN 758) used a Sea Ferret in an exercise with a Marine reconnaissance team, mirroring the *Chicago*'s earlier experiment. A Sea Ferret prototype was affixed to the wing of a Cessna light aircraft, which flew the course directed by the submarine. Although the exer-cise was successful, the Sea Ferret was not developed further.

In 1995 the U.S. Naval Research Laboratory in Washington, D.C., began studies into submarine-launched drones. The Submarine-launched Tactical Airborne Reconnaissance Expendable (STARE) drone would be launched from a six-inch countermeasure canister. It was to be propelled by an elec-tric motor for a 30-minutes flight. The 25-pound UAV would be expendable, obviating the need for complex recovery capabilities. Although the STARE drone did not enter the prototype stage, the laboratory continued studies into submarine-launched drones.[2]

A further submarine-drone experiment was carried out in June 2001, off the coast of San Diego. As part of a broader experimental Navy UAV exercise, the submarine *Jefferson City* (SSN 759) controlled two prototype Dakota UAVs. Launch and recovery was carried out on nearby San Clemente Island with the submarine directing the drones and receiving visual imagery while at periscope depth. Although a data link between the *Jefferson City* and the UAVs was established, both drones malfunctioned and crashed.[3]

The Lockheed Martin "Skunk Works"—famed for highly advanced aerospace projects—undertook a far more ambitious project: a large UAV that could be launched and recovered from a submerged submarine.[4] In 2003, that concept was selected by the Defense Advanced Research Projects Agency (DARPA) for further study, and a detailed design effort began in 2005. The resulting drone, named the Cormorant, was a most unusual aircraft.[5] Its angular, 19-foot-long fuselage hung from two "gull" wings with a large vertical stabilizer below the fuselage. A triangular air intake and sharp, faceted surfaces would minimize its radar signature.

The Cormorant's two weapons bays could accommodate 1,000 pounds of air-to-ground weapons, supplies for ground forces, or deployable sensors. The Cormorant also could act as a communications relay for ground forces.

The UAV could be deployed from converted *Ohio* (SSBN 726)-class ballistic missile submarines. In the early 2000s the four oldest *Ohio*-class submarines had their ballistic missile tubes deactivated and were redesignated SSGNs. The altered missile tubes could launch Tomahawk cruise missiles, carry equipment for Navy special forces, or deploy unmanned underwater vehicles.

The Cormorant was designed to fold into the 87-inch-diameter Trident launch tubes. To ensure that the aircraft was watertight and buoyant, the engine intake and exhaust were closed with inflatable seals, and voids in the airframe were filled with pressurized nitrogen gas and syntactic foam—a rigid, light material made of glass microspheres.

At a depth of 150 feet the Cormorant would be released and float to the surface. On the surface, two rocket boosters would send the UAV into the air before the turbofan engine started. After completing its mission, the Cormorant would fly back to the submarine and either descend on a parachute or perform a controlled stall to alight on the water. It would then activate an acoustic beacon and deploy a recovery cable. The submarine would deploy an unmanned underwater vehicle that could grab the cable and attach the drone to a launch/recovery mast projecting from the missile tube.[6]

Lockheed Martin planned to deliver the Cormorant to the Navy in 2010. In October 2006, the firm conducted tests of the Cormorant's launch and recovery systems. The tests were successful, but the Cormorant never reached flight testing: The project was cancelled in 2008.

While the Cormorant promised impressive performance, each of the 9,000-pound drones would cost an estimated $10 million. An expendable drone launched using modified cruise missile capsules could be produced much cheaper than the Cormorant, which had to rely on a convoluted recovery procedure and expensive and maintenance-intensive gas pressurization, inflatable seals, and syntactic foam to remain watertight.

The *Albany* (SSN 753) was the first U.S. submarine to launch a drone, albeit while on the surface. On 20 July 2005, she launched an AeroVironment RQ-14 Dragon Eye off the coast of Georgia. Although only able to be launched from the surface, the Dragon Eye's flight could be controlled while the submarine was submerged using an antenna fitted on the *Albany*'s Type 18 periscope. With an endurance of one hour and a range of 25 miles, the Dragon Eye was envisioned as an expendable reconnaissance platform to monitor special forces operations.[7]

Similarly, the AeroVironment FQM-151 Pointer UAV was considered for launch from surfaced *Ohio*-class SSGNs to support special forces operations. No SSGN was available for trials, thus the ballistic missile submarine *Alabama* (SSBN 731) launched and recovered the drone in November 2005.[8] Beyond their use in special operations, Dragon Eye UAVs have been used by SSBNs returning to port to screen the waters ahead for potential terrorist threats.[9]

In February 2008, the *Montpelier* (SSN 765) launched a Mission Technologies Buster UAV while surfaced in the Persian Gulf, marking the first operational use of a U.S. submarine-launched drone. Buster drones were deployed on the *Florida* (SSGN 728) later that year. However, the necessity to launch while on the surface remained a major limitation.

The first drone to be launched from a submerged U.S. submarine was a modified AeroVironment Switchblade in 2009.[10] Developed by the U.S. Army as a "loitering munition"—a *kamikaze* drone—the Switchblade was inexpensive and dispensable, alleviating the need for the intricate recovery process of previous drones.

The modified Switchblade was launched from the ten-inch-diameter trash disposal unit fitted in the bottom of the submarine. To clear the submarine's hull, the Raytheon-designed launch canister was initially negatively buoyant and sank. At a depth of 200 feet, a collar around the canister inflated, sending it up to the surface.[11] The canister deployed a water drogue to stabilize and a vane to orient it relative to the wind. The launch tube then tilted to a 35-degree angle and fired the drone into the air. The Switchblade was largely autonomous, with the submarine only providing updates to its mission profile.[12]

The Switchblade was tested again during the Trident Warrior exercise in June 2010.[13] Unlike earlier submarine-launched drones, which were intended to gather intelligence on activities ashore, the primary purpose of the Switchblade was to extend the submarine's range of vision for seeking out ship targets. During the two exercises the drone was used to provide targeting information on multi-ship formations from beyond the submarine's sensor horizon. The Switchblade was judged successful.[14]

After demonstrating the Switchblade to the Navy, AeroVironment began development of an improved model—the Blackwing 10C.[15] Endurance was increased from 15 minutes to one hour by lengthening the fuselage. The four-pound drone measures 19½ inches in length with a 27-inch wingspan. It is equipped with visible light and infrared cameras.[16]

Initially the Blackwing was launched from the six-inch countermeasure launchers external to the submarine's pressure hull. Subsequently a three-inch-diameter canister—the Hammerhead—was developed for the Blackwing to be deployed from the internal countermeasure launcher. The Hammerhead is much simpler than the ten-inch canister used to launch the Switchblade. Positively buoyant, the canister ascends to the surface and launches the drone into the air from a vertical orientation. A Blackwing-equipped submarine typically carries a set of six to 12 of the drones.[17]

The 2017 Navy budget included funding for 118 Blackwings, making it the first submarine-launched UAV to be acquired in significant numbers.[18] After several years of trials the Blackwing entered service in September, 2020, as the Submarine-Launched Unmanned Aerial System (SLUAS).

During an exercise in 2020, the submarine *Annapolis* (SSN 760) launched a Blackwing after gaining a long-range sonar contact on the littoral combat ship *Charleston* (LCS 18). Using the targeting data relayed back from the UAV, the *Annapolis* was able to simulate a torpedo attack on the *Charleston*.[19]

The U.S. Navy also has employed a second, larger model of UAV. Beginning in 2006, the XFC drone was developed by the Naval Research Laboratory.[20] In contrast to the short-endurance Blackwing, which was developed primarily to seek out naval targets, the XFC was developed for long-endurance missions.

The 19-pound XFC has a novel wing configuration: one of the wings is mounted under the fuselage, the other on top of it. When unfolded, the wings create an asymmetric X-shape. That unorthodox arrangement has excellent aerodynamics and high reliability to properly unfold.[21] Its hydrogen fuel cell provides up to ten hours of power for the motor, avionics, and sensors at a cruise speed of 35 mph.[22] The XFC is deployed by the Sea Robin launch system, which fits inside an empty Tomahawk cruise missile capsule.[23]

Time-lapse photo of the XFC drone being launched by the attack submarine *Providence* (SSN 719) on 12 December 2013. (U.S. NAVY)

The XFC's first test flight from a submarine occurred on 12 December 2013, when the submarine *Providence* (SSN 719) launched an XFC prototype from a torpedo tube.[24] In flight, the drone streamed four hours of video to the submarine before it landed in the Bahamas. The XFC subsequently became operational with 13 units included in the Navy 2017 budget.[25]

EUROPEAN DRONES

The development of submarine-launched drones has been proceeding in other countries, mostly driven by the efforts of private corporations. In 2008, the German firm Gabler Maschinenbau designed a modular submarine mast that could store and launch a small folding VOLANS drone, mount a machine gun, or deploy sensors.[26] However, that system was not procured by any navy.

In 2020 the French firm Diodon developed the HP30 waterproof quadcopter drone for submarine launch. The quadcopter is a rotary-wing drone with a motor and propeller at each of the four corners of the airframe. The drone is controlled by individually varying the speed of each propeller. The HP30's motors are mounted on inflatable outriggers, allowing the drone to float and to fold to fit in a watertight canister. The buoyant canister is launched via the submarine's escape trunk and springs open once it reaches the surface, creating a takeoff platform for the drone. The HP30 has an endurance of 30 minutes, a maximum range of five miles, and a top speed of 34 mph.

In May 2023 the HP30 was successfully deployed from the *Rubis*-class submarine *Améthyste* off Toulon.[27]

In 2022, the Israeli firm Spear exhibited the Ninox 103 drone, a folding quadcopter that can be launched from a submarine at depths up to 160 feet. The Ninox has an endurance of 50 minutes and a payload of 2.2 pounds.[28]

Russia also has shown interest in submarine UAV projects. In 2021, the Rubin design bureau publicized its Border and Offshore Submersible Sentry (BOSS) concept.[29] Intended as a hybrid between a submarine and a surface patrol vessel, the design would displace 1,300 tons on the surface and measure 236 feet in length. On the surface, the diesel-electric propulsion plant could power the submarine to 21 knots, with a range of 10,000 n.miles at 10 knots. Its tumblehome hull, optimized for surface running, would have a wave-piercing bow, a bulbous bow sonar dome, and a substantial superstructure deck.

The BOSS would be equipped with four 13-inch (324-mm) torpedo tubes, a retractable gun in the sail, and surface-to-air missile launchers. Two hangars built into the stern of the BOSS could store inflatable boats for boarding teams or unmanned aerial vehicles. Conceptual renderings show a helicopter UAV with a three-hour endurance. The UAV would expand the submarine's search

Rendering produced by the Rubin submarine design bureau of its BOSS design. Twin hangars aft of the sail would be able to carry UAVs or inflatable boats.
(RUBIN CENTRAL DESIGN BUREAU)

radius for border protection, coastal defense, and anti-piracy missions. The launch and recovery of the drone would be totally automated. The design was intended for export to smaller navies, although no orders were forthcoming when this volume went to press.[30]

Cruise missiles and drones launched from submarines represent the modern incarnation of a concept that began with the Imperial German Navy more than a century earlier. While submarine technology has greatly advanced during that time, the fundamental limit on their range of vision through the periscope is unchanged. Whether manned or autonomous, submarine-launched aircraft provide a submarine with significantly increased ability to perform reconnaissance and seek out targets, and to attack those targets. The difficulties of launching and recovery of manned aircraft resulted in the demise of the aircraft-carrying submarine after World War II, but the advances in UAV technology will enable the concept of submarine aircraft carriers to expand the submarine's capability into the 21st Century.

APPENDIX A

Aircraft-Carrying Submarines

Germany
U-9 class

Name	Laid Down	Launched	Completed	Notes
U-12		6 May 1910	13 Aug 1911	Sunk 10 Mar 1915 by British destroyers in North Sea

Displacement		
surface	493 tons	
submerged	611 tons	
Length	188 feet, 3 inches (57.4 m)	
Beam	19 feet, 8 inches (6.0 m)	
Draft	10 feet, 3 inches (3.15 m)	
Propulsion	4 kerosene engines, 1,000 shp; 2 electric motors, 1,160 shp; 2 shafts	
Speed		
surface	14.2 knots	
submerged	8.1 knots	
Range		
surface	3,300 n.miles at 9 knots	
submerged	80 n.miles at 5 knots	
Test depth	164 feet (50 m)	
Torpedo tubes	2 18-inch (450-mm) bow, 2 18-inch (450-mm) stern	
Torpedoes	6	
Guns	1 3.5-inch (88-mm)	
Complement	29	
Aircraft	1 FF 29a	

Britain

E class, Group 3

Name	Laid Down	Launched	Completed	Notes
E-22	25 Nov 1914	27 Aug 1915	8 Nov 1915	Sunk 25 Apr 1916 by German submarine *UB-18* in North Sea

Displacement	
surface	662 tons
submerged	835 tons
Length	181 feet (55.2 m)
Beam	23 feet, 6 inches (7.2 m)
Draft	12 feet 6 inches (3.8 m)
Propulsion	2 diesel engines, 3,200 shp; 2 electric motors; 1,680 shp; 2 shafts
Speed	
surface	16 knots
submerged	10 knots
Range	
surface	3,000 n.miles at 10 knots
submerged	65 n.miles at 5 knots
Test depth	100 feet (31 m)
Torpedo tubes	2 18-inch (450-mm) bow 2 18-inch (450-mm) beam 1 18-inch (450-mm) stern
Torpedoes	6
Guns	—
Complement	30
Aircraft	2 Sopwith Schneider

United States

S class

Name	Laid Down	Launched	Completed	Notes
S-1 (SS 105)	11 Dec 1917	26 Oct 1918	5 Jun 1920	Transferred to Royal Navy 20 Apr 1942, scrapped 14 Sept 1945

Displacement	
surface	908 tons
submerged	1,096 tons
Length	219 feet, 3 inches (66.8 m)
Beam	20 feet, 8 inches (6.3 m)
Draft	16 feet, 9 inches (5.1 m)
Propulsion	2 diesel engines, 1,200 shp; 2 electric motors, 760 shp;* 2 shafts
Speed	
surface	14.5 knots
submerged	11 knots
Range	
surface	5,000 n.miles at 10 knots
submerged	100 n.miles at 5 knots
Test depth	200 feet (61 m)
Torpedo tubes	4 21-inch (533-mm) bow
Torpedoes	12
Guns	1 4-inch (76-mm)
Complement	38
Aircraft	1 MS-1/XS-1/XS-2

*This figure is from "General Information U.S. Submarine Torpedo Boat S-1," dated September 1924. Other sources, such as the 1924 *Ships' Data: U.S. Naval Vessels*, give the total electric motor power as 1,500 shp.

Britain

M class

Name	Laid Down	Launched	Completed	Notes
M-2	13 Jul 1916	19 Oct 1918	14 Feb 1920	Lost 26 Jan 1932 in English Channel

Displacement	
surface	1,663 tons
submerged	1,950 tons
Length	295 feet, 7.5 inches (90.1 m)
Beam	24 feet, 6 inches (7.5 m)
Draft	17 feet, 7.5 inches (5.4 m)

Propulsion	2 diesel engines, 2,400 shp; 4 electric motors, 1,600 shp; 2 shafts
Speed	
surface	14 knots
submerged	8 knots
Range (nm/kn)	
surfaced	3,700 n.miles at 10 knots
submerged	24 n.miles at 4 knots
Test depth	200 feet (61 m)
Torpedo tubes	4 18-inch (450-mm) bow
Torpedoes	8
Guns	1 3-inch (76-mm)
Complement	65
Aircraft	1 Parnall Peto

France
Type Q5

Name	Laid Down	Launched	Completed	Notes
Surcouf	1 Jul 1927	18 Nov 1929	16 Apr 1934	Lost about 18 Feb 1942 in Caribbean

Displacement	
surface	3,304 tons
submerged	4,318 tons
Length	360 feet, 11 inches (110.0 m)
Beam	29 feet, 6 inches (9.0 m)
Draft	23 feet, 7 inches (7.2 m)
Propulsion	2 diesel engines, 7,600 shp; 2 diesel generators, 1,440 hp; 2 electric motors, 3,400 shp; 2 shafts
Speed	
surface	18.5 knots
submerged	8.5 knots
Range	
surface	10,000 n.miles at 10 knots
submerged	59 n.miles at 5 knots
Test depth	262 feet (80 m)

Torpedo tubes	4 21.5-inch (550-mm) bow
	2 21.5-inch (550-mm) external
	4 16-inch (400-mm) external
Torpedoes	14 21.5-inch (550-mm)
	8 16-inch (400-mm)
Guns	2 8-inch (203-mm)
	2 37-mm
Complement	118
Aircraft	1 MB 41 or MB 411

Italy

Agostino Barbarigo class

Name	Laid Down	Launched	Completed	Notes
Andrea Provana	16 Oct 1915	27 Jan 1918	10 Sept 1918	Damaged 30 Mar 1927 by accidental explosion, stricken 21 Jan 1928; conning tower on display in Turin

Displacement	
surface	784 tons
submerged	912 tons
Length	219 feet, 10 inches (67.0 m)
Beam	19 feet, 4 inches (5.9 m)
Draft	12 feet, 8 inches (3.9 m)
Propulsion	2 diesel engines, 2,600 shp; 2 electric motors, 1,300 shp; 2 shafts
Speed	
surface	16.8 knots
submerged	9.3 knots
Range (nm/kn)	
surface	1,607 n.miles at 9.3 knots
submerged	139 n.miles at 1.6 knots
Test depth	164 feet (50 m)
Torpedo tubes	4 18-inch (450-mm) bow
	2 18-inch (450-mm) stern
Torpedoes	10
Guns	1 3-inch (76-mm)
Complement	40
Aircraft	1 Dornier *Libelle II*

Italy

Ettore Fieramosca class

Name	Laid Down	Launched	Completed	Notes
Ettore Fieramosca	17 Jul 1926	14 Apr 1929	15 Dec 1931	Decommissioned 10 Apr 1941, stricken 18 Oct 1946

Displacement
    surface   1,531 tons
    submerged   1,934 tons

Length   270 feet, 3 inches (82.4 m)

Beam   26 feet, 4 inches (8.0 m)

Draft   17 feet, 5 inches (5.3 m)

Propulsion   2 diesel engines, 6,000 shp; 1 diesel generator, 325 hp; 2 electric motors, 2,000 shp; 2 shafts

Speed
    surface   15.5 knots
    submerged   9 knots

Range
    surface   4,605 n.miles at 8 knots
    submerged   78 n.miles at 3 knots

Test depth   327 feet (100 m)

Torpedo tubes   4 21-inch (533-mm) bow
                          4 21-inch (533-mm) stern

Torpedoes   14

Guns   1 4.7-inch (120-mm)

Complement   78

Aircraft   1 Macchi M.53 or Piaggio P.8*

*As built; aircraft hangar removed before commissioning. All other specifications as completed.

Germany

Type XI

Name	Laid Down	Launched	Completed	Notes
U-112–U-115				Ordered 17 Jan 1939, cancelled Sept 1939

Displacement

surface	3,140 tons
submerged	3,930 tons

Length   377 feet (115 m)

Beam   31 feet, 2 inches (9.5 m)

Draft   20 feet, 3 inches (6.2 m)

Propulsion   8 diesel engines, 17,600 shp; 2 diesel generators, 400 hp; 2 electric motors, 2,200 shp; 2 shafts

Speed

surface	23.3 knots
submerged	7 knots

Range

surface	15,800 n.miles at 12 knots
submerged	50 n.miles at 4 knots

Test depth   328 feet (100 m)

Torpedo tubes   4 21-inch (533-mm) bow
2 21-inch (533-mm) stern

Torpedoes   12

Guns   4 5-inch (127-mm)
2 37-mm
1 20-mm

Complement   117

Aircraft   1 Ar 231

Germany
Type IXD2

Name	Laid Down	Launched	Completed	Notes
U-177	25 Nov 1940	1 Oct 1941	14 Mar 1942	Sunk 6 Feb 1944 by U.S. aircraft in South Atlantic
U-178	24 Dec 1940	25 Oct 1941	14 Feb 1942	Scuttled 25 Oct 1944 at Bordeaux
U-179	15 Jan 1941	18 Nov 1941	7 Mar 1942	Sunk 8 Oct 1942 by British destroyer *Active* in South Atlantic
U-181	15 Mar 1941	30 Dec 1941	9 May 1942	Taken over by Japan 5 May 1945, renamed *I-501* 15 July 1945, scuttled 15 Feb 1946 by British in South China Sea
U-182	7 Apr 1941	3 Mar 1942	30 Jun 1942	Sunk 16 May 1943 by USS *MacKenzie* (DD 614) in North Atlantic

Name	Laid Down	Launched	Completed	Notes
U-196	10 Jun 1941	24 Apr 1942	11 Sept 1942	Lost about 1 Dec 1944 in Indian Ocean
U-197	5 Jul 1941	21 May 1942	10 Oct 1942	Sunk 20 Aug 1943 by British aircraft in Indian Ocean
U-198	1 Aug 1941	15 Jun 1942	3 Nov 1942	Sunk 12 Aug 1944 by British and Indian warships in Indian Ocean
U-199	10 Oct 1941	11 Jul 1942	28 Nov 1942	Sunk 31 Jul 1943 by U.S. and Brazilian aircraft in South Atlantic
U-200	3 Nov 1941	10 Aug 1942	22 Dec 1942	Sunk 24 Jun 1943 by British aircraft in North Atlantic
U-847	23 Nov 1941	5 Sept 1942	23 Jan 1943	Sunk 27 Aug 1943 by aircraft from USS *Card* (CVE 11) in North Atlantic
U-848	6 Jan 1942	6 Oct 1942	20 Feb 1943	Sunk 5 Nov 1943 by U.S. aircraft in South Atlantic
U-849	20 Jan 1942	31 Oct 1942	11 Mar 1943	Sunk 25 Nov 1943 by U.S. aircraft in South Atlantic
U-850	17 Mar 1942	7 Dec 1942	17 Apr 1943	Sunk 20 Dec 1943 by aircraft from USS *Bogue* (CVE 9) in North Atlantic
U-851	18 Mar 1942	15 Jan 1943	21 May 1943	Lost late Mar or early Apr 1944 in North Atlantic
U-852	15 Apr 1942	28 Jan 1943	15 Jun 1943	Damaged 2 May 1944 by British aircraft in Arabian Sea, beached and scuttled 3 May 1944 in Somalia
U-859	15 May 1942	2 Mar 1943	8 Jul 1943	Sunk 23 Sept 1944 by British submarine *Trenchant* in Indian Ocean
U-860	15 Jun 1942	23 Mar 1943	12 Aug 1943	Sunk 15 Jun 1944 by aircraft from USS *Solomons* (CVE 67) in South Atlantic
U-861	15 Jul 1942	29 Apr 1943	2 Sept 1943	Surrendered 9 May 1945 in Norway, scuttled 31 Dec 1945 by British off N. Ireland
U-862	15 Aug 1942	8 Jun 1943	7 Oct 1943	Taken over by Japan 5 May 1945, renamed *I-502* 15 Jul 1945, scuttled 15 Feb 1946 by British in South China Sea
U-863	15 Sept 1942	29 Jun 1943	3 Nov 1943	Sunk 29 Sept 1944 by U.S. aircraft in South Atlantic
U-864	15 Oct 1942	12 Aug 1943	9 Dec 1943	Sunk 9 Feb 1945 by British submarine *Venturer* in North Sea
U-871	14 Nov 1942	7 Sept 1943	15 Jan 1944	Sunk 26 Sept 1944 by U.S. aircraft in North Atlantic
U-872	23 Dec 1942	20 Oct 1943	10 Feb 1944	Damaged 29 Jul 1944 by U.S. aircraft at Bremen, stricken 10 Aug 1944

Name	Laid Down	Launched	Completed	Notes
U-873	17 Feb 1943	11 Nov 1943	1 Mar 1944	Surrendered 16 May 1945 in Maine, used for U.S. Navy trials in 1946, scrapped Mar 1948
U-874	17 Mar 1943	21 Dec 1943	8 Apr 1944	Surrendered 9 May 1945 in Norway, scuttled 31 Dec 1945 by British off N. Ireland
U-875	11 May 1943	16 Feb 1944	21 Apr 1944	Surrendered 9 May 1945 in Norway, scuttled 31 Dec 1945 by British off Norway
U-876	5 Jun 1943	29 Feb 1944	24 May 1944	Damaged 9 Apr 1945 by British aircraft in Germany, scuttled 3 May 1945

Displacement
  surface   1,616 tons
  submerged   1,804 tons

Length   287 feet, 5 inches (87.6 m)

Beam   24 feet, 7 inches (7.5 m)

Draft   17 feet, 9 inches (5.4 m)

Propulsion   2 diesel engines, 4,400 shp; 2 diesel generators, 1,160 hp, 2 electric motors, 1,000 shp; 2 shafts

Speed
  surface   19.2 knots
  submerged   6.9 knots

Range
  surface   23,700 n.miles at 12 knots
  submerged   57 n.miles at 4 knots

Test depth   295 feet (90 m)

Torpedo tubes 4 21-inch (533-mm) bow
             2 21-inch (533-mm) stern

Torpedoes   24

Guns   1 4.1-inch (105-mm)
             1 37-mm
             4 20-mm (2 twin)

Complement 57

Aircraft   2 Fa 330*

*One stored externally in the superstructure, one stored inside the pressure hull.

Japan
Kiraisen Type

Name	Laid Down	Launched	Completed	Notes
I-21	20 Oct 1924	30 Mar 1926	31 Mar 1927	Renamed *I-121* 1 Jun 1938, surrendered Sept 1945, scuttled by U.S. 30 Apr 1946

Displacement	
surface	1,383 tons
submerged	1,768 tons
Length	280 feet (85.2 m)
Beam	24 feet, 5 inches (7.2 m)
Draft	14 feet, 5 inches (4.4 m)
Propulsion	2 diesel engines, 2,400 shp; 2 electric motors, 1,100 shp; 2 shafts
Speed	
surface	14.5 knots
submerged	7 knots
Range	
surface	10,500 n.miles at 8 knots
submerged	40 n.miles at 4.5 knots
Test depth	200 feet (61 m)
Torpedo tubes	4 21-inch (533-mm) bow
Torpedoes	12
Mine tubes	2 33.9-inch (861-mm) stern
Mines	42
Guns	1 5.5-inch (140-mm)
Complement	75
Aircraft	1 Kugisho No. 1 or No. 2

Japan
Kaidai 1 Type

Name	Laid Down	Launched	Completed	Notes
I-51	6 Apr 1921	29 Nov 1921	20 Jun 1924	Stricken 1 Apr 1940

Displacement

surface	1,535 tons
submerged	2,430 tons

Length 300 feet (91.4 m)

Beam 28 feet, 1 inch (8.6 m)

Draft 14 feet, 1 inch (4.3 m)

Propulsion 4 diesel engines, 5,200 shp; 4 electric motors, 2,000 shp; 4 shafts*

Speed

surface	20 knots
submerged	10 knots

Range

surface	7,500 n.miles at 10 knots
submerged	100 n.miles at 3 knots

Test depth 200 feet (61 m)

Torpedo tubes 6 21-inch (533-mm) bow
2 21-inch (533-mm) stern

Torpedoes 24

Guns 1 4-inch (120-mm)

Complement 60

Aircraft 1 Kugisho No. 2

*Refitted with two diesels and two shafts in 1932.

Japan
Junsen 1 Type Modified

Name	Laid Down	Launched	Completed	Notes
I-5	30 Oct 1929	19 Jun 1931	31 Jul 1932	Sunk 19 Jul 1944 by USS *Weyman* (DE 36) near Guam

Displacement

surface	2,243 tons
submerged	2,921 tons

Length 319 feet, 11 inches (97.5 m)

Beam 30 feet, 3 inches (9.2 m)

Draft 16 feet, 6 inches (5.0 m)

Propulsion 2 diesel engines, 6,000 shp; 1 diesel generator, 603 hp; 2 electric motors, 2,600 shp; 2 shafts

Speed

surface	18 knots
submerged	8 knots

Range

surface	24,000 n.miles at 10 knots
submerged	60 n.miles at 3 knots

Test depth   265 feet (80 m)

Torpedo tubes   4 21-inch (533-mm) bow
2 21-inch (533-mm) stern

Torpedoes   20

Guns   1 5.5-inch (140-mm)

Complement   93

Aircraft   1 E6Y1 or E9W1

Japan

Junsen 2 Type

Name	Laid Down	Launched	Completed	Notes
I-6	14 Oct 1932	31 Mar 1934	15 May 1935	Accidentally rammed and sunk 16 Jun 1944 by Japanese freighter south of Japan

Displacement

surface	2,243 tons
submerged	3,061 tons

Length   323 feet, 2 inches (98.5 m)

Beam   29 feet, 9 inches (9.1 m)

Draft   17 feet, 6 inches (5.3 m)

Propulsion   2 diesel engines, 8,000 shp; 1 diesel generator, 603 hp; 2 electric motors, 2,600 shp; 2 shafts

Speed

surface	20 knots
submerged	7.5 knots

Range

surface	20,000 n.miles at 10 knots
submerged	60 n.miles at 3 knots

Test depth   265 feet (80 m)

Torpedo tubes	4 21-inch (533-mm) bow
	2 21-inch (533-mm) stern
Torpedoes	17
Guns	1 5.5-inch (140-mm)
Complement	97
Aircraft	1 E6Y1 or E9W1

Japan

Junsen 3 Type

Name	Laid Down	Launched	Completed	Notes
I-7	12 Sept 1934	3 Jul 1935	31 Mar 1937	Damaged 22 Jun 1943 by USS Monoghan (DD 354) and scuttled off Kiska
I-8	11 Oct 1934	20 Jul 1936	5 Dec 1938	Sunk 31 Mar 1945 by U.S. destroyers off Okinawa

Displacement	
surface	2,525 tons
submerged	3,583 tons
Length	358 feet, 7 inches (109.3 m)
Beam	29 feet, 10 inches (9.1 m)
Draft	17 feet, 3 inches (5.2 m)
Propulsion	2 diesel engines, 11,200 shp; 1 diesel generator, 603 hp; 2 electric motors, 2,800 shp; 2 shafts
Speed	
surface	23 knots
submerged	8 knots
Range	
surface	14,000 n.miles at 16 knots
submerged	60 n.miles at 3 knots
Test depth	328 feet (100 m)
Torpedo tubes	6 21-inch (533-mm) bow
Torpedoes	21
Guns	1 5.5-inch (140-mm)
	5 13-mm (2 twin, 1 single)
Complement	100
Aircraft	1 E9W1

Japan

Type A

Name	Laid Down	Launched	Completed	Notes
I-9	25 Jan 1938	20 May 1939	13 Feb 1941	Sunk 13 Jun 1943 by USS *Frazier* (DD 607) off Kiska
I-10	7 Jun 1938	29 Sept 1939	31 Oct 1941	Sunk 4 July 1944 by U.S. warships off Saipan
I-11	10 Apr 1939	28 Feb 1941	16 May 1942	Lost about 20 Mar 1944 off Tuvalu

Displacement		
surface	2,919 tons	
submerged	4,149 tons	
Length	372 feet, 9 inches (113.7 m)	
Beam	31 feet, 4 inches (9.5 m)	
Draft	17 feet, 6 inches (5.3 m)	
Propulsion	2 diesel engines, 12,400 shp; 1 diesel generator, 603 hp; 2 electric motors, 2,400 shp; 2 shafts	
Speed		
surface	23.5 knots	
submerged	8 knots	
Range		
surfaced	16,000 n.miles at 16 knots	
submerged	90 n.miles at 3 knots	
Test depth	328 feet (100 m)	
Torpedo tubes	6 21-inch (533-mm) bow	
Torpedoes	18	
Guns	1 5.5-inch (140-mm)	
	4 25-mm (2 twin)	
Complement	114	
Aircraft	1 E9W1 or E14Y1	

Japan
Type B

Name	Laid Down	Launched	Completed	Notes
I-15	25 Jan 1938	7 Mar 1939	30 Sept 1940	Sunk 10 Nov 1942 by USS *Southard* (DMS 10) in Solomons
I-17	18 Apr 1938	19 Jul 1939	24 Jan 1941	Sunk 19 Aug 1943 by NZ minesweeper *Tui* and U.S. aircraft off Nouméa
I-19	15 Mar 1938	16 Sept 1939	28 Apr 1941	Sunk 25 Nov 1943 by USS *Radford* (DD 446) off Makin
I-21	7 Jan 1939	24 Feb 1940	15 Jul 1941	Sunk 29 Nov 1943 by USS *Chenango* (CVE 28) off Tarawa
I-23	8 Dec 1938	24 Nov 1939	27 Sept 1941	Lost about 28 Feb 1942 off Oahu
I-25	3 Feb 1939	8 Jun 1940	15 Oct 1941	Sunk 25 Aug 1943 by USS *Patterson* (DD 392) off Vanuatu
I-26	7 Jun 1939	10 Apr 1940	6 Nov 1941	Lost about 27 Oct 1944 off Leyte
I-27	5 Jul 1939	6 Jun 1941	24 Feb 1942	Sunk 12 Feb 1944 by British destroyers *Paladin* and *Petard* off Maldives
I-28	25 Sept 1939	17 Dec 1940	6 Feb 1942	Sunk 17 May 1942 by USS *Tautog* (SS 199) off Truk
I-29	20 Sept 1939	29 Sept 1940	27 Feb 1942	Sunk 26 Jul 1944 by USS *Sawfish* (SS 276) in Luzon Strait
I-30	7 7 Jun 1939	17 Sept 1940	28 Feb 1942	Sunk 13 Oct 1942 by British mine off Singapore
I-31	6 Dec 1939	13 Mar 1941	30 May 1942	Sunk 12 May 1943 by USS *Farragut* (DD 348) and USS *Edwards* (DD 619) off Attu
I-32	20 Jan 1940	17 Dec 1940	26 Apr 1942	Sunk 24 Mar 1944 by U.S. warships off Wotje
I-33	21 Feb 1940	1 May 1941	10 Jun 1942	Lost 13 Jun 1944 in training accident off Kure, salvaged Jun 1953
I-34	9 Jan 1941	24 Sept 1941	31 Aug 1942	Sunk 13 Nov 1943 by British submarine *Taurus* off Penang
I-35	2 Sept 1940	24 Sept 1941	31 Aug 1942	Sunk 23 Nov 1943 by USS *Meade* (DD 602) and USS *Frazier* (DD 607) off Tarawa
I-36	4 Dec 1940	1 Nov 1941	30 Sept 1942	Surrendered Aug 1945, scuttled 1 Apr 1946 off Goto

Name	Laid Down	Launched	Completed	Notes
I-37	7 Dec 1940	22 Oct 1941	10 Mar 1943	Sunk 19 Nov 1944 by USS *Conklin* (DE 439) and USS *McCoy Reynolds* (DE 440) off Palau
I-38	19 Jun 1941	15 Apr 1942	31 Jan 1943	Sunk 13 Nov 1944 by USS *Nicholas* (DD 449) off Palau
I-39	19 Jun 1941	15 Apr 1942	22 Apr 1943	Sunk 26 Nov 1943 by USS *Boyd* (DD 544) off Tarawa

Displacement
    surface   2,584 tons
    submerged   3,654 tons

Length   356 feet, 8 inches (108.7 m)

Beam   30 feet, 6 inches (9.3 m)

Draft   16 feet, 9 inches (5.1 m)

Propulsion   2 diesel engines, 12,400 shp; 1 diesel generator, 603 hp; 2 electric motors, 2,000 shp; 2 shafts

Speed
    surface   23.5 knots
    submerged   8 knots

Range
    surface   14,000 n.miles at 16 knots
    submerged   96 n.miles at 3 knots

Test depth   328 feet (100 m)

Torpedo tubes   6 21-inch (533-mm) bow

Torpedoes   17

Guns   1 5.5-inch (140-mm)
    2 25-mm (2 single)

Complement   94

Aircraft   1 E9W1 or E14Y1

Japan
Type B Mod. 1

Name	Laid Down	Launched	Completed	Notes
I-40	18 Mar 1942	10 Nov 1942	31 Jul 1943	Lost about 25 Nov 1943 off Makin
I-41	18 Mar 1942	10 Nov 1942	18 Sept 1943	Sunk 18 Nov 1944 by USS *Lawrence C. Taylor* (DE 415) and aircraft from USS *Anzio* (CVE 57) in Philippine Sea
I-42	18 Mar 1942	10 Nov 1942	3 Nov 1943	Sunk 23 Mar 1944 by USS *Tunny* (SS 282) off Palau
I-43	27 Apr 1942	25 Oct 1942	5 Nov 1943	Sunk 15 Feb 1944 by USS *Aspro* (SS 309) off Guam
I-44	11 Jun 1942	5 Mar 1943	31 Jan 1944	Sunk 29 Apr 1945 by aircraft from USS *Tulagi* (CVE 72) off Okinawa
I-45	15 Jul 1942	6 Mar 1943	28 Dec 1943	Sunk 29 Oct 1944 by USS *Whitehurst* (DE 634) in Philippine Sea

Displacement
  surface   2,624 tons
  submerged   3,700 tons

Length   356 feet, 8 inches (108.7 m)

Beam   30 feet, 6 inches (9.3 m)

Draft   17 feet (5.2 m)

Propulsion   2 diesels, 11,000 shp; 1 diesel generator, 603 hp; 2 electric motors, 2,000 shp; 2 shafts

Speed
  surface   23.5 knots
  submerged   8 knots

Range
  surfaced   14,000 n.miles at 16 knots
  submerged   96 n.miles at 3 knots

Test depth   328 feet (100 m)

Torpedo tubes   6 21-inch (533-mm) bow

Torpedoes   17

Guns   1 5.5-inch (140-mm)
                     2 25-mm (1 twin)

Complement   114

Aircraft   1 E14Y1

Japan
Type B Mod. 2

Name	Laid Down	Launched	Completed	Notes
I-54	1 Jul 1942	4 May 1943	31 Mar 1944	Sunk 28 October 1944 by U.S. destroyers off Leyte
I-56	29 Sept 1942	30 Jun 1943	8 Jun 1944	Sunk 18 Apr 1945 by U.S. destroyers off Okinawa
I-58	26 Dec 1942	30 Jun 1943	7 Sept 1944	Surrendered Sept 1945 at Kure, scuttled 1 Apr 1946 off Goto by U.S.
#633–636				Ordered Nov 1941, cancelled 1943
#5101–5114				Ordered Sept 1942, cancelled 1943

Displacement
    surface   2,607 tons
    submerged   3,688 tons

Length   356 feet, 8 inches (108.7 m)

Beam   30 feet, 6 inches (9.3 m)

Draft   17 feet (5.2 m)

Propulsion   2 diesel engines, 4,700 shp; 1 diesel generator, 603 hp; 2 electric motors, 1,200 shp; 2 shafts

Speed
    surface   17.8 knots
    submerged   6.5 knots

Range
    surface   21,000 n.miles at 16 knots
    submerged   105 n.miles at 3 knots

Test depth   328 feet (100 m)

Torpedo tubes   6 21-inch (533-mm) bow

Torpedoes   19

Guns   1 5.5-inch (140-mm)
                  2 25-mm (1 twin)

Complement   101

Aircraft   1 E14Y1

Japan
S49A

Name	Laid Down	Launched	Completed	Notes
#5115–5132				Ordered Sept 1942, cancelled 1943

Displacement	
surface	2,330 tons
submerged	
Length	349 feet, 5 inches (106.5 m)
Beam	31 feet, 8 inches (9.6 m)
Draft	17 feet, 5 inches (5.3 m)
Propulsion	2 diesel engines, 11,000 shp; 2 electric motors, 2,400 shp; 2 shafts
Speed	
surface	22.4 knots
submerged	8 knots
Range	
surface	14,000 n.miles at 16 knots
submerged	80 n.miles at 3 knots
Test depth	328 feet (100 m)
Torpedo tubes	8 21-inch (533-mm) bow
Torpedoes	16
Guns	1 5.5-inch (140-mm) 4 25-mm (2 twin)
Complement	
Aircraft	1 E14Y1

Japan
Type A Mod. 1

Name	Laid Down	Launched	Completed	Notes
I-12	5 Nov 1942	3 Aug 1943	25 May 1944	Lost Jan 1945 north of Marshall Islands

Displacement

surface	2,934 tons
submerged	4,172 tons

Length   372 feet, 9 inches (133.7 m)

Beam   31 feet, 6 inches (9.5 m)

Draft   17 feet, 6 inches (5.3 m)

Propulsion   2 diesel engines, 4,700 shp; 1 diesel generator, 603 hp; 2 electric motors, 1,200 shp; 2 shafts

Speed

surface	17.7 knots
submerged	6.2 knots

Range

surface	22,000 n.miles at 16 knots
submerged	70 n.miles at 3 knots

Test depth   328 feet (100 m)

Torpedo tubes 6 21-inch (533-mm) bow

Torpedoes   18

Guns   1 5.5-inch (140-mm)
                  4 25-mm (2 twin)

Complement   114

Aircraft   1 E14Y1

Japan
S48

Name	Laid Down	Launched	Completed	Notes
#5094–5096				Ordered Sept 1942, cancelled 1943

Displacement

surface	2,330 tons
submerged	

Length   364 feet, 2 inches (111.0 m)

Beam   32 feet, 3 inches (9.8 m)

Draft   18 feet, 1 inch (5.5 m)

Propulsion   2 diesel engines, 11,000 shp; 2 electric motors, 2,400 shp; 2 shafts

Speed

surface	22.4 knots
submerged	8.0 knots

Range

surface	16,000 n.miles at 16 knots
submerged	80 n.miles at 3 knots

Test depth	328 feet (100 m)
Torpedo tubes	6 21-inch (533-mm) bow
Torpedoes	18
Guns	1 5.5-inch (140-mm) 4 25-mm (2 twin)
Complement	
Aircraft	1 E14Y1

Japan
Type A Mod. 2

Name	Laid Down	Launched	Completed	Notes
I-13	4 Feb 1943	30 Nov 1943	16 Dec 1944	Sunk 16 Jul 1945 by USS *Lawrence C. Taylor* (DE 415) and aircraft from USS *Anzio* (CVE 57) east of Japan
I-14	18 May 1943	14 Mar 1944	14 Mar 1945	Surrendered Aug 27 1945 off Japan, transferred to Pearl Harbor 6 Jan 1946, scuttled 28 May 1946 off Oahu
I-15	30 Apr 1943	12 Apr 1944		Converted to tanker submarine Jun 1945, 80% complete by Aug 1945, scuttled Apr 1946 off Japan
I-1	24 Jun 1943	10 Jun 1944		Construction stopped Mar 1945 at 40% completion, sank 18 Sept 1945 in storm at Kobe, salvaged and scrapped Apr 1947

Displacement

surface	3,603 tons
submerged	4,762 tons

Length	372 feet, 9 inches (113.7 m)
Beam	38 feet, 5 inches (11.7 m)
Draft	19 feet, 4 inches (5.9 m)
Propulsion	2 diesel engines, 5,200 shp; 2 diesel generators, 1,207 hp; 2 electric motors, 2,950 shp; 2 shafts

Speed

surface	16.8 knots
submerged	5.5 knots

Range

surfaced	21,000 n.miles at 16 knots
submerged	60 n.miles at 3 knots

Test depth   328 feet (100 m)

Torpedo tubes   6 21-inch (533-mm) bow

Torpedoes   16

Guns   1 5.5-inch (140-mm)
7 25-mm (2 triple, 1 single)

Complement   118

Aircraft   2 M6A1 *Seiran*

Japan

Sentoku Type

Name	Laid Down	Launched	Completed	Notes
I-400	18 Jan 1943	18 Jan 1944	30 Dec 1944	Surrendered 27 Aug 1945 off Japan, transferred to Pearl Harbor 6 Jan 1946, scuttled 4 Jun 1946 off Oahu
I-401	26 Apr 1943	11 Mar 1944	8 Jan 1945	Surrendered 29 Aug 1945 off Japan, transferred to Pearl Harbor 6 Jan 1946, scuttled 31 May 1946 off Oahu
I-402	20 Oct 1943	5 Sept 1944	24 Jul 1945	Converted to tanker submarine June 1945, surrendered Sept 1945, scuttled 1 Apr 1946 off Goto
I-403				Cancelled Oct 1943
I-404	8 Nov 1943	7 Jul 1944		Construction stopped 4 Jun 1945 at 95% completion, damaged in air raid and scuttled 28 Jul 1945, salvaged 1951 and scrapped 1952
I-405	27 Sept 1944			Construction stopped Jan 1945
#5237				Ordered Sept 1942, cancelled Oct 1943
#5238	20 Dec 1943			Construction stopped shortly after keel laying
#5239–#5240				Ordered Sept 1942, cancelled Oct 1943
#5241–#5248				Ordered Sept 1942, cancelled Jul 1943

Displacement
    surface   5,223 tons
    submerged   6,560 tons

Length   400 feet, 3 inches (122 m)

Beam   39 feet, 4 inches (12 m)

Draft   23 feet (7.0 m)

Propulsion   4 diesel engines, 9,000 shp; 2 diesel generators, 1,072 hp; 2 electric motors, 4,290 shp; 2 shafts

Speed
    surface   18.7 knots
    submerged   6.5 knots

Range
    surfaced   37,500 n.miles at 14 knots
    submerged   60 n.miles at 3 knots

Test depth   328 feet (100 m)

Torpedo tubes   8 21-inch (533-mm) bow

Torpedoes   20

Guns   1 5.5-inch (140-mm)
    10 25-mm (3 triple, 1 single)

Complement   204

Aircraft   3 M6A1 *Seiran*

United States

Fleet Snorkel (*Balao* class)

Name	Laid Down	Launched	Completed	Notes
Sennet (SS 408)	8 Mar 1944	6 Jun 1944	22 Aug 1944	Decommissioned and stricken 2 Dec 1968

SSP (*Balao* class)

Name	Laid Down	Launched	Completed	Notes
Perch (SSP 313)	5 Jan 1943	12 Sept 1943	7 Jan 1944	Decommissioned and stricken 1 Dec 1971
Sealion (SSP 315)	25 Feb 1943	31 Oct 1943	8 Mar 1944	Decommissioned 20 Feb 1970, stricken 15 Mar 1977

	Fleet Snorkel	*SSP*
Displacement		
surface	1,570 tons	1,525 tons
submerged	2,410 tons	2,610 tons
Length	311 feet, 9 inches (95.0 m)	311 feet, 9 inches (95.0 m)
Beam	27 feet, 3 inches (8.3 m)	27 feet, 3 inches (8.3 m)
Draft	15 feet, 3 inches (4.6 m)	15 feet, 3 inches (4.6 m)
Propulsion	4 diesel generators, 4,610 hp;	2 diesel generators, 2,700 hp;
	2 electric motors, 2,740 hp; 2 shafts	2 electric motors, 2,740 shp; 2 shafts
Speed		
surface	18 knots	15 knots
submerged	9 knots	8.4 knots
Range		
surface	11,000 n.miles at 10 knots	10,300 n.miles at 10 knots
submerged	108 n.miles at 3 knots	100 n.miles at 3 knots
Test depth	400 feet (122 m)	400 feet (122 m)
Torpedo tubes	6 21-inch (533-mm) bow 4 21-inch (533-mm) stern	— —
Torpedoes	24	—
Guns	—	1 5-inch (127-mm) 1 40-mm
Complement	80	74-185
Aircraft	1 helium balloon	1 HTL helicopter

APPENDIX B

Submarine-Launched Aircraft

FIXED WING AIRCRAFT

Country	Germany	Britain	Germany	Germany
Manufacturer	*Friedrichshafen*	*Sopwith*	*H.-B.*	*LFG*
Type	*FF 29a*	*Schneider*	*W 20*	*V 19*
Operational	1914	1914	1917	1918
Number built	44	136	3	1
Engine				
number	1	1	1	1
type	Mercedes D.II*	Gnome Monosoupape	Oberursel U.0	Oberursel UR.II
configuration	inline-6	rotary-9	rotary-7	rotary-9
horsepower	120	100	80	110
Weight				
empty	2,046 lb.	1,220 lb.	871 lb.	1,058 lb.
loaded	3,086 lb.	1,770 lb.	1,250 lb.	1,521 lb.
Length	34 ft. 1 in. (10.4 m)	22 ft. 10 in. (10 m)	19 ft. 5 in. (5.9 m)	21 ft. 8 in. (6.6 m)
Wingspan	53 ft. 6 in. (16.3 m)	25 ft. 8 in. (7.8 m)	22 ft. 4 in. (6.8 m)	31 ft. 4 in. (9.6 m)
Height	13 ft. 9 in. (4.2 m)	10 ft. (3.0 m)	9 ft. 6 in. (2.9 m)	9 ft. 2 in. (2.8 m)
Wing area	642 sq. ft.	240 sq. ft.	170 sq. ft.	140 sq. ft.
Max. speed	59 mph	104 mph	105 mph	106 mph
Range	280 miles		137 miles	224 miles
Endurance	4–6 hr.	2.3 hr.	1.3 hr.	2 hr.
Armament	—	1 7.7-mm MG	—	—
Crew	2	1	1	1

*An Argus As II inline-6 engine (120 hp) was installed on some aircraft.

Country	Germany	United States	United States	United States
Manufacturer	Caspar-Heinkel	Martin	Cox-Klemin	Loening
Type	U 1	MS-1	XS-2	XSL-2
Operational	1922	1923	1926	1931
Number built	5	6	1	1
Engine				
number	1	1	1	1
type	Siemens-Halske Sh 4	Lawrence L-4	Lawrence L-4	Menasco B-6
configuration	radial-5	radial-3	radial-3	inline-6
horsepower	60	60	60	160
Weight				
empty	794 lb.	657 lb.	700 lb.	1,229 lb.
loaded	1,124 lb.	1,007 lb.	1,050 lb.	1,684 lb.
Length	20 ft. 4 in. (6.2 m)	17 ft. 8 in. (5.4 m)	18 ft. 2 in. (5.5 m)	31 ft. (9.5 m)
Wingspan	23 ft. 7 in. (7.2 m)	18 ft. (5.5 m)	18 ft. (5.5 m)	27 ft. 2 in. (8.3 m)
Height	7 ft. 8 in. (2.3 m)	8 ft. (2.4 m)	8 ft. (2.4 m)	7 ft. 10 in. (2.4 m)
Wing area	150 sq. ft.	99 sq. ft.	99 sq. ft.	148 sq. ft.
Max. speed	90 mph	100 mph	115 mph	116 mph
Range	224 miles	239 miles	238 miles	
Endurance	2 hr.	3.4 hr.	3 hr.	
Armament	—	—	—	—
Crew	1	1	1	1

Country	Britain	France	France	Germany
Manufacturer	Parnall	Besson	Besson	Dornier
Type	Peto	MB 35	MB 411	Libelle II
Operational	1926	1926	1935	1921
Number built	2	6	2	16
Engine				
number	1	1	1	1
type	Armstr. Sidd. Mongoose IIIC	Salmson 9AC	Salmson 9ND	Siemens-Halske Sh 5
configuration	radial-5	radial-9	radial-9	radial-7
horsepower	169	120	175	80
Weight				
empty	1,229 lb.	1,191 lb.	1,676 lb.	992 lb.
loaded	1,730 lb.	1,687 lb.	2,249 lb.	1,653 lb.
Length	22 ft. 6 in. (6.9 m)	23 ft. (7.0 m)	27 ft. 1 in. (8.3 m)	24 ft. 6 in. (7.5 m)
Wingspan	28 ft. 5 in. (8.7 m)	32 ft. 3 in. (9.8 m)	39 ft. 4 in. (12 m)	32 ft. 2 in. (9.8 m)
Height	8 ft. 11 in. (2.7 m)	8 ft. 3 in. (2.5 m)	9 ft. 4 in. (2.9 m)	7 ft. 9 in. (2.4 m)
Wing area	174 sq. ft.	178 sq. ft.	237 sq. ft.	169 sq. ft.
Max. speed	113 mph	99 mph	118 mph	90 mph
Range	120 miles	186 miles*	249 miles	
Endurance	2 hr.	3.3 hr.*	7 hr.	
Armament	—	—	—	—
Crew	2	2	2	1+2 passengers

*With pilot and observer. With only the pilot, the range and endurance were 500 miles and seven hours, respectively.

Country	Italy	Italy	USSR	Poland
Manufacturer	Macchi	Macchi	Chetverikov	Nikol
Type	M.53	P.8	SPL	A-2
Operational	1928	1929	1935	1939
Number built	1	1	1	1
Engine				
number	1	1	1	1
type	ADC Cirrus Mk. II	ADC Cirrus Mk. II	Shvetsov M-11	de Havilland Gipsy Major
configuration	inline-4	inline-4	radial-5	inline-4
horsepower	75	75	110	129
Weight				
empty	1,067 lb.	1,175 lb.	1,389 lb.	1,389 lb.
loaded	1,507 lb.	1,618 lb.	1,750 lb.	2,094 lb.
Length	18 ft. 7 in. (5.7 m)	23 ft. 1 in. (7.0 m)	24 ft. 5 in. (7.5 m)	25 ft. 3 in. (7.7 m)
Wingspan	35 ft. 4 in. (10.8 m)	39 ft. 2 in. (12 m)	31 ft. 2 in. (9.5 m)	41 ft. 4 in. (12.6 m)
Height	9 ft. (2.8 m)	8 ft. 4 in. (2.6 m)	8 ft. 11 in. (2.7 m)	10 ft. 2 in. (3.1 m)
Wing area	172 sq. ft.	205 sq. ft.	144 sq. ft.	231 sq. ft.
Max. speed	89 mph	93 mph	116 mph	91 mph
Range		373 miles	250 miles	373 miles
Endurance	4 hr.	4 hr.	2.2 hr.	
Armament	1 7.7-mm MG	1 7.7-m MG	—	—
Crew	1	1	2	2

Country	Germany	Japan	Japan	Japan
Manufacturer	Arado	Kugisho	Kugisho	Watanabe
Type	Ar 231	No. 1	E6Y1 Type 91	E9W1 Type 96 "Slim"
Operational	1941	1927	1931	1936
Number built	6	1	10	36
Engine				
number	1	1	1	1
type	Hirth HM 501	Le Rhône 9c	Gadsuden Jimpu	Hitachi GK2 Tempu 11
configuration	Inline-6	rotary-9	radial-7	radial-9
horsepower	160	80	160	340
Weight				
empty	1,837 lb.	882 lb.	1,257 lb.	1,940 lb.
loaded	2,315 lb.	1,146 lb.	1,951 lb.	2,756 lb.
Length	25 ft. 7 in. (7.8 m)	20 ft. 4 in. (6.2 m)	22 ft. 7 in. (6.9 m)	25 ft. 1 in. (7.6 m)
Wingspan	33 ft. 5 in. (10.1 m)	23 ft. 7 in. (7.2 m)	26 ft. 3 in. (8 m)	32 ft. 9 in. (10 m)
Height	10 ft. 3 in. (3.1 m)	7 ft. 10 in. (2.4 m)	9 ft. 3 in. (2.8 m)	10 ft. 10 in. (3.3 m)
Wing area	164 sq. ft.	164 sq. ft.	182 sq. ft.	253 sq. ft.
Max. speed	106 mph	96 mph	104 mph	144 mph
Range	310 miles	200 miles	380 miles	454 miles
Endurance	4 hr.	2 hr.	4.5 hr.	5 hr.
Armament	—	—	—	1 7.7-mm MG
Crew	1	1	1	2

Country	Japan	Japan	United States
Manufacturer	Kugisho	Aichi	Douglas
Type	E14Y1 Type 0 "Glen"	M6A1 Seiran*	Model 640
Operational	1942	1944	—
Number built	138	26	—
Engine			
number	1	1	1
type	Hitachi GK2 Tempu 11	Aichi Atsuta 32	Westinghouse J34-WE-36
configuration	radial-9	inverted V12	turbojet
horsepower	340	1,400	—
thrust	—	—	3,400 lbf.
Weight			
empty	2,469 lb.	5,712 lb.	4,051 lb.
loaded	3,197 lb.	9,722 lb.	7,800 lb.
Length	28 ft. (8.5 m)	38 ft. 2 in. (11.6 m)	32 ft. 11 in. (10.0 m)
Wingspan	36 ft. (11 m)	40 ft. 3 in. (12.3 m)	25 ft. (7.6 m)
Height	12 ft. 1 in. (3.7 m)	15 ft. (4.6 m)	13 ft. 6 in. (4.1 m)
Wing area	205 sq. ft.	290 sq. ft.	134 sq. ft.
Max. speed	153 mph	286 mph	
Range	609 miles	955 miles	
Endurance	6 hr.	4.8 hr.	
Armament	1 7.7-mm MG 2 66-lb. bombs	1 13-mm MG 1,764-lb. bomb or 1 torpedo	1 Mk 7, Mk 11, or Mk 12 nuclear bomb
Crew	2	2	1

*Data for aircraft without floats fitted.

ROTARY WING AIRCRAFT

Country	Germany	Germany	France	United States
Manufacturer	Flettner	Focke Achgelis	Dorand	Bell
Type	Fl 282 Kolibri	Fa 330 Bachstelze	G 20	HTL
Operational	1942	1943	—*	1947
Number built	24	~200	1	179‡
Engine				
number	1	—	2	1
type	BMW 314	—	Renault 6Q-04	Lycoming O-435-6
configuration	radial-7	—	inline-6	opposed-6
horsepower	160	—	240	240
Weight				
empty	1,676 lb.	192 lb.	3,086 lb.	1,652 lb.
loaded	2,204 lb.	412 lb.	6,614 lb.	2,700 lb.
Length	21 ft. 6 in. (6.6 m)	14 ft. 8 in. (4.5 m)	36 ft 4 in (11.1 m)	32 ft. 4 in. (9.9 m)
Rotor diameter	39 ft. 4 in. (12 m)	23 ft. 11 in. (7.3 m)	50 ft. 6 in.† (15.4 m)	37 ft. 2 in. (9.8 m)
Height	7 ft. 3 in. (2.2 m)	5 ft. 6 in. (1.7 m)	10 ft. 3 in. (3.1 m)	9 ft .6 in. (2.9 m)
Max. speed	49.7 mph	50 mph	155 mph	83 mph
Range	104 miles	—	500 miles	200 miles
Endurance	2 hr.	—		
Armament	—	—	—	—
Crew	1 or 2	1	2	1+3 passengers

*Prototype completed in 1947; never flew.
†Upper rotor diameter; the lower rotor was 42 feet, 8 inches (13 m) in diameter.
‡Navy HTL models only; over 6,000 Bell Model 47/H-13 helicopters were produced.

APPENDIX C

Flights from Japanese Submarines during World War II

This list encompasses all flights from Japanese submarines logged in the Hackett and Kingsepp online database (http://www.combinedfleet.com/sensuikan.htm).

Date	Submarine	Aircraft	Location	Notes
30 Nov 1941	I-10	E9W	Suva, Fiji	Recon flight; airmen reported no ships in harbor; aircraft did not return
7 Dec 1941	I-25	E9W	Pearl Harbor, Hawaii	Aircraft damaged during launch; flight aborted
16 Dec 1941	I-7	E9W	Pearl Harbor, Hawaii	Predawn recon flight; airmen reported on damage and ships in the harbor; aircraft scuttled after landing
4 Jan 1942	I-19	E9W	Pearl Harbor, Hawaii	Night recon flight; catapult inoperative; I-19 sighted by patrol boat during launching and dived while aircraft took off; airmen reported on warships in the harbor; aircraft recovered
17 Feb 1942	I-25	E14Y	Sydney, Australia	Predawn recon flight; airmen reported on warships in the harbor; aircraft recovered
23 Feb 1942	I-9	E9W	Pearl Harbor, Hawaii	Night recon flight in preparation for Operation K; airmen unable to observe harbor through clouds; aircraft damaged during recovery
26 Feb 1942	I-25	E14Y	Melbourne, Australia	Predawn recon flight; aircraft sighted by Australian forces; airmen reported on warships in the harbor; aircraft recovered

Date	Submarine	Aircraft	Location	Notes
1 Mar 1942	I-25	E14Y	Hobart, Australia	Predawn recon flight; airmen reported on merchant ships but no warships in harbor; aircraft recovered
7 Mar 1942	I-25	E14Y	Wellington, New Zealand	Aircraft damaged during launch; flight aborted
8 Mar 1942	I-25	E14Y	Wellington, New Zealand	Predawn recon flight; aircraft sighted steamer en route; aircraft recovered
13 Mar 1942	I-25	E14Y	Auckland, New Zealand	Predawn recon flight; airmen reported on transports in harbor; aircraft recovered
16 Mar 1942	I-25	E14Y	North of New Zealand	Flight in search of cruiser and large merchant ship; ships not sighted; aircraft recovered
19 Mar 1942	I-25	E14Y	Suva, Fiji	Predawn recon flight; airmen reported on warships and merchant ships in harbor; aircraft sighted by British cruiser; aircraft recovered
7 May 1942	I-30	E14Y	Aden, Aden Colony	Recon flight; aircraft recovered
8 May 1942	I-30	E14Y	Djibouti, French Somaliland	Night recon flight; aircraft came under fire from warships; mission aborted; aircraft recovered
19 May 1942	I-21	E14Y	Suva, Fiji	Predawn recon flight; airmen reported on warships in harbor; aircraft recovered
19 May 1942	I-30	E14Y	Zanzibar and Dar es Salaam, Tanganyika	Recon flight; airmen reported on merchant ships in harbor; float damaged on landing; aircraft recovered
20 May 1942	I-10	E14Y	Durban, South Africa	Recon flight; airmen reported no target in harbor; aircraft detected by South African forces; aircraft recovered
23 May 1942	I-29	E14Y	Sydney, Australia	Dawn recon flight; aircraft sighted by Australian forces; airmen reported on warships in harbor; aircraft recovered
24 May 1942	I-9	E14Y	Kiska and Amchitka, Alaska	Dawn recon flight; airmen reported on potential landing sites and lack of U.S. forces; aircraft recovered
24 May 1942	I-21	E14Y	Auckland, New Zealand	Dawn recon flight; airmen unable to observe harbor through clouds; Auckland airport turned on runway lights; aircraft recovered
26 May 1942	I-19	E14Y	Bogoslof, Alaska	I-19 sighted by U.S. warship while launching at night; aircraft lost when sub dived

Date	Submarine	Aircraft	Location	Notes
26 May 1942	I-9	E14Y	Adak and Kanaga, Alaska	Predawn recon flight; troops sighted on Adak; aircraft recovered
26 May 1942	I-25	E14Y	Dutch Harbor, Alaska	Flight aborted due to weather
27 May 1942	I-25	E14Y	Dutch Harbor, Alaska	Predawn recon flight; catapult inoperative and flight nearly aborted when U.S. cruiser passed close aboard; catapult later repaired; airmen reported on warships in the harbor; aircraft recovered
29 May 1942	I-25	E14Y	700 miles WNW of Seattle, Washington	Morning flight in search of cruiser and transport in fog; airmen unable to sight ships; aircraft recovered
29 May 1942	I-21	E14Y	Sydney, Australia	Predawn recon flight in preparation for midget sub attack; airmen reported on warships in the harbor; aircraft sighted by Australian forces; aircraft capsized and scuttled after landing
29 May 1942	I-10	E14Y	Diego-Suarez, Madagascar	Night recon flight in preparation for midget sub attack; airmen reported on warships in the harbor; aircraft recovered
31 May 1942	I-10	E14Y	Diego-Suarez, Madagascar	Flight in search of midget subs after attack; midget subs not found; aircraft recovered
10 Jun 1942	I-29	E14Y	Nouméa, New Caledonia	Dawn recon flight; aircraft recovered
15 Jun 1942	I-9	E14Y	Kodiak, Alaska	Recon flight over Kodiak naval air station; aircraft recovered
28 Aug 1942	I-19	E14Y	Nendo, Santa Cruz Is.	Recon flight; airmen reported on seaplane tenders and flying boats in Graciosa Bay; aircraft recovered
29 Aug 1942	I-29	E14Y	Seychelles Is.	Recon flight; aircraft recovered
9 Sept 1942	I-25	E14Y	Brookings, Oregon	Predawn bombing mission; aircraft sighted by Forest Service; incendiary bombs dropped on forest; aircraft recovered
11 Sept 1942	I-31	E14Y	Nendo, Santa Cruz Is.	Dawn recon flight; airmen reported on destroyers and flying boats in Graciosa Bay; aircraft recovered

Date	Submarine	Aircraft	Location	Notes
13 Sept 1942	*I-31*	E14Y	Vanikoro, Santa Cruz Is.	Dawn recon flight; aircraft encountered squall and returned to *I-31*; aircraft capsized during recovery; crew rescued
29 Sept 1942	*I-25*	E14Y	Cape Blanco, Oregon	Predawn bombing mission; aircraft sighted by Forest Service; incendiary bombs dropped on forest; aircraft recovered
2 Oct 1942	*I-21*	E14Y	Espiritu Santo, New Hebrides Is.	Dawn recon flight over airfield; aircraft recovered
13 Oct 1942	*I-7*	E9W	Espiritu Santo, New Hebrides Is.	Dawn recon flight; airmen reported on warships, transports, and seaplanes off south coast; aircraft recovered
19 Oct 1942	*I-19*	E14Y	Nouméa, New Caledonia	Noon recon flight; aircraft damaged beyond repair during recovery
31 Oct 1942	*I-7*	E9W	Espiritu Santo, New Hebrides Is.	Aircraft damaged during launching; flight aborted
2 Nov 1942	*I-8*	E9W	Efate, New Hebrides Is.	Recon flight over Port Vila and Havannah; aircraft recovered
4 Nov 1942	*I-9*	E14Y	Nouméa, New Caledonia	Dawn recon flight; airmen reported on warships in the harbor; aircraft recovered
4 Nov 1942	*I-31*	E14Y	Suva, Fiji	Dawn recon flight; aircraft recovered
11 Nov 1942	*I-7*	E9W	Vanikoro, Santa Cruz Is.	Dawn recon flight; aircraft recovered
11 Nov 1942	*I-31*	E14Y	Pago-Pago, American Samoa	Dawn recon flight; airmen reported on transport in the harbor, Tafuna airfield, and Aunu'u lighthouse; enemy aircraft appeared during recovery but did not spot *I-31*; aircraft recovered
12 Nov 1942	*I-9*	E14Y	Espiritu Santo, Santa Cruz Is.	Dusk recon flight; airmen unable to observe harbor through clouds; aircraft recovered
24 Jan 1943	*I-10*	E14Y	Nouméa, New Caledonia	Night recon flight; airmen reported on warships and transports in the harbor; aircraft recovered
25 Jan 1943	*I-21*	E14Y	Sydney, Australia	Recon flight; airmen reported on warships in the harbor; aircraft recovered

Date	Submarine	Aircraft	Location	Notes
16 Feb 1943	*I-25*	E14Y	Espiritu Santo, New Hebrides Is.	Night recon flight; aircraft recovered
19 Feb 1943	*I-21*	E14Y	New South Wales, Australia	Photo-recon flight over coast; aircraft detected by Australian radar; aircraft recovered
21 Feb 1943	*I-11*	E14Y	Nouméa, New Caledonia	Recon flight; airmen reported on warships in the harbor; aircraft recovered
1 Mar 1943	*I-11*	E14Y	Chesterfield Reefs, New Caledonia	Recon flight over airfields; aircraft damaged during recovery
4 Jun 1943	*I-29*	E14Y	Penang, Malaya	ASW patrol to protect incoming submarine
8 Jun 1943	*I-29*	E14Y	Penang, Malaya	ASW patrol
25 Jul 1943	*I-11*	E14Y	Nouméa, New Caledonia	Night recon flight; airmen reported on warships in the harbor; aircraft recovered
23 Aug 1943	*I-25*	E14Y	Espiritu Santo, New Hebrides Is.	Recon flight; airmen reported on warships in the harbor; aircraft recovered
20 Sept 1943	*I-10*	E14Y	Perim Is., Aden Colony	Dawn recon flight in search of suspected airfield; airmen reported no airfield on island; aircraft recovered
25 Sept 1943	*I-32*	E14Y	Nouméa, New Caledonia	Catapult inoperative; flight aborted
8 Oct 1943	*I-21*	E14Y	Suva, Fiji	Night recon flight; aircraft recovered
11 Oct 1943	*I-37*	E14Y	Diego-Suarez, Madagascar	Recon flight; airmen reported on heavy defenses around the harbor; aircraft recovered
16 Oct 1943	*I-36*	E14Y	Pearl Harbor, Hawaii	Night recon flight; aircraft detected by U.S. forces; airmen reported on warships in the harbor; aircraft did not return
17 Nov 1943	*I-19*	E14Y	Pearl Harbor, Hawaii	Night recon flight; airmen reported on warships in the harbor; U.S. aircraft sighted during recovery; aircraft scuttled
17 Nov 1943	*I-37*	E14Y	Mombasa, Kenya	Recon flight; aircraft recovered

Date	Submarine	Aircraft	Location	Notes
3 Mar 1944	*I-37*	E14Y	Chagos Archipelago	Morning recon flight with 2 60-kg. bombs; no ships sighted and bombs discarded; aircraft recovered
15 Mar 1944	*I-37*	E14Y	Diego-Suarez, Madagascar	Night recon flight; airmen reported on warships in the harbor; aircraft recovered
30 Mar 1944	*I-8*	E9W	SE of Diego Garcia	Recon flight; airmen sighted merchant ship and vectored *I-8* toward it; aircraft recovered
7 Apr 1944	*I-37*	E14Y	Pemba, Zanzibar and Mombasa, Kenya	Night recon flight; airmen reported on merchant ships in Mombasa harbor; aircraft recovered
22 Apr 1944	*I-36*	E14Y	Majuro, Marshall Is.	Afternoon recon flight in preparation for Operation Yu-Go; airmen reported on warships in the anchorage; aircraft unable to locate *I-36*; aircraft found by *I-36* at dawn and scuttled
27 Apr 1944	*I-37*	E14Y	Penang, Malaya	Predawn escort flight for *I-37*
12 Jun 1944	*I-10*	E14Y	Majuro, Marshall Is.	Night recon flight; airmen reported anchorage empty; aircraft capsized and sank after landing; airmen rescued

NOTES

CHAPTER 1: THE EARLY EFFORTS

1. Eberhard Rössler, *Die deutschen U-Kreuzer und Transport-U-Boote* [*The German U-Cruisers and Transport U-boats*] (Bonn: Bernard & Graefe, 2003), 164.
2. R. D. Layman, "U-Boat with Wings," Naval Institute *Proceedings* (April 1968): 56.
3. Layman, "U-Boat with Wings," 57.
4. Ian Castle, *Zeppelin Onslaught: The Forgotten Blitz, 1914–1915* (Barnsley, England: Frontline Books, 2018), 35.
5. Thomas Fegan, *The "Baby Killers": German Air Raids on Britain during the First World War* (Barnsley, England: Pen & Sword, 2012), 46. The Friedrichshafen was intercepted over Erith, on the outskirts of London. Von Arnauld claimed they had bombed an oil depot at Sheerness, but in reality had dropped the payload near the Cliffe railway station, about ten miles to the east.
6. Karl Caspar, flying a Gotha Taube, claimed to have bombed Dover in October 1914; no evidence was found by the British. Caspar would go on to establish Caspar Werke, which built the Caspar-Heinkel U 1 (see Chapter 2).
7. "Kriegstagebuch 'U-12,' Angefangen: 1.I.15, Beendet: 16.I.15 [War Diary 'U-12,' Begun: 1 Jan. 1915, Ended: 16 Jan. 1915]," (German Navy).
8. Layman, "U-Boat with Wings," 58.
9. Forstmann left the *U-12* and Zeebrugge for the Mediterranean in early March to command the *U-39*. His second-in-command on the *U-39* was *Oberleutnant zur See* Karl Dönitz, future Commander-in-Chief of the U-boat arm and then of the German Navy during World War II, and, briefly at the end of the war, Adolph Hitler's successor. Forstmann went on to become the second highest-scoring submarine commander of both world wars, second only to von Arnauld's brother Lothar. Von Arnauld remained the commander of the Zeebrugge air group until December of 1915, when he was shot down near Dunkirk and taken prisoner by the French. He served as a *Luftwaffe* general during World War II.
10. Rössler, *Die deutschen U-Kreuzer und Transport-U-Boote*, 166.
11. "Kriegstagebuch 'U-22,' 16. bis 31. Mai 1915 [War Diary 'U-22,' 16 to 31 May 1915]" (German Navy).
12. *Kommandørkaptein* Hans Petter Oset, Royal Norwegian Navy, e-mail to Jacob Gunnarson, 14 January 2019.
13. Heinz J. Nowarra, Bruce Robertson, and P. G. Coorsley, *Marine Aircraft of the 1914–1918 War* (Letchworth, England: Harleyford, 1966), 189. The K-class was an unseaworthy

design, sometimes jokingly referred to as the "Kalamity" class after many groundings, collisions, and uncontrolled dives. Out of 19 completed, 6 sank in accidents.

14. David R. Winans, "Submarine Aircraft," *American Aviation Historical Society Journal* (Spring 1967): 41.

15. Cdr. Richard Compton-Hall, RN (Ret.), *Submarine Warfare: Monsters and Midgets* (Poole, England: Blandford, 1985), 59.

16. R. D. Layman, *Naval Aviation in the First World War* (Annapolis, Md.: Naval Institute, 1996), 38. Adm. Arbuthnot was killed in the battle of Jutland in May 1916, while commanding a cruiser squadron.

17. See Dwight R. Messimer, *The Merchant U-boat: Adventures of the Deutschland 1916–1918* (Annapolis, Md.: Naval Institute, 1988); and Paul König, *Voyage of the Deutschland: The First Merchant Submarine* (Annapolis, Md.: Naval Institute, 2001). König commanded the *Deutschland* on her two voyages to the United States in 1916; his account originally was published in 1917.

18. Rössler, *Die deutschen U-Kreuzer und Transport-U-Boote*, 164.

19. Ibid., 167. Lothar von Arnauld became the most successful U-boat commander of all time: He sank 194 ships totaling 454,000 tons and did so always strictly according to existing rules. After the war von Arnauld served in the Turkish Navy in the 1930s and from 1939 again in the German Navy. He died in an aircraft accident at Le Bourget airport in France in 1941. Lothar and Friedrich appear to have occasionally spelled the French part of their last name as de la Pierrère.

20. Peter M. Grosz, "A Study in Contrasts: German Submarine Aircraft of World War One," *Air Enthusiast* 33 (May–August 1987): 3.

21. Terry C. Treadwell, *Submarines with Wings* (London: Conway, 1985), 8–10.

22. Layman, *Naval Aviation in the First World War*, 92–93.

23. Gotthard Baatz, "The Seaplane of the Aircraft Company Ltd. (L.F.G.) Stralsund," AL-380147-01, Technical Reference Files: Aircraft, NASM.

24. Nowarra et al., *Marine Aircraft of the 1914–1918 War*, 34.

25. The Hansa-Brandenburg aircraft were allocated Navy numbers 2590–2592; the numbers for the LFG and Zeppelin aircraft are unknown.

26. Gerrard Terry, "The LFG Roland V19: Submarine-borne Spotter Aircraft," *Cross and Cockade* 18, no. 2 (1987): 70.

27. The Project 50 submarine had four bow torpedo tubes, two amidships tubes, two angled stern tubes, and two stern tubes firing directly aft. The two amidships torpedo tubes were fixed to a swiveling mount inside the pressure hull and could be rotated to mate with a set of muzzle doors on either the port or starboard side depending on the direction of the target from the submarine's bow.

28. Eberhard Rössler, *The U-boat: The Evolution and Technical History of German Submarines*, trans. Harold Erenberg (Annapolis, Md.: Naval Institute, 1989), 73–75.

29. The Junkers J 1, nicknamed the *Blechesel* (Sheet Metal Donkey), built in 1915, generally is considered the world's first all-metal aircraft.

30. Baatz, "Seaplane of the Aircraft Company Ltd. (L.F.G.) Stralsund."

31. Terry, "LFG Roland V19," 72–74. After the war, the aircraft was renamed the V 19 Putbus after a town near the LFG factory in Stralsund.

32. Terry, "LFG Roland V19," 70.

33. William B. Clark, *When the U-boats Came to America* (Boston: Little, Brown, 1929), 78–79.

34. Charles W. Duke, "Will the U-boats Come to America This Summer?" *Washington Post*, 2 June 1918, 1.

35. "City Lights out in Air Raid Test," *New York Times*, 5 June 1918, 1. The only lights allowed to remain lit were streetlamps and lights in residences.

36. Steven H. Jaffe, *New York at War: Four Centuries of Combat, Fear, and Intrigue in Gotham* (New York: Basic Books, 2012), 210.

CHAPTER 2: BETWEEN THE WARS—UNITED STATES

1. Grosz, "A Study in Contrasts," 4.

2. Ibid., 2–3.

3. House Committee on Naval Affairs, *Sundry Legislation Affecting the Naval Establishment 1921*, 77th Congress, 1st Session (Washington, D.C.: 1921), 207.

4. Gotthard Baatz, "Das Schiffsflugzeug der Luft-Fahrzeug Gesellschaft mbH Werft Stralsund [The Seaplanes of the Luft-Fahrzeug Gesellschaft Company Stralsund]," *Illustrierte Flug Welt* (5 July 1922).

5. S. Y. Dyme, "Trois nouveaux hydravions L.F.G. [Three New L.F.G. Seaplanes]," *L'Aéronautique* 41 (October 1922): 314–15. It is not believed that a buyer was found.

6. Cdr. John D. Alden, USN (Ret.), *The Fleet Submarine in the U.S. Navy: A Design and Construction History* (Annapolis, Md.: Naval Institute, 1985), 14, 18.

7. William F. Trimble, *Admiral William A. Moffett: Architect of Naval Aviation* (Washington, D.C.: Smithsonian Institution, 1994), 99–102.

8. Eberle Board hearing, 30 September 1924, Roll 19, Entry UD 5: Secret and Confidential Correspondence, 1919–1927, RG 80, NARA I.

9. Norman Friedman, *U.S. Submarines through 1945* (Annapolis, Md.: Naval Institute, 1995), 172, 348.

10. Rodney P. Carlisle, *Where the Fleet Begins: A History of the David Taylor Research Center, 1898–1998* (Washington, D.C.: Naval Historical Center, 1998), 74.

11. Bureau of Construction and Repair, "Prel. Design Sketches for Submersible Cruiser," 17 February 1921, Box 19, Entry P37, Item S-11, RG 19, NARA II.

12. Senior Member Present (General Board) to Secretary of the Navy, "Building Program, 1925; Characteristics for Cruiser Submarines," 19 April 1923, Box 109, GB 420-15, General Board Subject Files, RG 80, NARA I. The cited information is from an undated and unsigned attachment to this file prepared by the Bureau of Construction and Repair titled "History of Design of Cruiser Submarines."

13. The Conference on the Limitation of Armament, signed in Washington, D.C., on 6 February 1922, by representatives of the British Empire, France, Italy, Japan, and the United States.

14. Bureau of Aeronautics, "Material Division Progress Report," 1 December 1921, Roll 25, Entry UD 5: Secret and Confidential Correspondence, 1919–1927, RG 80, NARA I.

15. The XS-1 aircraft had bureau numbers A-6515 to A-6520; the MS-1 aircraft had bureau numbers A-6521 to A-6526. The MS-1 used in the brief 1923 trials was A-6525. The XS-2 used in the 1926–1927 trials was A-6519.

16. Eventually seaplanes were deployed on U.S. destroyers, albeit briefly; see Norman Polmar, "A Floatplane on a . . . What?" *Naval History* (December 2018): 58–59.

17. BuAer also purchased three J. V. Martin K-IV and Macchi M.16 floatplanes at about the same time. Never intended for use on board submarines, they probably were intended to give the Navy experience with small floatplanes. See E. R. Johnson, *United States Naval Aviation, 1919–1941: Aircraft, Airships and Ships Between the Wars* (Jefferson, N.C.: McFarland, 2011).

18. Christiansen would serve as a *Luftwaffe* general during World War II; after the war he was convicted of war crimes.

19. Ernst Heinkel and Jürgen Thorwald, *Stürmisches Leben* [*Stormy Life*] (Stuttgart: Europäischer Buchklub, 1953), 97–98.

20. Heinkel and Thorwald, *Stürmisches Leben*, 101.

21. Director of Naval Intelligence to Bureau of Aeronautics, "Caspar Demountable Seaplane, Type U-1," 26 August 1922, AC-120150-01, Technical Reference Files: Aircraft, NASM.

22. Svenska Aero [Caspar-Werke], "Beschreibung des Unterseeboot-Flugzeuges U.1, Type Heinkel [Description of the Submarine-Aircraft U.1, Type Heinkel]," 1922, AC-120150-01, Technical Reference Files: Aircraft, NASM. The U 1 required a hangar 19 inches longer than that installed on the *S-1*, thus it is unclear if the submarine could have accommodated the U 1.

23. Director of Naval Intelligence to Bureau of Aeronautics, "Caspar Demountable Seaplane, Type U-1."

24. Heinkel and Thorwald, *Stürmisches Leben*, 100. Many secondary sources claim that the U 1s built for Japan were designated U 2 and were built with rotary engines. However, there appears to be no primary source evidence for those claims. See Günter Frost, "Die Flugzeuge der Caspar-Werke in Travemünde [The Aircraft of Caspar Werke in Travemünde]," Arbeitsgemeinschaft Dt. Luftfahrthistorik, https://adl-luftfahrthistorik.de/dok/caspar-flugzeugwerke-travemuende-werksgeschichte-flugzeugtypen-2023-05.pdf.

25. After several mergers, that company would become Svenska Aeroplan AB (SAAB).

26. "The Caspar Sport Seaplane," *Flight* (14 June 1923): 315–16; and "Gothenburg International Aero Exhibition 1923," *Flight* (2 August 1923): 432–53. The German U 1 was registered as D-293.

27. Frost, "Die Flugzeuge der Caspar-Werke in Travemünde."

28. Aircraft history cards for BuAer No. A-6434 and A-6435, Reel 4, Aircraft History Cards, 1911–1949, EBNAL; and BuAer Material Division Progress Reports, October 1922–January 1923, April–July 1923, and October–December 1923, Roll 25, Entry UD 5: Secret and Confidential Correspondence, 1919–1927, RG 80, NARA I.

29. General Board hearing, "Submarine V-4 (SM1)—Conference on Plans of," 26 August 1924, Roll 18, Proceedings and Hearings of the General Board of the U.S. Navy 1900–1950, RG 64, NARA II.

30. Eberle Board hearing, 6 October 1924, Roll 19, Entry UD 5: Secret and Confidential Correspondence, 1919–1927, RG 80, NARA I.

31. General Board hearing, "Characteristics of Cruiser Submarines," 8 May 1925, Roll 18, Proceedings and Hearings of the General Board of the U.S. Navy 1900–1950, RG 64, NARA II.

32. General Board to Secretary of the Navy, "Building Program, 1925; Characteristics for Cruiser Submarines."

33. Before they were laid down, the *V-5* and *V-6* hull numbers were changed to SC 1 and SC 2 (SC—Cruiser Submarine). The *V-4/Argonaut* was allocated the hull number SS 166 but was never so designated. See Alden, *Fleet Submarine in the U.S. Navy* for the design history and naming of those submarines.

34. Those were the largest caliber guns ever fitted in U.S. submarines.

35. The hangar installation is detailed in Bureau of Construction and Repair, "General Information U.S. Submarine Torpedo Boat S-1," September 1924, Box 2, Entry P13: Submarine General Information Books and Related Documentation, 1913–1961, Item S-68, RG 19, NARA II.

36. "Logbook U.S.S. S-1: Jan. 1 1922 to Dec. 31 1922," Logbooks of U.S. Navy Ships, ca. 1801–1940, RG 24, NARA I.

37. Adm. Montgomery M. Taylor to General Board, "Aircraft on Submarines," 23 September 1924, Box 109, GB 420-15, General Board Subject Files, RG 80, NARA I.

38. General Board hearing, "Submarine V-4 (SM1)—Conference on Plans of."

39. Eberle Board hearing, 6 October 1924.

40. Bureau of Aeronautics, "Material Division Progress Report," April–June 1925 and April–June 1926, Roll 25, Entry UD 5: Secret and Confidential Correspondence, 1919–1927, RG 80, NARA I.

41. General Board to Secretary of the Navy, "Submarine V-4 (SM1)—Conference of plans of," 8 September 1924, Box 109, GB 420-15, General Board Subject Files, RG 80, NARA I.

42. Senior Member Present (General Board) to Secretary of the Navy, "Building Program, 1926—Fleet Submarine—Cruiser Type," 13 May 1925, Box 109, GB 420-15, General Board Subject Files, RG 80, NARA I.

43. Adm. Edward W. Eberle was Chief of Naval Operations from July 1923 to November 1927.

44. Eberle board hearing, 6 October 1924.

45. General Board hearing, "Submarine V-4 (SM1)—Conference on Plans of."

46. Ibid.

47. "Logbook U.S.S. S-1: Jan. 1 1926 to Dec. 31 1926," Logbooks of U.S. Navy Ships, ca. 1801–1940, RG 24, NARA I.

48. Lt. C. B. Momsen to CNO, 5 October 1926, Box 292, Subject Files, NHHC.

49. "Logbook U.S.S. S-1: Jan. 1 1926 to Dec. 31 1926."

50. Lt. G. Bannerman to CNO, "Airplane, Submarine Experimental Type, Report on," 1 August 1926, Box 109, GB 420-15, General Board Subject Files, RG 80, NARA I.

51. Senior Member Present (General Board) to Secretary of the Navy, "Airplane—Submarine Experimental Type—Report on," 28 September 1927, Box 109, GB 420-15, General Board Subject Files, RG 80, NARA I.

52. The McCann chamber was used to rescue the crew of the submarine *Squalus* (SS 192) when she sank in 1939, and was employed as a diving bell during the salvage of the *Squalus*; derivatives of the McCann chamber still are in use by the U.S. Navy.

53. Bureau of Aeronautics, "Material Division Progress Report" May 1922, Roll 25, Entry UD 5: Secret and Confidential Correspondence, 1919–1927, RG 80, NARA I. The early flying boats were designs No. 21 (pusher configuration) and 22 (tractor configuration).

54. Bureau of Aeronautics, "Material Division Progress Report" January–March 1924, Roll 25, Entry UD 5: Secret and Confidential Correspondence, 1919–1927, RG 80, NARA I and General Board hearing, "Submarine V-4 (SM1)—Conference on Plans of."

55. Bureau of Aeronautics, "Material Division Progress Report," April–June 1925, Roll 25, Entry UD 5: Secret and Confidential Correspondence, 1919–1927, RG 80, NARA I.

56. Bureau of Aeronautics, "Report on XSL-1 Loening Single Place Submarine Plane (Boat Type)," 25 April 1931, AL-540270-01, Technical Reference Files: Aircraft, NASM.

57. Bureau of Aeronautics, "Detail Specification for Model XSL-1 Airplane," 25 March 1930, AL-540270-03, Technical Reference Files: Aircraft, NASM.

58. Aircraft history card for BuAer No. A-8696, Reel 6, Aircraft History Cards, 1911–1949, EBNAL. Loening's first company, Loening Aeronautical Engineering, was founded in 1917 and bought by Keystone Aircraft in 1928. He founded the new Grover Loening Aircraft Company in 1929.

59. See Patricia T. Groves, "The Loening Monoplanes," *American Aviation Historical Society Journal* (Winter 1984): 242–55; and Box 135, Aircraft Files, NHHC. Some sources claim the Loening Kitten and Cat were intended for use on board submarines, but that assertion is not borne out by primary sources.

60. "Folding Plane Tried Here, Fits Tube of Submarine," *New York Herald Tribune*, 5 February 1931. The aircraft was assigned Bureau number A-8696.

61. Grover Loening, Airplane, Patent No. 1,859,306, filed 7 November 1930.

62. Treadwell, *Submarines with Wings*, 40.

63. Bureau of Aeronautics, "Report on XSL-1 Loening Single Place Submarine Plane (Boat Type)."

64. Bureau of Aeronautics, "Air Force and Moment for Proposed Flying Boat for Submarines," 31 May 1933, AI-600030-01, Technical Reference Files: Aircraft, NASM. Based on the drawing numbers referenced in the report, the design likely was designated the N-3 by Amphibions, next in the sequence after their N-1/N-2 Neptune flying boat.

65. The General Board was abolished in 1951.

66. "Funds Held Lacking for Submarine Plane," *U.S. Daily* (7 October 1930).

67. Aircraft history card for BuAer No. A-8696. *Submarines with Wings* by Treadwell states that the XSL-2 was irreparably damaged in a flood at Anacostia in March 1933, when it was actually at the Loening factory on Long Island at that time. (Anacostia did flood during a hurricane in late August 1933.) The only incident recorded on the aircraft history card was an aileron damaged at Anacostia on 11 September 1933.

CHAPTER 3: BETWEEN THE WARS—EUROPE

1. Fisher served as First Sea Lord—the senior officer in the Royal Navy—from 1904 to 1910 and in 1914–1915.

2. Martin H. Brice, *M-class Submarines* (London: Outline, 1983), 3–4.

3. Some sources claimed that "M" stood for "monitor"; however, M was the next letter in the alphabetical series designation of British undersea craft. The M-class submarines were referred to as "mutton boats" because their bulbous superstructure and gun had the appearance of a lamb chop.

4. The M-1 and M-2 had 18-inch torpedo tubes; the M-3 and uncompleted M-4 had 21-inch torpedo tubes, which increased their overall length by seven feet and submerged displacement by 84 tons.

5. See Thomas A. Adams, "The M Class Submarine Monitors," *Warship* VII (London: Conway, 1983), 25–29.

6. Brice, *M-class Submarines*, 7–9.

7. Norman Friedman, *British Submarines in Two World Wars* (Barnsley, England: Seaforth, 2019), 174.

8. Compton-Hall, *Submarine Warfare*, 35–36. When the tampion was opened, an indicator flipped up and was visible through the aiming periscope.

9. The Mark VIII 12-inch/35 caliber guns weighed 46 tons and had a range of 27,000 yards (13.3 n.miles).

10. Don Everitt, *K-Boats: Steam-Powered Submarines in World War I* (Annapolis, Md.: Naval Institute, 1999), 111–12. For secrecy, the M class were referred to by the names of the K-class submarines that they were laid down in place of: *K-18* (M-1), *K-19* (M-2), *K-20* (M-3), and *K-21* (M-4).

11. Friedman, *British Submarines in Two World Wars*, 174.

12. Commander-in-Chief, Atlantic Fleet to Secretary of the Admiralty, "Seaplane-Carrying Submarine," 27 July 1923, ADM 1/8724/90, TNA; and Compton-Hall, *Submarine Warfare*, 59. According to Compton-Hall, Horton's proposal was forwarded verbatim by CINC Atlantic Fleet to the Admiralty in the above memorandum, which is quoted here.

13. Capt. Max Horton to Commander-in-Chief, Atlantic Fleet, "Seaplane-Carrying Submarine—Additional Memo," 10 August 1923, ADM 1/8724/90, TNA.

14. Controller of the Navy, M.0855/23, 11 February 1923, ADM 1/8724/90, TNA.

15. A. N. Harrison, *The Development of HM Submarines from Holland No. 1 (1901) to Porpoise (1930)*, BR 3043 (London: Ministry of Defence, 1979), 12.7.

16. Brice, *M-class Submarines*, 19. Initially the *M-1* was expected to undergo the conversion.

17. Rear Admiral (Submarines) to Secretary of the Admiralty, "Seaplane-Carrying Submarine—'M' class," 20 September 1923, ADM 1/8724/90, TNA.

18. K. J. Meekcombs and E. B. Morgan, *The British Aircraft Specifications File: British Military and Commercial Aircraft Specifications, 1920–1949* (Tonbridge, England: Air Britain), 81–83.

19. Kenneth E. Wixley, *Parnall Aircraft since 1914* (Annapolis, Md.: Naval Institute, 1990), 147. The Peto probably was named for Lt. Cdr. Henry F. M. Peto, who commanded the *M-2* in 1922–1924.

20. The floats were initially Saunders "Consuta" floats made of mahogany plywood sewn together with copper wire. They were later replaced by duralumin floats with water rudders.

21. The aircraft were temporarily fitted with the wheeled undercarriage from the Parnall Pike for land test flights. Both aircraft originally were fitted with 128-horsepower Bristol Lucifer IV radial engines with one rebuilt with a 169-horsepower Armstrong Siddeley Mongoose IIIC radial. Some sources incorrectly claim that either six or eight production Petos were built in addition to the two prototypes. This confusion is likely due to the changing wing, strut, and float design of the prototypes.

22. Brice, *M-class Submarines*, 21, 29. Designed by R. Falkland Carey of the elevator manufacturer Weygood-Otis, the catapult was specified to launch a 7,000-pound aircraft at 45 mph. The *M-2* was the second Royal Navy ship to mount a catapult after a similar design was fitted to the light cruiser *Vindictive*.

23. "A Submarine Aircraft Carrier," *Flight* (31 July 1931): 759–60.

24. Brice, *M-class Submarines*, 22.

25. Treadwell, *Submarines with Wings*, 24.

26. Rear Admiral (Submarines) to Secretary of the Admiralty, "H.M. Submarine 'M.2,'" 17 July 1930, ADM 116/3484, TNA.

27. Brice, *M-class Submarines*, 22; and Rear Admiral (Submarines) to Secretary of the Admiralty, "H.M. Submarine 'M.2.'"

28. Rear Admiral (Submarines) to Secretary of the Admiralty, "H.M. Submarine 'M.2.'"

29. Winans, "Submarine Aircraft," 43. Peto N181 did not fly from the M-2 after the bathhouse incident. It was repaired and sold to a civilian with the register mark G-ACOJ, but likely never flew. It was put into storage after 1935 and probably scrapped.

30. Wixley, *Parnall Aircraft since 1914*, 153.

31. Lt. Cdr. John Leathes, "H.M. Submarine 'M.2'—Report on Air Work," 4 April 1931, ADM 116/3484, TNA.

32. Director of Tactical Division, TD3514/30, 11 November 1930, ADM 116/3484, TNA. In May 1931 the Director of Naval Construction sketched two schemes for modifying the submarine *Thames* to carry a Peto: Scheme A mirrored the M-2 arrangement, with a hangar and catapult forward of the hangar; Scheme B was inspired by the U.S. Navy's S-1, with an aft-mounted hangar and no catapult. Except for the increase in vulnerability due to flooding of the hangar, the submarine's speed, range, and maneuverability were hardly altered.

33. Commander-in-Chief, Atlantic Fleet to Secretary of the Admiralty, "Tactical Uses of Submarines Which Carry Aircraft," 8 October 1930, ADM 116/3484, TNA.

34. Director of Plans, M.03946/30, 10 October 1931, ADM 116/3484, TNA.

35. Friedman, *British Submarines in Two World Wars*, 190.

36. Director of Naval Air Division, M.02816/31, 24 December 1931, ADM 116/3484, TNA.

37. Admiralty to Rear Admiral (Submarines), M.02285/32, 21 October 1932, ADM 116/3484, TNA.

38. Director of Naval Construction, M.03946/30, 9 June 1933, ADM 116/3484, TNA.

39. M.03946/30, 10 July 1933, ADM 116/3484, TNA.

40. John Jordan, "French Submarine Development between the Wars," in *Warship 1991*, ed. Robert Gardiner (Annapolis, Md.: Naval Institute, 1991), 59–60.

41. Capt. Claude Huan, French Navy (Ret.), *Le croiseur sous-marin* Surcouf *(1926–1942)* [*The Submarine Cruiser* Surcouf *(1926–1942)*] (Bourg-en-Bresse: Marines Éditions, 1996), 23, 33.

42. Capt. Claude Huan, French Navy (Ret.), *Le sous-marins français, 1918–1945* [*French Submarines, 1918–1945*] (Bourg-en-Bresse: Marines Éditions, ca. 1995), 20.

43. Huan, *Le croiseur sous-marin* Surcouf, 20–33.

44. Ibid., 28.

45. The submarine was named after French privateer Robert Surcouf.

46. The *Surcouf*/Project Q was one of two French cruiser submarine projects planned in 1922. The other was the smaller and faster "grand patrol" Project M submarine armed only with torpedoes; that design became the 1,500-ton *Redoutable* class.

47. Jordan, "French Submarine Development between the Wars," 62, 73. The participants in the London conference in 1930 were France, Great Britain, Italy, Japan, and the United States.

48. The treaty definition of standard displacement for submarines was the surface displacement loaded for a combat patrol, but without fuel, oil, fresh water, or ballast water.

49. Those guns, as the Model 1924, were the main battery of the French heavy cruisers of the *Suffren* and *Duquesne* classes.

50. Jordan, "French Submarine Development between the Wars," 61.

51. Huan, *Le croiseur sous-marin* Surcouf, 54. The wine cellar was under the deck plating, forward of the reload torpedo storage in the bow torpedo room.

52. Huan, *Le croiseur sous-marin* Surcouf, 52.

53. Roger Branfill-Cook, *X.1: The Royal Navy's Mystery Submarine* (Barnsley, England: Seaforth, 2012), 113–18.

54. Huan, *Le croiseur sous-marin* Surcouf, 44–48.

55. Gérard Bousquet, *Les ailes françaises, l'Encyclopédie des avions de la Seconde Guerre Mondiale* [*The French Wings, Encyclopedia of WWII*], vol. 3, *Les hydravions à flotteurs, 1ère partie* [*Floatplanes, Part 1*] (Paris: Artipresse, 2012), 1. As built, the *Surcouf*'s hangar was 30 ft., 10 in. long and 6 ft., 7 in. in diameter.

56. Alain Marchand and Claude Huan, "'Passe-Partout,' l'avion du sous-marin ['Go Anywhere,' the Submarine Aircraft]," *Le Fana de l'Aviation* 314 (January 1996): 17.

57. Ibid., 19.

58. The cruisers that embarked the MB 35 were the *Jeanne d'Arc, Duguay-Trouin, Lamotte-Piquet, Primauguet, Edgar Quinet,* and *Jules Michelet.*

59. That aircraft also was referred to as the MB 410.

60. Marchand and Huan, "'Passe-Partout,'" 21.

61. Huan, *Le croiseur sous-marin* Surcouf, 47, 58, 62–63.

62. Ibid., 33, 51.

63. Ibid., 32.

64. Achille Vigna, "Idrovolanti per i sommergibili italiani [Seaplanes for Italian Submarines]," *Storia Militare* (June 2012): 59. The *Libelles* were given military aircraft numbers 56 and 57.

65. Ibid., 61–63.

66. Director General of Construction and Procurement, "Idro M.53 per Sommergibili: Istruzione per il montaggio e regolazione [M.53 Seaplane for Submarines: Instructions for Assembly and Maintenance]" (Ministry of Aeronautics); and Director General of Construction and Procurement, "Idro P.8: Istruzione per il montaggio e per le regolazione [P.8 Seaplane: Instructions for Assembly and Maintenance]" (Ministry of Aeronautics).

67. The M.53 prototype was given military aircraft number 94; the P.8 prototype was number 95.

68. Umberto Ruzzier, "L'aviazione sottomarina [Submarine Aviation]," *Rivista Marittima* (May 2007): 64.

69. Alessandro Turrini, Ottorino Miozzi, and Manuel Minuto, *Sommergibili e Mezzi d'Assalto Subacquei Italiani* [*Italian Submarines and Underwater Assault Craft*] (Rome: Ufficio Storico Marina Militare, 2010), 593–600.

70. Capt. Paolo M. Pollina, Italian Navy, *I Sommergibili Italiani: 1895–1962* [*The Italian Submarines: 1895–1962*] (Rome: Ufficio Storico Marina Militare, 1963), 214–18.

71. Allesandro Turrini, "Breve storia del 'sommergibile cannoniere,' e in particolare di quello italiano [Brief History of the 'Cannon Submarines,' in Particular Those of Italy]," *Rivista Marittima* (December 2011): 127–39.

72. Norman Polmar and Jurrien Noot, *Submarines of the Russian and Soviet Navies: 1718–1990* (Annapolis, Md.: Naval Institute, 1991), 87, 264–66.

73. V. A. Lesnichenko and A. N. Gusev, *Samolet i podvodnaya lodka: Ocherki k istorii podovodnoy aviatsii* [*Aircraft and Submarine: Essays on the History of Submarine Aviation*] (St. Petersburg: Galeya, 2001), 68.

74. Bill Gunston, *Aircraft of the Soviet Union: The Encyclopedia of Soviet Aircraft since 1917* (London: Osprey, 1983), 80–81. The SPL could be stowed in a cylinder 8 ft., 4 in. in diameter and 24 ft., 5 in. in length.

75. Polmar and Noot, *Submarines of the Russian and Soviet Navies*, 87, 264–66. The Type K submarine was designated Project 41 and the Type KE was Project 41a.

76. Lesnichenko and Gusev, *Samolet i podvodnaya lodka*, 70.

77. The SPL was given to the Society for Assistance to Defense, Aviation, and Chemical Construction, a paramilitary sport organization that focused on aircraft, boats, and automobiles. The aircraft was renamed *Gidro-1* and set several records for its class.

78. TsKBS = *Tsentral'noye konstruktorskoye byuro spetsial'nogo (podvodnogo) sudostroyeniya* [Central Design Bureau for Special (Undersea) Shipbuilding].

79. A. V. Platonov, *Lineynye sily podvodnogo flota* [*Forces of the Line of the Undersea Fleet*] (St. Petersburg: Galeya, 1998), 12–17.

80. Przemyslaw Budzbon, "Pride of Poland: The *Orzel* Class Submarines: Construction," *Warship* (April 1987): 74–82.

81. With Polish input, the Nederlands Vereenigde Scheepsbouw Bureaux designed the submarines, which were built in Vissinigen (*Orzeł*) and Rotterdam (*Sęp*).

82. Andrzej Morgała, *Samoloty w polskim lotnictwie morskim* [Aircraft in Polish Naval Aviation] (Warsaw: Wydawnictwo Komunikacji, 1985), 156–58.

CHAPTER 4: EUROPE AT WAR

1. The source for the *Surcouf*'s World War II activities is primarily Huan, *Le croiseur sous-marin* Surcouf.

2. Rear Adm. Paul Auphan, French Navy (Ret.), and Jacques Mordal, *The French Navy in World War II* (Annapolis, Md.: Naval Institute, 1959), 124–25.

3. "Facts by Request—The *Surcouf*'s Seaplane," *Flying Review International* (August 1967): 812. Also see John Gaylard, "Last at Poole," *Flight* (20 June 1959): 887; K. W. Clark, "Poole Identification," *Flight* (25 July 1958): 153; and John Gaylard, "Poole Petrel," *Flight* (15 August 1958): 240. That aircraft was MB 411 no. 2; MB 411 no. 1 remained in France and was captured by the Germans.

4. Huan, *Le croiseur sous-marin* Surcouf, 80–81.

5. Auphan and Mordal, *French Navy in World War II*, 167–68.

6. James Rusbridger, *Who Sank* Surcouf? *The Truth about the Disappearance of the Pride of the French Navy* (London: Century, 1991), 186.

7. Ibid., 195–96. The aircraft took off at 0800 and landed at 0935. The cruise speed of the A-17 and B-18 was about 170 mph, thus the attack must have occurred within a 135-mile radius of Rio Hato. The Gulf of San Blas is within that distance and also outside the *Surcouf*'s moving haven.

8. Ibid., 193.

9. See, for example, Capt. Frederick H. Hallett, USN (Ret.), "The Loss of the *Surcouf*: Solving an Old Mystery," *Submarine Review* (Winter 2012): 76–89, and (Spring 2012), 77–97.

10. Rössler, *The U-boat*, 112.

11. Rössler, *Die deutschen U-Kreuzer und Transport-U-Boote*, 207.

12. The design was begun in mid-1937 and the requirement to carry an aircraft was added in 1938. Early iterations of the Type XI designs had space reserved for an aircraft under the deck forward of the conning tower.

13. R. D. Layman, "Question 42/89," *Warship International* 2 (1992): 204.

14. Steve Coates and Jean-Christophe Carbonel, *Helicopters of the Third Reich* (Hersham, England: Classic, 2002), 23–25.

15. J. R. Smith and Antony L. Kay, *German Aircraft of the Second World War* (Baltimore, Md.: Nautical & Aviation, 1972), 584.

16. Seekriegsleitung [Naval War Staff], "'Flettner-Huber' für Marinezwecke ['Flettner-Helicopter' for Naval Purposes] (Neu 1.Skl. I L 2231/39 g.K.)," 19 December 1939; and Luftwaffen Inspektion der Seeflieger [Air Force Inspectorate of Naval Aviation], "Taktisch technische Forderungen für Hubschrauberentwicklung [Tactical Technical Requirements for Helicopter Development] (L.In.8 B.Nr.83/40 8c g.Kdos.)," 29 January 1940.

17. Theodore Mohr, "Flettner Fl 282 'Kolibri' Varianten: Die Geschichte einer erfolgreichen Hubschrauberentwicklung" [Flettner Fl 282 'Kolibri' Variants: The History of a Successful Helicopter Development]," *Flugzeug Profile* 14 (1991): 5.

18. Steve Coates, discussion with Jacob Gunnarson, 1 February 2023. Bode claimed that visit was sometime in 1942; examination of his flight log suggests that he visited Rechlin several times in October 1941, and not in early 1942.

19. Heinrich Wollé, H. A. Caspari, and Oskar Passoth, eds., *E-Stelle See: Die Geschichte der Flugerprobungsstellen Travemünde und Tarnewitz* [*Testing Station Sea: The History of the Travemünde and Tarnewitz Flight Test Stations*] (Steinebach-Wörthsee, Germany: Luftfahrt-Verlag Axel Zuerl, 1975), 154. The concept of a towed autogyro was actually put forward by designer Reinhold Gensel; see Coates and Carbonel, *Helicopters of the Third Reich*, 94.

20. The *Bachstelze*'s designation within Focke Achgelis was E 19. The prototypes were designated Fa 330 A-0, and the production machines Fa 330 A-1 (Coates and Carbonel, *Helicopters of the Third Reich*, 94, 100).

21. Fredi Lang, "Die Ausbildung am Tragschrauber FA-330 'Bachstelze' [Training on the FA-330 'Bachstelze' Towed Autogyro]," *Aero* 3 (March 1952). A larger rotor with a diameter of 28 feet, 3 inches was tested in late 1943 but probably never fitted to production Fa 330s.

22. U.S. Navy, Office of the Chief of Naval Operations, "Report on the Interrogation of Survivors from *U-177* Sunk 6 February 1944" (22 May 1944), 43.

23. U.S. Navy, Office of the Chief of Naval Operations, "Report on the Interrogation of Survivors from *U-841* Sunk 17 October 1943 and *U-848* Sunk 5 November 1943" (12 January 1944), 91.

24. "Tragschrauber-Flugzeug Fa 330 [Towed Autogyro Aircraft Fa 330]," *Luftfahrt International* 21 (May–June 1977): 3256. This article is a reproduction of an original Fa 330 manual.

25. O. L. L. Fitzwilliams, "Some Work with Rotating-Wing Aircraft," *Journal of the Helicopter Association of Great Britain* 1, no. 2 (October–December 1947): 16. Fitzwilliams was one of the British engineers to examine the Fa 330; he later was the head designer for helicopters at Westland.

26. Coates and Carbonel, *Helicopters of the Third Reich*, 150.
27. Ibid., 96–97. The wind-tunnel tests revealed a dangerous resonance in the flexible rotor blades, which was solved by stringing damper weights between the blades.
28. German Navy, "Kriegstagebuch 'U 523': 25 Juni 1942–16 April 1943" [War Diary 'U 523': 25 June 1942–16 April 1943]," (1943).
29. Wollé, Caspari, and Passoth, *E-stelle See*, 159–60.
30. Carl Bode, "Die Entwicklung der Focke FA-330 [The Development of the Focke FA-330]," *Der Flieger* 5 (1974): 204.
31. Royal Navy, Naval Intelligence Division, "History of U-boat Policy: 1939-1945 (CB 4501)," (February 1946), 30, 33. When the conversation turned to powered aircraft Hitler remembered that the French had difficulties with submarine-launched aircraft.
32. Norman Polmar and Floyd D. Kennedy, *Military Helicopters of the World* (Annapolis, Md.: Naval Institute), 61.
33. Coates and Carbonel, *Helicopters of the Third Reich*, 100.
34. Lang, "Die Ausbildung am Tragschrauber FA-330 'Bachstelze;'" and Gerhard Freund, *Himmelfahrtskommando "Bachstelze": Der Einsatz des antriebslosen Tragschraubers Fa 330 im U-boot-Krieg des Zweiten Weltkrieges* [Suicide Mission "Bachstelze": The Use of the Unpowered Autogyro Fa 330 in the U-boat Battle of the Second World War] (Steinau, Germany: Märchenstraßen, 2014), 41–43. The former French minelayer *Elsaß* and the destroyer *Theodor Riedel* took part in these training exercises.
35. Dorr Carpenter and Norman Polmar, *Submarines of the Imperial Japanese Navy* (Annapolis, Md.: Naval Institute, 1986), 37.
36. Lawrence Patterson, *Hitler's Grey Wolves: U-Boats in the Indian Ocean* (London: Greenhill, 2004), 71.
37. Carpenter and Polmar, *Submarines of the Imperial Japanese Navy*, 37.
38. Rössler, *The U-boat*, 114, 150.
39. The engines frequently overheated and soon were replaced with two standard diesels. The two Type IXD1 submarines that were built were converted to carry cargo by removing their bow torpedo tubes and using that compartment and the space freed up in the engine room to store cargo.
40. Patterson, *Hitler's Grey Wolves*, 45.
41. U.S. Navy, Office of the Chief of Naval Operations, "Report on the Interrogation of Survivors from *U-177* Sunk 6 February 1944," 37. The locations of the second aircraft and spare parts were: fuselage in the engine room; rotor blades and extra telephone box in the electric motor room; and extra set of rotor blades in the second munitions room, the petty officers' room, or the port stowage cylinder.
42. The *U-179*, *U-199*, and *U-200* were sunk before they could be modified to carry the Fa 330. It is unclear if *U-178* or *U-197* were ever modified, although it is certain from examination of their war diaries that neither used the Fa 330 operationally. Two Type IXD2/42 U-boats—a variant of the Type IXD2 with more powerful diesels—were built, but likely neither were equipped to carry the Fa 330.
43. Clay Blair, *Hitler's U-boat War: The Hunted, 1941–1945*, vol. 2 (New York: Random House, 1998), 300–301.
44. German Navy, "Kriegstagebuch 'U 177': 2. Feindfahrt [War Diary 'U-177': 2nd War Patrol]," (1943), 12.
45. Admiralty OIC to COMINCH, "COMINCH OIC Serial 410 from Admiralty," (20 April 1943), 3, and Admiralty OIC to COMINCH, "COMINCH OIC Serial 447

from Admiralty," (6 May 1943), 1. The messages between the Admiralty's Operational Intelligence Center/Submarine Tracking Room and the U.S. Navy's Atlantic Section Tracking Room updated their respective commanders, the First Sea Lord and Commander-in-Chief, U.S. Fleet (COMINCH), to U-boat intelligence gained through the breaking of German naval ciphers (Ultra).

46. "Kriegstagebuch 'U 849,'" 1.

47. "Kriegstagebuch 'U 177': 2. Feindfahrt," 120. Gysae also noted that flying in the Doldrums (near the equator in the Intertropical Convergence Zone) was impossible due to insufficient wind.

48. Blair, Hitler's U-boat War, 301–2.

49. Luftwaffe, "Kriegstagebuch der Bordfliegergruppe 196, Anfangen: 1 September 1943, Abgeschlossen: 31 Dezember 1943 [War Diary of Embarked Air Group 196, Beginning: 1 September 1945, Ending: 31 December 1943]," (1943), 32.

50. "Freie Jagd im Indische Ozean [Free Hunting in the Indian Ocean]," n.d., 9–10. This is an unpublished document created for a U-862 crew member reunion.

51. Patterson, Hitler's Grey Wolves, 222–24. An earlier trade may have been made for a Kugisho E14Y1 (Glen); see Coates and Carbonel, Helicopters of the Third Reich, 149.

52. Coates and Carbonel, Helicopters of the Third Reich, 149.

53. U.S. Navy, Office of the Chief of Naval Operations, "Report on the Interrogation of Survivors from U-177 Sunk 6 February 1944," 75.

54. Coates and Carbonel, Helicopters of the Third Reich, 100, 149, 151. One hundred eighty were delivered when production was cancelled, and it is unclear how many additional machines were completed.

55. U.S. Navy, Office of the Chief of Naval Operations, "Report on the Interrogation of Survivors from U-199 Sunk on 31 July 1944" (27 September 1943), 30. Survivor interrogations were not always accurate: British naval intelligence received erroneous reports that some Type IXs had hangars to carry the Arado Ar 196 floatplane.

56. On 13 March 1944 the U-852 sank the Greek steamer Peleus. The U-boat officers murdered the survivors in their rafts in an attempt to cover up the sinking. After the submarine ran aground and the crew was captured, three officers were tried and executed for war crimes, including the commander, Kapitänleutnant Heinz-Wilhelm Eck. Two other officers, including the Fa 330 pilot, Matrosenobergefreiter Wolfgang Schwender, were convicted and imprisoned.

57. Gordon Williamson, U-boat Tactics in World War II (Oxford: Osprey, 2010), 42.

58. Fitzwilliams, "Some Work with Rotating-Wing Aircraft," 14. The Fa 330 was examined at the Airborne Forces Experimental Establishment at Beaulieu, England.

59. Lesnichenko and Gusev, Samolet i podvodnaya lodka, 98, 102. That design, dated 28 June 1944, had a rotor diameter of 26 feet, 2 inches and loaded weight of 728 pounds.

60. Coates and Carbonel, Helicopters of the Third Reich, 201–6. The U.S. Army Air Forces tested an Fa 330 by towing it behind a jeep at Wright Field, Ohio. It was later evaluated by the Ryan Aeronautical Co. Another was towed behind a boat off MacDill Field in Florida, but that aircraft struck the water and sank. Thirteen Fa 330s have been on display or under restoration in museums in several nations.

61. Jean-Christophe Carbonel, "Sur une table de cuisine: La Marine teste le Fa 330 [On a Kitchen Table: The Navy Tests the Fa 330]," Aéro Journal 32 (August–September 2003): 62–65.

CHAPTER 5: JAPAN PREPARES FOR WAR

1. Gordon W. Prange, Donald M. Goldstein, and Chief Warrant Officer Katherine V. Dillon, U.S. Air Force (Ret.), *At Dawn We Slept: The Untold Story of Pearl Harbor*, 2nd ed. (New York: Viking, 1991), 12.
2. David C. Evans and Mark R. Peattie, *Kaigun: Strategy, Tactics, and Technology in the Imperial Japanese Navy, 1887–1941* (Annapolis, Md.: Naval Institute, 1997), 214.
3. The signatories of the treaty were each allowed to build three 2,800-ton submarines. The total displacement limit was 52,700 tons.
4. I (イ) is the first letter of the *Iroha* ordering of the *katakana* script and was applied to "first-class" submarines of more than 1,000 tons. Medium/second-class submarines used the next letter of the Japanese alphabet, RO (ロ) and coastal/third-class submarines used HA (ハ). In 1939, the names of older I-boats had 100 added to their number (e.g., the *I-21* became the *I-121*), and new submarines were given the old, lower numbers.
5. Ryusuke Ishiguro and Tadeusz Januszewski, *Kugisho E14Y Glen: The Aircraft That Bombed America* (Petersfield: Mushroom Model, 2012), 6–7.
6. The Air Technical Arsenal was known by two other contractions: Kusho (Naval Air Arsenal) and Ichigisho (1st Naval Air Technical Arsenal). Kugisho is frequently referred to simply as Yokosuka in Western publications.
7. Winans, "Submarine Aircraft," 46.
8. No Petos were purchased by Japan after the M-2 sank in 1932. Peto N225 was wrecked, and N181 was sold to a private British buyer.
9. Originally, the aircraft was to be fitted with a Hitachi *Kamikaze* engine.
10. Akira Terada, "Development of Japanese Submarines—Hull," *Sakai no Kasen* [*Ships of the World*] 469 (1993), 130. The *I-51* lacked the high-horsepower diesel engines developed by Germany during the war. To achieve high surface speed with less powerful Japanese-built engines, she had four 1,300-horsepower diesels each driving a shaft, becoming the first and only four-shaft submarine to be built. To accommodate four engines mounted abreast, most of her pressure hull had an unusual cross-section: three intersecting circles, creating a very wide hull. The cusps where the circles intersected were reinforced with pillars. The later Japanese *Sentoku* Type and German Type XI submarines would have "figure-eight" hulls, which had cross-sections constructed from two intersecting circles.
11. "Nippon Kaigun Kantei Shashin Shu [Japanese Navy Ship Photobook]," *Maru* 19 (1997): 36, 53.
12. E6Y1 was the "short" designation, similar to contemporary U.S. Navy designations: "E" for shipboard reconnaissance seaplane, "6" for the model (i.e., the sixth model of the reconnaissance seaplane), "Y" for Kugisho/Yokosuka, and "1" for the submodel. Navy aircraft were also given a designation with a "*Shi*" prototype number that corresponded to the year of reign of Emperor Showa (Hirohito), which began in 1926. The E6Y1 was developed to meet requirements issued in 1931 (imperial year 2,591), thus it was also designated 6-*Shi* Small Reconnaissance Seaplane, Type 91.
13. The E6Y1's designation within Kawanishi was the Type N.
14. Ishiguro and Januszewski, *Kugisho E14Y Glen*, 15. The *I-51* had her hangars and catapult removed after the trials and returned to fleet service.
15. Eberhard Rössler, *Die deutschen U-boote und U-bootentwürfe zwischen den Weltkriegen, 1922–1939* [*The German U-boats and U-boat Development between the World Wars, 1922–1939*] (Berlin: Edition Erich Gröner, 2013), 10.

16. Ishiguro and Januszewski, *Kugisho E14Y Glen*, 15.
17. Tsutomu Nakagawa, "History of Japanese Submarines," *Sakai no Kasen* [*Ships of the World*] 469 (1993), 56.
18. The project leader at Watanabe was Ryohachiro Higuchi.
19. Ishiguro and Januszewski, *Kugisho E14Y Glen*, 21
20. Watanabe developed a slightly larger version, designated WS-103S, for the Thai Navy with six delivered in 1938; they could not operate from submarines.
21. Zenji Orita and Joseph D. Harrington, *I-Boat Captain* (Canoga Park, Calif.: Major Books, 1976), 111.
22. The following models of the Kure Type No. 1 catapult were installed on board Japanese submarines:

Model 2	*I-51, I-5*
Model 3	*I-6*
Model 3 Mod.	*I-7*
Model 4	*I-8*, Type A, Type B

The models of catapult increased in length as the weight of the aircraft rose, and the Model 4 introduced a gunpowder booster to increase maximum takeoff weight for the E14Y1. The Kure Type No. 1 Model 1 was the first Japanese shipboard catapult, and was installed on the cruiser *Kinugasa* in 1928. Most Japanese surface ships used various models of the Kure Type No. 2 catapult.
23. The *Junsen 3* Type could operate the E6Y1, but likely only did so in the short time before the E9W1 entered service.
24. In 1943 the *I-8* was refitted with a twin 5.5-inch gun mount. She was converted to a *kaiten* "human torpedo" carrier in late 1944; her 5-inch guns, aircraft hangar, and catapult were removed, and she was fitted to carry four *kaitens*.
25. The full designation was Type 0 Small Naval Seaplane Model 1. It later was changed to Small Naval Reconnaissance Seaplane Model 11.
26. Watanabe was renamed Kyushu in 1943.
27. The E14Y1 apparently was difficult to operate from the *Junsen 3* Types, which only operated the E9W1 during World War II.
28. Carpenter and Polmar, *Submarines of the Imperial Japanese Navy*, 3.
29. The Type A submarine could be visually distinguished from the Type B by the twin 25-mm gun atop the Type A's hangar.
30. Ishiguro and Januszewski, *Kugisho E14Y Glen*, 29, 50–51.

CHAPTER 6: WAR IN THE PACIFIC—PART 1

1. The primary source for position data is "Tabular Records of Movement" of Japanese World War II submarines prepared by Robert Hackett and Sander Kingsepp. Those records combine Japanese and U.S. sources to provide the accounts of Japanese submarine actions; see http://www.combinedfleet.com/sensuikan.htm.
2. Orita and Harrington, *I-Boat Captain*, 111.
3. See Carpenter and Polmar, *Submarines of the Imperial Japanese Navy* for the structure of the Japanese submarine force, which was constantly changing due to losses, new construction, and periodic reorganizations.

4. Defense Research Institute, War History Branch, *Senshi Sosho* [*War History Series*], Vol. 98, *Sensuikan-shi* [*History of Submarines*] (Tokyo: Asagumo Shimbunsha, 1979), 94–95.

5. Carpenter and Polmar, *Submarines of the Imperial Japanese Navy*, 17.

6. There were eight battleships in Pearl Harbor at the time of the attack—one was damaged and ran aground, four were sunk, and three were damaged. Also sunk was the *Utah* (AG 16, ex-BB 31), a demilitarized, dreadnought-era battleship converted to a target and training ship.

7. Mark Felton, *The Fujita Plan* (Barnsley, England: Pen & Sword, 2006), 56.

8. The *I-17*'s attack was the second attack on the mainland United States since the Mexican-American War of 1846–1848. The first was the shelling of Orleans, Mass., by the German submarine *U-156* on 21 July 1918.

9. Warrant Flying Officer Nobuo Fujita, Japanese Navy (Ret.), and Chief Journalist Joseph D. Harrington, USN, "I Bombed the U.S.A.," Naval Institute *Proceedings* (June 1961): 64–69.

10. Ibid.

11. Originally the Sydney attack would be carried out by Unit B—the *I-27*, *I-28*, and *I-29*. Unit C—the *I-21*, *I-22*, and *I-24*—would attack merchant shipping off the east coast of Australia and New Zealand. Before either unit reached their destination, they were combined for the Sydney operation as the Eastern Unit.

12. All but 13 of the *I-30*'s crew of 100 men were rescued when she sank.

13. Details of those operations are in Naval History and Heritage Command, "H-Gram 033-1: *Yanagi* Missions and Submarine Atrocities" (July 2019).

14. The previous attacks on Canadian soil were the raids carried out by the U.S.-based Fenian Brotherhood, an Irish republican organization, in 1866 and 1870–1871.

15. Norm Hall and Carol Hall, "At a Crucial Hour: The Attack on Estevan Point," *The Beaver* 84, no. 2 (May 2004): 18–24.

16. The *I-25*'s navigator was using an outdated map from the 1920s showing a submarine base, which had been planned but not constructed at Tongue Point.

17. Fujita and Harrington, "I Bombed the U.S.A.," 64–69.

18. Felton, *Fujita Plan*, 95–99.

CHAPTER 7: WAR IN THE PACIFIC—PART 2

1. Fujita and Harrington, "I Bombed the U.S.A.," 64–69.

2. Felton, *Fujita Plan*, 142–43.

3. William McCash, *Bombs over Brookings: The World War II Bombings of Curry County, Oregon and the Postwar Friendship between Brookings and the Japanese Pilot, Nobuo Fujita* (Bend, Ore.: Maverick Publications, 2005), 26.

4. Fujita and Harrington, "I Bombed the U.S.A.," 64–69.

5. Ishiguro and Januszewski, *Kugisho E14Y Glen*, 91. The *I-21*'s Glen was similarly painted. Many of the Glens in submarine service had their white identification markings painted out.

6. Felton, *Fujita Plan*, 144. It had rained only 0.16 inches in the previous two months, but on 8 September it rained nearly half an inch.

7. Fujita and Harrington, "I Bombed the U.S.A.," 64–69.

8. After the war, Fujita incorrectly claimed that he had flown over Cape Blanco on the first raid and proceeded 50 miles southwest to the site of the bombing. Fujita's account conflicts with Tagami's testimony and with observations of eyewitnesses on the ground that the aircraft flew over Brookings on 9 September (see Ishigiro and Januszewski, *Kugisho E14Y1 Glen*, 74–75; McCash, *Bombs over Brookings*, 11–13).

9. McCash, *Bombs over Brookings*, 11. Several others heard, but did not see, the aircraft.

10. The only other aerial bombing of the contiguous United States in World War II was by balloon-borne bombs, which rode the jet stream from Japan to America. One of the 9,000 balloons released killed a woman and five children in Oregon, about 150 miles west of where Fujita and Okuda had dropped their bombs. The balloons failed to achieve any other success, and their existence was kept secret by the U.S. government, eliminating any possible propaganda value for the Japanese.

11. Fujita and Harrington, "I Bombed the U.S.A.," 64–69.

12. The first bomb site at Wheeler Ridge was probably the one found by the Forest Service.

13. McCash, *Bombs over Brookings*, 16–29.

14. "Japanese Bomb Found in Oregon Is Linked to Unidentified Seaplane," *New York Times*, 15 Sept. 1942, 1, 10.

15. Fujita incorrectly claimed that this flight began around midnight.

16. McCash, *Bombs over Brookings*, 41–42.

17. Fujita and Harrington, "I Bombed the U.S.A.," 64–69.

18. McCash, *Bombs over Brookings*, 43–46. There are reports that pieces of the bomb were recovered, but were not officially confirmed.

19. These bombings are often called variously the Brookings air raids (for the coastal town closest to the site of the first bombing) or the Lookout air raids (for the Forest Service lookouts). Fujita returned to Brookings in 1962 when invited by the community and assured that he would not be tried as a war criminal. He brought his family's sword with him; it was reported that he planned to commit suicide if the people of Brookings were hostile toward him. His reception was mostly positive and respectful, and the sword was given to the city as a gesture of goodwill. Fujita made several subsequent trips to Brookings, and was involved in cultural exchanges between Japan and the city. He died in 1997 at the age of 85.

20. Civil defense and the Army prepared for bombings in the summer of 1943, possibly influenced by Fujita's attack. However, the greatest threat was expected from bombers flying from Kiska in the Aleutians, although a bulletin did caution observers to look out for submarine-launched aircraft. Once the United States recaptured all of the Aleutians, the West Coast air defenses were relaxed (McCash, *Bombs over Brookings*, 52–53).

21. The *I-7* shelled Espiritu Santo in the New Hebrides on 14 and 23 October 1942.

22. Ishiguro and Januszewski, *Kugisho E14Y Glen*, 112.

23. Some of the submarines would carry the Type 4 torpedo-armed landing craft.

24. David Dickson, Bob Hackett, and Sander Kingsepp, "Yu-Go: The Japanese Plan for a Second Pearl Harbor Surprise Attack," www.combinedfleet.com/U-GO.htm.

25. Ishiguro and Januszewski, *Kugisho E14Y Glen*, 36.

26. U.S. Navy, U.S. Naval Technical Mission to Japan, "Ship and Related Targets: Japanese Navy Diesel Engines" (December 1945), 7.

27. U.S. Navy, U.S. Naval Technical Mission to Japan, "Ship and Related Targets: Characteristics of Japanese Naval Vessels: Article 1—Submarines" (January 1946), 7.
28. At the Battle of Midway in early June 1942, the Japanese lost four fleet carriers and one heavy cruiser. The U.S. Navy lost the large carrier *Yorktown* and a destroyer, both sunk by the submarine *I-168*.
29. Japanese submarine designs were given plan numbers (analogous to Soviet Navy project numbers and U.S. Navy Ship Characteristics Board numbers):

Type	Plan No.
Kaidai 1	S22
Junsen 1 Mod.	S23 or S24 (possibly)
Junsen 2	S32
Junsen 3	S33
A	S35A
A Mod. 1	S35B
A Mod. 2	S35C
B	S37A
B Mod. 1	S37B
B Mod. 2	S37C
Sentoku	S50

30. Carpenter and Polmar, *Submarines of the Imperial Japanese Navy*, 29.
31. Ibid., 35.
32. Dickson, Hackett, and Kingsepp, "Yu-Go."
33. At that time Cdr. Takakazu Kinashi was commanding officer of the *I-29*, which had sailed to France on one of the *Yanagi* missions.
34. U.S. Navy, U.S. Naval Technical Mission to Japan, "Ship and Related Targets: Japanese Submarine Operations" (February 1946), 1.

CHAPTER 8: THE ULTIMATE UNDERWATER CARRIERS

1. John J. Geoghegan, *Operation Storm: Japan's Top Secret Submarines and Its Plan to Change the Course of World War II* (New York: Crown, 2013), 27. That quote originates from the memoir of Nobukiyo Nambu, captain of the *I-401*.
2. Prange, Goldstein, and Dillon, *At Dawn We Slept*, 13.
3. Geoghegan, *Operation Storm*, 29.
4. Henry Sakaida, Gary Nila, and Koji Takaki, *I-400: Japan's Secret Aircraft-Carrying Strike Submarine* (Crowborough, England: Hikoki, 2006), 16.
5. R. J. Francillon, *Japanese Aircraft of the Pacific War* (London: Putnam, 1970), 292.
6. Tetsukuni Watanabe, "Aichi M6A1 Rikujo-Ki No Shinso [The Truth about the Aichi M6A1 Land-Based Aircraft]," *Koku Fan* 564 (December 1999): 77. The name *Seiran* references the 17th-Century *Awazu Seiran* woodblock print by Hiroshige, which depicts a mountain fog after a storm. See Thomas S. Momiyama, "All and Nothing," *Air & Space* (October/November 2001): 24.
7. Momiyama, "All and Nothing," 28.
8. Ibid.

9. Aichi Aircraft Company, "M6A1 Seino Keisansho [M6A1 Performance Calculation Book]," 5 October 1943. The floats could not be jettisoned in flight as some sources claim. With the floats, its maximum speed dropped from 286 mph to 254 mph and its range was reduced from 955 miles to 702 miles.

10. Aichi Aircraft Company, "M6A1 Rikujo Ki Keikaku Setsumeisho [M6A1 Land-Based Aircraft Planning Manual]," 21 January 1944. The landing gear was lowered and raised by a hand crank. Many sources incorrectly use the designation M6A1-K *Nanzan* for the land-based trainer. In original documents it was only referred to as the *Seiran* or M6A1 *Rikujo Ki* (Land-Based Aircraft).

11. Watanabe, "Aichi M6A1 Rikujo-Ki No Shinso," 77. One of the 27 was used as a structural test article and never flew. The aircraft on display at the Smithsonian National Air and Space Museum is *Seiran* no. 28.

12. When on the *I-37*, Takahashi was ordered to shoot the survivors of the merchant ship *British Chivalry*. He was not prosecuted for that war crime.

13. Sakaida, Nila, and Takaki, *I-400*, 25.

14. Geoghegan, *Operation Storm*, 167.

15. Momiyama, "All and Nothing," 25. Allied intelligence probably surmised it was an experimental aircraft. As a result, it never received an Allied reporting name.

16. U.S. Navy, Pacific Fleet and Pacific Ocean Areas, "CINCPAC-CINCPOA Bulletin No. 108-45: Japanese Naval Vessels: Special Translation Number 64" (18 May 1945), 8, 66.

17. U.S. Navy, Office of Naval Intelligence, "The Japanese Navy" (June 1945), 85.

18. The *Okha* was designed with the help of the University of Tokyo's Aeronautical Research Institute.

19. Thomas S. Momiyama, "Racing Against Invasion: Engineering a Kamikaze 'Cruise Missile,'" *Air Power History* 56, no. 2 (Summer 2009): 6–8.

20. The first number in the *Okha*'s model number corresponded to the airframe version and the second number corresponded to the engine (1 for rockets, 2 for motorjet, and 3 for turbojet).

21. The only surviving *Ohka* Model 22 is on display at the National Air and Space Museum's Udvar-Hazy Center in Chantilly, Va.

22. Tadeusz Januszewski, *Japanese Submarine Aircraft* (Redbourn: Mushroom Model, 2002), 14.

23. Francillon, *Japanese Aircraft of the Pacific War*, 479. The only surviving Model 43B is an MXY7-K2 two-seat trainer held by the Smithsonian Air and Space Museum in Washington, D.C.

24. Januszewski, *Japanese Submarine Aircraft*, 84.

25. Francillon, *Japanese Aircraft of the Pacific War*, 482.

26. Koji Takaki, *I400 To Seiran Zen Kiroku: Kaitei zoho-ban* [*Complete Record of the I-400 and Seiran: Revised and Expanded Edition*] (Tokyo: Futabasha, 2017), 295–97. A similar configuration was previously used in the Japanese *Kaidai 7* Type attack submarines, but they had only two tubes in the upper torpedo room.

27. The only submarines to have separate, parallel pressure hulls were the Cold War-era Soviet Project 941/*Akula* (NATO Typhoon) SSBN and Dutch *Dolfijn* SS. The design of those submarines was not influenced by the *Sentoku* Type, as is sometimes claimed.

28. Thomas O. Paine, "The Last Voyage of a Submarine Aircraft Carrier," *Submarine Review* (April 2006): 55–56. Paine was the executive officer of the *I-400*'s prize crew and would later head NASA during the Apollo 11 lunar landing.

29. U.S. Navy, U.S. Naval Technical Mission to Japan, "Ship and Related Targets: Japanese Naval Vessels Own Ship's Noise" (January 1946), 10–11. Postwar tests by the U.S. Navy determined that compared to a U.S. fleet submarine the *Sentoku* submarines were noisier and had significantly stronger radar and active sonar returns; see Christopher C. Wright, "The U.S. Navy's Operation of the Former Imperial Japanese Navy Submarines *I-14*, *I-400* and *I-401*: 1945–1946," *Warship International* 37, no. 4 (2000): 375–76.

30. U.S. Navy, U.S. Naval Technical Mission to Japan, "Ship and Related Targets: Japanese Submarine Equipment" (January 1946), 9.

31. Sakaida, Nila, and Takaki, *I-400*, 105.

32. Paine, "Last Voyage of a Submarine Aircraft Carrier," 56; and Geoghegan, *Operation Storm*, 149.

33. Geoghegan, *Operation Storm*, 151–52.

34. Paine, "Last Voyage of a Submarine Aircraft Carrier," 57.

35. U.S. Navy, U.S. Naval Technical Mission to Japan, "Ship and Related Targets: Characteristics of Japanese Naval Vessels: Article 7—Submarines, Supplement II" (January 1946), 60–61

36. Momiyama, "All and Nothing," 28.

37. Sakaida, Nila, and Takaki, *I-400*, 133. The *Sentoku* Type and Type A Mod. 2 had the Type 4 No. 1 Model 10 catapult, which could launch a 11,023-pound aircraft every four minutes.

38. Geoghegan, *Operation Storm*, 72–73.

39. Ibid., 78.

40. The beams of the *South Dakota* (BB 57) and *Iowa* (BB 61) battleship classes were 108 feet, 2 inches, and 108 feet, 3 inches, respectively; the width of the canal locks was 110 feet.

41. Sakaida, Nila, and Takaki, *I-400*, 36. After the war, the U.S. Naval Technical Mission to Japan incorrectly reported that a fourth aircraft could be carried in disassembled form.

42. Geoghegan, *Operation Storm*, 80–81.

43. Designated Type AM in many English-language sources.

44. Carpenter and Polmar, *Submarines of the Imperial Japanese Navy*, 110.

45. Geoghegan, *Operation Storm*, 166.

46. Ibid., 167, 170.

47. Robert Hackett and Sander Kingsepp, "IJN Submarine *I-8*: Tabular Record of Movement," http://www.combinedfleet.com/sensuikan.htm.

48. Geoghegan, *Operation Storm*, 202–7.

49. See, for example, Peter Williams and David Wallace, *Unit 731: Japan's Secret Biological Warfare in World War II* (New York: Free Press, 1989).

50. Dennis Warner, Peggy Warner, and Cdr. Sadao Sendo, JMSDF (Ret.), *The Sacred Warriors: Japan's Suicide Legions* (New York: Van Nostrand Reinhold, 1982), 282–83.

51. Sakaida, Nila, and Takaki, *I-400*, 46. The great-circle route from Japan to Ecuador would take them into the North Pacific, away from the majority of U.S. Navy forces.

52. Sakaida, Nila, and Takaki, *I-400*, 46–49.

53. Gen. Douglas MacArthur, USA, *Reports of General MacArthur*, vol. 1, part 2 (Washington, D.C.: Government Printing Office, 1966), 609.

54. The reconnaissance mission was named Operation *Hikari* (Light).

55. As specified in Article 23 of the 1899 and 1907 Hague Conventions.

56. Momiyama, "All and Nothing," 31.

57. Hackett and Kingsepp, "IJN Submarine *I-14*: Tabular Record of Movement."

58. Ibid.

59. Ibid.

60. Geoghegan, *Operation Storm*, 281, 284–85.

61. Ibid., 283–92.

62. Also being inspected at Pearl Harbor were two *Sentaka* (High Speed Submarine) Type submarines, which had superior underwater performance to the German Type XXI.

63. U.S. Navy, U.S. Naval Technical Mission to Japan, "Ship and Related Targets: Characteristics of Japanese Naval Vessels: Article 7—Submarines, Supplement II," 61.

64. The floatplane is on display at the National Air and Space Museum's Udvar-Hazy Center, Chantilly, Va., and is the only *Seiran* in existence (the land-based *Seiran* was scrapped).

65. Norman Polmar and K. J. Moore, *Cold War Submarines: The Design and Construction of U.S. and Soviet Submarines* (Dulles, Va.: Potomac, 2003), 247–48.

66. The wrecks of all three submarines have been located, all in several thousand feet of water off of Oahu.

CHAPTER 9: UNDERWATER TANKERS—PART 1

1. Polmar and Noot, *Submarines of the Russian and Soviet Navies*, 78, 255.

2. M. E. Morozov and K. L. Kulagin, *Sovetskiy podvodnyy flot 1922–1945 gg: O podvodnykh lodkakh i podvodnikakh* [*The Soviet Submarine Fleet 1922–1945: On Submarines and Submariners*] (Moscow: Tranzitkniga, 2006), 40–41.

3. "Nippon Kaigun Kantei Shashin Shu," 4–5.

4. See Capt. Edwin T. Layton, USN, "Rendezvous in Reverse," Naval Institute *Proceedings* (May 1953): 478–85.

5. Steven Horn, *The Second Attack on Pearl Harbor: Operation K and Other Japanese Attempts to Bomb America in World War II* (Annapolis, Md.: Naval Institute, 2005), 69–70.

6. Elliot Carlson, *Joe Rochefort's War: The Odyssey of the Codebreaker Who Outwitted Yamamoto at Midway* (Annapolis, Md.: Naval Institute, 2011), 176–79.

7. Six days after Operation K, the two Emilies reconnoitered Midway. Hashizume's aircraft was shot down, but Sasao returned with photos of the American base.

8. Lt. Wilford Holmes, USN (Ret.), *Double Edged-Secrets: U.S. Naval Intelligence Operations in the Pacific during World War II* (Annapolis, Md.: Naval Institute, 1979), 60.

9. Alec Hudson [Lt. Wilford Holmes, USN (Ret.)], "Rendezvous," *Saturday Evening Post* 214, no. 5 (2 August 1941), 9–11, 70–72, and Alec Hudson, "Rendezvous," *Saturday Evening Post* 214, no. 6 (9 August 1941), 30, 32, 71–75.

10. Capt. Wilford J. Holmes, USN (Ret.), "Discussion, Comments, and Notes: Rendezvous in Reverse," Naval Institute *Proceedings* (August 1953).

11. Carlson, *Joe Rochefort's War*, 179–81.

12. Ibid., 212.

13. Several sources indicate that the conversion to submarine tanker took place in 1940 and the fuel tanks did not replace the submarines' minelaying equipment. However, none of the three submarines appear to have laid mines after Operation K-2 and some Japanese sources claim the tanks replaced the mine chutes.

14. Carpenter and Polmar, *Submarines of the Imperial Japanese Navy*, 24.

15. The *I-121* and *I-123*, later joined by the *I-122*, continued to patrol the area around the Shoals for several days before departing for Kwajelein.

16. Carl Boyd and Akihiko Yoshida, *The Japanese Submarine Force and World War II* (Annapolis, Md.: Naval Institute Press, 1995), 79.

17. Anthony Tully and Lu Yu, "A Question of Estimates: How Faulty Intelligence Drove Scouting at the Battle of Midway," *Naval War College Review* 68, no. 2 (Spring 2015): 94.

18. Carl Boyd, "American Naval Intelligence of Japanese Submarine Operations Early in the Pacific War," *Journal of Military History* (April 1989): 181.

19. Ibid., 183.

20. For a comprehensive discussion of the Japanese perspective of the Battle of Midway, see Jonathan B. Parshall and Anthony P. Tully, *Shattered Sword: The Untold Story of the Battle of Midway* (Washington, D.C.: Potomac, 2005).

21. Some sources claim, incorrectly, that the aircraft were refueled at the Indispensable *Reefs*, a chain of atolls about 200 nautical miles south of the Indispensable Straight. The Jakes would not have had enough fuel to patrol the Solomons from this remote location.

22. Nakagawa, "History of Japanese Submarines," 78.

23. Hackett and Kingsepp, "IJN Submarine *I-351*: Tabular Record of Movement."

24. Much of this section is based on the logbook for the *U-255*'s 2nd Patrol.

25. German Navy, "Kriegstagebuch '*U255*' fur die Zeit vom 16/7 bis 9 September 1942" [War Diary '*U255*' from 16 July to 9 September 1942]," (1943).

26. That operation was variously referred to as *Wunderland II*, *Südwind* (Southwind), and *Dudelsack* (Bagpipes).

27. Gerhard Koop and Klaus-Peter Schmolke, *Pocket Battleships of the Deutschland Class* (Barnsley, England: Seaforth, 2014), 56.

28. Lawrence Patterson, *Steel and Ice: The U-boat Battle in the Arctic and Black Sea, 1941–45* (Annapolis, Md.: Naval Institute, 2016), 201.

29. Much of this section is based on the logbook for the *U-255*'s 7th Patrol.

30. Jak P. Mallmann Showell, *Swastikas in the Arctic: U-boat Alley through the Frozen Hell* (Stroud: Fronthill, 2014), 186–89.

CHAPTER 10: UNDERWATER TANKERS—PART 2

1. William F. Trimble, *Attack from the Sea: A History of the U.S. Navy's Seaplane Striking Force* (Annapolis, Md.: Naval Institute, 2005), 31.

2. "Aviation Gasoline in Submarines," 7 October 1940, Roll 24, Proceedings and Hearings of the General Board of the U.S. Navy 1900–1950, RG 64, NARA II. As the tank was backfilled with seawater, only about 18,000 gallons could be delivered to minimize the risk of water contamination in the PBYs' fuel tanks. The gasoline storage tank was between frames 28 and 32, replacing main ballast tanks 3D and 3C.

3. Commander Patrol Wing 2 to Commander-in-Chief, U.S. Fleet, "USS *Nautilus*— Plane Refueling Exercises on 9 October 1940," 11 December 1940, Submarine Patrol Reports, San Francisco Maritime National Historic Park, San Francisco, Calif.

4. Submarine Patrol and Attack Force (RED Fleet), "Operation Plan No. 8-38," 18 March 1939, Roll 24, Records Relating to United States Navy Fleet Problems I to XXII, RG 64, NARA II.

5. Roy A. Grossnick, *United States Naval Aviation: 1910–1995* (Washington, D.C.: Naval Historical Center, 1997), 94.

6. Naval History and Heritage Command, "Dictionary of American Fighting Ships: *Nautilus II* (SS-168)," and Adm. Ignatius J. Galantin, USN (Ret.), *Submarine Admiral: From Battlewagons to Ballistic Missiles* (Champaign: University of Illinois, 1997), 50.

7. "Narrative, U.S.S. *Nautilus*," 18 to 23 April 1940, Roll 34, Records Relating to United States Navy Fleet Problems I to XXII, RG 64, NARA I.

8. Commander Scouting Force (Acting) to Commander-in-Chief, U.S. Fleet, "Plane Refueling Exercise 9, October 9, 1940," 21 December 1940, Submarine Patrol Reports, San Francisco Maritime National Historic Park, San Francisco, Calif.

9. Chairman General Board to Secretary of the Navy, "Facilities for Carrying Aviation Gasoline in Submarines under Contract," 9 October 1940, Box 113, GB 420-15, General Board Subject Files, RG 80, NARA I; and Norman Friedman, *U.S. Submarines since 1945: An Illustrated Design History*, 2nd ed. (Annapolis, Md.: Naval Institute, 2018), 280.

10. Roscoe Creed, *PBY: The Catalina Flying Boat* (Annapolis, Md.: Naval Institute, 1985), 65; and Commander Task Force Nine (Commander Patrol Wing Two) to Commander-in-Chief, U.S. Pacific Fleet, "Operations on December 7, 1941," 20 December 1941.

11. The *Argonaut* received the designation APS 1 after the conversion.

12. George Poulos, "At War Part II: Recollections of a VP Pilot," *Naval Aviation News* (September 1982): 35–36.

13. Commanding Officer USS Amberjack to Commander Task Force 42, "War Patrol Report," 31 October 1942, Submarine Patrol Reports, San Francisco Maritime National Historic Park, San Francisco, Calif.

14. Friedman, *U.S. Submarines since 1945*, 280.

15. Ernest G. Stout, "Development of High-Speed Water-Based Aircraft," *Journal of the Aeronautical Sciences* 17, no. 8 (August 1950): 457–59.

16. Glenn L. Martin Company, "A Plan for Seaplane Handling for the United States Navy," July 1953, Box 1, Entry P21 (Item S-11), RG 19, NARA II.

17. See Steve Ginter, *Convair XP5Y-1 & R3Y-1/2 Tradewind* (Simi Valley, Calif.: Steve Ginter, 1992).

18. Stout, "Development of High-Speed Water-Based Aircraft," 479.

19. Matthew Willis, "From Skate to Sea Dart: Convair & the USA's Seaplane Striking Force, Part 1, 1946–52," *Aviation Historian* 25 (October 2018): 100–109.

20. Capt. Lloyd Harrison to Chief, BuAer, "Model VF Seaplane Night Fighter—Recommendations on Design Competition," 5 April 1949, Box 167, Aircraft Collection, NHHC Archives, Washington, D.C.

21. Cdr. D. O. Ness, "Air Board Presentation," 7 July 1952, Box 292, Aircraft Collection, NHHC Archives, Washington, D.C.

22. Robert E. Bradley, *Convair Advanced Designs: Secret Projects from San Diego, 1923–1962* (North Branch, Minn.: Specialty, 2010), 71–77.

23. Internally the Sea Dart was designated Y2-2 (the Skate was Y2-1). Although the project was canceled before the tri-service aircraft designation change, the Sea Dart retroactively had its designation changed to YF-7A in 1962 [see Norman Polmar, "A Dart from the Sea," *Naval History* (December 2012): 12–13].

24. See B. J. Long, *Convair XF2Y-1 and YF2Y-1 Sea Dart* (Simi Valley, Calif.: Steve Ginter, 1992).

25. Of those five Sea Darts, only three flew. The other two were fully complete, but never received their engines.

26. Matthew Willis, "Son of Sea Dart: Convair & the USA's Seaplane Striking Force, Part 2, 'The Tactical F2Y,'" *Aviation Historian* 26 (January 2019): 79–84. Alternative improved Sea Dart designs for the interceptor role (e.g., with single engines and internally carried Sidewinder air-to-air missiles) were also studied.

27. Capt. Richard Hoffman, USN (Ret.), *The Martin P5M Patrol Seaplane* (Simi Valley, Calif.: Steve Ginter, 2007), 2.

28. Francis J. Allen, "Poseidon's Giant: The Story of the Martin P6M Seamaster," *Air Enthusiast* (March/April 2001): 18.

29. Bureau of Aeronautics, "Standard Aircraft Characteristics: YP6M-1 'Seamaster,' Martin" (U.S. Navy, 15 April 1957).

30. Bureau of Ships, "Circular of Requirements for Conversion of a Fleet Type Submarine to Submarine Oiler SSO: Part 1—Hull," 15 September 1948, Box 39, Entry UD 1027-A, Item S-18, RG 19, NARA II. Her initial conversion was under Ship Characteristics Board Project 39. Her beam was increased from 27¼ feet to 38 feet.

31. Lt. D. P. Dakos, USNR, "Seagoing Service Stations," *Naval Institute Proceedings* (October 1957): 1098–1105.

32. Hoffman, *The Martin P5M Patrol Seaplane*, 66–73.

33. Allen, "Poseidon's Giant," 27.

34. Chief, BuShips to Chief, BuAer, "Applicability of Naval Vessels for Water Based Seaplane Support," 7 October 1955, Box 1, Entry P21 (Item S-11), RG 19, NARA II.

35. Friedman, *U.S. Submarines since 1945*, 89.

36. BuShips Preliminary Design Branch, "Exploratory Studies for Nuclear Seaplane Support," 10 October 1956, Box 1, Entry P21 (Item S-11), RG 19, NARA II.

37. G. A. Cheremukhin, *Dal'she. Vyshe. Bystreye: vospominaniya o rabote v aviapromyshlennosti, o tekhnike i yeye sozdatelyakh* [*Further. Higher. Faster: Memories of Working in the Aviation Industry, On Technology and its Creators*], ed. N. G. Georgiyevoy (Moscow: Prospekt, 2011), 55–58.

38. N. V. Yakubovich, *Samolety R. L.Bartini* [*Aircraft of R. L. Bartini*] (Moscow: Rusavia, 2006), 76–78.

39. G. S. Panatov, A. N. Zablotskiy, and A. I. Sal'nikov, *Samolety TANTK im. G. M. Berieva: 1945–1968* [*Aircraft of the G. M. Beriev Taganrog Aviation Scientific Technical Complex: 1945–1968*] (Moscow: Restart+, 2001), 140.

40. The Tupolev design bureau and the Central Aerohydrodynamic Institute (TsAIG) were also tasked with developing designs.

41. Panatov, Zablotskiy, and Sal'nikov, *Samolety TANTK im. G. M. Berieva: 1945–1968*, 141–43. SD-MBR = *Sverkhzvukovoy Dal'niy Morskoy Bombardirovshchik-Razvedchik* (Supersonic Long-Range Maritime Reconnaissance Bomber).

42. A. A. Bruk, K. G. Udalov, S. G. Smirnov, A. V. Arkhipov, and B. L. Puntus, *Illyustrirovannaya Entsiklopediya Samoletov OKB B. M. Myasishcheva* [*Illustrated Encyclopedia of the Aircraft of OBK V. M. Myasishchev*], vol. 2, part 3, ed. V. K. Novikov (Moscow: Aviko Press, 2001), 215–19.

43. Ibid., 221.

44. Panatov, Zablotskiy, and Sal'nikov, *Samolety TANTK im. G. M. Berieva: 1945–1968*, 141; and Konstantin Udalov, "Sverkhzvukovy, dal'niy, okeanskiy: O proyekte

unikal'nogo gidrosamoleta [Supersonic, Long-Range, Oceanic: On a Unique Seaplane Project]," *Kryl'ya Rodiny* 11 (2000): 7–8.

45. Yakubovich, *Samolety R. L.Bartini*, 83–88. Bartini's A-58 design was a revised version of the A-57.

46. *Istoriya otechyestvyennogo sudostroyeniya* [*History of Domestic Shipbuilding*], ed. I. D. Spasskiy, vol. 5 (St. Petersburg: Sudostroyeniya, 1996), 89. Project 613B was designed by the SKB-112 bureau (later named Lazurit).

47. TsKB-16 was renamed "Volna" in 1966; the bureau was merged with SKB-143/Malachite in 1974.

48. Forty 21-inch and 20 16-inch torpedoes could be carried by the submarine.

49. Polmar and Moore, *Cold War Submarines*, 229, 231.

50. Panatov, Zablotskiy, and Sal'nikov, *Samolety TANTK im. G. M. Berieva: 1945–1968*, 148–49, 153.

51. Polmar and Moore, *Cold War Submarines*, 231, 233.

CHAPTER 11: COLD WAR CONCEPTS

1. Polmar and Moore, *Cold War Submarines*, 228–29. TsKB-18—later named Rubin—designed most of the Soviet Union's ballistic and guided missile submarines, as well as most diesel-electric submarines. Rubin continues to design submarines for the Russian Navy.

2. Polmar and Moore, *Cold War Submarines*, 249–50.

3. Central Intelligence Agency, "Information Report: New Soviet Long-Range Aircraft Carrying Submarines," 3 September 1954, CIA-FOIA.

4. Polmar and Moore, *Cold War Submarines*, 94.

5. Panatov, Zablotskiy, and Sal'nikov, *Samolety TANTK im. G. M. Berieva: 1945–1968*, 10, 13.

6. Boris Gubarev, "Sverkhlegkiy Ka-56 [Ultralight Ka-56]," *Vertolet* 4 (1999): 16–17. Gubarev was the deputy chief designer of the Ka-56.

7. Central Intelligence Agency, "Balloon Overflights—Stereo Camera Operations," 12 November 1954, CIA-FOIA.

8. Central Intelligence Agency, "Joint USN/CIA Balloon Launching Tests from Submarine," 3 January 1955, CIA-FOIA. One of the Navy's liaisons for the project was Lt. Cdr. Malcolm Ross, USN, Balloon Projects Officer at ONR. Ross later set several altitude records for manned balloons, demonstrated the feasibility of an airborne astronomical observatory, and tested the Mk IV pressure suit, which would be used by NASA for Project Mercury.

9. Central Intelligence Agency, "Balloon Overflights—Stereo Camera Operations," 27 January 1955, CIA-FOIA.

10. Richard Douglass, telephone discussion with Jacob Gunnarson, 19 September 2018.

11. Richard Douglass, "Before the U-2 Spy Plane: The Covert Operations Manned Balloon Gets to Work, Part 2," *Ballooning* 51, no. 4 (July/August 2018): 36–39.

12. There were suggestions of storing the helium inside the air flasks of ten torpedoes, or using the submarine's forward bank of high-pressure air flasks. Of the former, "it [would be] improbable that the Bureau of Ordinance would allow it," and the latter would interfere with the submarine's supply of high-pressure air.

13. Central Intelligence Agency, "Joint USN/CIA Balloon Launching Tests from Submarine." The Key West Tests were Navy Project FL/A106/ZZ; the CIA project name remains classified. The *Albatross* was built as the YMS 80, completed in 1942. From 1944 she was involved in target retrieval and in experimental work, being designated E-YMS 80. Subsequently, in 1947 she was named *Albatross* and redesignated AMS 1; that was changed to E-AMS 1 that same year and to E-MSC(O) in 1955, the "O" indicating "old." She was decommissioned and stricken in 1958.

14. Central Intelligence Agency, "Balloon Overflights—Stereo Camera Operations," 12 November 1954, CIA-FOIA.

15. Richard Douglass, "Submarine Operations: The Covert Operations Manned Balloon Gets to Work, Part 3," *Ballooning* 51, no. 5 (September/October 2018): 36–39; Richard Douglass, telephone discussion with Jacob Gunnarson, 19 September 2018.

16. Central Intelligence Agency, "Project [redacted]," 1 July 1955, CIA-FOIA.

17. Central Intelligence Agency, "Project [redacted]—Balloon Overflight," 26 August 1955, CIA-FOIA.

18. Gregory W. Pedlow and Donald E. Welzenbach, *The Central Intelligence Agency and Overhead Reconnaissance: The U-2 and OXCART Programs, 1954–1974* (Washington, D.C.: CIA, 1992), 85. One of the Genetrix balloons was viewed by one of the authors of this book in the KGB/FSB museum in Moscow.

19. Central Intelligence Agency, "Concurrence in Letter Contract No. SS-100 with Convair, San Diego, California, Project CHAMPION," 9 June 1958, CIA-FOIA.

20. See Convair Division, General Dynamics Corp., "Project Hazel: Aircraft Design (ZP-253)," October 1958, CIA-FOIA, and "Project Hazel: Aerodynamics (ZA-282)," October 1958, CIA-FOIA.

21. The Marquardt ramjet was constructed from fiberglass with a metal honeycomb inner layer; the Pratt & Whitney engine was all-metal.

22. Clarence L. Johnson, "Development of the SR-71 Blackbird," 29 July 1981, CIA-FOIA.

23. Paul A. Suhler, *From RAINBOW to GUSTO: Stealth and the Design of the Lockheed Blackbird* (Reston, Va.: American Institute of Aeronautics and Astronautics, 2009), 103–6.

24. Ibid., 113.

25. See Polomede Ferrari and Enrico Miglioli, Combined Hydroaeroplane and Submergible Craft, Patent No. 1,288,860, filed 7 March 1918; Joseph Ardo, Submersible Flying Boat, Patent No. 1,421,369, filed 28 October 1921; Guido Brogelli, Aeroplane with Detachable Body, Patent No. 1,797,713, filed 28 May 1929; Earl Briggs and Herbert C. Redding, Wing Folding Arrangement for Submersible Aircraft, Patent No. 2,444,332, filed 7 December 1944; and Houston Harrington, Design for a Combination Airplane and Submarine, Patent Design No. 143,313, filed 17 April 1945.

26. Gennadiy Petrov, "Letayushchaya . . . podvodnaya lodka [Flying . . . Submarine]," *Vestnik vozdushnogo flota* 3 (1995): 52–53.

27. Lesnichenko and Gusev, *Samolet i podvodnaya lodka*, 173–76.

28. Ibid., 184–85. Kovalev was quoted in the 11 January 1997 issue of *Sankt-Peterburgskie Vedomosti*.

29. Ibid., 186–87.

30. Donald V. Reid, Flying Submarine, Patent No. 3,092,060, filed 17 January 1958, issued 4 June 1963.

31. Ansel E. Talbert, "Designers Study Flying Submarine," *New York Herald Tribune*, 28 October 1955.

32. The Soviets never planned to conduct a third battle of the Atlantic, instead relying on their large submarine force to protect Soviet home waters and Soviet ballistic missile submarines, and to seek out Western ballistic missile submarines. NATO intelligence only became aware of the Soviets' true intentions in the early 1980s through espionage activities.

33. Convair, General Dynamics Corp., "Proposed Study of a Flying-Submersible ASW Vehicle, HP-62-016)" (December 1962).

34. Convair, General Dynamics Corp., "Flying Submersible Vehicle: Technical Proposal (GDC-64-104)" (April 1964). Additionally, the craft would have to be able to take off in one to three-foot waves and be able to hover while submerged.

35. Eugene Handler, letter to Norman Polmar, 8 August 1979. Handler, an engineer with the Airframe Design Division of BuWeps at the time, was involved with the hydrodynamics of the Sub-Plane.

36. Convair, "Proposed Study of a Flying-Submersible ASW Vehicle, HP-62-016"; and Robert E. Bradley, *Convair Advanced Designs: Secret Projects from San Diego, 1923–1962* (North Branch, Minn.: Specialty, 2010), 115–18.

37. Eugene Handler, untitled document. Each additional foot of depth would require an additional pound of structure.

38. Polmar and Moore, *Cold War Submarines*, 260. The turbojets would be Rolls Royce RB.162-1s and the turbofan would be a General Electric CF700-2B.

39. The electric propulsion system would be similar to that used in the *Aluminaut*, a research submersible with an aluminum hull.

40. Eugene Handler, "The Flying Submarine," Naval Institute *Proceedings* (September 1964): 144–45.

41. Senate Armed Services Committee, Military Authorizations and Defense Appropriations for Fiscal Year 1966, 89th Congress, 1st Session (Washington, D.C.: 1965), 439, 1220, 1222.

42. Electric Boat Division, General Dynamics Corp., "Interim Report: Preliminary Design of a Small, High-Density, Hydro-Ski Equipped Seaplane," U419-66-103 (September 1966); Electric Boat Division, General Dynamics Corp., "Towing Basin Tests with a One-Eleventh Scale Model of a High-Density Seaplane Configuration," U419-67-011 (September 1967); and Electric Boat Division, General Dynamics Corp., "Proposed Mission Analysis Study for a Small High Density Seaplane," SD-207-1 (April 1969).

43. By that time BuWeps had been succeeded by the Naval Air Systems Command (NavAir).

44. This section is based on Scott Lowther, "Convair Submersible Nuclear Ramjet," *U.S. Bomber Projects* 21 (2018): 5–6.

45. Roger P. Johnson, Henry P. Rumble, and Albert J. Tenzer, "Submersible Aircraft: Potential Missions, Selected Systems Operations, and Costs RM-4183-PR," RAND Corp. (November 1964).

46. Defense Advanced Research Projects Agency, Strategic Technology Office, "Broad Agency Announcement: Submersible Aircraft" (DARPA-BAA-09-06), (3 October 2008).

47. Rick Goddard and Jonathon Eastgate, "Submersible Aircraft Concept Study" (Bethseda, Md.: NSWC Carderock Division, August 2010).

CHAPTER 12: THE ATOMIC AGE

1. U.S. Navy, U.S. Naval Technical Mission to Japan, "Ship and Related Targets: Japanese Submarine Operations," 24–25.
2. The SSP designation was subsequently changed to ASSP, APSS, and finally LPSS.
3. "Shipbuilding Program, Fiscal Years 1951–1960," 8 November 1948, Roll 27, Proceedings and Hearings of the General Board of the U.S. Navy 1900–1950, RG 64, NARA II.
4. Norman Polmar, *The American Submarine*, 2nd ed. (Annapolis, Md.: Nautical and Aviation, 1983), 89. HTL was the Navy designation of Army's H-13 Sioux, which was based on the Bell Model 47.
5. Polmar and Moore, *Cold War Submarines*, 237.
6. The *Perch* and *Sealion* were the last U.S. Navy submarines to have deck guns. The *Perch* used her 40-mm cannon and .50-caliber machine guns to provide covering fire for special operations during the Vietnam conflict, probably the last submarine to use deck guns in combat.
7. An earlier, smaller exercise with helicopters took place on 4 May off the Little Creek amphibious base in Virginia Beach, Va. The Marine exercise (Phase 1 of Reconnaissance Exercise 3-56) took place in July. The HRS helicopter was designated the H-19 Chickasaw in Army service.
8. Capt. Don Walsh, USN (Ret.), discussion with Jacob Gunnarson, Springfield, Va., 22 January 2020.
9. Norman Polmar and Capt. John O'Connell, USN (Ret.), *Strike from the Sea: The Sea-Launched Cruise Missile* (Annapolis, Md.: Naval Institute, 2020), 51. JATO = Jet-Assisted Takeoff.
10. David K. Stumpf, *Regulus: America's First Nuclear Submarine Missile* (Paducah, Ky.: Turner, 1996), 14.
11. Excerpt from "General Information U.S. Submarine Torpedo Boat S-1 [September 1924]," Box 62, Entry P62 (Item S-13), RG 19, NARA II.
12. Redesignated RUM-6 after 1962.
13. Friedman, *U.S. Submarines since 1945*, 178. The hangar was in the path of the missile's jet blast, and a saltwater spray system was devised to keep it cool. However, the salty mist found its way into the missile's intake, damaging its engine. The cooling system was quickly replaced by a blast deflector aft of the ramp.
14. Bureau of Naval Weapons, *Handbook: Service and Launching Instructions Navy Model SS-N-8 Guided Missile (Regulus)* (U.S. Navy, 1961), 64–83.
15. Polmar and O'Connell, *Strike from the Sea*, 36.
16. The submarines were outwardly similar, but not identical. Mare Island's *Grayback* was originally an improved *Tang*-class (SCB 2A), whereas Portsmouth's *Growler* was based on a modified *Darter* design (SCB 124).
17. To expedite her construction, the *Halibut* was nearly identical from the reactor compartment aft to the *Skate*-class attack submarine *Sargo* (SSN 583), the first nuclear submarine built at Mare Island.
18. See Sherry Sontag, Christopher Drew, and Annette Lawrence Drew, *Blind Man's Bluff: The Untold Story of American Submarine Espionage* (New York: PublicAffairs, 1998).
19. See Norman Polmar and Michael White, *Project Azorian: The CIA and the Raising of the K-129* (Annapolis, Md.: Naval Institute, 2010).

20. "Sub. Aircraft Carrier," ca. Dec. 1952, Box 1, Entry P37 (Item S-11), RG 19, NARA II.

21. Heinemann would go on to design the A3D Skywarrior bomber, F3D Skynight and F4D Skyray fighters, the Skystreak and Skyrocket experimental aircraft, and the Mk 80 series of low-drag bombs.

22. Cdr. D. O. Ness, USN, "Air Board Presentation," 7 July 1952, Box 292, Aircraft Collection, NHHC.

23. Ed Heinemann, foreword to *Submarines with Wings*, by Terry C. Treadwell (London: Conway, 1985), ix–x. The Skyhawk resembled an enlarged Model 640, but with a revised fuselage and delta wings.

24. BuShips Code 420 [Preliminary Design Section] to BuShips Code 400 [Assistant Chief for Ships], "Status of Submarine Design Work," 9 December 1946, Box 1, Entry P37 (Item S-11), RG 19, NARA II.

25. Friedman, *U.S. Submarines since 1945*, 292–93. The A2J (originally designated ARD-45A by North American) was an improved, turboprop-powered version of the piston-engine AJ. Only one prototype XAJ2 prototype was built before the project was cancelled.

26. Norman Polmar and Robert S. Norris, *The U.S. Nuclear Arsenal: A History of Weapons and Delivery Systems since 1945* (Annapolis, Md.: Naval Institute Press, 2009), 81–83, 145–46. By 1952, the Banshees could carry the 1,700-lb. B7 and 3,200-lb. B8 bombs.

27. BuShips Code 400 [Assistant Chief for Ships] to BuShips Code 100 [Chief, BuShips], "Aircraft-Carrying Submarine," 27 May 1952, Box 1, Entry P37 (Item S-11), RG 19, NARA II.

28. The power plant was probably intended to be two Submarine Advanced Reactors (later designated S4G). The *Triton*'s twin S4G plant produced only 34,000 shaft horsepower; she was the only U.S. two-reactor submarine.

29. A sponson in the outer hull would enable the outboard-opening door to clear the elevator when open and also serve to longitudinally strengthen the submarine in way of the elevator well. Hangar No. 1 would be 57 ft. long; hangars No. 2 and No. 3 would be 62 ft. long.

30. Electric Boat Division, General Dynamics Corp., "Feasibility Report: Reactor Located in Bow" (20 May 1953), Box 1, Entry P37 (Item S-11), RG 19, NARA II.

31. BuShips Code 400 [Assistant Chief for Ships] to BuShips Code 101 [Deputy and Assistant Chief], "Design studies for third nuclear submarine," 5 May 1953, Box 1, Entry P37 (Item S-11), RG 19, NARA II.

32. Friedman, *U.S. Submarines since 1945*, 183, 192. The aircraft specifications were a weight of 30,000 lb., maximum speed of 500 kn, and a 1,000-mile combat radius. BuShips only considered the project worthwhile if the aircraft could carry megaton nuclear weapons.

33. Norman Friedman, *Fighters over the Fleet: Naval Air Defence from Biplanes to the Cold War* (Barnsley, England: Seaforth, 2016), 215.

34. See Norman Polmar, "The Tail Sitters, Part 1—Lockheed," *Naval History* (June 2013), and Norman Polmar, "The Tail Sitters, Part 2—Convair," *Naval History* (August 2013).

35. Friedman, *U.S. Submarine since 1945*, 183.

36. Boeing Airplane Company, "Flying Carpet Feasibility Study: Submarine Carrier (D3-1870-8)," 18 December 1958.

37. Boeing documents specify the engine as a Wright SE-105 with 23,000 lb. of thrust.

38. Polmar and Moore, *Cold War Submarines*, 251.

39. Defence Research Policy Committee, "Dipper," ca. February 1963, DEFE 10/454, TNA. The aircraft were to be 40 ft. long, with a 25-ft. wingspan and weight of 25,000 lb.

40. Electric Boat Division, General Dynamics Corp., "Submersible Aircraft Carrier for Naval Strike Operations: A Preliminary Outlook (C417-63-047)," 3 November 1963.

41. Small—44 ft. long, 20,000 lb.; Medium—56 ft. long, 30,000 lb.; Large—70 ft. long, 35,000 lb.

42. See C. C. Abt, "The Submarine-Aircraft Carrier," Naval Institute *Proceedings* (October 1963), and Donald Kelley, "The Submarine Aircraft Carrier," *Our Navy* (February 1969).

CHAPTER 13: SAILING INTO THE FUTURE

1. Vincent Vigiotti, "Demonstration of Submarine Control of an Unmanned Aerial Vehicle," *Johns Hopkins APL Technical Digest* 19, no. 4 (1998): 501–12.

2. Jay Gundlach and Richard J. Foch, *Unmanned Aircraft Systems Innovation at the Naval Research Laboratory* (Reston, Va.: American Institute of Aeronautics and Astronautics, 2014), 57–59.

3. Steve Weinstein, Tom Sachse, and William McGannon, "Submarine Unmanned Vehicle System . . . Past, Present, and Future Efforts," paper presented at AIAA's 1st Technical Conference and Workshop on Unmanned Aerospace Vehicles, Portsmouth, Va., 20–23 May 2002.

4. Robert A. Ruszkowski, "MPUAV: Advanced Development Programs Team Makes Splash with Successful Underwater Recovery of a Unique Aircraft," *LM Aeronautics Star* 8, no. 1 (2007): 4–5.

5. The Cormorant was also referred to as the Multi-Purpose UAV (MPUAV).

6. Robert A. Ruszkowski (Lockheed Martin Corp.), Immersible Unmanned Air Vehicle and System for Launch, Recovery, and Re-Launch at Sea, Patent No. 7,097,136, filed 13 April 2004, issued 29 August 2006.

7. Petty Officer 1st Class Jennifer Spinner, USN, "USS *Albany* Launches Experimental UAV," *Undersea Warfare* 7, no. 5 (Fall 2005): 4–5.

8. Petty Officer 1st Class Michael Howlett, USN, "Joint Spec Ops: Air Force, Navy Test Rescue Scenario," *Undersea Warfare* (Spring 2006): 5–7.

9. Petty Officer 2nd Class Christina Shaw, USN, "Submarine Force Tests UAV Technology to Enhance Force Protection," *Undersea Warfare* 7 (Summer 2005): 6–7.

10. U.S. Navy, "Exhibit R-2, RDT&E Budget Item Justification: PB 2012 Navy," February 2011.

11. Thomas D. Futch, "An Analysis of the Manpower Impact of Unmanned Aerial Vehicles on Subsurface Platforms" (M.S. thesis, Naval Postgraduate School, 2012), 18.

12. Geoff Fein, "Navy, Raytheon Effort Deploys Sub Launched UAV Out with the Trash," *Defense Daily*, 5 November 2008; and Graham Warwick, "Raytheon to Launch UAV from Submarine," *Aviation Week*, 30 October 2008. The launch system and modified Switchblade were developed under the SOTHOC (Submarine Over the Horizon Organic Capabilities) program.

13. Robert Pursell, "Trident Warrior 2010 Leads the Way in Maritime Experimentation," *CHIPS Magazine* 28, no. 3 (July–September 2010): 51–52.

14. U.S. Navy, "Exhibit R-2, RDT&E Budget Item Justification: PB 2015 Navy" (March 2014).

15. The Blackwing was developed under the AWESUM (Advanced Weapons Enhanced by Submarine Unmanned aerial vehicles against Mobile targets) program.

16. The Blackwing may be able to fit a warhead to serve as a self-defense weapon against anti-submarine helicopters and small surface vessels that cannot be engaged with torpedoes; see Capt. Chad Muse, USN, Presentation at 19th NDIA Expeditionary Operations Conference (19 November 2014), Norfolk, Va.

17. Department of Defense Inspector General, "Audit of Department of Defense Middle Tier of Acquisition Rapid Prototyping and Rapid Fielding Programs," 28 September 2021, 11–12.

18. Vice Adm. Joseph Tofalo, USN, "Commander's Intent for the United States Submarine Force and Supporting Organizations," *Submarine Review* (June 2016): 80.

19. Richard R. Burgess, "Admiral: Submarine-Launched UAS Proving 'Awesome Capability,'" *Sea Power* (18 November 2020).

20. "Surveillance Vehicles Soar on Fuel Cell Power," *Naval Research Laboratory Spectra* (Fall 2010): 3.

21. Gundlach and Foch, *Unmanned Aircraft Systems*, 385–87.

22. Vice Adm. Joseph Tofalo, USN, "34th Annual Symposium," *Submarine Review* (March 2017): 17.

23. The Sea Robin, designed and built by Oceaneering International, is 18 inches in diameter and 8 feet long.

24. Daniel Parry, "Navy Launches UAV from Submerged Submarine," *Naval Research Laboratory Spectra* (Winter 2014): 30.

25. Tofalo, "Commander's Intent," 80.

26. VOLANS = Verdeckte Optische Luft-Aufklärung Navalisiertes System (Covert Optical Navalized Air-Reconnaissance System).

27. Jean-Marc Tanguy, "Innovation: un drone aérien lancé depuis un sous-marin en plongée [Innovation: An Aerial Drone Launched from a Submerged Submarine]" *Le Marin* (1 June 2023).

28. Seth J. Frantzman, "Spear unveils submarine-launched Ninox 103 drone," *Defense News* (10 June 2022).

29. Rubin Central Design Bureau, "The Sentry Submersible Patrol Ship Developed for Foreign Customers," press release, 12 April 2021.

30. Rubin Central Design Bureau, "The BOSS: New Look, New Features," press release, 9 February 2022.

BIBLIOGRAPHY

ARCHIVAL SOURCES

CIA-FOIA Central Intelligence Agency, Freedom of Information Act Electronic Reading Room, https://www.cia.gov/library/readingroom/home.

EBNAL Emil Buehler Naval Aviation Library, National Naval Aviation Museum, Pensacola, Fla.
Aircraft History Cards, 1911–1949.

NASM Smithsonian National Air and Space Museum, Chantilly, Va.
Technical Reference Files: Aircraft.

NARA I National Archives and Records Administration, Washington, D.C.
U.S. Navy. Bureau of Navigation. Entry 118: Logbooks of U.S. Navy Ships, ca. 1801–1940, Record Group 24.
U.S. Navy. Department of the Navy. Entry 281: General Board Subject Files, 1900–1947, Record Group 80.
U.S. Navy. Department of the Navy. Entry UD 5: Secret and Confidential Correspondence, 1919–1927, Record Group 80.

NARA II National Archives and Records Administration, College Park, Md.
General Services Administration. National Archives and Records Service. Records Relating to United States Navy Fleet Problems I to XXII, Record Group 64.
National Archives and Records Administration. Proceedings and Hearings of the General Board of the U.S. Navy 1900–1950, Record Group 64.
U.S. Navy. Bureau of Ships. Entry P13: Submarine General Information Books and Related Documentation, 1913–1961 (Item S-68), Record Group 19.
U.S. Navy. Bureau of Ships. Entry P21: Records Relating to the Design of a Nuclear-Powered Seaplane Tender, Ship Preliminary Design History and Data Files (Item S-11), Record Group 19.
U.S. Navy. Bureau of Ships. Entry P37: Records Related to Preliminary Design Books, 1904–1957, Ship Preliminary Design History and Data Files (Item S-11), Record Group 19.
U.S. Navy. Bureau of Ships. Entry P62: Records Relating to Ship Hull Design History, 1940–1966 (Item S-13), Record Group 19.
U.S. Navy. Bureau of Ships. Entry UD 1027-A: Specifications for Ships and Ship Machinery (Item S-18), Record Group 19.

NHHC   Naval History and Heritage Command Archives, Washington, D.C.
         Aircraft Collection.
         Naval Air Systems Command Collection.
         Subject File Collection.
TNA   The National Archives, Kew, England
         Admiralty of the Royal Navy. ADM 116/3484: Submarines carrying
            aircraft.
         Admiralty of the Royal Navy. ADM 1/8724/90: Conversion of an "M"
            class submarine for aircraft carrying; and the design of a suitable
            seaplane.
         Ministry of Defence. DEFE 10/454: Defence Research Policy Commit-
            tee Papers, 1963.

DOCUMENTS IN ENGLISH

Admiralty of the Royal Navy. Naval Intelligence Division. "History of U-boat Policy: 1939–1945 (CB 4501)." February 1946.

Boeing Airplane Company. "Flying Carpet Feasibility Study: Submarine Carrier (D3-1870-8)." 18 December 1958.

Consolidated Vultee Aircraft Corp. "Class VF Seaplane Night Fighter: Standard Aircraft Characteristics." January 1949.

Convair Division, General Dynamics Corp. "Flying Submersible Vehicle: Technical Proposal (GDC-64-104)." April 1964.

———. "Project Hazel: Aerodynamics (ZA-282)." October 1958.

———. "Project Hazel: Aircraft Design (ZP-253)." October 1958.

———. "Proposed Study of a Flying-Submersible ASW Vehicle (HP-62-016)." December 1962.

Defense Advanced Research Projects Agency. Strategic Technology Office. "Broad Agency Announcement: Submersible Aircraft (DARPA-BAA-09-06)." 3 October 2008.

Electric Boat Division, General Dynamics Corp. "Interim Report: Preliminary Design of a Small, High-Density, Hydro-Ski Equipped Seaplane (U419-66-103)." September 1966.

———. "Proposed Mission Analysis Study for a Small High Density Seaplane (SD-207-1)." April 1969.

———. "Submersible Aircraft Carrier for Naval Strike Operations: A Preliminary Outlook (C417-63-047)." 3 November 1963.

———. "Towing Basin Tests with a One-Eleventh Scale Model of a High-Density Seaplane Configuration (U419-67-011)." September 1967.

Futch, Thomas D. "An Analysis of the Manpower Impact of Unmanned Aerial Vehicles on Subsurface Platforms." M.S. thesis, Naval Postgraduate School, 2012.

Goddard, Rick, and Jonathon Eastgate. "Submersible Aircraft Concept Study." Bethseda, Md.: NSWC Carderock Division, August 2010.

Johnson, Roger P., Henry P. Rumble, and Albert J. Tenzer. "Submersible Aircraft: Potential Missions, Selected Systems Operations, and Costs (RM-4183-PR)." RAND Corp., November 1964.

Pedlow, Gregory W., and Donald E. Welzenbach. *The Central Intelligence Agency and Overhead Reconnaissance: The U-2 and OXCART Programs, 1954–1974*. Washington, D.C.: Central Intelligence Agency, History Staff, 1992.

U.S. Congress. House. Committee on Naval Affairs. *Sundry Legislation Affecting the Naval Establishment 1921*. 77th Cong., 1st sess., 4 March to 9 November 1921.

U.S. Congress. Senate. Committee on Appropriations. *Department of Defense Appropriations, 1966: Hearings before the Subcommittee on the Department of Defense*. 89th Cong., 1st sess., 24 February to 15 March 1965.

U.S. Navy. Bureau of Aeronautics. "Standard Aircraft Characteristics: YP6M-1 'Seamaster,' Martin." 15 April 1957.

U.S. Navy. Bureau of Naval Weapons. *Handbook: Service and Launching Instructions Navy Model SS-N-8 Guided Missile (Regulus)*. 1961.

U.S. Navy. General Board. "Shipbuilding Program, Fiscal Years 1951–1960." 8 November 1948.

U.S. Navy. Office of the Chief of Naval Operations. "Report on the Interrogation of Survivors from *U-177* Sunk 6 February 1944." 22 May 1944.

———. "Report on the Interrogation of Survivors from *U-199* Sunk on 31 July 1944." 27 September 1943.

———. "Report on the Interrogation of Survivors from *U-841* Sunk 17 October 1943 and *U-848* Sunk 5 November 1943." 12 January 1944.

U.S. Navy. Office of Naval Intelligence. "The Japanese Navy." ONI 222-J, June 1945.

U.S. Navy. Ship Characteristic Board. "Second Preliminary Characteristics (Revised) for Conversion of Fleet Submarine to SSO—Shipbuilding Project No. 39." 30 March 1948.

U.S. Navy. "Ships' Data, U.S. Naval Vessels." 1 July 1924.

U.S. Navy. United States Pacific Fleet and Pacific Ocean Areas. "CINCPAC-CINCPOA Bulletin No. 108-45: Japanese Naval Vessels Special Translation Number 64." 18 May 1945.

U.S. Navy. U.S. Naval Technical Mission to Japan. "Ship and Related Targets: Characteristics of Japanese Naval Vessels: Article 1—Submarines," no. S-1-01. January 1946.

———. "Ship and Related Targets: Characteristics of Japanese Naval Vessels: Article 7—Submarines, Supplement II," no. S-1-07. January 1946.

———. "Ship and Related Targets: Japanese Naval Vessels Own Ship's Noise," no. S-43. January 1946.

———. "Ship and Related Targets: Japanese Navy Diesel Engines," no. S-42. December 1945.

———. "Ship and Related Targets: Japanese Submarine Equipment," no. S-19. January 1946.

———. "Ship and Related Targets: Japanese Submarine Operations," no. S-17. February 1946.

DOCUMENTS IN GERMAN

The following German war diaries (KTBs) were consulted:

    Bordfliegergruppe 196 (1 September to 31 December 1943)

    U-12 (1 January to 16 January 1915)

    U-22 (16 to 31 May 1915)

U-177, 2nd Patrol (1 April to 1 October 1943)

U-255, 2nd Patrol (16 July to 9 September 1942)

U-255, 7th Patrol (30 April to 19 September 1943)

U-523 (25 June 1942 to 16 April 1943)

U-703, 9th Patrol (3 August to 10 October 1943)

U-849, 1st Patrol (11 March to 2 October 1943)

Kriegsmarine. Seekriegsleitung [Naval War Staff]. "'Flettner-Huber' für Marinezwecke ['Flettner-Helicopter' for Naval Purposes] (Neu 1.Skl. I L 2231/39 g.K.)." 19 December 1939.

Luftwaffe. Luftwaffen Inspektion der Seeflieger [Air Force Inspectorate of Naval Aviation]. "Taktisch technische Forderungen für Hubschrauberentwicklung [Tactical Technical Requirements for Helicopter Development] (L.In.8 B.Nr.83/40 8c g.Kdos.)." 29 January 1940.

DOCUMENTS IN ITALIAN

Ministry of Aeronautics. Director General of Construction and Procurement. "Idro M.53 per Sommergibili: Istruzione per il montaggio e regolazione [M.53 Seaplane for Submarines: Instructions for Assembly and Maintenance]." n.d. [ca. 1930].

———. "Idro P.8: Istruzione per il montaggio e per le regolazione [P.8 Seaplane: Instructions for Assembly and Maintenance]." n.d. [ca. 1930].

DOCUMENTS IN JAPANESE

Aichi Aircraft Company, "M6A1 Rikujo Ki Keikaku Setsumeisho [M6A1 Land-Based Aircraft Planning Manual]." 21 January 1944.

———. "M6A1 Seino Keisansho [M6A1 Performance Calculation Book]." 5 October 1943.

BOOKS IN ENGLISH

Alden, John D., USN (Ret.). *The Fleet Submarine in the U.S. Navy: A Design and Construction History*. Annapolis, Md.: Naval Institute, 1985.

Amerson, A. Binion, Jr. *The Coral Carrier—French Frigate Shoals, Northwest Hawaiian Islands: A History*. Dallas, Tx: Binion Amerson, 2012.

Auphan, Rear Adm. Paul, French Navy (Ret.), and Jacques Mordal. *The French Navy in World War II*. Annapolis, Md.: Naval Institute, 1959.

Blair, Clay. *Hitler's U-boat War*. Vol. 2, *The Hunted, 1941–1945*. New York: Random House, 1998.

Boyd, Carl, and Akihiko Yoshida. *The Japanese Submarine Force and World War II*. Annapolis, Md.: Naval Institute, 1995.

Bradley, Robert E. *Convair Advanced Designs: Secret Projects from San Diego, 1923–1962*. North Branch, Minn.: Specialty, 2010.

Branfill-Cook, Roger. *X.1: The Royal Navy's Mystery Submarine*. Barnsley, England: Seaforth, 2012.

Brice, Martin H. *M-class Submarines*. London: Outline Publications, 1983.

Carlisle, Rodney P. *Where the Fleet Begins: A History of the David Taylor Research Center, 1898–1998.* Washington, D.C.: Naval Historical Center, 1998.

Carlson, Elliot. *Joe Rochefort's War: The Odyssey of the Codebreaker Who Outwitted Yamamoto at Midway.* Annapolis, Md.: Naval Institute, 2011.

Carpenter, Dorr, and Norman Polmar. *Submarines of the Imperial Japanese Navy.* Annapolis, Md.: Naval Institute, 1986.

Castle, Ian. *Zeppelin Onslaught: The Forgotten Blitz, 1914–1915.* Barnsley, England: Frontline Books, 2018.

Clark, William B. *When the U-boats Came to America.* Boston: Little, Brown, 1929.

Coates, Steve, and Jean-Christophe Carbonel. *Helicopters of the Third Reich.* Hersham, England: Classic Publications, 2002.

Compton-Hall, Cdr. Richard, RN (Ret.). *Submarine Warfare: Monsters and Midgets.* Poole, England: Blandford, 1985.

Evans, David C., and Mark R. Peattie. *Kaigun: Strategy, Tactics, and Technology in the Imperial Japanese Navy, 1887–1941.* Annapolis, Md.: Naval Institute, 1997.

Everitt, Don. *K-Boats: Steam-Powered Submarines in World War I.* Annapolis, Md.: Naval Institute, 1999.

Fegan, Thomas. *The "Baby Killers": German Air Raids on Britain during the First World War.* Barnsley, England: Pen & Sword, 2012.

Felton, Mark. *The Fujita Plan.* Barnsley, England: Pen & Sword, 2006.

Francillon, R. J. *Japanese Aircraft of the Pacific War.* London: Putnam, 1970.

Friedman, Norman. *British Submarines in Two World Wars.* Barnsley, England: Seaforth, 2019.

———. *Fighters over the Fleet: Naval Air Defence from Biplanes to the Cold War.* Barnsley, England: Seaforth, 2016.

———. *U.S. Submarines through 1945: An Illustrated Design History.* Annapolis, Maryland: Naval Institute, 1995.

———. *U.S. Submarines since 1945: An Illustrated Design History.* 2nd ed. Annapolis, Md.: Naval Institute, 2018.

Galantin, Adm. Ignatius J., USN (Ret.). *Submarine Admiral: From Battlewagons to Ballistic Missiles.* Urbana: University of Illinois, 1997.

Geoghegan, John J. *Operation Storm: Japan's Top Secret Submarines and Its Plan to Change the Course of World War II.* New York: Crown Publishers, 2013.

Ginter, Steve. *Convair XP5Y-1 & R3Y-1/2 Tradewind.* Simi Valley, Calif.: Steve Ginter, 1992.

Grossnick, Roy A. *United States Naval Aviation: 1910–1995.* Washington, D.C.: Naval Historical Center, 1997.

Gundlach, Jay, and Richard J. Foch. *Unmanned Aircraft Systems Innovation at the Naval Research Laboratory.* Reston, Va.: American Institute of Aeronautics and Astronautics, 2014.

Gunston, Bill. *Aircraft of the Soviet Union: The Encyclopedia of Soviet Aircraft since 1917.* London: Osprey, 1983.

Harrison, A. N. *The Development of HM Submarines from Holland No. 1 (1901) to Porpoise (1930), BR 3043.* London: Ministry of Defence, 1979.

Hoffman, Capt. Richard, USN (Ret.). *The Martin P5M Patrol Seaplane.* Simi Valley, Calif.: Steve Ginter, 2007.

Holmes, Capt. Wilfred J., USN (Ret.) *Double Edged-Secrets: U.S. Naval Intelligence Operations in the Pacific During World War II* (Annapolis, Md.: Naval Institute, 1979).

Horn, Steven. *The Second Attack on Pearl Harbor: Operation K and Other Japanese Attempts to Bomb America in World War II.* Annapolis, Md.: Naval Institute, 2005.

Ishiguro, Ryusuke, and Tadeusz Januszewski. *Kugisho E14Y Glen: The Aircraft That Bombed America.* Petersfield: Mushroom Model, 2012.

Jaffe, Steven H. *New York at War: Four Centuries of Combat, Fear, and Intrigue in Gotham.* New York: Basic Books, 2012.

Januszewski, Tadeusz. *Japanese Submarine Aircraft.* Redbourn, England: Mushroom Model, 2002.

Johnson, E. R. *United States Naval Aviation, 1919–1941: Aircraft, Airships and Ships Between the Wars.* Jefferson, N.C.: McFarland, 2011.

Jordan, John. "French Submarine Development between the Wars." In *Warship 1991*, edited by Robert Gardiner. Annapolis, Md.: Naval Institute, 1991.

König, Paul. *Voyage of the* Deutschland: *The First Merchant Submarine.* Annapolis, Md.: Naval Institute, 2001.

Koop, Gerhard, and Klaus-Peter Schmolke. *Pocket Battleships of the Deutschland Class.* Barnsley, England: Seaforth, 2014.

Layman, R. D. *Naval Aviation in the First World War.* Annapolis, Md.: Naval Institute, 1996.

Layton, Rear Adm. Edwin T., USN (Ret.), Captain Roger Pineau, USNR (Ret.), and John Constello. *And I Was There: Pearl Harbor and Midway—Breaking the Secrets.* New York: William Morrow, 1985.

Long, B. J. *Convair XF2Y-1 and YF2Y-1 Sea Dart.* Simi Valley, Calif.: Steve Ginter, 1992.

MacArthur, Gen. Douglas, USA. *Reports of General MacArthur.* Vol. 1, *Japanese Operations in the Southwest Pacific Area*, Part 2. Washington, D.C.: U.S. Govt. Printing Office, 1966.

Mallmann Showell, Jak P. *Swastikas in the Arctic: U-boat Alley through the Frozen Hell.* Stroud, England: Fronthill, 2014.

McCash, William. *Bombs over Brookings: The World War II Bombings of Curry County, Oregon and the Postwar Friendship between Brookings and the Japanese Pilot, Nobuo Fujita.* Bend, Ore.: Maverick Publications, 2005.

Meekcombs, K. J., and E. B. Morgan. *The British Aircraft Specifications File: British Military and Commercial Aircraft Specifications, 1920–1949.* Tonbridge, England: Air Britain.

Messimer, Dwight R. *The Merchant U-boat: Adventures of the* Deutschland, *1916–1918.* Annapolis, Md.: Naval Institute, 1988.

Nowarra, Heinz J., Bruce Robertson, and P. G. Coorsley. *Marine Aircraft of the 1914–1918 War.* Letchworth, England: Harleyford, 1966.

Orita, Zenji, and Joseph D. Harrington. *I-Boat Captain.* Canoga Park, Calif.: Major Books, 1976.

Parshall, Jonathan B., and Anthony P. Tully. *Shattered Sword: The Untold Story of the Battle of Midway.* Washington, D.C.: Potomac, 2005.

Patterson, Lawrence. *Hitler's Grey Wolves: U-Boats in the Indian Ocean.* London: Greenhill Books, 2004.

———. *Steel and Ice: The U-boat Battle in the Arctic and Black Sea, 1941–45.* Annapolis, Md.: Naval Institute, 2016.

Polmar, Norman. *The American Submarine.* 2nd ed. Annapolis, Md.: Nautical and Aviation, 1983.

———, and K. J. Moore. *Cold War Submarines: The Design and Construction of U.S. and Soviet Submarines.* Dulles, Va.: Potomac, 2003.

———, and Floyd D. Kennedy. *Military Helicopters of the World.* Annapolis, Md.: Naval Institute, 1981.

———, and Michael White. *Project Azorian: The CIA and the Raising of the K-129.* Annapolis, Md.: Naval Institute, 2012.

———, and Capt. John O'Connell, USN (Ret.). *Strike from the Sea: The Sea-Launched Cruise Missile.* Annapolis, Md.: Naval Institute, 2020.

———, and Jurrien Noot. *Submarines of the Russian and Soviet Navies: 1718–1990.* Annapolis, Md.: Naval Institute, 1991.

———, and Robert S. Norris. *The U.S. Nuclear Arsenal: A History of Weapons and Delivery Systems since 1945.* Annapolis, Md.: Naval Institute, 2009.

Prange, Gordon W., Donald M. Goldstein, and CWO Katherine V. Dillon, USAF (Ret.). *At Dawn We Slept: The Untold Story of Pearl Harbor.* 2nd ed. New York: Viking, 1991.

Rössler, Eberhard. *The U-boat: The Evolution and Technical History of German Submarines.* Translated by Harold Erenberg. Annapolis, Md.: Naval Institute, 1989.

Rusbridger, James. *Who Sank Surcouf? The Truth about the Disappearance of the Pride of the French Navy.* London: Century, 1991.

Sakaida, Henry, Gary Nila, and Koji Takaki. *I-400: Japan's Secret Aircraft-Carrying Strike Submarine.* Crowborough, England: Hikoki, 2006.

Smith, J. R., and Antony L. Kay. *German Aircraft of the Second World War.* Baltimore, Md.: Nautical & Aviation, 1972.

Sontag, Sherry, Christopher Drew, and Annette Lawrence Drew. *Blind Man's Bluff: The Untold Story of American Submarine Espionage.* New York: PublicAffairs, 1998.

Stern, Robert C. *Type VIIC U-boats.* Annapolis, Md.: Naval Institute, 1997.

Stille, Mark. *Midway 1942: Turning Point in the Pacific.* Oxford: Osprey, 2010.

Stumpf, David K. *Regulus: America's First Nuclear Submarine Missile.* Paducah, Ky.: Turner, 1996.

Suhler, Paul A. *From RAINBOW to GUSTO: Stealth and the Design of the Lockheed Blackbird.* Reston, Va.: American Institute of Aeronautics and Astronautics, 2009.

Swanborough, Gordon, and Peter M. Bowers. *United States Navy Aircraft since 1911.* Annapolis, Md.: Naval Institute, 1968.

Treadwell, Terry C. *Strike from beneath the Sea: A History of Aircraft-Carrying Submarines.* Stroud, England: History Press, 2009.

———. *Submarines with Wings.* London: Conway, 1985.

Trimble, William F. *Admiral William A. Moffett: Architect of Naval Aviation.* Washington, D.C.: Smithsonian Institution, 1994.

———. *Attack from the Sea: A History of the U.S. Navy's Seaplane Striking Force.* Annapolis, Md.: Naval Institute, 2005.

Warner, Dennis, Peggy Warner, and Cdr. Sadao Sendo, JMSDF (Ret.). *The Sacred Warriors: Japan's Suicide Legions.* New York: Van Nostrand Reinhold, 1982.

Williams, Peter, and David Wallace. *Unit 731: Japan's Secret Biological Warfare in World War II.* New York: Free Press, 1989.

Williamson, Gordon. *U-boat Tactics in World War II.* Oxford: Osprey, 2010.

Wixley, Kenneth E. *Parnall Aircraft since 1914.* Annapolis, Md.: Naval Institute, 1990.

BOOKS IN FRENCH

Bousquet, Gérard. *Les ailes françaises, l'Encyclopédie des avions de la Seconde Guerre Mondiale* [*The French Wings, Encyclopedia of WWII Aircraft*]. Vol. 3, *Les hydravions à flotteurs, 1ère partie* [*Floatplanes, Part 1*]. Paris: Artipresse, 2012.

Huan, Capt. Claude, French Navy (Ret.). *Le croiseur sous-marin Surcouf (1926–1942)* [*The Submarine Cruiser Surcouf (1926–1942)*]. Bourg-en-Bresse: Marines Éditions, 1996.

———. *Le sous-marins français, 1918–1945* [*The French Submarines, 1918–1945*]. Bourg-en-Bresse: Marines Éditions, ca. 1995.

BOOKS IN GERMAN

Freund, Gerhard. *Himmelfahrtskommando "Bachstelze": Der Einsatz des antriebslosen Tragschraubers Fa 330 im U-boot-Krieg des Zweiten Weltkrieges* [*Suicide Mission "Bachstelze": The Use of the Unpowered Autogyro Fa 330 in the U-boat Battle of the Second World War*]. Steinau, Germany: Märchenstraßen, 2014.

Heinkel, Ernst, and Jürgen Thurwald. *Stürmisches Leben* [*Stormy Life*]. Stuttgart: Europäischer Buchklub, 1953.

Rössler, Eberhard. *Die deutschen U-boote und U-bootentwürfe zwischen den Weltkriegen, 1922–1939* [*The German U-boats and U-boat Development between the World Wars, 1922–1939*]. Berlin: Edition Erich Gröner, 2013.

———. *Die deutschen U-Kreuzer und Transport-U-Boote* [*The German U-Cruisers and Transport U-boats*]. Bonn: Bernard & Graefe, 2003.

Wollé, Heinrich, H. A. Caspari, and Oskar Passoth, eds. *E-Stelle See: Die Geschichte der Flugerprobungsstellen Travemünde und Tarnewitz* [*Testing Station Sea: The History of the Travemünde and Tarnewitz Flight Test Stations*]. Steinebach-Wörthsee, Germany: Luftfahrt-Verlag Axel Zuerl, 1975.

BOOKS IN ITALIAN

Pollina, Capt. Paolo M., Italian Navy. *I Sommergibili Italiani: 1895–1962* [*The Italian Submarines: 1895–1962*]. Ed. Vice Adm. Aldo Cocchia, Italian Navy. Rome: Ufficio Storico Marina Militare, 1963.

Turrini, Alessandro, Ottorino Miozzi, and Manuel Minuto. *Sommergibili e Mezzi d'Assalto Subacquei Italiani* [*Italian Submarines and Underwater Assault Craft*]. Rome: Ufficio Storico Marina Militare, 2010.

BOOKS IN JAPANESE

Defense Research Institute, War History Branch. *Senshi Sosho* [*War History Series*]. Vol. 98, *Sensuikan-shi* [*History of Submarines*]. Tokyo: Asagumo Shimbunsha, 1979.

Takaki, Koji. *I400 To Seiran Zen Kiroku: Kaitei Zoho-ban* [*Complete Record of the I-400 and Seiran: Revised and Expanded Edition*]. Tokyo: Futabasha, 2017.

BOOKS IN POLISH

Morgała, Andrzej. *Samoloty w polskim lotnictwie morskim* [*Aircraft in Polish Naval Aviation*]. Warsaw: Wydawnictwo Komunikacji, 1985.

BOOKS IN RUSSIAN

Bruk, A. A., K. G. Udalov, S. G. Smirnov, A. V. Arkhipov, and B. L. Puntus. *Illyustrirovannaya Entsiklopediya Samoletov OKB B. M. Myasishcheva* [*Illustrated Encyclopedia of the Aircraft of OBK V. M. Myasishchev*]. Vol. 2, Part 3. Edited by V. K. Novikov. Moscow: Aviko Press, 2001.

Cheremukhin, G. A. *Dal'she. Vyshe. Bystreye: vospominaniya o rabote v aviapromyshlennosti, o tekhnike i yeye sozdatelyakh* [*Further. Higher. Faster: Memories of Working in the Aviation Industry, About Technology and Its Creators*]. Edited by N. G. Georgiyevoy. Moscow: Prospekt, 2011.

Istoriya otechestvennogo sudostroyeniya [*History of Domestic Shipbuilding*]. Vol. 5, *Sudostroyeniye v poslevoyennyy period 1946–1991 gg.* [*Shipbuilding in the Postwar Period, 1946–1991*]. Edited by I. D. Spasskiy. St. Petersburg: Sudostroyeniya, 1996.

Lesnichenko, V. A., and A. N. Gusev. *Samolet i podvodnaya lodka: Ocherki k istorii podovodnoy aviatsii* [*Aircraft and Submarine: Essays on the History of Submarine Aviation*]. St. Petersburg: Galeya, 2001.

Morozov, M. E., and K. L. Kulagin. *Sovetskiy podvodnyy flot, 1922–1945 gg: O podvodnykh lodkakh i podvodnikakh* [*The Soviet Submarine Fleet, 1922–1945: On Submarines and Submariners*]. Moscow: Tranzitkniga, 2006.

Panatov, G. S., A. N. Zablotskiy, and A. I. Sal'nikov. *Samolety TANTK im. G. M. Berieva: 1945–1968* [*Aircraft of the G. M. Beriev Taganrog Aviation Scientific Technical Complex: 1945–1968*], Moscow: Restart+, 2001.

Platonov, A. V. *Lineynye sily podvodnogo flota* [*Forces of the Line of the Undersea Fleet*]. St. Petersburg: Galeya, 1998.

Razletov, B. K. *Istoriya Sankt-Peterburgskogo morskogo byuro mashinostroyeniya "Malakhit"* [*History of the Saint Petersburg Naval Engineering Bureau "Malakhit"*]. Vol. 1, *Spetsial'noye konstruktorskoye byuro No. 143—Soyuznoye proyektno-montazhnoye byuro mashinostroyeniya: 1948–1974 gody* [*Special Design Bureau No. 143—United Design-Assembly Engineering Bureau: 1948–1974*]. Ed. V. V. Klimov. St. Petersburg: Gangut, 2002.

Yakubovich, N. V. *Samolety R. L.Bartini* [*Aircraft of R. L. Bartini*]. Moscow: Rusavia, 2006.

ARTICLES IN ENGLISH

Abt, C. C. "The Submarine-Aircraft Carrier." *Naval Institute Proceedings* (October 1963).

Adams, Thomas A. "The M Class Submarine Monitors." *Warship* VII (London: Conway, 1983).

Allen, Francis J. "Poseidon's Giant: The Story of the Martin P6M Seamaster." *Air Enthusiast* (March/April 2001).

———. "*Surcouf* under refit." *Warship* VII (London: Conway, 1983).

Boyd, Carl. "American Naval Intelligence of Japanese Submarines Early in the Pacific War." *Journal of American Military History* (April 1989).

Budzbon, Przemyslaw. "Pride of Poland: The Orzel Class Submarines: Construction." *Warship*, no. 42 (April 1987).

Burgess, Richard R. "Admiral: Submarine-Launched UAS Proving 'Awesome Capability.'" *Sea Power* (18 November 2020).

"The Caspar Sport Seaplane." *Flight* (14 June 1923).

Clark, K. W. "Poole Identification." *Flight* (25 July 1958).

"City Lights out in Air Raid Test." *New York Times* (5 June 1918).

Dakos, Lt. D. P., USNR. "Seagoing Service Stations." Naval Institute *Proceedings* (October 1957).

Douglass, Richard. "Before the U2 Spy Plane: The Covert Operations Manned Balloon Gets to Work, Part 2." *Ballooning* 51, no. 4 (July/August 2018).

———. "Submarine Operations: The Covert Operations Manned Balloon Gets to Work, Part 3." *Ballooning* 51, no. 5 (September/October 2018).

Duke, Charles W. "Will the U-boats Come to America This Summer?" *Washington Post* (2 June 1918).

"Facts by Request—The *Surcouf*'s Seaplane." *Flying Review International* (August 1967).

Fein, Geoff. "Navy, Raytheon Effort Deploys Sub Launched UAV Out with the Trash." *Defense Daily* (5 November 2008).

Fitzwilliams, O. L. L. "Some Work with Rotating-Wing Aircraft." *Journal of the Helicopter Association of Great Britain* 1, no. 2 (October–December 1947).

"Folding Plane Tried Here, Fits Tube of Submarine." *New York Herald Tribune* (5 February 1931).

Fujita, Warrant Flying Officer Nobuo, IJN (Ret.), and Chief Journalist Joseph D. Harrington, USN. "I Bombed the U.S.A." Naval Institute *Proceedings* (June 1961).

Gaylard, John. "Last at Poole." *Flight* (20 June 1959).

———. "Poole Petrel." *Flight* (15 August 1958).

"Gothenburg International Aero Exhibition 1923." *Flight* (2 August 1923).

Grosz, Peter M. "A Study in Contrasts: German Submarine Aircraft of World War One." *Air Enthusiast* 33 (May–August 1987).

Groves, Patricia T. "The Loening Monoplanes." *American Aviation Historical Society Journal* (Winter 1984).

Hall, Norm, and Carol Hall. "At a Crucial Hour: The Attack on Estevan Point." *The Beaver* 84, no. 2 (May 2004).

Hallett, Capt. Frederick H. USN (Ret.), "The Loss of the Surcouf: Solving an Old Mystery," *Submarine Review* (Winter 2012): 76–9.

——— "The Loss of the Surcouf: Solving an Old Mystery," *Submarine Review* (Spring 2012), 77–7.

Handler, Eugene. "The Flying Submarine." Naval Institute *Proceedings* (September 1964).

Holmes, Capt. Wilfred J., USN (Ret.) "Discussion, Comments, and Notes: Rendezvous in Reverse." Naval Institute *Proceedurings* (August 1953).

Howlett, Petty Officer 1st Class Michael, USN. "Joint Spec Ops: Air Force, Navy Test Rescue Scenario." *Undersea Warfare* (Spring 2006).

Hudson, Alec [Lt. Wilford Holmes, USN (Ret.)]. "Rendezvous." *Saturday Evening Post* 214, no. 5 (2 August 1941).

———. "Rendezvous." *Saturday Evening Post* 214, no. 6 (9 August 1941).

"Japanese Bomb Found in Oregon Is Linked to Unidentified Seaplane." *New York Times* (15 Sept. 1942).

Kelley, Donald. "The Submarine Aircraft Carrier." *Our Navy* (February 1969).

Layman, R. D. "U-Boat with Wings." Naval Institute *Proceedings* (April 1968).

———. "Question 42/89." *Warship International* 2 (1992).

Layton, Capt. Edwin T., USN. "Rendezvous in Reverse." Naval Institute *Proceedings* (May 1953).

Lowther, Scott. "American Submarine Aircraft Carriers." *Aerospace Projects Review* 1, no. 6 (2008).

———. "Convair Submersible Nuclear Ramjet." *U.S. Bomber Projects* 21 (2018).

Momiyama, Thomas S. "All and Nothing." *Air & Space* (October/November 2001).

———. "Racing Against Invasion: Engineering a Kamikaze 'Cruise Missile,'" *Air Power History* 56, no. 2 (Summer 2009).

"The New Trend in Naval Aircraft." *Aviation* (30 October 1922).

"The Paris Aero Show 1926." *Flight* (2 December 1926).

Paine, Dr. Thomas O. "The Last Voyage of a Submarine Aircraft Carrier." *Submarine Review* (April 2006).

Parry, Daniel. "Navy Launches UAV from Submerged Submarine." *Naval Research Laboratory Spectra* (Winter 2014).

Polmar, Norman. "A Dart from the Sea." *Naval History* (December 2012).

———. "A Floatplane on a . . . What?" *Naval History* (December 2018).

———. "The Tail Sitters, Part 1—Lockheed." *Naval History* (June 2013).

———. "The Tail Sitters, Part 2—Convair." *Naval History* (August 2013).

Poulos, George. "At War Part II: Recollections of a VP Pilot." *Naval Aviation News* (September 1982).

Pursell, Robert. "Trident Warrior 2010 Leads the Way in Maritime Experimentation." *CHIPS Magazine* 28, no. 3 (July–September 2010).

Ruszkowski, Robert A. "MPUAV: Advanced Development Programs Team Makes Splash with Successful Underwater Recovery of a Unique Aircraft." *LM Aeronautics Star* 8, no. 1 (2007).

Shaw, Petty Officer 2nd Class Christina, USN. "Submarine Force Tests UAV Technology to Enhance Force Protection." *Undersea Warfare* 7, no. 4 (Summer 2005).

Spinner, Petty Officer 1st Class Jennifer, USN. "USS Albany Launches Experimental UAV." *Undersea Warfare* 7, no. 5 (Fall 2005).

Stout, Ernest G. "Development of High-Speed Water-Based Aircraft." *Journal of the Aeronautical Sciences* 17, no. 8 (August 1950).

"A Submarine Aircraft Carrier." *Flight* (31 July 1931).

"Surveillance Vehicles Soar on Fuel Cell Power." *Naval Research Laboratory Spectra* (Fall 2010).

Talbert, Ansel E. "Designers Study Flying Submarine." *New York Herald Tribune*, 28 October 1955).

Terry, Gerrard. "The LFG Roland V19: Submarine-borne Spotter Aircraft." *Cross and Cockade* 18, no. 2 (1987).

Tully, Anthony, and Lu Yu. "A Question of Estimates: How Faulty Intelligence Drove Scouting at the Battle of Midway." *Naval War College Review* 68, no. 2 (Spring 2015).

Vigiotti, Vincent. "Demonstration of Submarine Control of an Unmanned Aerial Vehicle." *Johns Hopkins APL Technical Digest* 19, no. 4 (1998).

Warwick, Graham. "Raytheon to Launch UAV from Submarine." *Aviation Week* (30 October 2008).

Weinstein, Steve, Tom Sachse, and William McGannon. "Submarine Unmanned Vehicle System . . . Past, Present, and Future Efforts." Paper presented at AIAA's 1st

Technical Conference and Workshop on Unmanned Aerospace Vehicles, Portsmouth, Va., 20–23 May 2002.

Willis, Matthew. "From Skate to Sea Dart: Convair & the USA's Seaplane Striking Force, Part 1, 1946–52." *Aviation Historian* 25 (October 2018).

———. "Son of Sea Dart: Convair & the USA's Seaplane Striking Force, Part 2, 'The Tactical F2Y.'" *Aviation Historian* 26 (January 2019).

Winans, David R. "Submarine Aircraft." *American Aviation Historical Society Journal* (Spring 1967).

Wright, Christopher C. "The U.S. Navy's Operation of the Former Imperial Japanese Navy Submarines *I-14*, *I-400* and *I-401*: 1945–1946." *Warship International* 37, no. 4 (2000).

ARTICLES IN FRENCH

Carbonel, Jean-Christophe. "Sur une table de cuisine: La Marine teste le Fa 330 [On a Kitchen Table: The Navy Tests the Fa 330]." *Aéro Journal* 32 (August–September 2003).

Dyme, S. Y. "Trois nouveaux hydravions L.F.G. [Three New L.F.G. Seaplanes]." *L'Aéronautique* 41 (October 1922).

Marchand, Alain, and Claude Huan. "'Passe-Partout,' l'avion du sous-marin ['Go Anywhere,' the Submarine Aircraft]." *Le Fana de l'Aviation* 314 (January 1996).

ARTICLES IN GERMAN

Baatz, Gotthard. "Das Schiffsflugzeug der Luft-Fahrzeug Gesellschaft mbH Werft Stralsund [The Seaplanes of Luft-Fahrzeug Gesellschaft Inc. Works Stralsund]." *Illustrierte Flug Welt* (5 July 1922).

Bode, Carl. "Die Entwicklung der Focke FA-330 [The Development of the Focke FA-330]." *Der Flieger* 5 (1974).

Lang, Fredi. "Die Ausbildung am Tragschrauber FA-330 'Bachstelze' [Training on the FA-330 'Bachstelze' Towed Autogyro]." *Aero* 3 (March 1952).

Mohr, Theodore. "Flettner Fl 282 'Kolibri' Varianten: Die Geschichte einer erfolgreichen Hubschrauberentwicklung [Flettner Fl 282 'Kolibri' Variants: The History of a Successful Helicopter Development]." *Flugzeug Profile* 14 (1991).

"Tragschrauber-Flugzeug Fa 330 [Towed Autogyro Aircraft Fa 330]." *Luftfahrt International* 21 (May–June 1977).

ARTICLES IN ITALIAN

Ruzzier, Umberto. "L'aviazione sottomarina [Submarine Aviation]." *Rivista Marittima* (May 2007).

Turrini, Allesandro. "Breve storia del 'sommergibile cannoniere,' e in particolare di quello italiano [Brief History of the 'Cannon Submarines,' in Particular Those of Italy]." *Rivista Marittima* (December 2011).

Vigna, Achille. "Idrovolanti per i sommergibili italiani [Seaplanes for Italian Submarines]." *Storia Militare* (June 2012).

ARTICLES IN JAPANESE

Nakagawa, Tsutomu. "History of Japanese Submarines." *Sakai no Kasen* [*Ships of the World*] 469 (1993).

"Nippon Kaigun Kantei Shashin Shu [Japanese Navy Ship Photobook]." *Maru* 19 (1997).

Terada, Akira. "Development of Japanese Submarines—Hull." *Sakai No Kasen* [*Ships of the World*] 469 (1993).

Watanabe, Tetsukuni. "Aichi M6A1 Rikujo-Ki No Shinso [The Truth about the Aichi M6A1 Land-Based Aircraft]." *Koku Fan* 564 (December 1999).

ARTICLES IN RUSSIAN

Gubarev, Boris. "Sverkhlegkiy Ka-56 [Ultralight Ka-56]." *Vertolet* 4 (1999).

Petrov, Gennadiy. "Letayushchaya . . . podvodnaya lodka [Flying . . . Submarine]." *Vestnik vozdushnogo flota* 3 (1995).

Udalov, Konstantin. "Sverkhzvukovy, dal'niy, okeanskiy: O proyekte unikal'nogo gidrosa-moleta [Supersonic, Long-Range, Oceanic: On a Unique Seaplane Project]." *Kryl'ya Rodiny* 11 (2000).

WEBSITES

Dickson, David, Bob Hackett, and Sander Kingsepp. "Yu-Go: The Japanese Plan for a Second Pearl Harbor Surprise Attack." www.combinedfleet.com/U-GO.htm.

Frost, Günter. "Die Flugzeuge der Caspar-Werke in Travemünde [The Aircraft of Caspar Werke in Travemünde]." Arbeitsgemeinschaft Dt. Luftfahrthistorik. https://adl-luftfahrthistorik.de/dok/caspar-flugzeugwerke-travemuende-werksgeschichte-flugzeugtypen-2023-05.pdf.

Hackett, Bob, and Sander Kingsepp. "*SENSUIKAN!* Stories and Battle Histories of the IJN's Submarines." http://www.combinedfleet.com/sensuikan.htm.

Helgason, Gudmundur. "uboat.net." http://www.uboat.net.

Mason, Capt. Jerry, USN (Ret.). "U-boat Archive." https://www.uboatarchive.net/.

Naval History and Heritage Command. "Dictionary of American Fighting Ships." https://www.history.navy.mil/content/history/nhhc/research/histories/ship-histories/danfs.html.

Nikolayev, Andrey. "Shturm Glubiny [Deep Storm]." https://www.deepstorm.ru.

INDEX

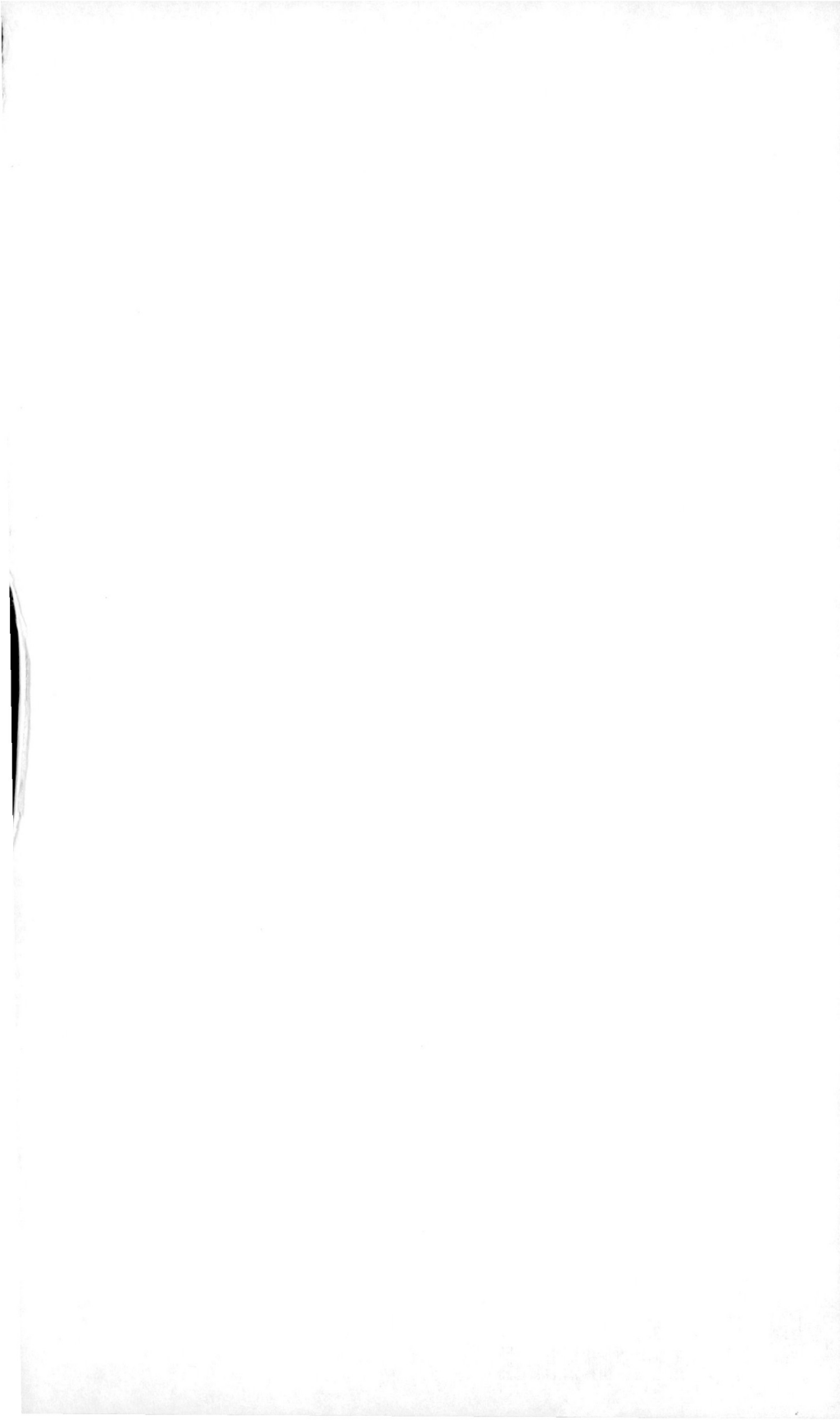